THE CHURCH UNDER THE LAW

THE CHURCH
UNDER THE LAW

JUSTICE, ADMINISTRATION
AND DISCIPLINE IN
THE DIOCESE OF YORK
1560–1640

RONALD A. MARCHANT

CAMBRIDGE
AT THE UNIVERSITY PRESS
1969

Published by the Syndics of the Cambridge University Press

Bentley House, 200 Euston Road, London N.W.1

American Branch: 32 East 57th Street, New York, N.Y.10022

Library of Congress Catalogue Card Number: 79–80819

Standard Book Number: 521 07460 6

Printed in Great Britain

at the University Printing House, Cambridge

(Brooke Crutchley, University Printer)

CONTENTS

PREFACE   *page* vii

INTRODUCTION   I

1 CHURCH COURTS   12
   The provincial courts of Canterbury   12
   Diocesan courts   13
   Diocese of Norwich   15
   The Commissary Court of the Archdeaconry of Suffolk   29
   Apparitors   31
   The High Commission   33
   The Bishop's legal secretary   35

2 THE CONSISTORY AND CHANCERY COURTS OF YORK   38
   The Lawyers   41
   The Consistory Court   60
   The Chancery Court   66
   The Archbishop's Legal Secretary   82

3 THE EXCHEQUER AND PREROGATIVE COURT   86
   Early history   87
   Probate and Rural Deans   88
   Office of Receiver-General   91
   Development of the Exchequer Court in the sixteenth century   92
   History of the Court in the seventeenth century   101
   The founding of the Prerogative Court   103
   Nature of litigation in the Exchequer   107
   Fees   111

4 VISITATIONS   114
   Diocesan and provincial Visitations   114
   Archdeaconry Visitations   122
   Disciplinary law   128
   Visitation procedure and fees   134

Contents

5 THE ARCHDEACONRY OF NOTTINGHAM   *page* 147
The Archidiaconate of John Lowth (1565–90)   147
Officials and Registrars   157
The jurisdiction of the Archdeacon   173
The Correction Court   178
Diocesan Visitations   185
The Nottingham Consistory Court   188
The Laudian period   195

6 CHURCH DISCIPLINE   204

CONCLUSION   236
The abolition of the York Legal Tradition   236
The laicization of Church administration   238
Civil Law and Common Law   239
Church discipline over morals   240
Criticisms of the church courts   243

APPENDICES
I   The Value of court offices   246
II   Advocates of the Consistory Court of York   247
III   Officials of the Archdeacon of Nottingham and their
     Principal Surrogates   252
IV   Proctors of the Consistory Court of Nottingham   253

BIBLIOGRAPHY   255

TABLE OF CASES   260

STATUTES AND CANONS   263

INDEX   265

MAPS

1   Ecclesiastical Yorkshire after the changes of Henry VIII   39
2   Archdeaconry of Nottingham   149

PREFACE

It is usual for an author to acknowledge in his Preface his indebtedness to others, and somewhere near the end of the list is his secretarial assistant. The present work has come through so many stages over the past ten years, and there has been so much rewriting of manuscript, that my helper, Miss Joan Pearce, is worthy of a much higher place.

This work originated as the middle part of the chronological sequence of an administrative history of the diocese of York which was financed by the Leverhulme Foundation in 1957. In the event the work was never published as intended, although the early and later sections were completed and may be consulted at the Borthwick Institute of Historical Research, St Anthony's Hall, York.

My first major revision was the chapter on the Exchequer Court, dealing with probate and allied matters. As a church historian I investigated this court as a routine chore and for the sake of completeness. It was only after reading the standard legal histories that I discovered that what I was reading in the Exchequer acts was very different from what legal historians would have expected to find there, and that the subject merited deeper research. Later work at Norwich enabled a quantitative estimate to be made to show the importance of testamentary jurisdiction to church administration, and also to gauge its effect on that administration's development. I hope that the non-legal reader may find the subject as interesting as I have, or at least not as recondite as he might have supposed.

The manuscript underwent further slight changes and was submitted for the degree of Bachelor of Divinity at Cambridge. It was only some time after this that I heard of the final collapse of the project for publishing the Leverhulme material, and I was left to turn my own section into a self-contained work if I wished. The result has been the addition of the Introduction, Chapter 1, much of Chapter 6, the Conclusion, and general revision of, and additions to, the B.D. thesis. In particular much Norwich material has been added for comparison with the situation in York.

As a result of this revision the book now sets out to achieve two purposes: to describe the diocesan and archidiaconal courts and administrations in the old diocese of York from the accession of Elizabeth I to the Civil War, and also to serve as a general introduction to this aspect of church history during the period. Much use has been made of material from diocesan archives to describe medieval church life, but surprisingly little has been done to put to historical service the even more abundant material from the same sources for the post-Reformation Church. It may be that the sheer bulk of the records has deterred investigators, and I have become convinced that the statistical use of visitation and some other sources of information is preferable to printing a few random samples in full, in view of the limited amount of money available for publication. My own statistics have become more sophisticated as I gained more experience, and some earlier tables have been dropped. Other students may be encouraged to develop the process, although there are many pitfalls for the unwary.

The broadening scope of this work owes much to stimulation from Christopher Hill's *Society and Puritanism in Pre-revolutionary England* (1964). Hill rehashed contemporary Puritan and common law attacks on the church courts, throwing in a welter of supporting material from modern printed sources. What he failed to do was to give a reasoned description of the courts themselves, and to place them within the legal framework of their day. I have therefore been provoked into attempting to remedy the deficiency. At the least Mr Hill's readers can now have a clearer picture of the beast from which Oliver Cromwell rescued the Puritan damsel, and at the same time discover pure economic reasons for certain phenomena which they had not suspected—even if they have reason to doubt some part of Mr Hill's thesis.

Contemporary criticisms have to be seen in their own contexts. The Puritan propagandists and Elizabethan and early Stuart parliaments added little to John Colet's criticisms made at the beginning of the sixteenth century, or the observations of the parliament of 1529. Canon CXXXIII of 1603 has sometimes been used as evidence of the unruly behaviour of proctors at that period, yet it is an almost verbatim reproduction of one of Archbishop Greenfield's statutes for the Consistory Court of York three hundred years before. It may be assumed that there were always deficiencies in the church court system and its officials, but evidence has yet to be produced that they were more serious than those in contemporary secular courts.

If the divines spurned church administration because it did not come up to the standards they found in the Bible, common lawyers affected to despise it because it used Roman (civil) law, rather than the common law of England. Their greatest champion, Sir Edward Coke, managed to ignore the whole of feudal law when tracing the history of common law back through Saxon law to an alleged origin more ancient even than the founding of Rome. The arbitrary way in which Coke and his allies used the facts of history and legal precedents does not create confidence in their pronouncements on the church courts. Their complaints that civil law courts were encroaching on those of the common law can be better appreciated when it is remembered that English common law was originally a law of land. Consequently when it tried to draw defamation, tithe, testamentary and mercantile matters into its own courts, it had first to appropriate some law about them from civil and canon law sources.

R. M. Jackson, Downing Professor of the Laws of England at Cambridge, has bluntly stated that in the early nineteenth century 'the English criminal law was the most brutal and savage of any civilised country' (*The Machinery of Justice in England*, 5th ed. 1967, p. 145). A few improvements had been made since the end of the seventeenth century, so it was men who operated this law in its rawest form who criticized the procedure of the church courts. How the right balance between prosecution and defence can be achieved is still a matter for debate, and it is not surprising that deficiencies can be found in the church court procedure. It has yet to be established that it was more unfair than that of contemporary secular courts. The standards of the time also leave something to be desired. If ecclesiastical officers took bribes (and some did), what is to be said of a Chief Baron of the Exchequer who accepted a bribe to acquit a murderer, and then gave him his livery to protect him from the relatives of the victim? Or what is to be said of Queen Elizabeth who ordered her Lord Chancellor to try a charge of manslaughter against a favourite in private during a vacation, so that the affair could be hushed up? (L. Stone, *The Crisis of the Aristocracy 1558–1641*, 1965, pp. 210, 233.) The church lawyers had to work in a world where such occurrences were sometimes held to be improper (Lord Chancellor Bromley resisted before he gave way), but in which they were not entirely unexpected or unknown, and from which the church courts were neither isolated nor immune.

The Church system not only needs placing within a legal context, but also within the context of secular administration. This meant remuneration largely by fees, nepotism, place-seekers, promotion through influence with the right people, sinecure offices, execution of office by deputy, sale of offices, etc. The imagination flinches before the thought of a state-run system of probate offices managed by the courtiers of James I, which must have been the only alternative to a church probate system. This book has not attempted more than a few parallels with secular fees. It seemed more important to give an idea of the volume of business transacted by the church courts. It is easy enough to produce a contemporary estimate of £200,000 a year as the cost of those courts at the end of our period (as Mr Hill does), but the figure is meaningless unless measured against the work which they undertook.

Preface

Professor Butterfield, who has made us familiar with the Whig interpretation of history, comes near to suggesting that the end justifies the means: although the reasoning of the common lawyers was unsound, yet their ideas were of great service to their country. This may be true, but their contribution has been over-rated. Just as Magna Carta only made England a place fit for Barons to live in, so the Parliamentary struggle resulted in more freedom for those whose lives were lived in a legal context—property owners, merchants, politicians, lawyers. The average Briton still lived under the domination of squire, employer, overseer, churchwarden, parson, manorial court, justice of the peace. He only secured his real freedom from the regulation of his life by others when he escaped into the towns and founded trades unions to protect his interests.

There is one last point about the contents of this work which needs to be made. The disciplinary side of church administration lay under the ultimate control of the Court of High Commission, a statutory court erected by Elizabeth to ensure that the royal will was carried out in the church. Dr Phillip Tyler has for some years been engaged in a study of this Court in the province of York which he hopes to publish. I have referred to the High Commission when necessary to elucidate the workings of the diocesan courts, but I have not attempted any general description.

In the preparation of this book I have been indebted to Professor A. G. Dickens of London and Mr D. E. C. Yale of Christ's College, Cambridge, for advice and friendly criticism; to Mr K. S. S. Train, Secretary of the Thoroton Society of Nottinghamshire, for checking references and providing information from the records at Nottingham; to the staffs of Nottingham University Library Archives Department, and of the Norfolk and Norwich Record Office for their help and courtesy; to Miss E. Brunskill for answering queries about material in the Chapter Library at York; and most of all to Mrs N. K. M. Gurney and the staff at the Borthwick Institute, York, for checking references, production of xerox copies of documents, answering numerous queries and for much general encouragement.

The usual addendum of an author that despite advice and help he must be entirely responsible for his mistakes is one particularly applicable in my case. In such a subject as this, one is inevitably largely self-taught. I had the good fortune to begin work at York when the Borthwick Institute was still in its infancy, and was able to browse at leisure through its archives. A similar situation existed at Nottingham, and in my early days at Norwich I had the run of the chapel of the old bishop's palace where the diocesan records were then stored (with no artificial light or heat). These fortunate chances enabled me to discover the relevance of each class of document, and to recover the system to which they bore witness, much more quickly and thoroughly than through any catalogues of documents. Archivists are uniformly helpful, and this work owes much to them, yet they exist as a barrier between a student and his material. Consequently this work is perhaps a period piece by being essentially a late product of the pre-archive office period in English historiography.

RONALD MARCHANT

Laxfield, September 1968

'...you are no longer under law,
but under the grace of God.'

Romans VI, 14 (*N.E.B.*)

GENERAL NOTES

A.B. = Act Book.

In the chapters on the York courts all references are to the York diocesan archives at St Anthony's Hall, York, unless otherwise stated. All MSS. with a reference number beginning with 'R' are at St Anthony's Hall.

In the chapter on the Nottingham court all references are to the Archdeaconry of Nottingham archives in the University Library, Nottingham, unless otherwise stated.

References to unprinted sources of records of the Norwich diocese are to the Norwich diocesan archives in the City Library, Norwich, unless otherwise stated.

All dates are given new style, i.e. the year beginning 1 January.

References to the 'Chancery Court' without any qualification refer to the Court of Audience or Chancery of the Archbishop of York.

INTRODUCTION

'The records of the Ecclesiastical Courts, particularly in the post-Reformation period, form one of the most intractable and forbidding of historical sources. Much labour is apt to produce little save material for an historical gossip column.'[1] This stricture, by an accomplished historian, is enough to deter any reader from even considering a book produced almost wholly from such material to be worth his while to peruse. Yet the church courts were never busier, nor ecclesiastical discipline more intense, than in the post-Reformation decades. The machinery of administration, discipline and litigation bequeathed to the Reformed Church of England by the Middle Ages, was taken over by Tudor and Stuart lawyers who tried to breathe into it the efficiency of Tudor and Caroline bureaucrats.

It is the object of the present work to describe how this machinery functioned, with special reference to a single diocese, that of York. The courts in their civil and disciplinary aspects were so much intertwined that no attempt has been made to separate them. The church historian will therefore find here much that is new to him, but he has to accept it as part of church life of the time. The same men were concerned with proving of a will, adjudicating a dispute over tithes, disciplining a person who led an immoral life, allocating a seat in church, divorcing a couple whose matrimonial life had become unbearable or enforcing the maintenance of a churchyard wall. For good or ill, all these activities came under the aegis of the Church, and her life and reputation were bound up with them. Theological disputes have captured the historian's attention during this period, and the life of the average person has been left to the chattier type of antiquary. It is hoped to show in this book that the systematic study of court records does bring its own rewards, and introduces a new dimension into the picture of church life at the time.

The developed medieval Church was as much a legal institution as it was a society preparing for a heavenly existence, and its lawyers and administrators were often better rewarded in this life than its theologians. The medieval legal scene was, to a modern observer, very complicated. In western Europe there were basically three systems of law operating at the same time—local customary law, Roman or civil law and canon law. There was cross-fertiliza-

---

[1] Canon Eric Kemp, in a review in the *Journal of Ecclesiastical History*, XIV, 266.

tion of ideas between them which served for mutual enrichment. During the sixteenth century there was a renewed interest in, and assimilation of, civil law, with a consequent supersession of local law. Throughout Europe this Reception of the civil law typified the gradual dying of medieval ideas and their replacement by the ideas of the Renaissance. Amid rising nationalism, the Renaissance supplied a common cultural background for the peoples of the new self-conscious states of western Europe. When, for instance, John Calvin's father took his son away from the study of theology at Paris in 1528 and sent him to Orleans to read law under one of the greatest expositors of the Reception in France, Pierre l'Estoile, he was only acting as a wise and far-seeing father should have done. Calvin later graduated as a doctor of law at that university, and although his own interests developed in other ways, his legal studies became part of his intellectual equipment, as they did of educated Europeans generally, whether Catholic or Protestant. In the British Isles, only Scotland shared in the Reception.

In medieval Europe, the different systems of law gave much scope for rivalry. The field of conflict was even wider because church and secular courts both existed and often disputed their respective jurisdictions. The rivalry was particularly evident between the canon and the civil law. Similar in many respects, with a common inheritance from the Roman Empire, they had each developed their own particular theories, assumptions, ideals and ethos. Their political differences, leading to the exaltation of the Pope and the Emperor respectively, are well known, but such differences were only one variety among many.

The scene in medieval England was similar to that on the continent of Europe. There were three systems of law practised—canon, civil and the common law, the latter being the customary law of England. Again there was both rivalry and cross-fertilization of ideas. Common law had its own peculiar ways of criminal investigation and procedure, but in non-criminal matters it was particularly concerned with land and non-moveable property (real estate). In these subjects it learned little from other sources , but it was from canon law that the developing court of equity, the Chancery Court, received some of its basic principles and also its method of procedure—not unnaturally as many of the medieval lord chancellors were clerics. Common law had no maritime law, so that when the court of the Lord High Admiral acquired the jurisdiction of cases concerning ships and the sea, it was natural that it should use civil law and civil lawyers. Church courts came to have jurisdiction in matters of probate of wills and administration of intestate estates (except for real estate subject to common law), and they likewise used civil law. These courts also were originally the only courts dealing with matrimonial, slander and tithe suits, using canon law together with customary law in matters of tithe.

It is necessary to emphasize that canon law was not simply an administrative code made up of individual canons, but was a system with its own principles, rules and methods, studied at the universities as a distinct discipline. It was unfortunate that the doctrine of papal monarchy explicit in canon law led Henry VIII to abolish its study in the universities. Obviously such a principle could not be taught when the king was Supreme Head of the Church, but it meant that the future of canon law was in the hands of men whose principles were those of civil law. Canon law became subjected not so much to internal development within the Reformed Church as to development by the body of civil lawyers whose inspiration was to be found in the political theories of the later Roman Empire. The sources of canon law were studied, but its application was influenced by civil law.

The use of Latin in teaching enabled the English universities to study the whole range of literature produced on civil law in Europe, and also allowed them to appoint noted jurists, such as Gentili, to the Regius Professorships which Henry VIII had founded. In this way, civil lawyers kept English legal studies abreast of developments elsewhere, which was particularly important in Admiralty work where litigants were often foreigners, and in negotiating trade and other agreements with foreign countries. Civil lawyers had already become sufficiently important for the advocates who practised in the courts in and around London to form themselves into an organized body about 1508, and to acquire permanent premises in 1565. This was the corporation known as Doctors' Commons (for the advocates at London had to be doctors of the civil law). In 1600 there were twenty-four practising advocates, but a list of members in 1639[1] has fifty-two names on it, for it included those in full-time employment elsewhere and also the judges of the London courts themselves. It was this body which in effect ruled the profession, and served the same purpose which the Inns of Court performed for the common law.

The Reformation in England was therefore of considerable benefit to the civil lawyers, for they took over all the work of the church courts, at a time when their business was beginning to expand. Besides increasing Admiralty work, civil lawyers were also appointed to influential posts as Masters in Chancery, where they assisted the Lord Chancellor in his judicial duties, they secured places as Masters (or judges) in the developing Court of Requests and in the Star Chamber Court. Civil law not only magnified the prerogatives of the monarch, but it had also been evolved to suit the need of a highly bureaucratized administrative system. As such, it fitted admirably

---

[1] R.VII.P.R.108, 109.

the needs of the developing monarchies of Europe, and helped to produce what is known as 'administrative law'. Something similar happened in England through the work of the Star Chamber, the Privy Council and its offshoots—the Councils in the North and of the Marches (for Wales). How far this English development can be ascribed to the influence of civil law is a moot point, for all these bodies had common law members also, but it cannot all be said to have developed by accident.

In the sphere of church administration, the combined influence of civil lawyer and practical administrator is best seen in the Court of High Commission, established by statute at the beginning of Elizabeth's reign. Being a statutory body it was not a court Christian but a secular court dealing with church discipline. It took over and adapted the procedure of the church courts, as it likewise used the civil lawyers practising in those courts, but its primary purpose was to see that the will of the government in religious affairs was enforced. To this end, it had its own machinery for arresting suspects, fining and imprisoning them. Students of the period will be familiar with the propaganda of the Puritans against the court's use of the *ex officio* oath.[1] This oath had a long and respected history behind it as used in the church courts, but the essential feature of canonical discipline was that it was intended not so much to punish as to reform the offender. If something stronger than admonition was needed, he was made to perform public penance. This was a punishment, and was so described, but it did not hurt his person, restrict his liberty, nor touch his wealth. Its primary purpose was to extract a public confession of guilt, an expression of contrition, a profession of reformation and, incidentally, to serve as a warning to others. The purpose of the High Commission was as much to punish as to reform; it was therefore right that exception should be taken to its use of an oath intended to extract from the accused an admission of his own guilt, based on his answers to charges of which he had no previous knowledge until his examination.

The ability of an accused person to testify under oath in his own defence was one of the advantages of the church court procedure (copied by Chancery) over that of the common law, and it was only in official prosecutions (not in civil causes or prosecutions by a private person) that the *ex officio* oath was used. In the church courts it does not often seem to have extracted much information which the accused would not have otherwise provided voluntarily, when pleading guilty. Cases where the accused was proved guilty after having denied the charge on oath do not seem to have been followed by a

---

[1] For the origins and use of this oath, and the attacks on it, see the essay by M. H. Maguire in *Essays in History and Political Theory in Honor of C. H. McIlwain* (Cambridge, Mass., 1936). The most substantial complaint was that the accused had no knowledge of the charges against him before his examination.

4

prosecution for perjury, to which technically they were liable. The limitations of the church court, despite the *ex officio* oath, are exemplified in the examination of a Puritan clergyman, John Birchall.[1] The court had power to order a re-examination for fuller and clearer answers, if not satisfied with the original ones. Birchall was strongly suspected of having given the Holy Communion to Puritan non-parishioners. Here are his two answers:

Original answer	*Fuller answer*
This Respondent hath ordinarily within the space of fouer, five or six or seven weeks or thereabouts had Communions upon Sundayes at the Church articulate, And he denieth that he hath given the Sacrament usually to divers persons which he hath knowne at that tyme to have absented themselves from prayers at their owne parrishe Church, or which he hath knowne not to receive at their owne parish Church, unles Mrs. Scott with her daughters.	Ever since this respondent came to be Parson of the parish Church of St. Martins in Micklegate articulate, which is for the space of three yeares ended at Easter next, there hath beene Communions att the sayd parish Church of St. Martins some time at the end of the moneth some time within the compasse of five, six, seaven, eight, nine, tenn or eleaven weeks for and during the time that he hath beene Parson before confessed but not alwaies monethly as is articulate [i.e. as stated in this article of the libel against him] yet this respondent denieth that he hath given the sacrament usually to divers persons which he hath knowne att that tyme to have absented themselves from prayers att their owne parish Church or which he hath knowne not to receive att their owne parish Church, unles Mrs. Scott with her daughters.

The second answer was certainly 'fuller' but it contained no extra relevant information, and the case was later transferred to the High Commission. What action was taken by the Commissioners in this case is not known owing to loss of records, but they had it in their power to bring pressure to bear on an accused person by remanding him in custody as long as they thought fit. It was probably this power which brought such violent opposition to the use of the *ex officio* oath by that court.

The detection and prosecution of a criminal always pose great problems if fairness to the accused (who may be innocent) is to be balanced against efficiency of investigation and the conviction of the guilty. It would be hard

[1] See my *Puritans and the Church Courts in the Diocese of York 1560–1642* (1959), pp. 74–92, and R.VII.H.2123.

to claim that the balance has been achieved even today, and it certainly did not exist in the sixteenth and seventeenth centuries in the secular courts. At that time torture was still used (as on Guy Fawkes) to extract confessions in important cases. In lesser matters the examining magistrates questioned the accused and the witnesses separately and in private, and made available the resulting depositions only to the prosecution. Thus the accused had no notice of the case against him until his trial began, and, as he was not allowed counsel, he had to undertake cross-examination of the prosecution's witnesses himself. He was further handicapped because he could not compel witnesses to attend on his behalf, and there were no 'rules of evidence' or 'Judges rules' as we know them. The division between detective and judge was not as clear as today. A High Court judge could still both supervise the preparation of the case against an accused and sit in judgement upon him.

Within its historical context, the church courts' procedure was not as out of line with contemporary standards of justice as is sometimes made to appear. The defendant in a church court enjoyed certain substantial advantages not enjoyed by a person accused in the secular courts of the time:

(1) He did not know the contents of the libel against him until he was examined, but he could only be examined on the specific charges itemized in the different articles of the libel. There was no equivalent of the general investigation carried out by Justices of the Peace where they could try to discover anything of which the accused might be guilty.

(2) After his examination he was allowed full legal representation in court.

(3) He could compel the attendance of witnesses on his behalf.

(4) He could secure copies of his own and all the witnesses' depositions, and of any documents exhibited in the case.

(5) Examination and cross-examination of the accused and all witnesses was undertaken by an officer of the court, usually the registrar, who was impartial. He read the articles, any later articles or questions submitted by either side, and then framed questions to elicit the required information which he wrote down. These depositions were then read over in the presence of the judge and each person had an opportunity of making any changes he deemed necessary. Each deposition was signed by the person making it and endorsed by the judge.

This method of examination was of considerable importance to the accused because of the standards of contemporary examination in secular courts. From Elizabethan times, the successful prosecution counsel was one who could most terrify his witnesses, reduce them to pulp, appear to make them contradict themselves, and only when they were suitably abject begin the process of extracting the evidence he really wanted.[1] The rooted objection, which still lingers in places, to giving evidence in court is a justifiable hangover from this unfortunate period in English legal history.

The only real lowering of standards in the York courts came during the few years of the Laudian regime before the Civil War. The standards which are observed by professional men are usually unwritten, and therefore are difficult to unearth from purely manuscript sources. This is particularly true of the detection and prosecution of crime, yet these standards can make the difference between a just and an unjust system. The church system, where the chancellor or archdeacon's Official was responsible both for the detection and bringing of offenders to trial, and also for trying them, was one particularly open to abuse if the standards were not maintained. Up to the time of the Laudian administration no real abuse of this system has been discovered. The Laudian lawyers, however, had a tendency to arraign a Puritan and charge him with certain specified nonconformist practices. These would be denied and no further proceedings would be taken. Evidently the evidence in the possession of the chancellor was insufficient to obtain a conviction, and it was hoped to secure what was needed from the accused himself. This was apparently as far as the York lawyers were prepared to go.

Lord Devlin has observed that the standards of the police in England are today maintained in part by the standards of the lawyers they have to employ. Few solicitors and even fewer barristers are engaged solely on the work of criminal prosecution. Most of those concerned with such cases also appear often for the defence and in civil suits and so do not become 'prosecution-minded'. The same was generally true of the ordinary church courts. At London there was a king's advocate and king's proctor (whose functions await examination), but at York and other courts official prosecutions were shared among the ordinary lawyers. A king's advocate was appointed at York by the Laudians, but he prosecuted only in the High Commission, he still had to allocate his cases among the proctors, and he carried on a normal legal practice as well. The effect must have been similar to that noted by Lord Devlin in contemporary England.[2]

[1] C. P. Harvey, *The Advocate's Devil* (1958), pp. 130–48. Sir James Stephen, *History of the Criminal Law*, I, 350, quoted by T. F. T. Plucknett, *Concise History of the Common Law* (5th ed. 1956), p. 434. The prisoner was allowed counsel to argue points of law, but he was not fully represented in treason trials until 1696 and in felonies until 1837. From 1702 he was allowed (in these cases) to produce his own witnesses and have them sworn, but not until 1898 was he allowed to give evidence on oath himself. In Elizabethan and Stuart times the judges issued warrants and conducted examinations in important cases (*W. S. Holdsworth, A History of English Law*, 7th ed. 1956, I, 296).

[2] P. Devlin, *The Criminal Prosecution in England* (1960), pp. 21–2. Because the advocates at York could practise throughout that province, even the king's advocate in the North could find himself defending clients before the Durham High Commission Court (*Acts of the High Commission Court within the Diocese of Durham*, Surtees Soc. vol. 34, pp. 181, 188 (Mottershed)).

It was in the small court at Nottingham, served only by three or four local lawyers, that standards really slipped. The king's advocate at York secured one lawyer (Hatfield Reckles) who would co-operate, and who thus obtained most of the work of official prosecution. The practice evolved here was to make a general accusation of evasion of duty (e.g. in the case of churchwardens, of not presenting the offenders, or of a private person for disturbing a service in an unspecified manner), in the hope that the accused would themselves supply the details, without which a conviction could not be obtained. Even so, among the many prosecutions begun at Nottingham at this time in the interests of ecclesiastical discipline, the great majority were quite properly conducted according to normal practice.[1] The fact that the king's advocate could use a doubtful legal expedient at Nottingham, but not at York, is a strong indication that the church officials did have to observe the standards of the lawyers of their courts where these were strongly established. They were not entirely free to do as they pleased. The protection which the traditional church court system gave to an incumbent, added to his common law freehold, secured the Puritan clergyman in his benefice provided that he was an outward conformist. Even notorious Puritans (such as Birchall) survived because of the inability of the church officials to secure enough evidence or an admission of guilt by the normal methods. One wonders how long these men would have survived examination by a seventeenth-century barrister under common law methods. Some credit for the protection of such men must be given to the church court procedures, for without them the principle of *cuius regio eius religio* must have applied in England as well as in the Holy Roman Empire.

The stress under which the church authorities operated as a result of Puritan attacks from within and without must be appreciated. They were as conscientious in their stand for the Church as were the Puritans for their different brands of Protestantism. They took what action was needed in a desperate situation, and their opponents naturally squealed. Today, in order to secure more convictions of those whom the police regard as guilty, the rule of unanimity of juries has been abolished (what would Lord Chief Justice Coke have said about that?). One result of the *ex officio* oath controversy was the principle enshrined in English law that 'no man may be compelled to give evidence against himself'. Yet the reluctance of twentieth-century magistrates and juries to deal adequately with driving while under the influence of drink, has caused the executive to compel a motorist to undergo tests which might incriminate him as effectively as oral evidence.[2] At the time

---

[1] For particulars of such cases, see my *Puritans and the Church Courts*, pp. 192–3.

[2] The compulsory samples legislation also has the feature of fixed penalties. Some ecclesiastical offences, e.g. illegal marriages and violence on consecrated ground, also carried the fixed penalty

nonconformity with the established religion was seen as a disruption of society, and needed the severest penalties. Likewise sexual immorality was thought to produce the same result, and was punished with equal or greater severity. There is always a tendency in society to turn currently fashionable sins (by which is meant sins which it is fashionable to denounce) into crimes. Today, immorality between consenting adults is officially considered to be their own concern, but the sin of discrimination against a person because of his race (long permitted when 'only' Jews suffered) has been turned into a crime.

The general history of the law during this period is one of rivalry between the courts. For many centuries the limitations of common law prevented its courts from encroaching on other courts' preserves, but already by the end of the Middle Ages it was seeking to extend its sphere of operations. Common law originally had no law of slander, but from the end of the fifteenth century its courts gradually appropriated much of the litigation in this field. They adopted the principle that the church courts had jurisdiction only where the defamation was of a crime cognizable in the church courts. The conflict between the common and civil law courts reached its peak during this period. To the modern observer, the morality of the common law attack seems to leave much to be desired. A highly righteous attitude towards the *ex officio* oath went hand-in-hand with an attack on the Admiralty Court. Common law courts had no law merchant themselves, but nevertheless tried to prevent the suitor taking his lawful remedy at the Admiralty. The result was to leave the suitor powerless to achieve justice. It was only gradually that the common lawyers absorbed the law merchant and remedied the wrong which they had created.

The method by which the common law judges attacked other courts was through the writ of prohibition. The litigant in a civil law court who could discover a pretext for suggesting that the court had exceeded its jurisdiction could sue out this writ and stay proceedings. He would go to a judge of one of the High Courts at Westminster in his chambers, and if the judge thought that there was any plausibility in the litigant's suggestion, he would grant a prohibition. The litigant had a statutory period of six months in which to prove his allegation, and the common law judges helped him by interpreting this period as exclusive of legal vacations. Some litigants of the period waged what can only be described as legal campaigns, going from court to court with their cases. Clever litigants managed to play off the old common law courts against the rising equitable royal Chancery Court. Similarly, they had

of excommunication. Judges mitigated this rigour by granting almost immediate absolution for technical irregularities or minor offences, but fees still had to be paid for sentence and absolution. The result was to add fuel to the criticism that church courts acted only for fees.

much success from the end of the sixteenth century in pitting these courts against those of the civil law. Especially when Sir Edward Coke sat on the bench (1606–16), the common law judges were only too ready to allow their suspicions of the other courts to over-ride the real demands of justice in each case. By the time James I came to the throne the church authorities had become seriously worried by the growing number of prohibitions, although they did not admit that the growing number of causes inevitably produced a rise in complaints to the common law judges. The departure of Coke from the bench removed the influence which had stiffened the other judges, and prohibitions were not granted quite so readily, but the result had been the erection of certain rules which limited the jurisdiction of the civil law courts and so made them less attractive to litigants.

The procedure in courts of civil and canon law was so different from our own legal processes that it is necessary to summarize it. Most disciplinary prosecutions resulted from presentments made by churchwardens at episcopal or archidiaconal visitations. Those presented were tried summarily. In consistory courts both civil and disciplinary causes were conducted by lawyers acting for the parties, and each cause progressed by a series of well-defined stages. Each stage was taken on one day in a formal session, and there was a delay of a fortnight or three weeks between stages while citations were issued, evidence was taken or documents exchanged. Later, when the facts had been established as far as possible, counsel argued the merits of the cause before the judge at 'informations' which were in public, but were not regarded as formal court sessions and were not entered in the acts of court. The judge prepared his verdict (which did not normally contain his reasons but only his decisions) and delivered it at a formal session. The acts for a court day therefore recorded the causes in progress and which stage was taken in each; only rarely did some interesting legal material get entered.

The method of promotion to the bench also differed from common law courts. In the latter the judges were, and are, restricted to able counsel who have proved themselves in arguing cases and handling points of law. Advocates who practised before the church courts were sometimes appointed to be chancellors of dioceses, but very often these ecclesiastical judges were drawn from men whose training had been almost entirely academic. For instance, at the beginning of the sixteenth century Archbishop Warham appointed Cuthbert Tunstal, afterwards Bishop of Durham, to be his chancellor, only three years after the completion of his university studies. But Tunstal's university education lasted for fourteen years, including six at Padua where he had taken his doctorate.[1] Nevertheless university training was not devoid

[1] C. Sturge, *Cuthbert Tunstal* (1938), pp. 8–17.

of the practice of the law. English students did not have to content themselves with 'moots', there were consistory courts at both Oxford and Cambridge where the law could be observed in action. Two of the last advocates to be admitted at York before the Civil War, Glisson and Worlich, were recorded as having attended the Ely Consistory Court (held in Great St Mary's church at Cambridge) when they were fellows of Trinity Hall, and Worlich sometimes acted as substitute for the chancellor at formal sessions.[1] This chancellor was Dr Thomas Eden, who had been successively civil law tutor at Trinity Hall, professor of law at Gresham College, London, an advocate of Doctors' Commons, judge of the Archdeaconry of Sudbury (Norwich Diocese), master of Trinity Hall and chancellor.[2] He had succeeded Dr Clement Corbett in the tutorship, professorship and mastership, in the latter post when Corbett left Cambridge to become chancellor of the diocese of Norwich in his home county of Norfolk. This complete freedom of movement between advocacy, academic study and the bench (and in places where there were more than one court it was possible for a judge in one to be an advocate in another) made for lawyers with a better appreciation of law as a whole. The connection of law with life, and of civil law with the continent, was maintained because (in part) of the demand for civil lawyers as technical experts in all negotiations with foreign countries, and they were often sent on missions abroad. It was still possible to study in European universities, and Sir Julius Caesar, one of the most eminent of Elizabethan civilians, took his doctorate at the University of Paris. The civil law school at Oxford was noted, through its professors, for the study of international law. Alberico Gentili pioneered its systematic study during his professorship (1587–1608), and Richard Zouche (1620–61) developed his work and that of the more famous Dutchman Grotius. Generally speaking, the horizons of the civilian were wider than those of the common lawyer.[3]

[1] University Library, Cambridge, Ely Diocesan Archives, D2/47.
[2] Eden was one of the most attractive of civilians. The High Church Archbishop Neile of York referred to him as 'my good friend' (see under Glisson in List of Advocates), yet Eden took the Parliamentary side in 1640 (H. E. Malden, *Trinity Hall*, 1902, pp. 136–7). Trinity Hall had been founded to promote the study of canon and civil law; the latter was continued until the abolition of civil law courts in the nineteenth century.
[3] M. H. Curtis, *Oxford and Cambridge in Transition 1558–1642* (1959), pp. 154–61.

1

CHURCH COURTS

Before beginning this study of the diocese of York, it may be helpful to set the stage by describing the situation as it existed generally in England and Wales. This can be most usefully achieved by outlining the organization which the Archbishop of Canterbury supervised in his province and diocese, and by taking a typical southern diocese, that of Norwich, and showing how its different legal responsibilities were discharged. By the time of the Reformation the different ecclesiastical jurisdictions had evolved, and most of the disputes between them had been settled. So we shall be reviewing a relatively stable organization, but one which was still capable of development when occasion demanded it, and which had not yet fossilized. The interplay between jurisdictions, and *ad hoc* compromises achieved at various times in their history, meant that there was no one pattern of diocesan administration uniformly observed throughout the country, yet this chapter will do something to provide a context into which the story of the York courts can be placed.

THE PROVINCIAL COURTS OF CANTERBURY

The Archbishop of Canterbury has always led a dual existence, as a diocesan bishop and as the head of his province, symbolized by his two official residences at Canterbury and London. His administration likewise became divided, with the diocesan Consistory Court and its officials being at Canterbury and his provincial administration at London. From this came the first difference between York and Canterbury, for York was itself the northern capital and consequently the courts and administrative officials there transacted both provincial and diocesan business. If we except the Court of Faculties, which was set up at the Reformation as an administrative department to issue faculties, licences and dispensations previously obtained from the Pope, there were three provincial courts of Canterbury—Audience, Arches and Prerogative. The latter supervised the rights of the archbishop in matters testamentary, for where a deceased person had *bona notabilia* (goods exceeding £5 in value) in more than one ecclesiastical jurisdiction (diocesan or peculiar), the necessary probate or administration had to be obtained from the archbishop. The Court of Arches was the normal appellate court for the province and had been established in London since *c.* 1300, but, like medieval bishops, the archbishop also kept a Court of Audience. The fact that the greater part of his work was provincial rather than diocesan caused his Audience Court to have provincial rather than diocesan jurisdiction. By the sixteenth century the Audience Court of a bishop had become the court of his vicar-general or chancellor, dealing with administrative matters (such as institutions to benefices) and the exercise of discipline. This was true also of that of the Archbishop of Canterbury, but in his Audience Court he also heard appeals. The result was that there was little practical difference between the Audience and Arches Courts.[1] Where one person was judge of both courts there was no conflict of jurisdictions, but Archbishop Grindal appointed one judge for each, and the resultant disputes seem only to have been settled when two subsequent judges were given joint patents to both courts and left to settle matters between themselves. Where two courts each exercised the same jurisdiction (as did the Audience and Arches in the hearing of appeals) they were said to exercise concurrent jurisdiction.

DIOCESAN COURTS

Another example of concurrent jurisdiction was in the diocese of Canterbury itself, where the Consistory Court of the archbishop and the Archdeacon of Canterbury's court both heard causes from the whole of the diocese, with the exception of some few parishes and in matrimonial causes.[2] In places where the archdeacon and bishop had such a concurrency, the bishop had the advantage that in the years of his visitation of the diocese (every fourth year) he could inhibit the archdeacon from acting in a judicial or administrative capacity (except at inductions) and so cause all business to come into his own court, or alternatively his chancellor could appoint a judge to sit in the archdeacon's court. A study of another concurrency has been made by Mr R. Peters in his *Oculus Episcopi* which describes the small archdeaconry of St Albans (formerly the peculiar jurisdiction of that abbey) during the years

---

[1] See I. J. Churchill, *Canterbury Administration*, 2 vols. (1933), and for the Arches and Audience Courts in the reign of Elizabeth especially pp. 594–605. It is possible that at this time there was still a distinction between them, in so far as the Audience Court alone could deal with benefice and disciplinary matters; after the Civil War both courts decided such causes, see M. D. Slatter, 'The Records of the Court of Arches', *Journal of Ecclesiastical History*, IV, 139–53, and H. Conset, *The Practice of the Spiritual Courts* (3rd ed. 1708), pp. 4–8.

[2] For these courts see B. L. Woodcock, *Medieval Ecclesiastical Courts in the Diocese of Canterbury* (1952).

1580–1625. The study is not a complete account of the court's workings, for little is said of the litigation in non-criminal suits, but the point is made that the court complained that it was losing business to the Consistory Court of London.[1] Clearly, where two courts were competing for business, the one which offered the greater facilities had the advantage.

In some dioceses this competition between the bishop and his archdeacons had been largely eliminated in the course of time by the bishop devolving some of his diocesan powers to local commissaries. The archdeacons appointed the respective commissaries to be their Officials. In this way, one judge served in each district, combining in himself all local ecclesiastical power and preventing any possible friction. Such arrangements were made in the large dioceses of Lincoln and Norwich, in part of the diocese of London and in certain other dioceses.[2] Although this removed any cause for disagreement between the bishop and his archdeacons, it did not altogether remove possibilities of friction between the diocesan consistory court and those of the commissaries.[3]

Enough has been said to show that, while church courts transacted a uniform type of business, there was no one uniform pattern for the country. The court to which one went for litigation or to obtain a licence varied from diocese to diocese. Over most of the country the situation depended on the way in which the bishop and his archdeacons had shared the work between them. One exceptional feature of the York diocese was the failure of the three Yorkshire archdeacons to secure any share of ecclesiastical administration or litigation, save only the summary discipline of their annual visitation courts. The outlying parts of the diocese, Nottinghamshire and, in the Middle Ages, the Archdeaconry of Richmond, had achieved some independence. Richmond's independence had eventually become virtually complete, but Henry VIII altered northern administration by including this archdeaconry in his newly founded diocese of Chester. By merging the archdeaconry into the bishopric, he eliminated Richmond's independence and the archdeaconry court became an episcopal consistory court. The Bishop of Chester was therefore probably unique in England in having two consistory courts instead of one. His position, however, was complicated not by archdeacon's rights but by the traditional rights of the rural deans to exercise some ad-

---

[1] Pp. 30, 80.

[2] The nature of the business done in the Consistory Court and the growth of the Commissary Courts in the diocese of Lincoln have been traced by C. Morris in two articles in the *Journal of Ecclesiastical History*, x, 50–65 and xiv, 150–59.

[3] *The Registrum Vagum of Anthony Harison*, trans. by T. F. Barton, Norfolk Record Soc. vol. xxxii (1963), contains the chancellor's complaints against the commissaries of Norwich diocese (vol. i, pp. 33–4) and the commissaries' complaints against the activities of the newly appointed apparitors of the Consistory Court (pp. 46–8).

ministrative and disciplinary powers. In the course of our study we shall notice how the archbishops of York eliminated these rights in their own diocese, and the reason why such divergence of development occurred has yet to be explained.

DIOCESE OF NORWICH

Despite the fact that it is impossible to speak of an 'average' church court because of local differences of custom, nevertheless it will be profitable to begin our study with a brief description of the Consistory Court of Norwich. One reason for this is that the type of document which has survived the march of time varies from court to court, and a survival in one place may illuminate a gap in another. Another reason is that the York courts were primarily concerned with diocesan business, and that therefore they merit comparison with the court at Norwich rather than with any of those of the Archbishop of Canterbury. Lastly, if the same things are found at both York and Norwich it increases the probability of their being normal in the country as a whole.

The best starting-point at Norwich is a registrar's account book of 1635–6, which contains entries for most of the work done in his office and the fees charged for the same.[1] It is true that the year 1635 was the one when Archbishop Laud's provincial visitation reached the diocese, but the registrar still carried out his usual routine and the book is a reliable guide to his activities. Table 1 shows the sources of his income (with the adjustments mentioned) for the year 1 March 1635 to 28 February 1636.

TABLE I

Principal sources of the Norwich Diocesan Registrar's income, 1635–6

	£	s.	d.
Court fees (litigation between parties)	89	5	4
Marriage licences	79	12	6
Probates and administrations	74	9	10
Other licences, sequestrations, etc.	10	17	0
Court fees from disciplinary cases	6	11	8
	260	16	4
Add fees from institutions (estimated)	15	9	4
	276	5	8

(Unless otherwise stated, the fees mentioned as payable at Norwich are those payable to the registrar only, not the total fees.)

The Consistory Court. The pattern at both York and Norwich is not quite the same—a gradual increase in litigation between parties throughout the six-

[1] COS/1.

teenth century, reaching a peak about 1590 is common to both, and also a gradual decline setting in from about 1600, but in the north there was a slight revival in the decade before the Civil War. The earliest complete legal year for which evidence is available is that for 1509–10[1] and the number and type of cause then heard is shown in Table 2.

TABLE 2

Norwich Consistory Court litigation, 1509–10

Testamentary (official prosecutions)	19
Defamation	17
Tithe	15
Disciplinary (official prosecutions)	15
Matrimonial	9
Disciplinary (private prosecutions)	7
Testamentary (actions between parties)	6
Not stated	4
Recovery of mortuaries	2
Recovery of legacies	2
	96

Five proctors are mentioned in the act book of the court and of these only three were active. Two out of the three were university graduates but one of these two did not appear in many cases. Cases were heard at two- or three-weekly intervals, and on two or three days in those weeks, with occasional hearings on other days.

If we now jump nearly a century, to late Elizabethan days, certain changes are at once apparent. Official prosecutions had become separated from litigation between parties. The hearings had been standardized to thirteen sessions a year, but each session lasted two days. Litigation had vastly increased: the 62 cases between parties begun in 1509–10 had risen to something like 200, and those from the western part of the diocese were heard at Ipswich when the chancellor attended there for the twice-yearly synods of the clergy. The number of proctors was now ten, of which eight actually practised.

Because figures of the number of cases heard in a court are frequently mentioned in this work, something must be said about how these figures are calculated. In the earliest Norwich court book the record of the production in court of the certificate that the defendant has been cited to court in such-

---

[1] ACT/1. Depositions of witnesses are found as early as 1499 and have been calendared by E. D. Stone, *Norwich Consistory Court: Depositions 1499–1512 and 1518–30* (Norfolk Record Society, vol. x, 1938), but these do not provide the complete record of the business before the court. This can only be traced in the court A.Bs. themselves.

and-such a cause has been entered. It is easy therefore to count the number of causes, and their type, introduced to the court in a given period. At York, the first act in a cause is easily identified, and the nature of the action is recorded in this first act. This seems to have been general practice, but not at Norwich in Elizabethan and later times. In the later act books at the Norwich court the first mention of a cause is not usually readily identifiable and its nature is not given. Because there were only thirteen sessions each year at Norwich, each case normally came up for hearing at each session and the number of cases before the court at any time can be simply counted. Thus in 1598 there were 436 causes, in 1602, 322, in 1605, 302, in 1635, 275, and in 1636, 298. These figures include causes where the defendant had not yet appeared and ones which were agreed or abandoned in course of time. If it is assumed that the average cause took eighteen months in court at Norwich, then about A.D. 1600 some 200 causes a year must have been commenced in the court, and a rather lower figure two or three decades later. There are two volumes of the articles on which each cause is based, together with the defendants' replies, for the years 1623–4 and 1636–7,[1] which should provide an indication of the number of contested causes. There were 129 such articles and replies for 1623–4 and 123 for 1636–7. The number of contested causes was about three-quarters of the total commenced,[2] so that the number of articles and replies is about what would be expected. Such a method of cross-checking is not available at York or Nottingham because northern practice was to fold up all the papers in a cause into a small roll rather than to file them in yearly volumes; inevitably some of these were lost, others came to pieces and parts were lost. The southern practice of binding all the articles and replies for one year in one volume, and all the witnesses' depositions in another, has meant that the records for complete years were either lost or preserved together.

The amount of business transacted in a court varied according to the area it served and to the facilities which it offered. The number of lawyers who practised in each court was normally fixed by that court's statutes. The proctors mentioned above were lawyers who conducted a cause through its formal stages in court and were responsible for drawing up all the documents connected with it. In courts other than those of the two archbishops, they also very often undertook the whole management of a cause, including legal argument before the judge. The advocates (who were similar in the functions

---

[1] CON/11 and CON/15.
[2] See 'Reasons against the late orders given to the Consistorie of Norwich...' inserted into the Deposition Book for 1602 (DEP/32): 'Theare be iiij hundred causes dependinge in the consistorie at Norwich whereof iij hundred of them be reasonable good causes, and ordinarilie called uppon...' This document refers to 1602 or 1603.

which they performed to the modern barrister) were an optional extra for a client in the lower courts, but had to be employed in causes in the courts of the two archbishops. Some proctors in the lower courts were graduates in law, but this did not necessarily mean that they were the most successful in their profession.

The figures given above show that about 1620 approximately 170 causes a year were begun in the Norwich Consistory Court. At the same time, 123 causes were begun in the Commissary Court at Bury St Edmunds for the Archdeaconry of Sudbury in the same diocese,[1] and somewhat earlier (1588–90) 57 new causes entered the Ely Consistory Court at Cambridge, rising to 149 in 1635–6.[2] There were eight proctors in active practice at Norwich, but some of these also worked in one or other of the two Commissary Courts for the archdeaconries in the county of Norfolk. The court at Bury St Edmunds had five proctors, but some of these also practised at Cambridge, where the Ely court also had five proctors.[3] Where church courts were reasonably close together a lawyer could secure a good practice if he was prepared to travel.

The Norwich Consistory Court was a busy one, and its fees made up the largest single item of the registrar's income. It seems to have attracted most of the litigation between parties in Norfolk, but little of the business in West Suffolk—the area furthest from Norwich—to judge by the activity of the Commissary Court at Bury St Edmunds. Nevertheless, this part of his work involved the registrar in the greatest amount of labour in proportion to the income produced by it. Each defendant was charged 9*d.* for his examination on the articles (or libel) of the case stated by the plaintiff, and a further 9*d.* was charged for a copy of his answers. The first witness for either plaintiff or defendant also cost 9*d.* but subsequent witnesses only 6*d.* each. Similar charges were made for copies of their depositions. In the thirteen court sessions in 1635–6, 91 defendants and 360 witnesses were examined. Despite the large number of causes involved, sentences were given in only 47 of them, at 3*s.* 4*d.* each. The only large fees charged were for the writing out of the whole papers of a cause which was being sent to the Arches or Audience of

---

[1] For details see below, p. 194, Table 22.

[2] Ely Consistory Court act book 1587–90 at Norwich, ACT/21. The acts for 1 May 1635–30 April 1636 are in the Ely Diocesan Records, D2/47 (Cambridge University Library).

[3] John Blomefield, LL.B., was a proctor in the Ely court in 1588 and in the Sudbury court in 1621. William Revell, LL.B., sued for fees in the Ely court in 1588 (? proctor in the Ely archdeaconry court) and was a proctor in the Sudbury court in 1603—see *Registrum Vagum* I, 29. The two other proctors named in the *Registrum Vagum* as practising in the Sudbury court are not found in the Ely acts for 1587–90. Revell sat as substitute for the Ely judge on one occasion in 1590. It should be possible to discover the activities of proctors more thoroughly as court records are increasingly being studied.

Canterbury on appeal. Many defendants did not answer to their first citation and were excommunicated, but the sentence was only a technical one, and the 32 persons involved paid only a nominal 3*d*. or 6*d*. for absolution. To the court fees recorded in the fee book, one substantial item has to be added, a sum of 2*d*. for the entry in the court acts of what happened in each case at each session. Estimating 275 causes in process of trial at this time, no less than £29. 15*s*. 10*d*. would have been added to the registrar's fees each year from these twopences, and this has been done in the figure given above. In addition, the fee for the issue of the original citation to the defendants (8*d*. each) has to be assumed in each of the 91 causes where they appeared. These fees were probably not entered in the fee book because a separate citation book was normally kept.

The church courts, like all other courts and government agencies during the Tudor and Stuart period, were the subject of contemporary attack for attempting to raise fees. They were forced to do so because of inflationary tendencies in the economy, which made traditional fees unrealistic. Even so, the fees charged at the Norwich Consistory Court in 1635–6 were the same as those charged at the beginning of the reign of Elizabeth, so that the litigant was in effect being provided with a service for less money, in real terms, as the years went by.[1] A cross-check on the fees recorded in the fee book is provided by a bill of expenses for a tithe suit in 1634. These expenses include the fees paid to the proctor and advocates by the successful defendant, which again were the same as those in use seventy years before.[2] If anything extra was taken it must have been on an unofficial basis, such as was not uncommon in those days. The fees charged varied slightly from court to court, but not in any significant amount, and the figures given above may be regarded as typical of any church court.[3]

The causes entering the Norwich Consistory Court in 1509–10[4] can be compared with those entering it in our period, as derived from the books of articles and replies. These are set out in Table 3.

The figures in Table 3 reflect the removal of official prosecutions to a separate court, and the dominance of suits of defamation and for tithes in

---

[1] *Registrum Vagum*, I, 69–73.

[2] Holmes *c*. Hanner, CON 13. The bill totalled £7. 14*s*. 9*d*. and was taxed by the chancellor at £6, but the bill included £1 for the witnesses' expenses and £1 for the party's own expenses. The case covered 24 court sessions (nearly two years), for which the proctor received in fees £2. 0*s*. 8*d*., and advocates £1. 10*s*.

[3] The principal difference between the Norwich Consistory and the Commissary Court of the Archdeaconry of Suffolk was that the proctor's fee per session was 1*s*. at Norwich and 2*s*. at the Commissary Court, and the fee for each act in each case at each session was 2*d*. and 4*d*. respectively—the Suffolk fees are printed in the *Registrum Vagum*, I, 73–5.

[4] Table 2 above, p. 16.

the work of the church courts. This latter feature will constantly recur in the following pages whenever the work of the courts is examined. The minor items fluctuated from year to year and the evidence of a single year is not altogether a reliable guide to their incidence.

TABLE 3

Norwich Consistory Court litigation, 1623–4 and 1636–7

	1623–4	1636–7
Defamation	38	69
Tithe	38	38
Disciplinary (private prosecutions)	23	9
Suits for unpaid legacies	13	nil
Testamentary (between parties)	13	6
Appeals	2	nil
Matrimonial	1	nil
Other	1	1
	129	123

Marriage Licences. All ordinaries, that is those who exercised the ordinary ecclesiastical jurisdiction over a particular area, were able to issue licences for marriages to be performed without the necessity of banns being called in the parish churches of the parties concerned, or for marriages in Advent or Lent. Normally this jurisdiction was exercised for the ordinaries by their legal officers. Some archdeacons or commissaries had also acquired the right through long use (prescription), or by arrangement with their chancellors. In the Norwich diocese the chancellor only admitted that the commissary of the Archdeaconry of Norwich, among the four commissaries in the diocese, had this right.[1] Nevertheless, in the sixteenth and seventeenth centuries the issuing of marriage licences was a growth industry, and any chancellor who knew his job took care to develop his retail outlets.

The retail outlets for this purpose with which we are familiar today are local clergymen who act as chancellors' surrogates for the sole purpose of issuing marriage licences. Such surrogates doubtless existed in seventeenth-century England, but they seem to have left few traces. The probabilities are that they were used in the diocese of York (excluding Nottinghamshire), but no evidence has been found. A book of legal forms in the Ely Diocesan Registry contains forms of a commission to issue licences to marry of the pre-Civil War period, which would appear to be the beginning of the surrogation system.[2] In the Norwich diocese the right was farmed out to the com-

[1] *Registrum Vagum*, I, 28.   [2] Cambridge University Library, F5/34, e.g. fo. 163.

missaries. The fee books of the commissary of Suffolk begin to record the issuing of licences from 1 June 1613, which suggests that an arrangement was then reached with the chancellor.[1]

The Norwich registrar's fee book shows the importance of marriage licence revenue, and helps to keep in perspective criticisms made of fees generally. No one was compelled to be married by licence, and the fees payable to the officiating minister and parish clerk were also higher than when marriage was by banns. Canon CI of 1603 restrained the issuing of licences to 'such persons only as be of good state and quality'; in other words a marriage licence was a status symbol. As the chancellor's fee was the same as that of the registrar, so that a licence cost 8–10s., it was only the middle and upper classes who could afford to be married in this way.

Table 4 analyses the licences issued by the chancellor of Norwich during the greater part of a normal year (1635) and during the time of a diocesan visitation. From the last few days of February until mid-July in a visitation year some at least of the jurisdictions in the diocese were inhibited, resulting in an increased demand for the chancellor's licences by about 100. For these months the fee scale was uplifted to that of the commissaries, and the combined effect of these two factors was to put an extra £30 in the pockets of both chancellor and registrar. The fact that the chancellor's normal fee scale was 1s. per licence lower than that of the commissaries suggests that his arrangement with the latter was that they paid him and his registrar 1s. each for each licence issued. If this was so, then there was a considerable extra source of income for these officers which is not mentioned elsewhere in the estimates of the registrar's fees in this chapter.

Normally, licences were (and are) only issued for marriage in the parishes where either of the two parties was resident. A tendency for ordinaries to issue licences for marriage anywhere within their jurisdiction was checked by the canons of 1597 and forbidden by Canon CII of 1603. These prohibitions were never respected in the diocese of Norwich, either by the chancellor or the commissaries, and it must be assumed that they had a prescript right to issue licences as they did, and so were protected by 25 Henry VIII c. 21. Not even the Archbishop of York had this right. These facilities doubtless increased the sale of licences, and they were so much in demand that even as late as 1648, when civil marriages were introduced, the registry issued fifty-nine in a year. However, by that time a licence was not so valuable as in the

---

[1] E. Suffolk and Ipswich Record Office, 1C/AA6/1. Fos. 89–91 of this volume, covering 12 April–1 June 1613, have been lost, so the issuing may have begun a little earlier. It is also possible that records of such earlier licences may have been previously preserved separately, but they were not being issued in 1603 (*Registrum Vagum*, 1, 28).

TABLE 4

Marriage licences issued by the chancellor of Norwich with fees paid to the diocesan registrar

Month	1635-6							1636-7						
	Free	Under 3s. 6d.	3s. 6d.	4s. 0d.	4s. 6d.	5s. 0d.	Total	Total	Free	Under 3s. 6d.	3s. 6d.	4s. 0d.	4s. 6d.	5s. 0d.
March	—	—	4	15	—	—	19	38	1	—	4	8	4	21
April	—	1	4	31	—	—	36	62	1	—	5	5	15	36
May	—	2	3	26	—	—	31	81	1	—	2	7	18	53
June	1	1	15	21	1	—	39	66	1	—	1	10	7	47
July	1	1	3	33	—	1	39	42	3	—	1	16	—	22
August	—	—	8	25	—	1	34	28	1	—	2	17	2	6
September	—	1	7	20	—	—	28	39	1	—	3	30	—	5
October	—	1	4	38	—	1	44	38	—	—	3	31	1	3
November	—	1	5	21	—	1	28	32	1	—	3	20	3	5
December	—	—	5	22	—	—	27	23	1	—	2	16	2	2
January	—	—	7	25	—	—	32	30	—	—	2	28	—	—
February	—	1	3	33	1	12	50	30	1	1	1	25	—	2
Total	2	9	68	310	2	16	407	509	12	1	29	213	52	202

| Receipts | £79. 12s. 6d. | | | | | | | £110. 0s. 0d. | | | | | | |

From 1 March 1595 to 28 February 1596 only 158 licences were issued, producing about £36. 5s. 4d. in fees; the majority of the licences (where the fee was recorded) being at 5s. (Fiat Book in SUN/2)

days of episcopacy, and its usual value was no more than 2*s*. 6*d*. or less to the registrar, a mere £6. 13*s*. in the year.

Probates and Administrations. The Church in England and Wales had gradually acquired the right to prove wills and grant administrations of the estates of deceased persons in all except a few places. Although this may seem to the modern reader a very peculiar circumstance, it had its advantages, for the church administration provided a better range of offices and courts to do the business than did any contemporary state agency or court. The connection between the Church and probate business, however, had certain important consequences. It was advantageous because it helped to maintain the Church's officers with a good regular income. The registering and storing of wills and accompanying documents involved considerable office work, but probably it was more profitable than the labours demanded by a Consistory Court. Where a court went on circuit (as disciplinary courts often did), probates and administrations could be dispatched at the same time and thus helped to share the overhead expenses. The chief disadvantage was that the Church was involved in the work of unearthing illegal administrations of the estates of the deceased, and where this was done officiously, added odium would fall on the courts.

In the Norwich diocese the chancellor proved the wills and granted administrations of knights, esquires, gentlemen, clergymen and those who died possessed of personal estate in more than one archdeaconry. The local commissaries proved the remaining wills in their respective jurisdictions. Out of the 25 testamentary causes in the Consistory Court in 1509–10, 19 were official prosecutions to enforce the law concerning probate and administration of estates. In later times this enforcement assumed much larger proportions. For instance, in the list of official prosecutions on 16 January 1593, out of 63 causes, 28 were testamentary.[1] Sometimes the proportion was even greater: on 2 October 1617 and 27 March 1618, all the causes were testamentary (8 out of 8 and 30 out of 30).[2] The series of act books of official prosecutions has many gaps and there is little information between 1618 and 1627. By the latter year, testamentary prosecutions had been abandoned (except on presentment at visitations), but a list of 17 was entered in February 1632.[3] These prosecutions were commenced on the instigation of the apparitors of the court, whose instructions were not to cite any administrator or executor until at least fourteen days after the death of the deceased—in order to give time for the voluntary undertaking of their duties by those concerned.[4]

[1] ACT/25. [2] ACT/45. [3] ACT/57.
[4] *Registrum Vagum*, I, 44, shows the apparitors' duties as contained in their oath *c.* 1603. The requirement to cite was still in the apparitors' duties in 1640 (FCB/1, 16 May).

The effect of this enforcement can be gauged by comparing the fee book record of 139 probates and 161 administrations for the year March 1635—February 1636, with the 117 probates and 127 administrations for the year 1648 when there was no ecclesiastical method of compulsion. In revenue to the registrar this represented a drop of only £6, due to increased fees from searches and miscellaneous items:

	Probates	Registering Wills	Administrations	Searches and copies	Other	Total
	£ s. d.	£ s. d.	£ s. d.	£ s. d.	£ s. d.	£ s. d.
1635–6	16 18 6	24 10 6	24 11 0	6 6 9	2 3 1	74 9 10
1648	14 15 2	20 0 0	18 5 0	8 13 4	6 3 8	67 17 2

(Certain items under 'other' in 1648 would be entered under Consistory Court fees if the court had been functioning in that year.)

The fees for probates and administrations were fixed by 21 Henry VIII c. 5, and are set out in Table 5.

TABLE 5

Statutory probate and administration fees

	Value of estate	To the judge	To the registrar
Probate	Under £5	nil	6d.
	£5–£40	2s. 6d.	1s. 0d.
	Over £40	2s. 6d.	2s. 6d. (or 1d. per ten lines of the will)
Administrations	Under £5	nil	nil
	£5–£40	2s. 6d.	2s. 6d.
	Over £40	not fixed	not fixed

The registrar's fee under this statute was evidently intended to include the registering of the will. The actual will was kept in the registry and the grant of probate was written on it, but the registrar also copied all wills into large volumes or registers of wills, where they could be more conveniently consulted. In practice, during our period, the registrars at Norwich charged a flat rate of 2s. 6d. for probate regardless of the value of the estate, although very occasionally they charged less than this amount. They also charged a fee for registering the will which was nowhere near to the ten lines for 1d. mentioned in the statute. It is difficult to determine exactly the basis for this extra charge because it varied so considerably. In a sample of twenty-five wills, the fee ranged from one-half a line for 1d. (15 lines: 2s. 6d.) to four lines for 1d. (54 lines: 12d.). Even wills of the same length were charged differently (54 lines: 3s. 4d. and 2s. 6d.; 45 lines: 3s. 6d.; 44 lines: 2s.; 90 lines: 3s.; 85 lines: 4s.). Nor does it seem that value was a major factor in calculating the fee, for an estate of £69 (54 lines) paid 3s. 4d. and one of £142 (51 lines) paid 3s. It will be seen from the itemized account that the registrar received more from the registration fee than he did from the probate fee itself.

The Norwich registrar charged a flat rate of 3s. 6d. for each administration, although the number of reduced fees for small estates was greater than in the case of probates (4 probates, 28 administrations in 1635–6). He did not take advantage of the fact that there was no fixed fee for estates over £40. The extra 1s. above the statutory 2s. 6d. was for the bond which the administrator had to give in to court.[1] No similar fee for the executors' bonds can be traced in the probate fees, although at York 3s. 6d. was charged for both probates and administrations.[2] Where a commission had to be issued to receive the oath of executor or administrator outside Norwich, Canon CXXXII of 1603 allowed the judge and registrar a fee of 3s. 4d. each in such a case, yet the fee book shows that out of thirty-four such commissions issued in 1635–6, only in six instances was a fee charged.[3] When allowance is made for the inflation of a century since the regulating statute, the legal fees of 7s. 6d. each for the probate of an average will of the upper classes in 1635 cannot be regarded as extortionate.[4] The effect of the commissary court system was to divide the probate work of the diocese between five different courts, so that each of them had a reasonable share of it. In comparison, the centralized administration at York provided enough business for a specialized Exchequer Court.

Other licences, etc. This heading includes preachers' and surgeons' licences (5s. each), curates', schoolmasters' and midwives' licences (2s. 6d.), sequestrations (5s.), faculties for pews (6s. 8d.) and for searches and copies from the bishop's registers. There is not sufficient evidence to give a reliable average figure for licences, as the only other evidence besides the fee book comes from

[1] Bonds are discussed below, p. 109.
[2] The York fees in 1572 are given at the end of Conset's *Practice of the Spiritual Courts*. No set fee is stated for engrossing wills and inventories.
[3] In 1648 when the registry was suffering from loss of business, only six out of eighteen commissions were issued free, and four at reduced fees.
[4] Judge 2s. 6d.; registrar 2s. 6d. plus the average registration fee of almost 2s. 6d. In the Commissary Court of Suffolk, where estates were normally of smaller value, the registrar's probate fees were usually either 1s. 10d. or 2s. 6d., and 1s. 6d. or 2s. 6d. for administrations—but occasionally 5s. was charged. He also charged a fee—3s.—for most commissions. In the Prerogative Court of Canterbury the average registration fee was 5s. (Notestein, Relf and Simpson, *Commons Debates 1621*, VII, 471). In the debates in this Parliament over fees for engrossing wills no criticism was made of court officials, although proctors' charges for seeking probate and engrossing wills were thought to be too heavy, see below p. 53 n.

a period when schoolmasters throughout the diocese were evidently having their credentials checked.[1] For what they are worth, the following figures give some indication of the situation:

	(March–February)					(March–July)
	1582–3	1583–4	1584–5	1595–6	1635–6	1636
Preachers	—	—	—	—	18	29
Surgeons	2	5	4	1	4	6
Curates	9	6	1	8	7	31
Schoolmasters	22	78	23	10	3	22
Midwives	—	1	—	—	—	32

The significance of the last column is that it concerns the months covered by a diocesan visitation, and at a time when the Laudian Church was tightening up its practice on the issue of licences. Such strictness was highly profitable to the registrar, for his income from such licences in these five months was no less than £20. The year 1635, although at the time of Laud's provincial visitation, probably reflected more normal conditions. The lack of preachers' licences in 1582–5 is probably to be explained by a separate register of these items.

Under this heading may also be placed sequestrations and faculties. The figures for the former need explanation to those acquainted with the modern practice of issuing a sequestration each time an incumbent vacates his benefice. In the year 1635–6 there were only fourteen and in the following twelve months twenty-two. In the calendar year 1636 there were thirty-two institutions, compared with twenty-two sequestrations of which four were due to court orders and not to vacancies. (Seven sequestrations brought no fee.) It was one of the duties of the apparitors to report vacancies, but evidently where a presentee appeared promptly for institution (and many benefices were promised by the patrons in advance of vacancies), no sequestration was made.

The only type of faculty issued at this period was for the erection of private pews. Lack of a pew in church may have prompted some applications, but the small but steady growth in the years before the Civil War suggests the rise of another status symbol. These faculties cost 13s. 4d. in all, divided equally between chancellor and registrar.

Disciplinary Causes. During our period official prosecutions (*ex officio mero*) were heard at sessions which were held at the same time as the thirteen Consistory Court sessions, unless the amount of business did not warrant a

[1] SUN/2. In Elizabethan times judge and registrar received only 1s. 8d. each for schoolmasters' licences (Fiat Book in the same bundle).

session being held. The total fees in normal times were not great, and the chancellor was probably correct when he said 'the process ex officio be not beneficial to the Judge aforesayde [i.e. the chancellor] or the Register'.[1] Fees from this source varied according to the prevailing official policy, whether offenders should be actively sought or whether discipline should be left to the churchwardens to present voluntarily, and whether any particular type of offender was being sought for a particular reason. The fees recorded show that on dismissal, for instance of a man and wife charged with ante-nuptial immorality, 2s. 6d. was paid (man and wife were treated as one case). If a person had not appeared until he was denounced excommunicate, he paid 2s. 8d. for the letter of excommunication, his absolution and his certificate letter of absolution in addition to the dismissal fee.

Institutions. To undertake a new benefice was an expensive item. The new incumbent was faced with the following charges:

(1) The possibility of having to pay the legal charges of the patron for drawing up the deed of presentation.

(2) The fees of institution, which were at least 24s. 8d. in the Norwich diocese (10s. to bishop, 5s. to chancellor, 9s. 8d. to registrar—no fee to the apparitor is mentioned).

(3) The fees of induction, 22s. (20s. to the Official of the Archdeacon and his registrar, 2s. to the apparitor).

(4) A sum equal to one year's income to the Crown, as it had been calculated at the time of Henry VIII's *Valor Ecclesiasticus* (first-fruits).

(5) A fee of 1s. 6d. each (in addition to normal fees) at the first visitation of bishop and archdeacon after his institution. This fee was for the registering of his letters of orders and institution and induction deeds.

(6) He had to survey his residence and barns (and, if a rector, the chancel of his church). If they were out of repair he had to settle with the previous incumbent (or his heirs) for the sum needed to put right the defects, or institute a suit in the Consistory Court for dilapidations—for if he did not do so, the responsibility would fall on him.

Due to inflation, the value of livings had grown considerably in money terms since the time of Henry VIII, nevertheless the need to travel to the bishop for institution (usually in the private chapel of whichever of his residences he was using at the time), together with all other charges, must have consumed about half the first year's income of an average benefice. If the new incumbent had the misfortune to be nominated shortly after harvest, he might have to wait for nearly a year before receiving any substantial

[1] *Registrum Vagum*, I, 33.

monetary reward, for the average incumbent still depended for most of his income on tithes or the produce of his glebe.

As the year 1635 was the year of Archbishop Laud's visitation of the diocese of Norwich, no records of institutions are available, but in the year 1636, thirty two are entered in the registers. It is on this number that the figure for institution fees given above is calculated.

Other Income. The registrar's principal additional source of income to those listed above was the fees received at diocesan visitations. There were two classes of fees, those received from persons who were required to attend visitations, and those charged offenders attending disciplinary courts by way of costs. The scale of fees remained constant throughout the period.[1] Each single-beneficed incumbent paid 9*d.*, a pluralist 1*s.* 8*d.*, a schoolmaster 6*d.*, a curate 4*d.*, a licensed preacher 3*d.*, and each parish 1*s.* Averaging 2*s.* for each of 1,300 parishes, the gross income from these fees was £130, divided between chancellor and registrar. Out of this income the administrative and travelling expenses of the visitation had to be met. Each offender had to pay 1*s.* 4*d.* costs (6*d.* chancellor, 6*d.* registrar, 4*d.* apparitor), and very few higher fees were in practice charged (as for absolution or for a schedule of the penance awarded to serious offenders). Allowing for remissions to paupers and bad debts, probably about 1,100 persons paid the standard fees, so that chancellor and registrar each received about £27. 10*s.* from this source, gross. After deducting expenses, including those of excommunicating the large number of non-attenders, of second citations of those not served the first time, and of correspondence about the cases, the net profit from this source must have been less than half the gross profit. The level of costs at Norwich was very modest compared with that at York, where 5*s.* for dismissal was charged in the seventeenth century, with substantially higher sums for additional items. The Norwich court, however, adopted a practice of charging the basic fee for each offence for which an offender was presented, thus slightly raising its income from this source.

One other small item may be mentioned under this heading. As the diocese maintained its right to issue marriage licences for marriages out of the parishes of the parties concerned, so it maintained its right to issue 'personal unions' of benefices—i.e. pluralities, a right not even possessed by the Archbishop of York.[2] The advantage to the incumbent was considerable, for not only was the diocesan registry more accessible than the Faculty Office in

---

[1] *Registrum Vagum*, I, 171 for Elizabethan fees; FCB/1, fo. 19 for those in 1636.
[2] The right was challenged, but was confirmed by the Justices of the Assizes at Bury St Edmunds, *temp.* Elizabeth I (*Registrum Vagum*, I, 172 ff.). It was generally recognized (cf. J. Johnson, *The Clergyman's Vade Mecum*, 2nd ed. 1707, 36), and was extensively used in the eighteenth century.

London, but the fee charged was 26*s*. 8*d*. compared with £4–£6 by the Faculty Office. The registrar issued an average of three 'personal unions' a year during the period 1578–1618,[1] an annual income of £2 each for the chancellor and himself.

Averaging the visitation profits over four years, and allowing for other items, the Norwich registrar had a yearly gross income of about £350–60. His net income would be hard to estimate.

THE COMMISSARY COURT OF THE ARCHDEACONRY OF SUFFOLK

Although the pre-Commonwealth acts of this court are lost, an idea of its work can be gained because of the preservation of some of its account books.[2] The earliest complete year (beginning 26 March) now extant is 1610–11, and the earliest complete year which includes marriage licence revenue is for 1616–17. Either one-quarter (the eighteenth-century figure) or one-fifth[3] of this revenue had to be paid to Norwich, and the larger sum is here assumed.

TABLE 6

Income of the registrar of the Archdeaconry of Suffolk, year 1610–11 unless otherwise stated

	£	s.	d	£	s.	d.
Consistory Court				21	1	8
Probates	33	16	9			
Registering wills	34	12	7			
Administrations	29	6	10			
				97	16	2
Commissions				5	1	2
Searches and copies				9	13	11
Inductions				8	19	4
Visitation fees (approximately)				10	0	0
Marriage licences (year 1616–17)				24	10	0
Other				2	17	6
				£179	19	9

The Consistory Court fees in Table 6 include an estimated £7 for the 4*d*. paid for the act of court in each cause at each session, but excluding the sum, probably 30*s*., for citation fees.

The number of marriage licences issued in 1616–17 was 137, producing

---

[1] *Registrum Vagum*, I, 55 ff., 108 ff.
[2] E. Suffolk and Ipswich Record Office, County Hall, Ipswich, series 1C/AA6/1–. The table of fees in this court, 1603, is in *Registrum Vagum*, I, 73–5.
[3] Above, p. 21.

£31. 3s. 3d. gross; by 1636–7 the number had grown to 264, which should have produced *pro rata* about £60 gross, £45 net to the registrar.

Although the division of fees between the three items of testamentary business has had to be estimated in a few cases, owing to the division not being specified in the account book, it is reasonably accurate. Allowing for the fact that some of the commissions and many of the searches concern testamentary matters, about £110 per annum was derived from the probate jurisdiction. As the only important source of income omitted from this list is the correction court business, the probate jurisdiction provided approximately half the court's income, and the next largest source was the licence revenue. This is the basis for the argument that it was on these two supports that the circuit system rested, for the Consistory Court business contributed a comparatively minor amount to the total fees.[1]

In the year under review twenty-two sentences were delivered in consistory causes, probably representing about thirty causes before the court at any one time. A similar number were being heard in the Archdeaconry of Norwich Commissary Court in 1625–9,[2] although this court travelled a circuit which extended from Kings Lynn to Great Yarmouth (56 miles), compared with the Ipswich to Yoxford circuit (22 miles) of the Suffolk court. The two Norfolk archdeaconries and the Archdeaconry of Suffolk could not compete with the better facilities offered by the diocesan Consistory Court. The case of the Archdeaconry of Sudbury court was different,[3] for not only was this area the furthest from Norwich, but it could attract the services of proctors (and probably advocates) from the Ely Consistory Court at Cambridge. It was only because of the other work done by the court officers that circuit courts for three or four causes in places outside of county towns were economic. Most of the Archdeaconry of Suffolk consistory business was heard at Ipswich (15 sessions in 1610–11), with a few causes at Snape (14 sessions), and Yoxford (9 sessions) or Blythburgh (1 session). It is also unlikely that it would have been economic for proctors to have travelled to these out-of-town courts if they had not been employed in other legal business, such as advising clients about their wills.

The visitation fee received by the registrar from each parish was 8d. at the beginning of the seventeenth century, i.e. about £10 from about 290 parishes. The one unknown source of his income was receipts from offenders at correc-

---

[1] Licence business generated a greater net profit than any other type. The probate jurisdiction was responsible for a sizeable proportion of the commissary's consistory business as well as his non-contentious work: out of the twenty-two judgments pronounced, as mentioned in the next paragraph, nine were on the validity of wills.

[2] Norwich Record Office, Archdeaconry of Norwich A.B. 1625–29.

[3] See above, p. 18.

tion courts, and it is difficult to estimate what these would be. At the same time as 8*d*. was being charged for the visitation fee, 8*d*. was also being charged for each offender, divided between judge and registrar. In 1627, at the diocesan visitation, 262 persons were amenable to church discipline, but as the commissary court received presentments all the year round, its total may have been as high as 400. If this was so, the registrar's income from this source would have been less than £7, plus a few extra pounds from other correction court fees. Certainly, he was not making any great fortune from this source, and neither, we may suspect, was the commissary.

Thomas Wilson, himself a civilian, writing on *The State of England Anno Domini 1600*, described the state of civilians in terms which were not entirely special pleading:

This State of all others is the weakest, they haveing no meanes but by practise in the arches and other the Bishops of Canterburyes Courts, and some small practise in some other consistories. There are of them some 24 belonging to the arches which gayne well, and every Bishop hath a Chancellor that liveth in some good creditt, the rest, god wot, are fayne to become powre Commissaryes and officials of deanes and archdeacons, which ride up and downe the Country to keepe Courts for correcting of bawdy matters etc. and take great paines for small gaynes.[1]

The commissaries of the three Norwich archdeaconries who were resident in the diocese and operated circuit systems might augment their incomes by acting as advocates in the diocesan consistory court, but they were unlikely to have become very rich men.

APPARITORS

In theory there was one apparitor for each of the deaneries into which the diocese was divided, but in practice there was more or less according to the size of the deanery. These officers were nominally employed to cite persons to court or to attend visitations, but they were used far more extensively than this simple function might suggest. About 1603 their duties were:

(1) To inform the churchwardens of a parish of any offenders against church law living in it, so that the churchwardens could present them to an ecclesiastical judge;

(2) to inform the bishop quarterly of any case where proceedings taken against offenders had been stopped for any reason;

(3) to inform the bishop quarterly where any public penance had been commuted for a payment by money;

(4) to send quarterly to the bishop lists of recusants, heretics and schismatics, and any record of their appearance before any court;

---

[1] Camden Miscellany, LXVI, 25.

(5) to send quarterly to the bishop lists of non-resident incumbents, of all chancels and parsonages needing repair, of any lack of services and sermons, of any unlawful marriages, of any sequestrations and of any legacies bequeathed to charitable uses;

(6) to cite any executor or administrator to prove a will or undertake an administration, provided that fourteen days had elapsed since the death of the deceased;

(7) to give notice to the bishop of the death of any incumbent or curate within six days.[1]

The apparitors were, in fact, the policemen of the diocese, keeping watch not only on clergymen and laymen, but also on the Commissary and other church courts (e.g. that of the Dean and Chapter which exercised control over some parishes). If they did not themselves issue citations they had only to inform the registrar and, if the chancellor approved, a citation was issued to call a suspect to court. As apparitors were paid by fees, the more offenders they could detect, the more income they earned. The system was open to abuse, as by bribery, and apparitors were frequently criticized in contemporary Puritan propaganda, but these criticisms need to be taken in their context.

A twentieth-century school was once building a swimming-pool by voluntary labour, and in a misguided moment the village policeman was asked to help. He readily agreed, being something of a handyman himself, and duly arrived one evening at the site. The first thing he did was to order the cement-mixer to be removed. This very necessary machine had been loaned by a farmer and was attached to the back of a farm tractor. The tractor was only licensed for agricultural purposes, and building a swimming-pool was not an agricultural purpose, so a conscientious policeman could not permit its presence. Carting farm manure to a worker's private garden was also not an agricultural activity, as the same policeman rightly pointed out, so most of it was delivered during his annual holiday, for the neighbouring village constable took a more lenient view of such rural customs. The village policeman in this story was not paid by fees, nor would his superiors regard him with a more favourable eye if they knew of his interpretation of the law; he simply believed in enforcing the letter of the law.

Human nature does not change greatly, and this type of policeman doubtless had his spiritual ancestor in some of the apparitors of the sixteenth and seventeenth centuries. The law had to be obeyed, and they kept an eye open for funerals so that they could be certain that the widow duly took out her administration. They likewise listened to the gossip to detect if a recently married couple were having a baby earlier than they should have done.

[1] *Registrum Vagum*, I, 43–4.

A single person involved in an incontinency prosecution might escape or remain excommunicated for contempt of court, but newly married parents were more likely to wish to remain on the right side of the law. Such persons were easy game for an apparitor, although neighbours left to themselves might have turned a blind eye when the time came to make presentments. After the reorganization that took place in Norwich in 1603, there were thirty-three apparitors, and it is unlikely that they all were equally efficient, honest, or lacking in officiousness. They did not have the advantage of being members of a police-force with a good tradition to maintain, as have policemen today. Yet, as the recent campaign mounted in certain quarters to denigrate the police has shown, it is easy enough to reveal weaknesses in even as well disciplined a body of men as the British police.[1]

The trouble which sparked off the reorganization of 1603 was due to the desire of the chancellor to have a body of apparitors directly responsible to himself, the deanery apparitors being also employed by the commissaries. The result had been the gradual increase in the total number of these officers to no less than fifty. The bishop cut the number by seventeen, although the chancellor did manage to retain a much reduced force of his own apparitors.[2] The action taken shows that a bishop could successfully intervene to deal with abuses when necessary, and that the good management of his courts was ultimately his responsibility.

THE HIGH COMMISSION

The Elizabethan government brought a new court into the traditional administration of the Church of England. The High Commissioners for Causes Ecclesiastical were empowered by the Act of Supremacy (1 Elizabeth c. 1) to undertake the enforcement of any ecclesiastical discipline that might be required. The result was the establishment of a court under the presidency of the Archbishop of Canterbury, armed with powers to fine and imprison not wielded by ordinary church courts. This court had a jurisdiction extending throughout the whole of the country, although it did not normally concern itself with the northern province. A separate body of commissioners was provided in the province of York, and the Archbishop of York presided over this court. In the northern province the special position of the Bishopric of Durham was recognized by the establishment there of a separate court under the bishop, the commissioners being drawn from the Durham mem-

---

[1] Modern police are not paid by fees, but results bring increased monetary reward by way of promotion. For doubtful police practices see F. T. Giles, *Open Court* (1964), pp. 92–8.

[2] *Registrum Vagum*, I, 29–30, 41–4.

bers on the northern list. The result was that the Archbishop of York was never able to use the High Commission to establish his authority in a diocese which was otherwise largely exempt from it. The fact that a southern court, headed by the Archbishop of Canterbury, could and did interfere in the northern province must have created difficulties for the Archbishop of York. Archbishops of Canterbury had previously exercised jurisdiction in the province of York only as papal legates.[1]

The advantage of the High Commission's powers was not only in its ability to use secular sanctions to enforce church law, but also in its ability to pursue a delinquent from one ecclesiastical jurisdiction to another. Previously, if a person escaped from one archdeaconry, and particularly from one diocese to another, he could only be cited through a cumbersome process whereby one court requested the assistance of another. The High Commissioners could send their pursuivants far and wide through the country. The establishment of this court provided the Archbishop of Canterbury with an authority throughout his province that he had lacked since the break with Rome and since the abolition of the office of papal legate which he had usually occupied. The High Commission Court was not only the longest of the long arms of church law, it was also an administrative agency which issued orders and expected the bishops to obey them. The reorganization of apparitors in the diocese of Norwich was the result of an order sent by the High Commission to the bishops concerning church courts.[2]

Towards the end of Elizabeth's reign the Bishop of Norwich and two other local High Commissioners began to act as a court at Norwich. The exact purpose of this local court cannot be determined. The record of its acts only exists from its first session in September 1595 until August 1598.[3] It is likely that it then ceased operations, and the attempt to control Puritanism and Romanism reverted completely to the central direction in London. A local High Commission would have been useful, as it was at Durham, to assist church discipline. The attempt to control nonconformity from London, working through information supplied by local sources, while the bishop was attempting to enforce his own policy, could not have led to efficiency.[4]

---

[1] A case of this nature was that of the Nottingham exorcist John Darrell. His activities were investigated by a commission established by the Archbishop of York. Its findings did not satisfy Darrell's opponents, who caused him to be called before the High Commissioners in London. The latter imprisoned him and degraded him from Holy Orders. See my article 'John Darrell—Exorcist' in *Transactions of the Thoroton Society of Nottinghamshire* (1960).

[2] *Registrum Vagum*, I, 24–6.

[3] ACT/31. The book also contains marriage authorizations for the clergy, and institutions and resignations performed before the bishop in person.

[4] Bound into the cover of one of Harison's MS. books, entitled simply 'Liber Anthonij Harison', is a list of Puritans and their offences which the chancellor had sent direct to the archbishop without

THE BISHOP'S LEGAL SECRETARY

It has been recently said of the office of bishop's legal secretary that 'it is of fairly recent origin and references to it are not found until the eighteenth century'.[1] In the Norwich diocesan archives are an important collection of official records of the time of Queen Mary made by William Mortimer,[2] and another by Anthony Harison, the latter of which has been published under the title of *The Registrum Vagum of Anthony Harison*. Both these men were legal secretaries to Bishops of Norwich, and their collections form an essential source for the study of the history of the diocese.

Harison was attorney and solicitor of the University of Cambridge when, at the age of thirty-nine, he was chosen by the newly-appointed Jegon to be his secretary. Like all private secretaries, the bishop's secretary had to be a man of discretion, for the bishop might well seek his advice on matters affecting his legal administration. Jegon's chancellor was Robert Redmayne, LL.D., who had 'risen from the ranks' having previously been commissary of the Archdeaconry of Suffolk, and had been appointed chancellor in 1590. He had thus been in office thirteen years when Jegon, on instructions from the High Commission, began to reform his courts. Our knowledge of the results is limited to the reduction in numbers of apparitors, for while Harison preserved this information, together with Jegon's questionnaires to the chancellor and commissaries and the answers to them, he did not note any further executive orders. It is unlikely, however, that Redmayne could have been pleased by the reduction in the number of his consistory apparitors from thirteen to eight, and in the whole proceedings Jegon must have leaned heavily on Harison's advice. The result was embittered personal relations between the chancellor and the secretary,[3] while those between the chancellor and his bishop were little better.[4] When the reorganized apparitors renewed their oaths they did so before the bishop, Harison and representatives of

---

consulting the bishop. 'This much distasted (*sic*) by Bp. Jegon and bred a greate variance betweene the Bp. and his Chancellour', noted Harison. Jegon was much more sympathetic to Puritanism than Whitgift and Bancroft.

[1] *Report of the Church Assembly's Commission on Fees and Faculties* (1959), p. 16.

[2] SUN/3.

[3] *Registrum Vagum*, I, 103. Harison also noted (p. 123) alleged injustices in Redmayne's treatment of one of the proctors.

[4] Above p. 34. On one occasion Jegon issued an inhibition to the chancellor ordering him to cease proceedings in a cause in the Consistory as it was before the bishop in his Audience—as the chancellor well knew, added the bishop (autograph note in the Consistory acts for 25 June 1605, ACT/37). The chancellor and registrar normally assisted a bishop in his Audience Court, but an act of the Audience, 2 Dec. 1603, entered by Harison in his Register, shows the bishop hearing the case alone, Harison acting as actuary, and an advocate pleading before them (Office *c*. Griffith *als*. Griffin, *Registrum Vagum*, I, 104).

three out of four of the Commissary Courts, but neither chancellor nor diocesan registrar was present.[1]

Besides giving advice on such matters, the legal secretary was sometimes called in to function as a notary when the bishop was performing a legal action such as an institution, or receiving an oral resignation from a benefice. The prevalence of forms and actions concerned with his temporalities in Harison's books indicates that the secretary had to supervise the bishop's relations with his manorial and other subordinate officers. He likewise handled the bishop's correspondence with the Crown (as Mortimer had done) and with the High Commission. He must have been one of the hardest working members of the bishop's administration. Harison was rewarded for his services by being appointed to a benefice and by being granted leases of episcopal lands. The latter was a common method of rewarding service, but we shall notice that at York the tendency was for legal secretaries to become registrars rather than clergymen.

Clement Corbett, LL.D. became Chancellor of the diocese of Norwich in 1625. He lived on to see the desolation of episcopal administration during the Civil War. But people continued to die and their earthly affairs had to be concluded in a legal manner: so we find Corbett functioning in matters of probate, first under the authority of the bishop; when the bishop died, under the authority of the king; when the king was beheaded, under the authority of the Lord Protector. It cannot be over-emphasized that the church administration was part of the state administration, and most of its officers whether clergymen or laymen thought no more about resigning their appointments with a change of government (Henry VIII's break with Rome, Edward VI's Protestantism, Mary's reaction, Elizabeth's moderation, Charles I's 'Laudianism', Cromwell's Puritanism, etc.), than a modern civil servant would think of resigning when a new government was returned at the general election. It is true that Corbett was eventually declared redundant when Cromwell made other arrangements for testamentary matters, but the majority of the clergy continued in their benefices. What later enraged Walker, when he recounted the sufferings of the clergy under the Commonwealth government, was not that they had had to resign on grounds of conscience from a non-episcopal church, but that they had been ejected. And what enraged Calamy when he looked back on 'Black Bartholomew Day' 1662 was not that Puritan clergy had been forced to resign from an episcopal church on grounds of conscience, but that the wicked bishops had ejected them. Even after that event, 80–85 per cent of the clergy who had been

---

[1] *Registrum Vagum*, I, 40.

beneficed in Cromwell's Church of England continued to serve in the Church of Charles II.

The administration of the English Church continued through the centuries, and it would not be surprising to discover manifestations of the civil service mentality. Underneath is to be found the spiritual life of the country, but the outer shell, and so often the only visible part, was the machinery that governed it. Bumbledom existed before Dickens, and in an age when clergy sometimes bought themselves benefices, the lay officers of the Church could not be expected to rise above the standards of the times.[1]

[1] For the near-simony of a Puritan clergyman see my *Puritans and the Church Courts*, pp. 100-2. Many other instances of near-simony could doubtless be discovered. The Faculty Office issued dispensations from the legal consequences of simony (e.g. Lambeth Palace Library, F.I.B., 18 Feb. and 5 Nov. 1591, one cost £6, the other £2).

Additional Note

The full text of Bishop Jegon's letter to his chancellor (above page 35, note 4) is worth quoting in full to show the bishop's full control over litigation of immediate ecclesiastical interest:

Sir yow knowe that longe since I called to myne owne audience the controversie about the charter of the towne of Wymondham and I presume yow are not ignorant that on Friday next the parties are assigned to alledge before me, what they can pro et contra. Notwithstandinge this (I am informed) yow assigne a sentence this Tewsdaye June the 25 to the prejudice of that my summarie equall hearinge and finall accordinge all parties. If yow deal in it (a matter of instance) as under me I require yow to reserve it to me, and to command the parties before me as they are allready formerly cyted. So fare yow well. Ludham, June 23, 1605.

Jo: Norwich

The case was down in the consistory list as Freeman *c*. Cullier *et* More. It was suspended that day and no further act was made in it in that court. The matter probably concerned the parochial rights of the parishioners in the former monastic church.

2

THE CONSISTORY AND CHANCERY COURTS OF YORK

There was a large number of courts at York in the days before the Civil War. Those to which reference is here made were:

(1) The Court of Audience or Chancery, the court normally presided over by the archbishop's vicar-general.

(2) The Consistory Court, presided over by the official principal.

The offices of vicar-general and official principal were normally held jointly by the same person called the chancellor.

(3) The Exchequer Court, the judge of which was called the Commissary of the Exchequer.

(4) The Courts of the Archdeacons, each headed by the Official of the archdeacon concerned. (The Official was in fact the archdeacon's chancellor.)

(5) The courts of peculiar jurisdictions; of these, by far the most important was that of the Dean and Chapter of York, which consisted of about thirty-five parishes over which they had direct control, and a further sixty-five parishes where the prebendaries individually had certain rights. Any person in this latter category of parish who wished to bring a suit had to do so in the Dean and Chapter's Court. The judge of the court was called the commissary or auditor. Other peculiars were those of the Chapter of Southwell, Nottinghamshire (28 parishes), of the Dean of York (20 parishes), of Allertonshire (divided into two, a peculiar of the Bishop of Durham, 8 parishes, and of the Dean and Chapter of Durham, 6 parishes), Howdenshire (13 parishes) and certain small jurisdictions.

(6) The Admiralty Court of York. This court was part of the network of vice-admiralty courts, subordinate to the High Court of Admiralty, which extended throughout the country. Normally the local vice-admiral appointed the judge of his court,[1] but, if the one precedent of the appointment preserved in the High Court of Admiralty Records is a guide, the judge of the court at

---

[1] P.R.O., HCA. 50/1, fo. 235.

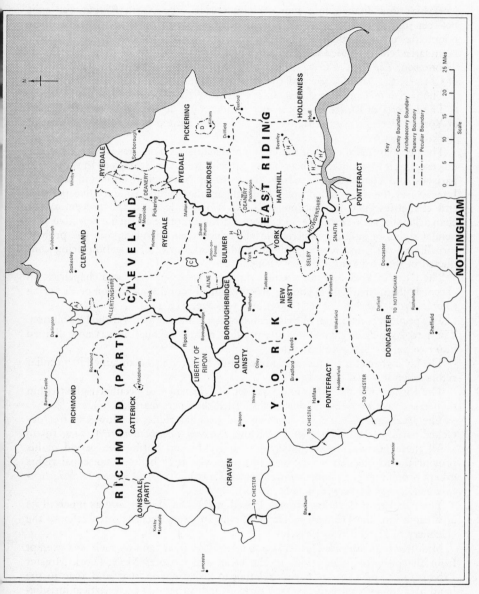

Map 1. Ecclesiastical Yorkshire after the changes of Henry VIII.

Yorkshire was divided into four archdeaconries. The North Riding was split between the Archdeaconries of Richmond and Cleveland, but otherwise their boundaries corresponded very nearly with the boundaries of the ridings. Deanery boundaries corresponded to those of a hundred or groups of hundreds (A. H. Thompson, *The English Clergy*, pp. 63–5). When Henry VIII founded the diocese of Chester, the Archdeaconry of Richmond was transferred to it.

The parish of Crayke (marked 'C') was part of the diocese of Durham.

The Liberty of Ripon was not in any archdeaconry or deanery. The Archbishop of York had certain secular rights in it, and it was treated as part of the diocese of York.

The peculiar jurisdiction of the Dean and Chapter of York was the largest in the diocese, but it is not marked because its parishes were very scattered. In thirty-five parishes and chapelries (of which six were in Nottinghamshire and three in Lancashire) the dean and chapter had full peculiar rights. In sixty-five parishes and chapelries (two in Nottinghamshire) two archdeacons, the precentor, the chancellor, the sub-dean, the succentor and the canons had their respective prebendal rights of summary correction of ecclesiastical offenders, and the probate jurisdiction over uncontested wills and administrations, all litigation being conducted in the Dean and Chapter's court.

The Dean of York had full peculiar rights in twenty parishes and chapelries, all except Kilham (marked 'D' on the map) grouped round Pocklington or Pickering (*Yorks Arch. Journal*, vol. 18 (1905), pp. 197–232, 313–41).

The peculiar jurisdiction of Selby Abbey passed into lay hands at the Dissolution. The new lay owners maintained the peculiar rights, although it was now divided into two parts—Selby and Snaith.

The lay owner of the Treasurership of York Minster also maintained its peculiar rights when it was dissolved (Alne).

The Bishop and the Dean and Chapter of Durham had peculiar rights within their respective parishes in Allertonshire (detached part marked 'A').

The Dean and Chapter of Durham had peculiar rights in Howdenshire (detached parts marked 'H'). (See F. Barlow, *Durham Jurisdictional Peculiars*, 1950.)

All these peculiars were subject to the archbishop during the period of his provincial and diocesan visitations, but otherwise they had full episcopal rights except ordination and confirmation. (See G. Lawton, *Collectio Rerum Ecclesiasticarum de Dioecesi Eboracensi*, 2 vols., 1840.)

The peculiar of Beverley Minster lapsed at the Dissolution, and as much of its area came into the Deanery of Harthill, contemporary records often refer to the 'Deanery of Harthill and Beverley'.

Middleham (Catterick Deanery) was a royal peculiar, and as such was exempt from all episcopal jurisdiction. In the Dean and Chapter MSS. (York Minster Library) C 1 and C 2, are papers relating to visitations in 1637 and 1640 in the hand of Thomas Squire jnr., a York proctor, indicating that ecclesiastical jurisdiction was exercised by York officials. (These MSS also have scattered prebendal visitation papers of the early seventeenth century.)

York was appointed directly by the Lord High Admiral, and its jurisdiction extended to Westmorland and the Scottish border.[1] The act books, files of cause papers and other records which would give the material for an account of the court are lost, but a few precedent papers and other scattered documents give the names of some officers of the court.

(7) The Council in the North. In its administrative capacity, under a Lord President, the Council was an extension of the Privy Council; in its judicial capacity, with permanent legal members (judges), an attorney-general, and a bar of practising barristers, it was almost a northern High Court of Chancery. Its jurisdiction extended from Yorkshire north to the Scottish border. The acts of the court are lost, but much valuable information was collected by Dr R. R. Reid in her *The King's Council in the North* (1921).

THE LAWYERS

From the time of Henry VIII, through all the troubles of Edward VI, Mary and the early years of Elizabeth I, the continuing influence in the diocese was the chancellor, John Rokeby, LL.D. His claim to fame has been enshrined in the family history written by his nephew, Ralph.[2] Rokeby, a Yorkshireman, had begun his career as an advocate at London, and had had the good fortune to be one of Henry's counsel in the divorce case. As a reward for his services —rejecting higher preferment in the south—he was given the chancellorship at York. His reputation as a judge spread to Europe, and was only exceeded by his reputation for probity at a time when judges frequently received 'presents' from suitors. Ralph stated that only once in thirty-two years as judge was a judgment for which he was responsible upset on appeal, and that was one given by a substitute. The tradition established by Rokeby must have done much to free the courts at York from those abuses which stained the justice of the period, and we shall see that there are indications that men were not wanting to carry on the tradition after his death.

The first Elizabethan archbishop, Young, was faced with tremendous administrative problems. Rokeby, by the nature of his ecclesiastical duties and by his membership of the Council in the North as well as by advancing age, was very much tied to residence in York. Walter Jones, D.C.L., was therefore appointed as additional vicar-general, to share the administrative

---

[1] P.R.O., HCA. 50/1,

[2] *Oeconomia Rokebiorum* (1565, revised 1593), printed in T. D. Whitaker, *History of Richmondshire* (1823), vol. I. The statement that Rokeby returned to the North simply because he was a northerner wanting to escape the fleshpots of London as quickly as he was able, is probably later piety. Henry VIII desperately needed completely reliable civil servants in that part of the country, and this capacity Rokeby filled admirably.

burden and the administration of church discipline. Both Rokeby and Jones became permanent legal members of the newly established High Commission Court, and Jones was made a prebendary of Southwell with special responsibility for Nottinghamshire.

Young's successor, Grindal, replaced Jones by a Lancashire man, John Gibson, LL.D., who succeeded to the chancellorship when Rokeby retired. Gibson had had only academic acquaintance with the law before his appointment (he had been a fellow of Trinity College, Cambridge). He was the first at York to set the fashion of lay lawyers in church courts. The tradition that the chancellor should be remunerated in part by ecclesiastical preferment was continued when Gibson became successively non-residentiary canon, precentor and residentiary canon (the two latter transferred from Rokeby on his death), for in early and mid-Elizabethan times such benefices without cure of souls were sometimes given to laymen. The Dean and Chapter of York appointed him likewise to succeed Rokeby as their Commissary, although he later quarrelled with them over his stipend as residentiary.[1]

These were the days when office-holding was still at the pleasure of the archbishop, so Archbishop Sandys replaced Gibson by a southerner, Robert Lougher, D.C.L. Gibson was made Archdeacon of the East Riding, evidently by way of compensation. The new chancellor was an able man, Regius Professor of Civil Law at Oxford, Chancellor of the Diocese of Exeter, an ecclesiastical pluralist and M.P. for Pembroke in various parliaments. On his appointment to York (1577) he resigned his professorship, but until 1580 was also principal of New Inn Hall, Oxford. The exact meaning of his appointment is hard to fathom. The diocese still needed constant care from its administrative officers, while the courts could not be properly supervised by one who was absent as often as Lougher. Much of his work had to be done by comparatively inexperienced substitutes, and the sessions of

---

[1] Gibson was dispensed (fee £6) to hold unordained the precentorship and prebend of Driffield annexed to it, 23 Jan. 1575, for seven years (Lambeth Palace Library, Faculty Office Muniment Book F.I.B., fo. 77v.). On 15 March 1581 he was dispensed for life under the Privy Seal, and also to enjoy the privileges and emoluments of a residentiary canon although non-resident (F.I.B., fo. 101v. Fee £9. 3s. 4d.). The latter dispensation was apparently secured because of an order in the Chancery Court (23 Aug. 1580) to attend the first session of the Easter Term 1581 to answer articles concerning deprivation from the precentorship. The precentorship was not in question, but Dean Hutton argued that to allow him to be paid as a residentiary although absent would in effect burden the other residentiaries, who could less afford it. Papers in the Bishopthorpe MSS, 28/21, 23 indicate that an agreement was reached in 1584 whereby Gibson received £20 p.a. in lieu of his full claim, but the dispute was still dragging on in 1586 (*Hutton Correspondence*, Surtees Soc. vol. 17, pp. 66–73). On going south, he soon began to amass offices, beginning in 1582 with the Deanery of the Canterbury peculiars of Shoreham and Croydon (I. J. Churchill, *Canterbury Administration*, 1, 609 n.), while the Bishopthorpe MSS just quoted show that he had been employed in the Queen's service before 1584.

Archbishop	Chancellor	Commissary of Exchequer	Principal Registrar	Registrar of Exchequer	Commissary of Dean and Chapter	Registrar of Dean and Chapter	Apparitor-General
1561 Thos. Young	John Rokeby (Walter Jones also Vicar-General)	1556 and before Robert Johnson 1558 George Palmes	Thomas Clerk before 1560-65† 1565 Richard Frankland	Not known	Before 1559 John Rokeby	Thomas Clerk 1566 Richard Frankland	Richard Smerthwaite (also pursuivant to High Commission)
1570 Edmund Grindal	Rokeby to 1572 1572 John Gibson (Vicar-General from 1571)	Rokeby 1570 Richard Percy			1573 John Gibson		Richard Plewman or Love (also pursuivant)
1577 Edwin Sandys	Robert Lougher 1585 Percy 1586-89 Edwin Sandys (Percy Surrogate)	1586 Percy and Miles Sandys	1587 Miles Sandys and Samuel Sandys	1579 Simon Hill and Samuel Sandys 1586 Thomas Sandys and Henry Sandys		1585 Frankland and John Atkinson sen.	1579 Thomas Southworth (also pursuivant until 1607)
1589 John Piers	Gibson and Benet Benet acted alone 1597-1604	1590 Sandys and Benet 1593 Benet and Wm Goodwin	1590 John Thacker sen. and John Thacker jnr.	1593 Wm. Benet and John Piers		1596 Atkinson sen. and John Atkinson jnr.	1603 Southworth and his son John
1595 Matthew Hutton	1604 Matthew Dodsworth (deputy)	1604 Benet and Henry Swinburne 1609 Swinburne and Wm. Ingram	1602 John Thacker and Robert Hall			1607 Atkinson jr. (Thos. Edmundson deputy)	
1606 Toby Matthew	1613 Benet alone	Easdall and Wm. Clarke	1612 Hall and Wm. Turbatts 1622 Turbatts and Stephen Hill	1613 Piers and John Benet jnr.	1613 Swinburne 1624 Edmund Mainwaring	1609 Atkinson and Edmundson 1613 Edmundson and Robt. Lupton 1619 Edmundson and John Ranson (Edmundson †1633)	1617 (Mar.-Nov.) Richard Metcalf 1617 Peter Hall 1625 Leonard Hall and son Robert
1628 Geo. Monteigne 1629 Samuel Harsnett 1632-40 Ric. Neile	1624 Dodsworth and Wm. Easdall 1627 Easdall and Mainwaring Easdall alone from c. 1631 1637 Geo. Riddell (Easdall continued to function as sole chancellor)	1632 John Levett		1637 Toby Worlich	1637 Edward Mottershed 1641 Toby Worlich		1637 Thos. Yorke (deputy in 1634)

43

the High Commission were rearranged to suit his convenience (the chancellor being *ex officio* its leading legal member).

Lougher died in 1585, and was succeeded by Percy (see list of advocates at the end of this study). Percy had had a long academic training at Oxford and was a practising advocate at York, as well as being Commissary of the Exchequer, but the reason for his appointment was probably to be a warming-pan for the archbishop's eldest son, Edwin. The latter was appointed to the office in the following year, and employed Percy as his surrogate. The Chapter of York, however, refused to register the patent until Edwin had proved himself fit to undertake the duties. As he was only twenty-five at the time, and it was three years more before he took his B.C.L., there was some reason in this.[1] The extent of Sandys nepotism may be seen in the list of Court Officers in Table 7.[2]

John Piers succeeded to the archbishopric in 1589 on the death of Sandys. It did not take him long to remove Edwin from the chancellorship and Miles and Samuel from the principal registrarship, but the family were not prised out of their Exchequer appointments until 1593.[3] Piers did much to revitalize the administration, one feature of his primacy being his two working chancellors. He thus reverted to the practice of Young, saving that his chancellors were on equal terms, sharing the work of the Consistory as well as the Chancery Courts. His senior chancellor was Gibson, who now returned from the south and worked at York until his appointment as judge of the Prerogative Court of Canterbury in 1597. His junior colleague was John Benet, another southerner, whose legal experience had been academic until he was promoted to the bench. He had studied twelve years at Oxford and proceeded to the degrees of both bachelor and doctor of civil law in the year he came to York. He was evidently held in esteem in that city because he was elected as M.P. for York in the last Parliament of Queen Elizabeth. In 1604 he succeeded Gibson as judge of the Prerogative Court of Canterbury, but did not resign his offices at York. One of the advocates, Matthew Dodsworth, judge of the Admiralty Court, became deputy-chancellor.

We may pause here to take stock of the position, and to say something more

[1] Chapter A.B., 24 April 1586. Dean Hutton was conservative in that he resisted a life patent to Lougher on the ground that it would prejudice Sandys' successors (Bishopthorpe MSS, 28/19). The Dean and Chapter's confirmation was required to life patents under 1 Eliz. c. 19, and it was eventually given to Lougher's patent on 30 July 1580.

[2] Sandys, as early as 1578, was having a dispute with Hutton over a patent for two lives to Percy and 'my son', probably Edwin. When Edwin was given the chancellorship, the Exchequer post was transferred to Miles.

[3] Bishopthorpe MSS. 28/18, and two unnumbered documents in bundle 24 which refer to the commissaryship of the Exchequer. Piers gave a half-interest in the Exchequer registrarship to one of his own family.

about a lawyer who has so far been mentioned only in passing, Richard Percy. When Grindal, still in London, completed the formalities of translation to York, his first duty was to issue patents to Rokeby, both to the chancellorship and to the commissaryship of the Exchequer. It is evident, however, that the latter appointment was merely temporary. When he arrived in York, he took time to assess the situation and appointed Percy to the Exchequer. We may reasonably speculate that Grindal took Rokeby's advice on whom to appoint, as he himself had had no personal knowledge of the lawyers at York. When Percy retired after twenty years in office, he was appointed to succeed Dean Hutton (now Bishop of Durham) as Rector of Settrington, four miles south-east of Malton. The benefice must have been doubly congenial to Percy, not only was it one of the most valuable in the archbishop's gift (£42 p.a. in the *Valor Ecclesiasticus*), but the village was the home of the Dodsworth family. Matthew's father, Simon, had been principal landowner and bailiff of the manor, and had bequeathed part of his estate to his son. Matthew's brother James in turn bequeathed part of his inheritance to Percy.[1] The exact extent of Matthew's fortune cannot be known as he did not leave a will, but it was sufficient to support the antiquarian researches of his more famous son, Roger, which formed the core of Dugdale's *Monasticon*.

In Elizabethan times one of the farmers in Settrington was John Swynburne, who may have been related to Henry Swinburne, the other notable York lawyer of this period. Swinburne's career can be traced through the act books —from clerk or apprentice in the registrar's office to actuary of the courts and, after an interval to graduate at Oxford, to be an advocate and commissary of the Exchequer. In 1590 he published his *Brief Treatise of Testaments and Last Wills* (which was still being reprinted as late as 1743). The preface contains laudatory references to Percy who, incidentally, is noted as having compiled a code of canon law suitable for the reformed Church of England. At that time a person could not rise in the world in the way Swinburne did unless he had a patron, and it seems likely that Percy filled this role. In the autumn and winter of 1604–5, when the plague swept York and forced all who could to flee, Swinburne tried to keep things going by holding an occasional court session for Dodsworth at Malton. At that time he was staying at Settrington, but whether with 'Swynburne', the Dodsworths or Percy's widow (who had married his successor as rector) cannot be said.[2]

[1] These details are taken from *A Survey of the Manor of Settrington* (Yorks. Arch. Soc. Record Series, CXXVI, 1962). For Dodsworth in the Admiralty, see R. VII. P.D. 49 (n.d.) and *Select Pleas in the Court of Admiralty* (Selden Soc. 1897), II, p. lii (1586). Consistory A.B., 21 July 1592, appeal *ex parte* Stanley *c.* Salisbury, shows Dodsworth was not then practising, although he was still attending the court as he witnessed an act on 25 Sept.
[2] Bishopthorpe MSS. 28/34.

Percy, with his younger contemporaries Dodsworth and Swinburne, maintained the traditions of the court at York, handed down and enhanced as they had been by Rokeby. Associated with them was Gibson, whose country seat at Welburn was only a few miles from Malton. When a perplexing problem arose, it was to Gibson that Swinburne turned for advice.[1] Dodsworth and Swinburne were made overseers of Gibson's will, being left 50s. each in gold to make a ring 'as a remembrance of an olde frende who loved them'. Some evidence of the attraction of this school of lawyers in its heyday may be seen in the List of Advocates (Appendix II). Lawyers who had no opportunity or intention of practising in the court attended there to complete their education, and to seal it by being admitted as an advocate.

The seventeenth century saw a transformation of the court at York. Unless the Consistory acts are deceptive, the courts ceased to attract students, and there were no admissions of supernumerary advocates. Dodsworth and Swinburne were judges for two decades, and there was little chance of promotion for advocates. Lynne, who was apparently a competent lawyer, was given no legal office and returned to the south to become a diocesan chancellor. Competition was so small that Thomas Crashawe, a schoolmaster with no legal degree, was able to build up a moderate practice. One of the advocate's places was retained by Swinburne himself who, although judge of the Exchequer Court, practised in all the other courts at York. The only advocate of importance (and a northerner) to join the court at this time was Edmund Mainwaring. He came from the other side of the Pennines, but his influence with the Bishop of Chester secured for him the post of judge of the Consistory Court at Richmond. In this way he was brought to Yorkshire and became also Official of the largest of the archdeaconries of the diocese of York, that of York itself. He would have been the natural successor to the chancellorship after Dodsworth and maintained the local connection, but it seems that at the crucial moment he became involved with the affairs of the Council in the North.

On its judicial side that Council's work was conducted by four councillors who were permanent, salaried judges. They were naturally chosen from common lawyers, sometimes from the northern bar, but were assisted by a civil lawyer who received a salary of twenty marks ($£13. 6s. 8d.$) for his services. John Rokeby had occupied the place from 1548 until his death, and had been followed by Gibson, Benet and William Ingram, LL.D. The tradition that the chancellor was the civilian judge was broken after Benet's resignation (1613), because Sir Arthur Ingram, who was secretary, wanted a deputy to do his work. By securing his brother William's appointment to the

---

[1] Bishopthorpe MSS. 28/34.

Council, he was able to use him as his deputy. William died in 1623, and there is no indication of who succeeded him either as civilian judge or as deputy secretary. At this time Sir Arthur's fortunes were in a precarious state, so he attached himself to the Savile faction in Yorkshire politics, a judicious move that won him restoration to membership of the Council and allowed him to appoint his son as his deputy. Dr R. R. Reid mentioned no change in the secretaryship until Sir John Melton's succession in 1633. The bitter opponents of the Saviles were the Wentworths, and it is most unlikely that Ingram's son would have been allowed to continue as deputy-secretary after Wentworth was appointed Lord President of the Council in December 1628. Mainwaring became the civilian member of the Council in 1629 and deputy-secretary at the same time—the latter is reasonably proved by the wording of a new patent for the High Commission in 1630, where one commissioner was to be 'Edmund Mainwaring, LL.B. and the Secretary of the Council of the North for the time being'. Such wording in similar instances implied that the man named then occupied the post mentioned.[1] Mainwaring's interests, therefore, lay wider than diocesan administration, and when he was appointed Chancellor of the diocese of Chester in 1634 he acted by deputy. Nevertheless, it must have assisted the Church's jurisdiction that such a prominent member of the Council remained, until 1638, as Official of the archdeaconry that included the whole of the West Riding of Yorkshire.

The aged Archbishop Matthew had perforce to look outside his own courts when, after 1623, he was seeking new judges. The first vacancy he had to fill was in the Exchequer where, after the manner of the time, one office was made to support two persons. The routine work was performed by Swinburne, the largely sinecure co-commissary was the William Ingram of the Council in the North probably in return for his services as a permanent member of the High Commission Court. On the latter's death in 1623, his place was given to William Boswell, Esq., M.A., fellow of Wadham College, Oxford. He seems to have had only an academic career, although later admitted an advocate at London. The Dean and Chapter refused to register his patent, for 'Mr. Best who came about the confirmacion of it refused to deliver it to be registered'.[2] Matthew evidently regarded it as valid for, on Swinburne's death in the following year, he renewed it to Boswell and to Thomas Boswell, fellow of Pembroke College, Cambridge.[3] A further patent

---

[1] *Acts of the High Commission Court within the Diocese of Durham* (Surtees Soc. vol. 34, p. 258). This implies he was acting as secretary, cf. 'William Easdall and the Chancellor of the Archbishop of York for the time being', 'Richard Palmer and the Precentor of York Minster for the time being', etc.   [2] Chapter A.B., 20 Dec. 1623.

[3] Presumably included because of William's interest with the archbishop because in 1622 Thomas was described as 'physic fellow'. Patent and confirmation given in full, R.VII.P. 4, fos. 155–8.

was issued, registered on 24 May 1624, to Thomas Levett, esquire, of High Melton, near Doncaster, and Richard Thornton, M.A., fellow of Lincoln College, Oxford. Levett, like many country gentry, had been educated at the Inns of Court and called to the bar, but it cannot be supposed that it was intended that he should be an ecclesiastical judge—he was rather a place-warmer for his son. Thornton may have studied law, but he never came to undertake his work. He was already ordained and was destined to follow the life of a country clergyman. Levett subscribed to the Three Articles on 28 May, but the patent was replaced by another, registered by the Chapter on 20 July. Those to emerge successfully from this welter of patents were two active lawyers, William Clark, LL.B., later an advocate at London and Judge of the High Court of Admiralty during the Commonwealth, and William Easdall, LL.D., a young advocate at London. Clark was not mentioned again and must have resigned his interest.

The confused situation revealed in the Exchequer is relevant to our main theme because similar complications were overtaking the chancellorship. Dodsworth had been made acting chancellor in 1623,[1] following the successful prosecution of Benet for bribery and corruption as judge of the Canterbury Prerogative Court. He was about seventy-three years old at the time, and the archbishop four years older: an injection of new blood was needed. Main-waring subscribed as chancellor on 21 January 1624, but his patent was not presented to the Chapter until 24 March and even then it was not registered. The other grantee in this patent was no less a person than Arthur Ducke, D.C.L., one of the foremost civil lawyers of his day and later Chancellor of the diocese of London. Two months later, Dodsworth and Levett subscribed as chancellors and their patent was registered by the Chapter, but after a further two months the Chapter registered yet another (20 July)—to Dods-worth and Easdall. On Dodsworth's resignation, he was replaced by Main-waring as co-patentee.[2] There is no hint as to the import of all these patents. What happened in court is that Dodsworth functioned alone until April 1627; from April to October Dodsworth and Easdall both sat as judges; from October Easdall sat alone. Easdall acted as sole judge in the diocesan visitation court of that year. He had subscribed on 23 August 1624, and sat in the Exchequer Court from April 1625, joining the High Commission in the same year when a new patent was issued.

The man who now became the supreme judge of the province of York was a typical Caroline bureaucrat of the school of Wentworth and of 'Thorough'. In his early years at York he had little opportunity to exercise his talents for

[1] 'Civil War Papers'; mandate dated 15 Jan. 1623.
[2] Registered by the Chapter, 7 June (A.B.) Patent to Duck and Mainwaring in R.VII.P. 4, fos. 146–8.

administration in that diocese, for he had the chancellorship of the diocese of Durham placed upon him (1628–32), and had to divide his time between the two dioceses.[1] When Richard Neile became archbishop in 1632, Easdall surrendered both his Durham appointment and his Exchequer post in order to concentrate on the administration of the diocese of York. Thence onwards his work was to enforce conformity to Laudian ideals of church order, and inevitably his Consistory Court routine had to be delegated to substitutes rather more often than under Dodsworth. The actual decisions in causes before him, however, were always made by himself.

We have noted that in Elizabethan times laymen took over from clergymen the judicial and administrative work done by the church courts. Although these lay officers were so assimilated into church affairs that they often functioned as proctors for the clergy in Convocation, yet clergymen always continued to play some part in ecclesiastical administration. Officials of archdeacons, for instance, continued to be drawn from both the clergy and the laity. The most important place for the clergy, however, was on the bench of the High Commission, where the canons residentiary of York in particular were frequent attenders. In Dodsworth's and Swinburne's old age, one of these, Phineas Hodson, D.D., Chancellor of York Minster, appears to have acted as vice-chairman (from 1622), and was appointed to the Council in the North in 1625. Hodson began his career as chaplain to the left-wing Archbishop Hutton, and although he trimmed his sails to the right-wing blasts of Neile, that archbishop replaced him as vice-chairman by Easdall. Archbishop Matthew's nephew, Henry Wickham, D.D., who was made Archdeacon of York, shared much of the work done in the High Commission by Hodson. When Easdall was in Durham these two clergymen usually deputized for him in the Consistory and Chancery Courts, while Hodson also deputized for some years in the Exchequer. The two were jointly commissioned to hear appeals from Easdall in the Durham Consistory made to the Consistory and Chancery Courts of York.[2] In the same year that Easdall assumed the chancellorship, the High Commission's sessions were increased from monthly to weekly intervals. The result was to make it practically impossible for laymen, except the chancellor, to attend, and more work was thrown on the ecclesiastical members. Under Neile, Hodson and Wickham were assisted by

---

[1] I would suggest that this was not a case of pluralism for the sake of money, but that Easdall was brought in to clear up the mess left by Chancellor Craddock. Craddock's conduct was examined by the Parliament of 1621 (see *Commons Debates 1621* (1935), ed. W. Notestein, F. H. Relf and H. Simpson, *passim* and especially III, 260–6, 382, 384; IV, 346–8), and he was only saved from prosecution because of his privileges as proctor in Convocation. He was arrested by the Star Chamber (*Acts of the High Commission of Durham*, 1–2) which evidently ended his career, for he was soon succeeded by Easdall.

[2] Consistory A.B., 8 Feb. 1628.

George Stanhope, D.D., Precentor of York Minster. After Hodson's resignation from the Exchequer, there was some trouble about who was to act for the absentee commissary. Eventually it was agreed that Stanhope should do the work. The inference seems to be that the High Church party, although it did as much as it was able to foster the practice of the civil law, felt that the laicisation of church administration had gone too far, and that clergymen should play a more effective part in this sphere of the Church's life.

Dodsworth and Swinburne apparently did little to foster a local circle of advocates which would have maintained the prestige of the York legal tradition. Easdall sat with Dodsworth on the bench for more than two terms, and one reason, or at least consequence, must have been that he was able to acquire a good working knowledge of the courts' customs in matters of procedure and administration of the law between parties. (In the same way Gibson had overlapped with Rokeby for a period.) Nevertheless, in matters of church discipline he was much more prone to use southern precedents. Inserted into the acts for September 1629 is a document headed 'The Manner and forme of proceedinge before his Majesties Commissioners Ecclesiasticall', almost certainly an import from the south. It says 'all mocions in the Courte are made by Advocates', and a little later the court actuary replaced the names of the proctors in the causes by those of the advocates. Later still, Laudian precedent led to the use of Letters of Assistance, whereby an ordinary judge could use his apparitors to arrest a person presented for a serious crime and hand him over to the High Commission for trial.[1]

In the period 1622–40, only one new advocate (Agar) was a local man, and the majority were southerners. This is worth noting because the effect of the policies of the archbishops after Matthew led to the embitterment of much local sympathy with the church courts. The connection between civic life at York and the courts was only maintained by the proctors. Their close society and apprenticeship system favoured integration in the local community. This connection, and the high standing of the proctors, is evidenced by the fact that in Elizabethan times two of their body (John Standeven and Edward Fawcett) were aldermen and sheriffs of York. Such civic honour was apparently not accorded to the proctors of the next generation, they were serving a body which was increasingly alienating itself from much popular goodwill. The indications are that the proctors maintained the forms of the court free from southern influence, but by themselves they could not keep the tradition of northern law alive, only fossilize it. Easdall and his cosmopolitan circle of advocates had no interest in maintaining that tradition in the living state necessary for its continued healthy development.

[1] R.X. 25 (the precedent), 20, 21, 22 (York letters).

One southern eruption into the York legal world who is worthy of notice was Edward Mottershed, D.C.L., son of the deputy-registrar of the London High Commission Court. In view of his father's position, his coming to York may well have been due to Easdall's influence or to his appointment as judge of the York Admiralty Court, the exact date of which is not known. He received more promotion than his contemporary advocates, even his seniors, which suggests official favour.[1] The office of King's Advocate in the North was created for him, involving the prosecution of all causes in the High Commission Court at York but not official prosecutions in the ordinary courts. He was also Official of two archdeacons, and in addition maintained a large ordinary practice as an advocate. He chose one of the clerks in the registry office, Francis Parker, to be his chief clerk. Parker survived his employer and lived to practise as a proctor at the Restoration. His papers, including many of those of Mottershed, were preserved in the diocesan registry among the precedent papers, and give valuable insights into church administration of the period, but little of importance about Mottershed's general practice.

The only fee officially received by an advocate at York, as shown in the tables of fees and bills of costs, was one of 10s. for each term, or part of a term, a cause was before the court. It was, however, usual for clients to give gratuities to their advocates and proctors. At the beginning of the seventeenth century about 575 causes involving counsel entered the civil law courts at York each year, made up as follows: Consistory 320, Chancery 50, Exchequer 50 (a 'written-down' figure to make it comparable with other courts for the majority of causes in this court did not last above a term), Dean and Chapter 35, other peculiars and the High Commission 40 (this is partly guess-work as the records of the peculiar courts at this time are not extant; many causes in the High Commission were summary and of short duration), Admiralty 60 (this figure is pure speculation, but the court seems to have been a flourishing one, and could hardly have had less business than this). About 125 causes probably terminated early and brought only one term's fees to the lawyers. As each of the remaining 430 causes involved double that number of counsel and lasted, on an average, at least three terms, the average advocate earned about £340 p.a. gross, out of which he had to pay for his chambers and office staff. He could also act in other northern church courts if clients wished to employ him.[2]

---

[1] For his career see my *Puritans and the Church Courts in the Diocese of York 1560–1642*, p. 53 and ch. 10.

[2] *Acts of the High Commission of Durham* p. 181 (Mottershed), p. 189 note *b* (Riddell). Lawyers were required to assist poor litigants *gratis*, and the judges had power to allocate advocates and proctors in such cases; and see letter from Chester to a York proctor asking him to accept reduced fees for

It is doubtful, however, whether an 'average' advocate ever existed. From two entries in the Consistory acts we learn that there was a clear distinction between senior and junior advocates,[1] so that a litigant who had feed both the seniors could be compelled by the judge to relinquish one of them to his opponent. If we knew more about the way in which advocates functioned, we might find that in practice the junior advocates earned their fees less by causes which they undertook on their own account than by acting as assistants to the seniors whose names actually appear on the articles. The List of Advocates shows that the more fortunate were able to augment their incomes by undertaking other legal appointments, although supervision of the minor peculiar jurisdictions probably brought little financial profit. Presumably, when a judge had to use a substitute to sit in court or examine witnesses, he had to pay the substitute a fee. This probably accounts for the practice of ecclesiastical judges using their vicar-choral for the purpose rather than advocates. Benet and Dodsworth also found these vicars convenient to use— they had the time to give to the work and, badly paid, a small gratuity would be sufficient. Advocates were usually mentioned in acts of substitution, but in fact they were rarely called upon to function as such. In the time of Neile the practice was reversed, presumably as a deliberate act of policy, and advocates replaced the vicars-choral as normal substitutes for the chancellor.

The necessity for advocates in London to be doctors of the civil law led those advocates to be referred to popularly as 'doctors'. Such a doctorate was a necessary professional qualification only in London. At York and elsewhere the bishops admitted such university graduates as they thought fit. The archbishops of York sometimes admitted masters of arts, innocent of any legal degree, but the average advocate there was a bachelor of laws. To gain admittance as an advocate was a costly business, although no exact figures have been preserved. To become a doctor of laws cost Mottershed £31. 18s. 2d.,[2] so that an advocate at London had to make a very considerable outlay before he could begin to earn. At York the rewards, if more modest, could start earlier.[3]

The Statutes of Archbishop Greenfield for the Consistory Court (1311)

a poor appellant with a good case (R.VII.PCC.19). Two cases have been noticed where an advocate sued for fees, but these may have been in connection with work in other courts. The *c.* 430 causes involving some appreciable litigation in the civil law courts at York *c.* 1600, may be compared with the *c.* 500 suits in the royal Chancery Court at the same date. The latter, however, were usually of a more complex nature (W. J. Jones, *The Elizabethan Court of Chancery*, p. 306).
[1] 25 Sept. 1567, Jobson *c.* Ricard; 18 June 1579, Constable *c.* Constable.
[2] R.VII.P.R.90c.
[3] The Norwich protest against the compulsory use of advocates was scathing about the London 'doctors': 'learning and creditt consisteth not in degrees and titles, but in substance of matter and soundness of knowledge'.

show that about three hundred years before our period the advocate received the same fee of 10s. per term per case.[1] At that time, however, there were normally twelve advocates to eight proctors, a proportion that suggests that over the centuries the burden of work was redistributed, for during the years from Elizabeth to the Civil War there were still the same number of eight proctors, but the normal number of advocates was only four. The proctors formed a strong body, and if there had been any attempt to increase their numbers with increasing work, they had successfully resisted it. They had also been strong enough, and perhaps increasing importance justified it, to double their fees from the 10s. per year of four terms in 1311 to 20s. in Elizabethan times. A more detailed study of the court system must be made before the precise significance of the static nature of the advocates' fee over nearly 350 years can be determined. It may be that the earlier advocates had an ecclesiastical income, certainly their successors had to handle a much greater number of causes and could not therefore devote so much time to each one. It is worth noting that advocates at both London and Norwich received the same fee as those at York, while the proctors at London only earned 13s. 4d. and those at Norwich, at 1s. per session, would normally receive 13s. per year for each cause. In addition to the flat terminal or session rate, proctors also received fees (unlike advocates in some courts) for particular acts, as drawing up the articles or libel on which a cause was founded, or attending witnesses at their examination. At York such extra fees probably averaged 30s. per cause.[2] Using the same rough calculations as in the case of advocates, the average proctor earned about £250 per annum gross, with gratuities in addition. Proctors also augmented their salaries by acting as registrars to archdeacons or other courts, as farmers of tithes,[3] and managers of the temporal estates of ecclesiastical bodies,[4] or as proctors in the church court at Richmond.[5]

---

[1] The Statutes are printed in D. Wilkins, *Concilia* (1737), II, 409–15, but I have used a late seventeenth-century copy in the Bishopthorpe MSS., 28/2.

[2] The fees were unchanged from *temp.* Henry VIII, and are printed in the *Ecclesiastical Courts Commission Report* (1832), pp. 522 f. At Norwich advocates received 10s. for informations, and 5s. for an appearance before a judge on a preliminary point of law. [3] R.VII.G.2074, James Stock.

[4] Fothergill and Claphamson successively Auditors of the Dean and Chapter's lands. In addition proctors acted for richer clients concerning their wills, and in matters of probate and administration. It was because of complaints against proctors for their charges for the latter that Sir Robert Floyd, Kt, M.P., was able to secure a patent for engrossing wills in the Prerogative Courts of Canterbury and York, 1620. Floyd knew, as did the proctors, that these wills were the best source of fees. The House of Commons censured the patent, expelled Floyd, and set up a select committee 'to prepare a Bill against the exactions of proctors about the engrossing, exhibiting and proving of wills and inventories'. The Privy Council suspended the patent, but the Bill was never produced (Notestein, Relf and Simpson, *Commons debates 1621, passim,* and esp. II, 250–5; VI, 460–1; VII, 469–71, 507–8).

[5] R.VII.G.2443 and R.VII.H.1054 and other appeals from Richmond.

The professional relationship between advocate and proctor is unknown, but it must have varied from court to court. It is unlikely that advocates personally appeared in the Nottingham Consistory Court, unimportant as it was, although their written advice was sometimes sought. In the Commissary Court of the Archdeaconry of Suffolk the only advocates' fee listed was for attending informations—the final stage in a cause before sentence, when the arguments on both sides were presented by counsel to the judge. The suggestion of this table of fees is that the advocate was sometimes brought in to the cause simply to present the facts and legal arguments for a party, the previous conduct of the cause being in the hands of the proctor. At Norwich, the situation was more complex. About 1601 orders were given that all libels must be endorsed by an advocate (indicating that he had approved them) and that informations must be conducted by advocates only. These orders produced a petition from the proctors, who objected to them on many counts, not least that it represented a change in practice of the court.[1] At the time of the petition the three senior advocates were at Doctors' Commons, and so not readily available, and the two juniors did not live in Norwich. It is unlikely that the Norwich court could have supported sufficient advocates to have made the proposed system work, neither did the infrequent sessions make their residence necessary. However, the one bill of expenses so far noticed, shows how advocates were being employed in the seventeenth century.[2] The cause covered twenty-four sessions, nearly eight terms, but one advocate, Dr Talbot, who was Commissary of the Archdeaconry of Norwich, received fees for two terms, and one who was not a doctor of law (and therefore not an advocate at Doctors' Commons) acted at informations and sentence. Under the system at York or London, an advocate would have to be retained continuously throughout the cause—which in this instance would have cost £4 in fees—while the Norwich system of payment only when he was used actually involved the unsuccessful litigant in a charge of 30s. The speedier handling of causes at York might have reduced the total cost of a suit as compared with those at Norwich, and partly offset this unbalance.

We have seen that in the Norwich Consistory Court the proctors consisted of graduates and non-graduates. One of their arguments against the compulsory use of advocates was that they were as well grounded in law as the 'doctors' from London, many of them being graduates. The latter probably were trained in court forms as well as in jurisprudence when at university. There is at Norwich a Book of Forms of eighteenth-century provenance, but which begins with a defamation suit taken through all its stages in an imaginary court at Cambridge in 1562, including writs of citation, libels and

---

[1] Norwich, loose paper in DEP/32.   [2] Norwich, CON/13, Holmes *c*. Hanner, 1634.

other processes, and the rules governing them. The cause of Sempronius *c*. Titium, with Ulpianus and Gaius as the famous (if resurrected) proctors, would be the type of cause which embryo civilians would learn at Cambridge so that they were as familiar with court forms and rules as the non-graduate proctors. The latter secured their training by apprenticeship. At York all the proctors were non-graduates, and served their apprenticeship either with an existing proctor or in the registrar's office. In one set of indentures, dated 1637, the premium was £100, for which training and board was provided for five years.[1] Acceptance as an apprentice was not a guarantee of succession to proctorial rank, but it would normally lead to a clerkship in the registrar's office and eventually, perhaps, to being an actuary of the court, or to a clerkship in the office of a proctor or advocate. In cities, as York and Norwich, where there were also archdeaconry, peculiar or commissary courts, a former clerk might be lucky enough to secure appointment as registrar of one of these if he had set up his own practice as a lawyer.

We may assume that there was a recognized order of succession to vacancies in the proctorial body, but it cannot be easily identified from the evidence available. Court actuaries, who acted under the principal registrar as the registrar of a court, sometimes became proctors (Fawcett, Fothergill, Grysdale), sometimes remained as actuaries (Atkinson). Stocke, from the registrar's office, became a proctor without ever being regularly employed as an actuary. The only intrusion on the regular succession came, as might be guessed, in the time of Archbishop Sandys. One of the archbishop's first acts was to appoint his legal secretary, John Theaker (or Thacker), as a supernumerary with right of succession to the next proctorial vacancy. Theaker, a Londoner, exhibited his admission in court,[2] the advocates and proctors testifying that there was then no vacancy. Knowing that he trod on delicate ground, he attempted to conciliate the proctors by conceding that if the then actuary (Proctor) should subsequently be admitted a proctor, he should have seniority over Theaker—suggesting that the actuary was acknowledged as the next candidate for a vacancy according to the custom of the court. At the time, there were only seven proctors attending the court, of whom Mason had not yet begun to work. The following year Proctor was admitted a supernumerary,[3] with right of succession to the next vacancy notwithstanding Theaker's admission, showing that the lawyers had won an important victory over the archbishop. Mason had by now begun work, but as another proctor had ceased to function, there were still only seven active proctors. Sandys made his retort on 2 October 1580 when he admitted at

[1] R.VII.P.R.122, 123.
[2] Consistory A.B., 30 March 1577.
[3] *Ibid.* 20 Feb. 1578.

Bishopthorpe John Fryckley, a literate person, to the next vacancy occurring after Proctor's and Theaker's admission. The seven continued alone until the beginning of the Michaelmas Term 1587 when Edmund Lindley was admitted and commenced working. It is quite likely that the non-active proctor was continued on the court books simply to bar the admittance of Theaker. After Lindley's admission, the succession of proctors reverted to normal and Proctor continued as actuary; Theaker was satisfied by appointment to the principal registrarship in 1590.[1]

The legal personnel of the courts worked harmoniously together. At least, if there was any friction (except during the time of Sandys) it was hidden below the surface. The few incidents which have left their marks may be briefly mentioned. The reason why Proctor never became a working proctor until 1595 may have been that he did not wish to give up the regular income of an actuary for the more uncertain rewards of practice, or it may have been due to dislike of his activities by the authorities. Archbishop Grindal suspended him from his place as actuary,[2] and he had to wait until the next archbishop was appointed before he could take it up again. Much later in his life he was ordered by the archbishop and the chancellor (having often been requested and not having obeyed) to remove the High Commission records from his house and put them in the Commission's office.[3] Archbishop Sandys had to reprimand the actuary of the Exchequer for executing certain deeds on his own account, without the commissary's authority.[4] Chancellor Gibson suspended Fawcett for seventeen days from his function as proctor, for allegedly infringing the archbishop's inhibition during a visitation, Fawcett being the registrar of a peculiar.[5] In one case a proctor successfully applied for the articles in two causes to be withdrawn and resubmitted in a new form, on the grounds that because of the negligence of the advocate they had been badly drawn.[6] These few incidents compare well with the many years when the courts functioned smoothly.

The records themselves tell us little about the professional relationship between the two branches of the profession. At York and London, where advocates were well-established, it may be presumed that each had a well-defined sphere of work. One feature, suggested by the evidence in the case of Steel *c*. Mell, is different from the solicitor-barrister relationship as it is today. Whereas today the lay client of a barrister can only approach him through a solicitor, in Elizabethan days there was nothing to prevent anyone

---

[1] I think this reading of the evidence is correct, but there was a period *c*. 1610–20 when again only seven proctors were active, and one of those had remarkably few causes in the Consistory Court.
[2] Chancery A.B., 26 Aug. 1574.   [3] Consistory A.B., 18 Jan. 1602.
[4] Exchequer Probates and Administrations, York City, 3 July 1577.
[5] Consistory A.B., 13 and 30 June 1575.   [6] *Ibid.* 28 Nov. 1560.

from seeking the advice of an advocate by the simple procedure of making an appointment with him directly. Steel sought the advice of the advocate on whether to undertake an action for defamation. If such a course was at all typical, the proctor would tend to become the nominee of the advocate, and the latter would have been the dominant partner in the profession.[1] Such primary consultation was probably exceptional however. There exist among the precedent papers two letters to a proctor simply stating the clients' experiences of being defamed, with the relevant details, and instructing him to issue the necessary citations.[2] Such entire lack of consultation with one's lawyers, or attempt to secure a settlement before the commencement of legal action, may be the reason why so many causes were dropped or settled while the action was in progress. In these two cases there is no mention of advocates, and the proctors were apparently free to engage whom they chose.

In other consistory courts outside of London, proctors probably managed all cases by themselves, until Elizabethan times. If the protest of the Norwich proctors was correct, no advocates were admitted to that court until about 1570. Even then, no one was compelled to employ them until the government orders of 1601. By this time the encouragement of the study of civil law by Henry VIII was bearing fruit, and the government and church authorities were compelled to find useful employment for a body of lay experts who had to live entirely by the law. As the proctors were the lawyers who lived locally, it would appear that in the normal consistory court they would advise the lay client and themselves seek the assistance of whichever advocate they thought most suitable. The Norwich case quoted above[3] shows that the proctors' original fears were not well-founded, and that they were not compelled to employ an advocate on a termly fee throughout the case. Likewise the acts of the Norwich Archdeaconry Commissary Court for 1626, which show only twenty-seven causes of instance being heard in that court, prove that the fears of the consistory proctors that causes would be heard in the Commissary Courts (where advocates were not needed) were groundless. Yet the necessity for employing the help of advocates in framing libels, and for arguing the merits of the case at informations, must have effectively lowered the professional standing of consistory proctors generally and enhanced that of the advocate.

The organization of the courts and the efficient running of their business depended largely on the ability of the registrar and his deputies. The arch-

---

[1] R.VII.G.1555, Steel *c*. Mell. This cause was essentially an attempt by a widow to force a York incumbent to marry her, now he was not compelled to remain celibate. It also showed a young, bachelor advocate, recently admitted and with little work, getting into questionable company—although his own character was not blackened by the case.

[2] R.VII.PCC.15 and 18.   [3] Holmes *c*. Hanner.

bishop's principal registrar was responsible for the Consistory and Chancery Courts. The two earliest registrars in our period—Clerke and Frankland—appeared personally in court on occasion, but left most of the actual management of routine duties to the actuaries.[1] Later in his life, Frankland retired from active work and appointed his actuaries as his deputies,[2] and Theaker also acted through deputies.[3] There are enough documents of the time of Turbatts still extant to show that he was a working registrar, as witnessed by his endorsements on them, although he never appeared in court himself. That the actuaries had a recognized place in the court organization is shown by the fact that they had recognized fees apart from those of the registrar himself.[4] Another demonstration of their status occurred during the first vacancy in the archbishopric after a long period when the same lawyer had been registrar both to the Archbishop and the Chapter of York: it was Turbatts' actuary, not Turbatts himself, who sued the Chapter registrar for the right to act as actuary *sede vacante*.[5] In the latter part of our period (from 1607) the Consistory and Chancery Courts had the same actuary, but in the earlier part (1567–74) Proctor and Fothergill worked as joint actuaries in both courts. After Proctor's dismissal he was succeeded by the young Swinburne in the Consistory Court and by John Atkinson in the Chancery. When Swinburne left to go to Oxford, Proctor secured his reappointment in the Consistory but Atkinson spent thirty-two years as Chancery actuary. (In the latter part of his life he was also registrar of the Dean and Chapter.) The then Consistory actuary, Giles Fenay, managed to reunite the two posts on Atkinson's death in 1607.

The court offices were in a building on the south side of the Minster, convenient for the courts which were held in the latter. A document of about 1613 describes the Consistory office as being the right-hand ground-floor room, the room over it the registry of the Chapter, and the left-hand upstairs room the Chancery office, leaving us to speculate that the left-hand downstairs room was used by the Exchequer.[6] The document mentions that the Chancery room was 'now' divided into two parts, most probably in order to create room for a High Commission office when Proctor was made to move the records.

Working under the direction of the chancellor and the principal registrar was the apparitor-general. There are few references either to him or his staff in the court acts, but it is likely that the dual system noted in the Norwich

[1] Consistory A.B., 16 Oct. 1567, contains the record of Frankland's constitution of actuaries.
[2] R.VII.P.R.16. [3] Consistory A.B., 24 Sept. 1590.
[4] *Ecclesiastical Courts Commission Report* (1832), 519 ff. column headed 'Deputy Registrar and Clerks'.
[5] Chapter A.B., 4 Jan. 1633; R.VII.P.R.18–24. [6] R.VII.P.R.19.

diocese existed here. A suggestion of this system can be detected in Nottinghamshire, where the local apparitors, one for each deanery, worked in conjunction with the archdeacon's court. Yet in the churchwardens' accounts of Upton, near Southwell, under 1629 is the item, 'to George Stokes for the besshopes arteckell, 4*d*.'. That represented the payment to the diocesan apparitor for the articles of enquiry at the archbishop's visitation. This Stockes was not an archdeaconry apparitor, but he promoted certain disciplinary prosecutions in the archdeacon's court about this time. In Yorkshire, the apparitors in the rural deaneries, like the rural deans themselves, were appointed by the Commissary of the Exchequer. They were not necessarily full-time officers: in 1576 one apparitor described himself as a tailor, another as a tanner.[1]

There are no indications in the York records of any trouble with apparitors because of their lack of probity. Except at the time of visitations their work was generally confined to civil and not criminal causes. The apparitor-general was an important official, usually a lawyer. Until the time of James I, the apparitor-general was also pursuivant to the High Commissioners, which involved similar work, and here again, the actual service of citations or arresting of suspects was carried out by his staff, not by himself personally. Robert Hall evidently did not appreciate the extra work put upon his organization by Easdall's administration, although he had previously shown himself disobliging. Part of the task of the apparitor's office was to distribute official communications to the parishes, and in 1628 he had been suspended for refusing to distribute prayers for the well-being of the navy. Three years later the High Commissioners again suspended him, and likewise Chancellor Easdall in 1633.[2] Eventually, he appointed a deputy who acted for him and later succeeded him. This deputy, Yorke, worked well with Easdall, and was used by him to inspect churches and as sequestrator of benefices whose incomes had been sequestrated by court order.[3]

One concluding observation may be made about the courts. Compared with secular courts there was a marked lack of sinecure posts, paid for by the fees of litigants. Certain offices were held jointly, one occupant presumably drawing a share of the fees for doing no work, but the only recognized sinecure was the registrarship of the Exchequer. If it ever becomes possible

---

[1] I have used a transcript of the Upton accounts made by W. A. James and kindly lent to me by the incumbent. Stockes' prosecutions are in the archdeacon's archives, LB 224, A 28, 14 Dec. 1621, A 29, 17 Jan. 1622, and in the York visitation act book, R.VI.A.20, fo. 315. R.VII.G.3258 (Office *c.* Elithorpe *et al.*) for the apparitors of Harthill and Beverley.

[2] Chancery A.B., 4 Oct. 1628; High Commission A.B., 22 June 1631; Chancery A.B., 27 May 1633 (for not serving citation on a Nottinghamshire Puritan clergyman). The last suspension was relaxed on 1 July.

[3] Yorke had previously been registrar of the Dean of York's peculiar (Chancery A.B., 7 Dec. 1627).

to compare costs between church and secular courts, it will probably be found that the success of the church courts was in part due to their relative cheapness, as well as to their convenient geographical situation for litigants.

THE CONSISTORY COURT

The Consistory Court was the court which heard suits between parties and thus had the greatest amount of business, but it is rather a dull prospect for the historian, changing little over the years. Its procedure has been adequately described elsewhere and need not be repeated here.[1] Its one interesting period was under Chancellor Rokeby.

Tudor England inherited the medieval system of administration through judicial processes and bodies, and its genius was to develop the executive side of government with its own administrative organs independent of the judiciary. Briefly, Rokeby tried something in this direction and failed. One cannot say for certain what he had in mind, but the indications are all in one direction. At the conclusion of the royal visitation of the diocese in February 1560, Rokeby became Commissary of the Chapter, *sede vacante*, for fifteen months. During that time all business was transacted in the Consistory. When he became Young's Chancellor, the Chancery was revived, but it had little to do. Disciplinary causes, even involving the clergy except in abnormal cases, benefice causes and other matters pertaining to the office of vicar-general, were all heard in Consistory. The effect was to make the Consistory the one normal court of law for the diocese, the Chancery Court becoming, in effect, an administrative organ. If an administrative cause required litigation, it could be transferred to the Consistory.[2] Exceptional causes were still heard in Chancery, however, where they were regarded as being more under the direct observation of the archbishop. The same procedure had been traditional in the Exchequer, but it was even more marked at this time, all matters litigious being transferred to the Consistory until the Exchequer became merely an administrative office.

Even during this period, however, the difference in functions between vicar-general (as deputy for the archbishop) and official principal (judge of the Consistory) was not forgotten. When Jones sat in the Consistory it was either as Rokeby's deputy, or else only for those disciplinary causes which he could determine as vicar-general. Rokeby, when he passed sentence of deprivation on a clergyman in the Consistory, is noted as doing it in his

[1] C. A. Ritchie, *The Ecclesiastical Courts of York* (1956). This book is rather less reliable in its more abbreviated notice of the courts themselves.
[2] E.g. office *c.* Oglethorpe and Allen, 3 Oct. 1567.

capacity as vicar-general alone.[1] Under Rokeby's successor, Gibson, the more normal usage of the courts was restored. Disciplinary and other causes pertaining to the office of vicar-general were heard normally in Chancery. Rokeby's experiment could only have been successful if it had been carried to its logical conclusion of separating the two offices by appointing different men to each. The failure to do this resulted in the Church having no defence to the charge that the man responsible for detecting breaches of ecclesiastical law was the same as the man who tried them—the policeman tried the criminal.

Rokeby made one other change worth noting. Before 1560, the public sessions of the Consistory Court had been held on the mornings of Tuesday, Thursday and Saturday, but in 1562 the Tuesday session was abandoned. As the number of causes steadily increased until about 1590, the reduction must have been accompanied by a streamlining of the formal routine of court. The acts always state that the court was held from 9.0 to 11.0 a.m., but can one believe that at a later date when a hundred or more causes were on the list for a single session, they were all heard in 120 minutes—even if some of them were merely continued *in status quo*? The Tuesday thus set free was used by the more energetic proctors for attending the court at Richmond, and by proctors and advocates for informations.[2] The other courts were held on Fridays, the Chancery in the morning, the Exchequer in the afternoon.

Table 8 shows how the number of causes grew during the period. For comparison, a check of the legal year 1541–2 shows that only 136 new causes entered the court; in 1543–4, 159; and in 1550–1, 108. The only type of cause which shows a marked overall decline (taking the two courts together) is the matrimonial suit. The change in marriage customs, simpler rules and a stricter enforcement of them, had its welcome result. After Rokeby, the only disciplinary causes remaining in the court were proceedings for contempt. The amount of litigation aroused by slander was a phenomenon of the age. Church courts had cognizance of any slander which, if true, would have rendered the person slandered liable to prosecution for an ecclesiastical offence. The majority of slanders were, therefore, concerned with alleged immorality, blasphemy, cursing and witchcraft. The proctors apparently employed their clerks in their spare time by drawing up standard sets of articles for use in defamation causes, leaving spaces for the insertion of the details when a client's instructions were received. Occasionally, as today,

[1] A.B., 14 and 15 May 1562.
[2] Rokeby's authority can be compared with the situation at Norwich where 300–400 causes were still being heard on the medieval ration of 13 court days *a year*, and the chancellor felt himself unable to increase them, although he knew an increase was needed (Norwich Episcopal MSS., loose paper in Deposition Book for 1602).

TABLE 8

Causes entering the Consistory Court of York

Year	Tithe	Defamation	Legacy	Probate etc.	Matrimonial	Rates	Procurations, synodals, pensions, mortuaries etc.	Dilapidations	Proctor's fees	Disciplinary	Appeals	Remitted by other courts	Not stated	Total
1561-2	13	1	11	8	7	—	3	—	—	16	16	2	136	213
1571-2	54	60	14	6	31	2	—	4	—	1	10	11	18	211
1581-2	72	114	18	2	46	2	4	3	5[1]	14	16	7	3[2]	306
1591-2	96	170	14	1	36	4	4	5	1	2	16	5	3[3]	357
1601-2	133	159	17	—	20	1	5	—	2	—	9	3	1	350
1611-12	143	164	23	—	12	—	15	3	3	—	14	1	1	379
1621-2	130	107	7	—	12	—	17	—	5	—	10	1[4]	1[3]	290
1626-7	132	134	8	—	5	—	2	1	6[1]	3	12	2	—	305
1634-5	101	159	11	1	7	—	5	—	5	—	18	—	1	308
1638-9	126	127	8	—	4	—	9	—	11	1[5]	11	—	8[6]	305

Years begin on the first day of the Michaelmas term. The acts for 1631 are in too bad a condition to be examined. 'Rates' includes church, curate's and parish clerk's rates.

[1] Includes one suit by an advocate.
[2] Includes a civil suit relating to a rector's responsibilities in a chapel-of-ease.
[3] Includes one suit concerning churchwardens' accounts.
[4] Not stated to be remitted, but defendant lived in the diocese of Carlisle.
[5] Subsequently transferred to Chancery Court.
[6] Seven of these not known due to defective MS.

there was a more serious case which really deserved litigation, as when the parish clerk of Dewsbury alleged that the registrar of the archdeaconry, and a former proctor, had had six bastards.[1]

L. W. Stone, in his *Crisis of the Aristocracy 1558–1641*, has compiled figures to show that land sales more than doubled from 1560 to about 1614, declined somewhat to about 1625, and then levelled off until the civil war (p. 37). As this rise and fall is very similar to that observed in the number of tithe causes, it suggests that there may be a connection between these and land sales. A tithe owner might try and tighten up on a new owner before the latter became established, and a new owner able to afford better legal advice might resist demands which had been customary. Land sales were by no means the only influence on the number of tithe causes, but their decline after 1614 suggests caution in ascribing the decline in tithe causes simply to attacks by the common law courts, or to rivalry from the royal Chancery Court. Tithe causes had one or more of three objects in view: (1) debt collecting—the tithe had not been paid; (2) new crops, reclaimed land, and other matters caused a conflict concerning whether tithes were payable, or the method of tithing; (3) to secure greater monetary payments from compositions outdated by rising inflation. Lay tithe owners used the York courts as frequently as clergymen. For instance 20 out of 42 causes were begun by laymen in the first three terms of 1591, and 37 out of 54 in the same period of 1634.

Testamentary causes were withdrawn from the Consistory during the chancellorship of Lougher, when Percy established the Exchequer as a court of law. The one variety of these causes which remained was the suit for an unpaid legacy. The grant of probate was a prerogative of the Ordinary, and therefore suits concerning probate involved promoting the office of the judge. Once the will had been proved, a suit for a legacy was regarded as a civil suit, that is an instance cause pure and simple, and it was presumably for this reason that such causes remained in the Consistory. The change in the relationship between the two courts is discussed in the next chapter.

The other causes need little comment. Suits for the recovery of ecclesiastical dues were sometimes heard in the Consistory, but those for church rates were eventually transferred to the Chancery. Causes remitted from other courts concerned a bishop or court official, were of particular complexity, concerned matters over which there might be a conflict of jurisdictions,[2] or were from the High Commission as better determined by the ordinary court.[3]

[1] R.VII.H.875, Stock *c*. Tingle.
[2] E.g. consistory A.B., 5 March 1575, Wharton *et al. c*. Garthe *et al.* remitted jointly from Dean and Chapter and from Richmond courts.
[3] E.g. *ibid.* 2 Aug. 1575, case of Robert Darrell and his wife remitted for divorce.

During early Elizabethan times there were frequent remissions, but as the other courts became better served with lawyers (especially their own advocates) the number declined.

Appeals came to the courts at York from the two Consistory Courts of the diocese of Chester, from the Consistory Courts of Durham and Carlisle, from the inferior courts within the diocese itself, and from the archbishop's jurisdiction of Hexhamshire within the diocese of Durham. The division between the Consistory and Chancery of appeals to the archbishop was usually made according to the subject of the cause, consequently tithe, defamation, testamentary and matrimonial appeals normally were heard in the Consistory. (The Exchequer had no appellate jurisdiction.) It is not difficult, however, to find exceptions and the courts' statutes (which are not extant) can hardly have contained any clear directions on the subject.[1] The appellate jurisdiction was generally accepted and only one case of contempt has been noticed.[2] Appeals from the Consistory, Chancery and Exchequer Courts themselves went directly to the High Court of Delegates in London, so that for causes begun in the diocesan courts there was only one stage of appeal. It may be observed that there is no sign that the York courts ever attempted to attract business from other church courts in the province, a practice of which the Court of Arches was sometimes accused.

There is one procedural matter which may be mentioned here, that of excommunication. In past centuries the judge of a church court, being in holy orders, had simply pronounced sentence himself. The advent of lay judges posed difficulties. Appeals were made against the excommunications of the first lay Official of the Archdeaconry of Nottingham.[3] The device, which became standard practice, was for a clergyman to sit with the lay judge and pronounce the sentence when it was decreed.[4] Even this did not please some persons in the Carlisle diocese, who objected to it on the grounds that a lay judge did not have the power to decree the penalty in the first place.[5] At York, the long-established use of some vicars-choral to assist the chancellor easily solved the problem. The first actual direct reference to the practice does not come until 1598 when Chancellor Benet appointed 'assessors', and the Chancery actuary thereafter noted that John Richardson, vicar-choral, sat with Benet and pronounced excommunications. The Consistory actuary never troubled to record the matter, and even the Chancery actuary ceased

[1] E.g. appeals concerning pews, R.VII.H.426, 427, 466; concerning discipline, R.VII.G.2071, H.836—Chancery jurisdiction normally, but heard in Consistory. See further in next section on the reverse process.
[2] The Chancellor of Durham ignored an inhibition in 1586, R.VII.G.2231 and cf. 2293.
[3] Consistory A.B., 6 June 1578, *ex parte* Chollerton; 6 Oct. 1578 *ex parte* Wright.
[4] Ordered by Canterbury Convocation in 1571, 1585 and 1597.
[5] Consistory A.B., 15 Dec. 1582, *ex parte* Johnson.

doing so when Dodsworth became judge, but it was evidently the accepted procedure. It was also standard form in the province.[1]

Church courts were notorious for the length of time causes took to pass through them, but then no contemporary court was free from this criticism. In any court, a complicated case will take much time to prepare, even if only a day or two is actually involved in hearing it. The way in which the church courts conducted their cases meant that much of the preparatory work that is now done before the case is heard would then be done while it was proceeding through the court. The only true measure of a court's efficiency is to take the time from when the action which gave rise to the litigation occurred until the sentence was pronounced. The simplest causes before the Consistory Court were those of defamation. In a random sample of thirty such causes spread over the years 1592–1637, the average time from the last date on which the slander was alleged to have been uttered until sentence was given was nine months. Twenty-one of the causes were of this duration or less, the shortest two took only four months. The longest cause was twenty-one months, but of this only about seven months was actually in court. Tithe causes necessarily often involved much more prolonged litigation, very often it was found necessary to introduce additional matter on either side, sometimes two sets of articles after those on which the cause was founded. The shortest tithe cause (in court) which has been noticed was one concerning tithes of the 1637 harvest; the defendant admitted liability at the first hearing in March 1640 and sentence was given the following month. The longest cause noticed was one concerning the harvest of 1604; litigation began in the Michaelmas term 1606 and sentence was delivered in February 1608. Appeals naturally progressed at a slow pace, and two years was common for a cause of this nature. The slow coming and going between the lawyers and the courts in different parts of the North must have been very trying even in those days. For instance, a testamentary cause which had spent three months in Chester Consistory Court was three years in York from the registering of appeal to sentence.[2] A student of the court acts cannot but be impressed by the number of causes in which the usual formalities of articles, defence replies, evidence of witnesses proceeded without any hitch, only to be followed by successive continuations *in status quo.* Appearances suggest that delays occurred more in bringing causes for legal argument by advocates before the judge, or by the judge being tardy in writing his sentence, rather than in the court procedure itself, somewhat cumbersome though it was.

---

[1] E.g. at Chester, R.VII.P.S.11; at Richmond, R.VII.H.1054.

[2] R.VII.H.467. Court formalities (including a fortnight to lodge an appeal) usually extended the length of a cause by a month after sentence. The more complicated suits heard in the royal Chancery Court lasted, on average, three years (W. J. Jones, *The Elizabethan Court of Chancery,* p. 306).

THE CHANCERY COURT

The archbishop's Court of Audience or Chancery was by nature a maid-of-all-work. It dispensed civil, criminal and administrative justice, and performed administrative functions such as supervising institutions to benefices, issuing licences and faculties, and proving wills and granting administrations of estates of deceased clergymen beneficed in the diocese. The amount of disciplinary work transacted depended very much on current policy. The great powers of the High Commissioners made them so much more effective in enforcing church discipline than the ordinary court that they completely overshadowed it. The historian of Roman recusancy will find little to interest him in the acts of this court, while the historian of Puritan nonconformity has only one or two cases of information in the desert of the years before Archbishop Neile. The High Commissioners were meant to investigate and punish major crimes only, and this distinction between their purpose and that of the ordinary court was never completely forgotten. There were, however, complications. Some obscure curate performing a clandestine marriage between two poor people was not committing a major offence, but clandestine marriages were a social evil of considerable proportions and the High Commissioners normally dealt with these cases. An ordinary offence might become a major problem if perpetrated by an important or wealthy person, and therefore would be tried by the High Commissioners. Nevertheless, they often dealt with causes which seem in themselves to be trivial: not catechizing (8 June 1585), serving a cure unlicensed (17 October 1586), baptizing a child in a private house (4 October 1592—perhaps Roman recusancy was suspected however), not providing a curate (23 April 1593), not paying state taxes (7 August 1594), causing damage to a pew (28 and 29 November 1595), non-payment of stipend to a curate (1 April 1600), not maintaining a chancel and rectory house in repair (19 January 1608), altering an entry in a parish register (3 October 1615). The powers of the court to arrest, fine and imprison were so superior to the ordinary weapon of excommunication, that there was always a temptation to use them on any occasion when it was thought that difficulties might arise.

In the period from 1561 to *c.* 1590, the work performed by the Chancery Court was usually of modest proportions. During 1563-4 the vicars-general and Richard Barnes, suffragan Bishop of Nottingham, were specially deputed to examine and license schoolmasters, and their acts were entered in the Chancery records. A sudden influx of cases for payment of clerical taxes to the state sometimes occurred.[1] In Rokeby's time, disciplinary and benefice

[1] E.g. in the Michaelmas term 1572.

causes needing full legal process were heard in the Consistory; simple causes and summary causes of this kind, some (clerical) testamentary and benefice causes, causes heard before the archbishop personally and extra-ordinary appeals (e.g. one concerning a claim to the Archdeaconry of Northumberland, 25 October 1566) were heard in Chancery. Gibson, as has been mentioned, heard all disciplinary and benefice causes in Chancery but the volume of business was small. Up to about 1590, an average of twenty-five causes entered the court yearly, and the number on the list at any one session was usually less than six, unless inflated by a spate of prosecutions for ecclesiastical dues or some particular 'run' of disciplinary prosecutions. These latter appear as summary *ex officio* causes, resembling presentments, which some of them may have been. In Table 9 they are given a separate column because they are not clearly presentments. Many probably originated from information given to the court by apparitors, clergymen or other reliable sources.[1]

During the later years of Hutton's episcopate, the Chancery Court was opened to many criminal prosecutions of a summary nature—i.e. without the formal processes and interrogation of witnesses—of the type normally found in visitation courts. A large proportion were for sexual immorality. After Hutton's death, the number rapidly diminished, being revived normally only in years of diocesan visitations when some presentments were heard at Chancery sessions, or when minor offenders were transferred from the High Commission. The situation changed about 1625 because of restrictions placed on the High Commission. Up to that time there seems to have been little outside control on the way the Commissioners managed the court. This is not to say that they abused their position by acting in a tyrannical way, but they had never been checked, as had the High Commissioners in London, by the secular courts. The York court felt the weight of prohibition from the secular court as a result of a disciplinary cause promoted by a private person against the Vicar of Halifax, John Clay, D.D. This clergyman was himself a High Commissioner, but there is no doubt that his recent appointment was unpopular both in Halifax and among the church authorities, for he was a careerist rather than a man of God. He was accused: (1) he read the Bible in an irreverent and unfitting manner, (2) he neglected to preach, (3) he used the Communion vessels in his own house, (4) he retained the services of a drunken and immoral curate, (5) he did not catechize, but retailed printed catechisms at a profit, (6) he took money from persons sentenced to perform public penance and let them escape performance, (7) he undertook servile labours, unbefitting a clergyman, such as gelding a

---

[1] E.g. 22 Feb. 1583, office *c.* Crawe and seven others, fornicators, according to the information of Southworth, apparitor-general.

TABLE 9
Causes entering the Chancery Court in the years shown

Year	Presentments	Ex Officio	Promoted	Defamation	Rates	Stipends	Other financial	Testamentary	Benefice	Administration	Matrimonial	Appeals	Churchwardens and Sequestrators A/cs	Pews	Other	Total
1571–2	—	7	1	—	—	—	—	2	8	3	1	2	2	—	1	27
1581–2	—	15	2	—	—	—	1	1	2	—	—	2	—	1	1	25
1592–3	15	48	22	—	1	2	1	1	1	2	—	—	3	1	—	97
1594–5	2	64	14	1	—	1	—	1	3	1	—	2	1	—	—	90
1597–8	5	69	18	1	—	—	1	2	5	1	—	1	1	1	—	105
1599–1600	46	42	35	4	—	—	2	—	—	—	1	—	1	2	—	134
1602–3	49	39	18	6	1	1	—	2	3	—	2	1	1	2	—	124
1606–7	17	15	15	19	1	2	—	—	3	1	—	2	—	3	4	82
1610*	—	3	14	31	5	1	—	2	1	3	2	2	—	3	1	68
1617–18	—	14	16	22	8	6	—	5	2	2	2	5	4	2	—	88
1627–28	3	19	14	36	4	3	—	5	—	3	1	8	6	12	—	114
1634–5	10	76	19	38	12	—	3	3	—	9	—	14	—	14	5	203

* Hilary to Michaelmas Terms.

68

pig, (8) ordered his curate to perform an irregular marriage, (9) certain minor matters. Clay was a southerner and knew what to do. He first secured an opinion from the London Commissioners that their colleagues in York were not competent to hear the cause, and when this produced no effect, he secured a prohibition, issued because the High Commissioners could only try major misdemeanours, heresies, 'and the like'.[1]

Thus it came about that Archbishop Neile and his chancellor were compelled to use the Chancery Court as the means whereby they enforced their High Church policies, as well as for much of their disciplinary and criminal proceedings. The large number of *ex officio* causes in Table 9 for 1634–5 is in part due to prosecutions of churchwardens and rectors for repairs and other deficiencies in churches and chancels, but the Laudians did try also to enforce the moral discipline of the Church with something of the severity of the Elizabethan officials. The logical step was taken by the court actuary in 1635 when he began to keep two court act books, one for promoted (i.e. civil) causes, and one for *ex officio* (i.e. administrative, disciplinary and criminal) causes. The worst offences continued to be heard by the High Commissioners; for instance, adultery was an offence for the Chancery Court, incest (except technical incest with the deceased wife's sister, etc.) for the High Commission.

The ordinary court acts and other documents show the machinery of church administration working along clearly defined procedures, with the formalities well respected. Only occasionally does it seem that the disciplinary powers of the chancellor were used in such a way as to suggest that they were abused. The chancellor's position in society was a high one, and he expected to be obeyed. One instance of how Easdall enforced obedience was shown in the prosecution of Elias Kidd, Parish Clerk of Holy Trinity, Micklegate, York.[2] The trouble arose over the digging of a grave for the corpse of John Scadlocke in February 1636. Kidd was in the churchyard when a friend or relative of the deceased, Nicholas Fisher, asked him to make the grave. The articles in the cause continued, 'whereupon yow, upon your own temeritie and insolense and rashness, answered that yow would not provide or make the said grave until your own tyme. And then clapt your hand on your tale.' This did not satisfy Fisher, who thereupon said he would report Kidd to the chancellor for his 'irreverent Carriage'. Kidd, continued the articles, 'did againe Clapp your hand on your Arse, and answered that yow did not care a fart to the greate Contempt of us (*sc*. the chancellor)'.

The articles evidently reflect the story told to Easdall by the aggrieved Fisher, but Kidd's reply to them was probably more accurate, while omitting

---

[1] J. Godolphin, *Repertorium Canonicum* (1678), p. 189.　　　　[2] R.VII.H.2128.

the derogatory remarks about the chancellor. The burden of the parish clerk's story was that when he was asked why the grave was not ready, he replied that it would be finished by the set time for the funeral. Fisher then angrily commanded Kidd to dig the grave at once, saying, 'Sirra gett it done or I'le have yow to appeare before Doctor Easdall'. The clerk replied that he had other things to do, but that it would be ready in time.

Fisher departed to the chancellor, and was back in half-an-hour. The time taken to see Easdall and return implies that he gained almost immediate access to the chancellor. The latter sent an unwritten order by Fisher to the effect that Kidd should come at once to see him. Kidd refused, saying in his answer to the articles that he did not believe that Easdall 'would send for him by any such fellowes as the said Fisher'. Fisher, for his part, alleged that Kidd 'againe Clapt your hand on your tale and refused to come'. It is quite clear that Easdall had unwittingly become involved in a pre-existing quarrel between the two men. Apparently there were no witnesses, and the necessity for Kidd to answer, even if he incriminated himself (by virtue of the *ex officio* oath), did not produce any significant admission. Kidd's statement that he had the grave ready half-an-hour before the burial was not controverted. What was at stake, therefore, was simply his admitted refusal to obey an oral command.

It had originally taken three months for Easdall to launch his prosecution against the parish clerk, and when he was unable to secure a conviction by the latter's own answers, he had to consider whether or not to proceed with the case. Investigation of Kidd's activities was made, resulting in another article being added to the original ones, and totally unconnected with them. It was alleged that he 'sung or caused to be sung divers psalmes in meeter in tyme of divine service otherwise then the prescript form of Common prayer hath appointed'. Kidd admitted in detail that he had sung or caused to be sung a metrical psalm after the second lesson at Morning and Evening Prayer, 'beinge sometimes willed thereto by the parishioners, which he did through ignorance only'. The substitution of psalms for the canticles was a common Puritan practice, one which was corrected by Archbishop Neile in his primary visitation, and it is surprising to discover it still in use in York at this date. It is equally surprising to discover responsibility for it being laid at the door of the parish clerk, instead of at that of the minister (as was usual).

Easdall, or Mottershed who was acting as his advocate, put a large cross beside this admission of Kidd, and two further articles were produced enlarging on the offence. Kidd simply admitted both of them, and it was presumably this submissive manner, continued in court, which resulted in his being allowed to go free without payment of costs, after judgment had been pronounced against him (15 and 22 July). The chancellor had upheld his dignity, the parish clerk had submitted, and presumably Fisher was suitably elated by the success of his original complaint. The chancellor had no lawful authority to order men to come and explain their conduct to him, but the statutory and canonical requirements were so extensive that it would be difficult not to find one which someone had not broken. Hence there was always a probability that if a man did not obey an oral order, he could be coerced in some way, so it behoved him to do what he was told first time.

This multiplicity of detailed regulations not only provided the authorities with an opportunity of bringing a successful prosecution to reinforce their other orders, but it also opened the court to many private disciplinary actions. If two men quarrelled, it was only too easy for one of them to discover something which could be used in an action against the other. As an example of a private prosecution of this type, the case of Robert Constable, gentleman, *c*. Thomas Simpson may be cited.[1] There was a disturbance outside Thwing churchyard on Easter Day, 1608, when Simpson, standing inside the boundary wall hit Constable with a riding crop. Apparently there had been an altercation between Simpson's father and Constable, and Simpson alleged Constable drew a dagger and so he hit him. One may suppose that Simpson senior was really to blame, for Constable indicted him at Quarter Sessions, he was fined 20s. and had to sit in the stocks in Thwing churchyard from Morning to Evening Prayer one Sunday. Simpson junior, being within the churchyard, fell under ecclesiastical jurisdiction and was prosecuted in the Chancery Court. Under 5 Edward VI c. 4, he was liable to excommunication for three years for violence in a churchyard, and was so sentenced. As he would have to pay his own and Constable's costs, together with his fees for absolution if he petitioned for it before the expiry of the three years, he would be at least 50s. out-of-pocket, say £50 in modern money. In this way Constable was able to secure victory over both his opponents.

Turning from disciplinary cases, properly the concern of the vicar-general's court, it is surprising to discover that the next most numerous type of cause was defamation. In order to explain this phenomenon, it is necessary to take a close look at this branch of canon law. H. Conset, in his *Practice of the Spiritual Courts* (3rd ed. 1708), p. 335, states that an action cognizable in the church courts is

a cause of defamation or reproach. And observe that this word (*convitii* or reproach) is wont to be writ in every citation, together with the word (defamationis or defamation), the reason is...because if the plaintiff doth not prove that the defendant uttered words, which of their own nature were defamatory, yet if he

[1] R.VII.H.448.

proves that the words were reproachful, he shall obtain the victory...the reason is, because these words were uttered out of a malicious and angry mind, and besides, against all fraternal charity.

It will be gathered from this that the church courts entertained actions which were something more than mere slander cases. The legal basis for these prosecutions was the constitution *Authoritate Dei Patris Omnipotentis* which stated: 'we excommunicate all them which for cause of lucre, hatred or favour, or for any other cause put upon any man maliciously any manner of crime, by means whereby he is defamed...'.[1] Actions under this constitution were not subject to the one-year limitation normally in force, after which a defamation suit could not be commenced. These actions and those specified as 'against the rule of charity' were theoretically disciplinary, and therefore the office of the judge was promoted. Slanders of witchcraft (heresy) and involving blasphemy (e.g. calling someone a devil) were also disciplinary and so heard in Chancery.

Exceptions can, of course, be found to these general rules, as will be noticed, but the main feature of these causes is the rise of the 'Chancery type' cause in the Consistory, followed by their transference to the Chancery when Benet was acting alone (from 1594 onwards). Twenty-six articles of defamation causes have been examined in the years 1580–3, all except one are simple accusations of immorality, drunkenness, etc. The exception is:

(Case described as words of cursing and defamation against the rule of charity), 'Did earnestly wyshe and desyre that she might see an evyll end of the said Robert Criplinge. And further desyred that the devyle mighte fetche the said Robert Criplinge sainge fye of the thowe hayst undone me and taken my farmhoulde over my heade'.[2]

Sixteen articles of causes in 1586–7 have also been examined, and even though it is only three years removed from the earlier period, no less than five examples of the more general type of malicious accusation remain:

'An ill man and the worst that ever dwelte in farndaile'.[3]
'Lier and brabelar'.[4]
'What is Ramsden, he is a chylde or servante of the devill or one of the devills'.[5]
'Thou art a mischevous man, thou art worse than the devill, and the devill ys better than thou'.[6]
'A slave and a Runygate slave'.[7]

All of these five are simply described as causes of defamation. At a slightly later date, 1593–5, twenty-five articles have been examined, revealing

---

[1] Lyndwood, *Provinciale*, V, 17, 1, from Archbishop Langton's Constitutions (1222), No. 1.
[2] Criplinge *c*. Pearson, R.VII.G.2086. [3] Hoggerd *c*. Wood, R.VII.G.2232.
[4] Browne *c*. Nevill, R.VII.G.2249. [5] Ramsden *c*. Staynton, R.VII.G.2252.
[6] Broadeheade *c*. Bull, R.VII.G.2241. [7] Thurston *c*. Hobman, R.VII.G.2275.

twenty-one normal Consistory causes and four of the more general type. This is a transitional period, two being heard in each court. The Chancery ones were:

(Words of cursing and defamation.) 'An evill plague might light upon the...fye upon the I ask a vengeance of the...and that an evill end may come upon the as ever did to man.'[1]

(Malicious words against charity and defamatory words.) 'Thou arte a Toade face, Thy face is freckled lyke a Toade and Thowe arte blacke in the face, and thowe lookest lyke the devill.'[2]

Those heard in the Consistory were:

'Pocky Rascall, vagabond Fox faced Readeheaded Rascall villan and Rascallie villan.'[3]
'Periured man and mainsworn man.'[4]

As will be seen from the table of causes, Benet was the first chancellor who allowed defamation actions, but it was not until the time of Dodsworth that they became an important part of Chancery business. The reason may have been procedural, office causes were by now very much the exception in the Consistory, or it may have been due more to the very practical need to shed some of the load from the Consistory list on to the much less busy Chancery. To most of the lawyers it mattered little, they worked in both courts, but it is interesting that it was not only Dodsworth's succession to the bench which occurred at the time when these causes begin in large numbers in the Chancery, but also the time (1607) when the Consistory actuary, Giles Fenay, took over the Chancery Court from Atkinson. Fenay was the only person who had had a financial interest in keeping as many causes as possible in the Consistory. It may be questioned why this more general form of action, against the rule of charity, did not become more popular if it permitted a greater chance of success? This is particularly relevant, for an examination of the Dean and Chapter Court acts reveals that in that peculiar court towards the end of our period the greater number of defamation causes were in this form. As it was, Chancery actions never accounted for more than a quarter of defamation causes in the diocesan courts.

Two examples of late Consistory suits may be given to make it clear that there was never a completely rigid demarcation of causes between the two courts. The first, begun in 1636, was partly a disciplinary cause, for brawling in Scarborough churchyard; the slander was:

[1] Office promoted Cooke *c.* Lickbarrowe, R.VII.G.2802.
[2] Office promoted Dallamye *c.* Brayne, R.VII.G.2827.
[3] Oldfielde *c.* Adamson *alias* Crosse, R.VII.G.2838.
[4] Beverleye *c.* Hawkes, R.VII.G.2822.

(Opprobrious, scandalous and disgraceful speeches.) 'Proude beggerlye knave and slave, and willed him to goe and pay his debts...he wore silver and gold lace but he hungered and starved his servants so that they were forced to goe from shipp to shipp to begg their meate.'[1]

The second example is a cause remitted by Mainwaring from the Richmond Consistory Court—and in which he then acted as advocate for the plaintiff:

The plaintiff and his wife 'were married by a priest, meaninge as the hearers did understand him, by a Seminary priest or a Romishe masse priest', and had had a child before their marriage.[2]

The 'breach of the rule of charity' actions involved many causes being tried in Chancery where the words complained of were simple Consistory type slanders. One example may suffice. In office promoted Howe *c*. Hill (1636-7) the words were 'scurvy pocky queane' and 'scurvy filthy pocky faced jade', expressions which reappear many times in Consistory causes. Three witnesses were produced, two deposed that they had heard the noise of a brawl and the third had heard the words but knew nothing to connect them with the plaintiff. It was evidently the intention to prove that the abuse had led to a breach of charity, the evidence being so slender, but the action failed.[3]

There were so many defamation suits in the sixteenth and seventeenth centuries that even the secular courts had to take steps to limit their number. At York, there does not seem to have been any procedural device available to the church courts to effect this purpose, but occasionally the judge inserted into his judgment an order that the expenses are to be 'moderately taxed'.[4] Comparatively few bills of expenses remain in the cause paper files, but one found in a defamation cause suggests that taxing was used as a disincentive without formal promulgation. In Lamberte *c*. Holmes, the bill's total is 77*s*. 8*d*. If Lamberte's expenses in attending court and serving citations are deducted, 59*s*. 4*d*. of genuine expenses—as they appear to be—remain. Dodsworth only allowed 40*s*.[5] Where the judge decided that the slander was particularly bad, he adopted the opposite course. In the Consistory cause of Bateman *c*. Barwick (alderman of Doncaster) the plaintiff failed, and for his

---

[1] Peacocke *c*. Clarke, R.VII.H.2175. [2] Barton *c*. Taylor, R.VII.H.1361. [3] R.VII.H.2182.
[4] R.VII.H.477. Westrop *c*. Watkin and Watkin *c*. Westrop, both sentences decree moderate taxation. R.VII.H.2178, Winder (Vicar of Acaster Malbis) *c*. Gill, 'the greatest moderation in taxing expenses'; this was a special case where Winder had been licensed to teach in place of Gill, there had been a disturbance and Gill had continued to teach; the slander was not proved, only that he had 'irreverently treated' his spiritual pastor.
[5] R.VII.H.419. Slander was: 'arrand whore and bitche'; the defendant's proctor admitted it. In Foster *c*. Daie (Dean and Chapter Court, R.As. 7B/8, 1637-8) Daie's expenses were submitted at £5. 2*s*. 5*d*. of which £3. 16*s*. 2*d*. appear to be normal legal expenses (lawyers' standard terminal fees, court fees, etc.), but Mottershed only taxed them at £2, so he was still appreciably out of pocket although he had made a successful defence.

impudence in challenging an alderman he was condemned to be taxed at the maximum.[1]

The one type of cause which still regularly occupies Consistory Courts is that occasioned by a request for a faculty. The ordinary has jurisdiction over all consecrated buildings, a right which is normally delegated to his vicar-general, so that faculty causes are to be found at York in the Chancery Court. There is nothing remaining among the records of the court to compare with the fine set of faculty books at Norwich which run uninterrupted from 1633 to the present day. A previous registrar of the diocese of York has stated that 'our first faculty was in 1736'.[2] In our period faculties as they are known today did not exist. The churchwardens had a duty to keep their churches in repair, and to furnish them according to the canons and current episcopal injunctions. If there were defects or deficiencies they had to present them at visitations, and pay the court fees for an appearance at a correction court. Provided they kept their churches repaired and properly furnished, they were normally free to provide such fittings and ornaments of a quality and design to suit themselves. Nobody had yet invented the modern practice of making them pay faculty fees *before* they did their duty; the churchwardens of olden times had only to pay if they failed to do their duty. A faculty was a grant, like a marriage licence, of a special privilege to a particular person or group of persons. It was in no way part of the chancellor's normal administrative processes as it is today, as the provision of canonically ordered ornaments and furnishings was a duty to be enforced, not a privilege to be granted.

The early Elizabethan archbishops altered their churches to Reformed standards by orders issued and enforced at visitations, with only a few supplementary causes in Chancery. One of the latter involved the last interdict to be placed on a parish in the diocese.[3] At the end of our period, Chancellor Easdall used the court extensively for the enforcement of his orders concerning churches, some derived from visitation presentments, but many evidently the result of his own personal inspection.[4]

The faculty cause as it was known in the seventeenth century concerned only the rightful ownership of pews. Disputes of this kind were not an innovation of Stuart or Elizabethan England, as Dr Purvis has shown,[5] but they did not make much impact on the York courts until the last decade of the

[1] R.VII.H.456. Slander was: 'whoremaster, bastard-getter and father of his servant's child'.
[2] In P. Winckworth, *A Verification of the Faculty Jurisdiction* (1953), p. 74.
[3] Chancery A.B., 15 Oct. 1563, parish of 'Sherburne'.
[4] Those for Nottinghamshire are printed in my article 'The Restoration of Nottinghamshire Churches 1635–40' in the *Transactions of the Thoroton Society of Nottinghamshire* (1961), pp. 57–93. [5] *Yorkshire Archaeological Journal*, CXLVI (1949), 165 ff., 182 ff.

sixteenth century. Until that time, churchwardens' powers of allocation had been sufficient to prevent all but exceptional disputes, but if any trouble had occurred they presented it at visitations. Litigation by private persons was so exceptional that only the most eminent engaged in it and took their disputes to the High Commission.[1] The one cause before 1590 which was entered in the Chancery acts was one where eventually the archbishop realized the matter was very complex, visited the church personally, and pronounced sentence himself.[2] Suits over pews took four forms:

(1) Presentment by churchwardens was obviously unsatisfactory as it was difficult to argue the real matter at issue—ownership. Litigants, therefore, started to promote disciplinary actions ostensibly over physical disturbances which had happened in church, but practically to determine who actually was the rightful owner. If no physical violence had been used, there had usually been some oral altercation which permitted an action for defamation under the breach of charity rule. Sometimes the judge sentenced one party as being responsible for the disturbance without reference to the right to the pew,[3] but usually it is directly stated or sufficiently implied who had the right, based on evidence on the matter given in the course of the action. This type of cause continued when other types were developed.

(2) A simple contest, where both parties set out their arguments and submitted to adjudication.

(3) By petition for the grant of a licence or faculty to confirm ownership. A citation against all and singular who claimed ownership of the pew was taken out of court and read in the church concerned, any person who claimed interest was required to enter an appearance in court on a certain day. These causes were usually uncontested.[4] The first recorded use of this procedure which has been noticed concerned the church at Sutton-cum-Lound, Nottinghamshire, 23 June 1613. The case of a faculty was different from an action to determine ownership, for a faculty is a form of licence which can be withdrawn or altered at any time, it is not a judgment which can only be upset by appeal. Hence, if a faculty was granted unopposed, it could subsequently be challenged in the same court on the ground that it had been issued on inaccurate information.[5]

[1] E.g. R.VII.G.1158 and 3198.
[2] Water and Water *c.* Hobman, R.VII.G.2037 and Chancery A.B., 17 June 1582.
[3] E.g. R.VII.H.660, 778.
[4] If a person gave notice of objection to the proposed faculty, it was listed like this example: office promoted by Harland *c.* all and singular, etc., Piers intervening for his interest.
[5] E.g. R.VII.H.2000, office promoted by Pawson (to revoke a letter of confirmation previously granted) *c.* Cooke; and cf. Chancery A.B., 5 May 1614, where a licence granting ownership of a choir in a church was cancelled after investigation. The form of faculty used at this time can be found in R.VII.P.A. 176.

(4) The least used form of action was to obtain from the Chancery office a monition directed against a specified person or persons to allow peaceable possession or else to attend on a specified day to show cause.[1]

The number of faculty causes remained small for many years, the reason being that the churchwardens' directions were normally obeyed without question. For instance, evidence in one case in 1633 described how, thirty years before, the seating at Leeds parish church had been allocated by the churchwardens on their own authority after it had been rearranged.[2] Archbishop Neile's enforcement of standardized seating, in orderly rows of pews of uniform height, meant a much closer official control over seating. Many churches had to renew their pews on a large scale. In small churches the churchwardens were allowed or commissioned[3] to continue to allocate pews by themselves, in larger churches others were joined with them including, in corporate towns, civic officials.[4]

Neile's policy had a levelling effect, as the richer parishioners could no longer erect special pews to their own designs to serve as status symbols. It must have aroused considerable resentment and some opposition, and for that reason the cause of the office *c.* Haber (1635) has every appearance of being a test case, designed to assert the archbishop's power of ordering churches.[5] The first feature which attracts attention is that it is a prosecution *ex officio mero*; although the authorities must have received some complaint from local sources, they decided to undertake an official prosecution, rather than leave it to the aggrieved parishioners themselves. The second feature is that the pew in question was erected in 1633, that is, after Neile's primary visitation, when his directions on these matters were made known. Lastly, it is noteworthy that Easdall chose his test case carefully—the pew was very large and ornate, much out of keeping with the others in the church, decorated with 'mottoes' and the names of Haber and his wife, and it had offended the local knight and other parishioners.

The prosecution alleged: (1) the canons of 1603, specifying that pews should be uniform and comely; (2) that no private person should alter existing seats and/or erect new ones without the permission of the ordinary— no reference to churchwardens. In the written evidence there is no mention of any reply to the first point, that was a legal matter to be argued by advo-

---

[1] E.g. office promoted Carr *c.* Marsh, Chancery A.B., 21 Oct. 1614.
[2] Office promoted Mathew *c.* Hudson jnr., R.VII.H.1987.
[3] A form of commission is in R.VII.P.A.125; the actual allocation by the churchwardens at Guiseley was recorded in the parish register (printed by the Yorkshire Parish Register Society).
[4] At Luddenham, two clergymen and two laymen, R.VII.H.2021. At St John's, Beverley, the mayor, recorder, two clergymen, Sir Michael Wharton and another, R.VII.P.A.154.
[5] R.VII.H.2060.

cates as to its relevance in this case. But Haber did contest the second, by alleging that seats could be erected or altered with the consent of the minister and churchwardens, without permission of the ordinary, reserving only to the latter his right to decide disputes. The prosecution's third argument was that the pew interfered with the convenience with which the knight and others could see and hear what was done in church, a contention which Haber denied. Needless to say, Haber was found guilty. In this case Easdall had done two things. He had asserted the Church's authority over the individual who thought he could have his own way in church, and use his pew to enhance his social status. He had also reasserted his own authority in churches over that of the churchwardens, for there is little doubt that Haber's contention represented the existing state of affairs.

The Chancery Court traditionally had some jurisdiction over matrimonial causes, for instance in 1546 there can be found in its acts causes to prove a marriage, to compel cohabitation and to enforce a contract of marriage. In early Elizabethan times the monopoly of the Consistory in contested causes removed these actions from the Chancery and it was not until the time of Benet that they reappeared there. The only noteworthy exception is the sole matrimonial cause in Table 9 for 1571–2. This was the breach of promise case involving a beneficed clergyman of York city, involving an allegation of intimacy between the parties in the study of an advocate. The substance of the cause no doubt made the archbishop direct that it be heard in Chancery.[1] Three other matrimonial causes have been noticed: Tocketts *c*. Twenge (8 January 1567), which has no distinguishing features in the acts; Ashburn *c*. Lascye (18 February 1573), involving another clergyman and begun before the archbishop in person; and *in re* Wilkinson, where a secular court had required an enquiry into the validity of a marriage (11 August 1579). From the time of Benet the Chancery exercised concurrent jurisdiction with the Consistory over causes moving the office of the judge to prove the validity of a marriage. It is quite easy to see why these office causes were brought back into Chancery, less easy to understand why they were continued unchecked in the Consistory.

This last problem is even more difficult to answer when it is compared with suits for church rates. These had been predominantly heard in Consistory, but under Benet were transferred almost entirely to Chancery.[2] A similar concentration of suits for stipends of curates (against parishioners who were rated for them, not against employing incumbents!) and parish

---

[1] R.VII.G.1555, office promoted Steel *c*. Mell.
[2] As always, there were exceptions to the rule, e.g. Consistory A.B., 27 Oct. 1614, office promoted by the churchwardens of St Saviour's, York *c*. Russells.

clerks, and for other ecclesiastical dues, likewise took place under Benet. Payments to the archbishop, archdeacons and Chapter of York continued to be recovered in the Consistory in civil actions.[1] The item in Table 9 of causes 'other financial' refers principally to the recovery of state taxes (the clerical subsidy) against defaulting clergymen. The administrative causes refer to the issue of licences and other administrative orders issued under the guise of a legal action. Testamentary causes concerned the estates of clergy beneficed in the diocese, and of those beneficed in the province who had goods or chattels in more than one diocese or peculiar jurisdiction, together with estates of the deceased of peculiar jurisdictions who died during the regular diocesan visitations every fourth year, when the peculiar jurisdictions were inhibited.

The appellate jurisdiction of the court was not large. All appeals in disciplinary and benefice causes came into Chancery, and it shared with the Consistory testamentary and, until the time of Easdall, pew appeals. As the Consistory alone dealt with suits for non-payment of legacies, appeals of this kind went to that court, otherwise testamentary appeals seem to have been heard in both courts without any settled rule. Even when Lougher was trying to maintain the Consistory jurisdiction in these matters, a probate appeal was heard in Chancery,[2] although two years later a similar appeal went into Consistory.[3] If ever there was a time when one might have expected to discover a rule in operation, it would be in the time of Easdall, yet he heard appeals concerning grants of administration and executors' accounts in both courts.[4]

Easdall, however, did make one apparent alteration in the rules concerning appeals, relating to pew suits. These appeals, the earliest which has been noticed being of the time of Lougher,[5] began before the York courts were much troubled with this type of cause from their own diocese and so naturally followed the majority of appeals into the Consistory. The first such appeal which has been noticed in Chancery did not arrive until 1616, the next one following in 1624,[6] but without exception the appeals after 1627, which have been examined either in the cause paper files or in the act books, were in

---

[1] The usual exceptions can be found; e.g. a suit for procurations to the archbishop against a long list of clergy from the Deanery of Retford, Chancery A.B., 8 June 1604.

[2] A.B., 2 May 1584, R.VII.G.2025; *ex parte* Harte *alias* Punchon *c.* Punchon.

[3] R.VII.G.2231, 2293, *ex parte* Shafto *c.* Blenkinsopp *et al.*

[4] Administration: Chancery A.B., 4 Nov. 1633, *ex parte* Farrington *c.* Hobbs *alias* Meare; Consistory A.B., 14 Jan. 1637, *ex parte* Done *c.* Wilbraham.
    Accounts: Chancery A.B., 18 May 1636, *ex parte* Millbank *alias* Emerson *c.* Wharton; Consistory A.B., 1 March 1637, *ex parte* Middleton *c.* Blacket.

[5] R.VII.G.3064, n.d., *ex parte* Brearton *c.* Massye.

[6] Chancery A.B., 2 Sept. 1616, R.VII.H.1344, *ex parte* Dinnock *c.* Lloyd; A.B., 27 Nov. 1624, *ex parte* Smith *c.* Harte.

Chancery. As the Chancery had long since established its jurisdiction in pew causes, this was only a logical development.

Enough has been said to demonstrate that although the general pattern of the distinctions between the two courts is clear, yet exceptions in many classes of business blur the distinctions. The earlier history of the courts from the time of Henry VII has still to be written but in the time of his son the Chancery list, although relatively small, was varied. Causes of instance were mingled with office causes, defamation and tithe causes among them. Even so, it is difficult to account for a solitary tithe cause obtruding itself so late in our period as 1614,[1] while at the same time a disciplinary appeal was being heard in the Consistory.[2]

We have so far been reviewing the litigation in Chancery, but in terms of productivity the Chancery registry was more concerned with non-litigious administration than with court cases. The record of its work in this sphere was kept in the institution books and in the licence books. The proportion of administrative work done by the Norwich episcopal registrar has been noted,[3] and, although there is no fee book of this period extant, a sample of the work done may be gathered from the one licence book that remains.[4] The largest single item was marriage licences. The licence book covers a period of twenty-one complete months during 1618–20, and at this time about 425 licences were being issued per annum (ignoring licences issued because of the 1619 diocesan visitation). Paver's transcripts show that by the 1630s about 560 licences were being issued per annum.

The chancellor's jurisdiction covered the whole of the province, that is, he could grant a licence for a marriage where a party lived anywhere in the province of York, regardless of diocese or peculiar jurisdiction. One part of the Chester diocese, around Colne in Lancashire, particularly took advantage of his jurisdiction, presumably because communications with York were as convenient, or more so, as those with Chester. In the ten months covered by the licence book outside the 1619 visitation period, 49 licences were issued through the chancellor's provincial jurisdiction. This jurisdiction was par-

---

[1] A.B., 23 Sept. 1614, Dawney *c.* Copland, R.VII.H.1143.
[2] R.VII.H.836, *ex parte* Denton *c.* Woodward (Chancellor of Carlisle).   [3] Above, p. 26.
[4] R.VI.C.3, fos. 11–33v. apparently contains the Chancery receipts for Feb. 1539–March 1541. The other licence books have disappeared. William Paver (1803–71), a former registrar of births and deaths at York, copied the marriage licences from these books (British Museum, Add. MSS. 29667–8) and these have been printed (see Bibliography). The originals have apparently not been seen since he borrowed them. (Information kindly supplied by Mrs N. K. M. Gurney.) His early entries are evidently not complete. The extant book shows 484 licences in 1619 (about 30 due to the visitation of that year). Paver gives 270–300 annually in 1614–16, then suddenly jumps to 448 in 1617. Thereafter his entries are probably accurate.

ticularly useful to him because of the existence of the peculiars in his own diocese. He often issued licences for marriages in these areas, and especially in the fashionable churches in the City of York which were in the Dean and Chapter's jurisdiction (St Michael-le-Belfrey and St Martin's, Coney Street).

We have noted above[1] that one of the features of the Norwich administration was the way it issued marriage licences for marriage outside the place of residence of the parties, regardless of the canons of 1597 and 1603. The practice was growing at York, judging by the evidence of Paver's transcripts, but was never considerable. In 1590, five such licences were issued; in 1591, six; in 1592, fifteen; in 1597, seventeen. Thereafter very few licences attempted to avoid the canonical prohibition, although occasionally the form 'W.N. of Saxton, son of E.N. of Church Fenton and T.C. of Hatfield' covered a licence to marry in any of the three places, and similarly with 'A.B. of Kildwick and C.W. now of Ilkley, late of Maltby', at those three places. The interpretation of Paver's transcripts needs care, for what often appears to be a licence to marry in any of three churches, turns out on closer scrutiny to include a chapel and a parish church within the same parish. Neile's administration was much more strict. The alternative of parish church or local chapel appeared much less frequently, and in the seven years 1632–8 (inclusive) only two clear cases of marriage *extra parochiam* can be discovered.[2]

For want of more certain information, it may be assumed that the licence fee at York approximated to the 10s. which was normal throughout the country, chancellor and registrar sharing the sum.[3] Consequently in the early part of the century each of these officials received about £100 per annum from this source, rising to £140 per annum in the years before the Civil War, and occasional small bonuses at the times of visitation. For the chancellor in particular this was almost entirely unearned income. Marriage licences were normally issued (as today) by the registrar as a routine function of his office. Out of 746 licences entered in the extant act book, covering a period of under two years, only nineteen had been referred to the chancellor and are noted as being issued with his authority. Some harmless fun can be had by persons with local knowledge of Puritan families in spotting their names among marriage licensees, for it was the Puritan opposition who were most loud in their attacks on the rapacity of church court officers. Among those to be found in Paver's transcripts are the great Puritan merchant

[1] P. 21.

[2] Yorks. Arch. Soc. Record Series, XL, 19, 71. The effect of the canons of 1597 in preventing the issue of such licences can also easily be traced in the peculiar of the Dean and Chapter of Westminster, Harleian Soc. vol. 23 (1886).

[3] At Nottingham the archdeacon's Official received 5s., the registrar 5s. 4d. (R.VII.P.O.30).

families of York, the Micklethwaites, Breareys, Vauxes, Tophams, Bradleys, Hoyles and Brookes. Among others were Christopher Copley, later a colonel in the Parliamentary army; Robert Jenison, Puritan lecturer at Newcastle-on-Tyne and deprived by the High Commission under Archbishop Neile; the father of Major-General John Lambert, the Parliamentary army commander; and William Alder, Vicar of Aughton, Yorkshire, who at the time of his licence was under suspension for his Puritan non-conformity.

The other administrative acts of the Chancery registrar may be briefly reviewed. During the years 1612–19 there were an average of 41 institutions each year, these are not entered in the licence books but in separate act books. The extant licence book shows that during a period of twenty-one months there were 22 sequestrations, 39 curates' licences, 39 readers' licences and 52 schoolmasters' licences issued. Many of the curates were in fact incumbents of parishes where no vicarage had been ordained, and the curate was a stipendary of a lay rector. If any licences of surgeons or midwives were issued they were recorded in a separate series of books now lost. In addition, the Chancery registrar was responsible for the probate and administration business of deceased incumbents. One other administrative item, revealed by the subscription books, was the issue of preachers' licences at a yearly average (1612–19) of 12 diocesan and nearly 3 provincial licences. The fact that they appeared in the subscription books indicates that they were issued personally by the archbishop.

THE ARCHBISHOP'S LEGAL SECRETARY

The records show that the normal licence and sequestration business was done in the registrar's office in York, but there was an overlap with the work done by the archbishop himself. The latter was responsible for consecrations, ordinations and institutions as well as licences to preach, and the legal work involved was supervised by the archbishop's legal secretary, who also acted in these matters as a deputy of the registrar. Hence an entry in the Chancery accounts of an earlier time, 'Recevyd of John wright the xiiij daye of Februarie Anno 1539 in parte of payment of the Recepts in thoffice of the Registreshipe receyvd by him at Cawodde £3'.[1] The legal secretary necessarily had a very personal connection with his master, and would therefore be a keen candidate for the registrarship itself should opportunity arise.

Archbishop Sandys' attempt to intrude John Theaker, a London proctor, into the body of proctors at York is most probably to be explained by assuming that he was Sandys' secretary. Theaker apparently continued in that

---

[1] R.VI.C.3. fo. 11. Cawood Castle was then the archbishop's principal residence.

position under the next archbishop, Piers, who appointed him to the registrarship. Archbishop Hutton appointed his secretary, Robert Hall, to succeed Theaker in 1602.[1] Archbishop Matthew similarly appointed his own secretary, William Turbatts, to succeed Hall.[2] It is with the coming of Turbatts that documentary evidence begins for the work performed by the secretary.

From the beginning of Matthew's primacy two distinct records of institutions survive—one the series kept by the registrar in York, which include other administrative detail; the other a 'pocket' sized series, with the earlier entries in Turbatts' own handwriting. The latter was paralleled by a complementary series of subscription books. Later in his life, Turbatts' own writing in the institution book ceased, but he supervised its contents and occasionally corrected an entry. It was in this corrected form that it was entered into the registrar's acts.

Turbatts' active connection with the legal secretary's office came to an end in 1628 on Matthew's death. In 1622, presumably on Hall's death, his share of the registrarship passed to Stephen Hill, and as Hill and Turbatts lived on into the Civil War Archbishop Neile was never able to promote his own secretary. Turbatts lived in York, maintained general oversight of his registry and signed necessary documents.[3] It is likely, in view of there being no known church lawyer of this name in York, that Archbishop Matthew had originally appointed Turbatts to be his secretary when he was Bishop of Durham, and it was as Bishop of Durham that Archbishop Neile first engaged his last secretary, Edward Liveley, esquire, notary public.

Liveley played a more active part in court proceedings in Durham than at York, and he may have been a member of the registrar's staff when Neile took him into his own employment.[4] He was elected to the Parliament of 1629 as member for Berwick-on-Tweed, although Neile had by this time been translated to Winchester.[5] It was here that he acquired what is now a comparative

---

[1] R.VII.P.R.14 (Theaker), P.R.9 (Hall).

[2] R.VII.P.R.6. The appointment was in return for Turbatts' 'good and faithfull service'.

[3] O. Heywood, the Presbyterian minister, in his *Diaries* (ed. J. H. Turner, 1882), III, 209–11, recorded the gossip of Restoration Yorkshire concerning the then registrar, George Aislaby. This man was Turbatts' clerk and married the widow on his master's death. He thereby not only became possessed of a £20,000 fortune, but also of his master's books. With these, he secured the registrarship at the Restoration of Charles II. Heywood said that the registrar's profits were £500 p.a. In the extant records Aislaby comes very late into the picture—he witnessed a resignation from a benefice in Turbatts' house in Coney Street, York, 23 June 1642.

[4] *Acts of the Durham High Commission* (Surtees Soc. vol. 34, 1858), *passim*.

[5] The constituency was probably one of the bishop's pocket boroughs. Sir J. E. Neale in his *Elizabethan House of Commons* (1949), p. 242, suggests this in one of his rare lapses: 'Moreover, displaying a curious ignorance for a principal minister of State and an M.P. of long standing, he [*sc.* Sir Robert Cecil] asked the Bishop of Durham for two borough seats, assuming that the County Palatine of Durham was represented in Parliament. Surely the merest tyro ought to have

rarity among the precedent books which old lawyers have bequeathed to the present day. Most registrars, proctors and advocates had such books containing precedents of court procedure, typical articles in different causes and other forms normally employed by them; but Liveley's book is the book of a bishop's legal secretary. Begun by the secretary to Bishop Watson of Chichester, it was continued by Lancelot Andrewes' secretary and carried by him to Ely and Winchester, where Lively secured it.

Liveley's precedent book is of interest because it shows the wide range of work with which a legal secretary had to deal. It included matter concerning benefices, visitations and patents to ecclesiastical offices, such as were found in the registrar's books, but excluded court procedure and almost all the normal business of a proctor. There are forms connected with the bishop's relation with the Crown, writs for attendance at Parliament, Convocation matters, episcopal dilapidations, consecrations of churches, confirmation of appointments, episcopal licences, monetary dues to the bishop, the administration of secular estates and appointments to secular offices in the bishop's gift. To these, Liveley added at York forms relating to the work of an archbishop. When he died in 1639, the book was handed to his successor, Barnabas Barker, who continued to make entries. Whatever, therefore, had been the previous practice at York, it would be safe to say that under Neile much of the higher administration of the diocese and province was conducted through the archbishop's own office and not through the Chancery registry, although the latter was formally responsible for issuing and registering the necessary documents.

That Liveley undertook more work for Neile than had been customary for archbishops' secretaries at York is suggested by his institution book. He abandoned the 'pocket' sized format of Turbatts (so handy for carrying around) but it is the scope of the contents that impresses the modern reader. Turbatts had only very rarely entered anything other than institutions, but Liveley's book became a miniature register—certificates of recusants' conformity, consecrations of chapels, confirmation of archdeacons' patents, archiepiscopal patents, consecrations of bishops, certain licences and, in institution acts, a record of the ordination of each incumbent.[1]

The overall responsibility for the courts of the diocese remained with the archbishop. Only in the Consistory Court is there no record of his personal

recognized the absurdity of this!' Sir Robert's knowledge of Elizabethan England does not deserve this stricture. Northumberland and Berwick were within the Bishopric but not within the County Palatine of Durham.

[1] Turbatts kept his own private register or precedent book of documents, both secular and ecclesiastical, issued during his secretaryship (R.VII.P.4).

intervention at some time. In the Exchequer, Archbishop Holgate, with legal help, heard a cause, 12 and 20 June 1553; Archbishop Sandys revoked an administration of the estate of a deceased person and granted a new one, 20 January 1582; Archbishop Neile called causes before him in 1639. Details have been given above of the archbishops' actions in certain Chancery causes, and such acts also occurred in Chancery type causes in the Consistory under Chancellor Rokeby (15 January 1562, 16 March 1564). The alternative title of the Chancery—'Court of Audience'—shows that in causes of church discipline and administration the archbishop's right to hear and determine causes himself was recognized. Chancellors acted as independent judges only in causes of a secular nature in the Consistory—causes which are now tried in secular courts.

Additional Note

One procedural change appears to have been made by Easdall when he became chancellor at York, and which had not been noticed at the time the above was written. The High Court of Delegates' A.B.s (at the P.R.O.) show that the practice at London was to enter formally the registration of each appeal in the A.B. The appeal came before the judges in chambers, usually at Doctors' Commons, and they assumed jurisdiction, inhibited the judge in the lower court, and issued a citation against the other party. The whole entry took up nearly a page of the acts, and such entries began at York in the time of Easdall. He either caused an entry to be made which had before been omitted, or, as is more likely, began the formalities in chambers as an improvement on existing practice at York.

3

THE EXCHEQUER
AND PREROGATIVE COURT

In the twentieth century we are familiar with the concept of the 'image' produced in the public mind by corporate bodies. People in the sixteenth century did not think in these terms, but the effect must still have been there. Part of the 'image' created by the Church of England was derived from the way in which it administered its testamentary jurisdiction, the probity and efficiency of its officers and the manner in which they charged and collected fees. Testamentary jurisdiction, however, was neither some relic of medieval religion nor a device for lining the pockets of church lawyers. In the seventeenth century best-seller, Bishop Lewis Bayley's *Practice of Piety* (chapter 28), the sick man was encouraged to make his will, and in doing so to devote some part of his estate to charity, and urged to take legal advice in framing it. If he had already made his will, then he was to have it produced and read over, and to ensure that the witnesses present knew it for what it was. The sick man was also warned of the ways of executors, of how legal quibbles had overthrown the intentions of testators, and urged to distribute as much of his estate as possible before his death. (Advice which was against the professional interests of the church lawyers.)

The rubrics of the Order for the Visitation of the Sick in the Book of Common Prayer likewise direct that the minister should use his influence towards the making of wills including provision for the poor. The religious motives behind these directions were, first, to free the minds of the sick from further concern for their temporal affairs, so that they could concentrate on spiritual matters, and also to discharge the Church's duty in urging Christians to be charitable for the well-being of their souls. One can also detect the attitude that a Christian man, who has properly organized his life under the guidance of God, does not leave his affairs in a mess, so causing trouble to his executors and breeding contention among creditors, debtors, legatees and members of his family. The advantage to the community at large in having the Church to keep a watchful eye on charitable bequests must have been considerable. Many such small legacies may well have been lost if the church courts had not accepted the duty of prosecuting *ex officio mero* (usually on the presentments of churchwardens) when executors failed to make payment.

EARLY HISTORY

The Exchequer Court of York has preserved its administrative records—registers (and originals) of wills, grants of administrations and inventories—which are common to all probate offices, but only a few of the court act books of the pre-Commonwealth period remain to show the nature and extent of its jurisdiction. These, however, provide ample material from which may be derived many points of interest to the historian. First, the concentration of testamentary business in the hands of the diocesan administration, removing one good motive for the archdeaconry courts to go on circuit as did the commissary courts elsewhere. Secondly, the comparative lack of compulsory administrations (as compared with Norwich), producing a better 'image' of church courts in the north. Thirdly, the survival in the north, in good working order, of a system in this branch of law which was at once better than English common law and also nearer to Roman civil law. Fourthly, a record of change and development within the church courts which shows them to have been by no means moribund.

The lack of other records means that our earliest knowledge of the work of the Exchequer has to be derived from a study of the patents to offices granted by the archbishop. As early as 1374 Archbishop Neville appointed an officer to transact the testamentary business of the diocese who was neither his vicar-general nor official principal,[1] but the latter officers usually had such power included in their patents in the fifteenth century.[2] Archbishop Savage issued a separate patent for a Commissary of the Exchequer and receiver-general in 1501,[3] an act which was continued by his successor Bainbridge in 1508,[4] and so became established practice. Archbishop Wolsey specifically limited the probate rights of his vicar-general to the estates of deceased beneficed clergymen, and so introduced a distinction which became permanent.[5] In this way the same official became responsible for testamentary business and for collecting the ecclesiastical revenues of the see of York.

The volume of testamentary business during the Middle Ages could not

---

[1] A. H. Thompson, *The English Clergy* (1947), p. 189 gives the patent in full. R. L. Storey in his *Diocesan Administration in the Fifteenth Century* (St Anthony's Hall Publications. no. 16, 1959), shows how before this date the probate administration was in the hands of archdeaconry sequestrators or diocesan sequestrators-general.

[2] Thompson, *op. cit.* pp. 190, 193.   [3] Given *ibid.* pp. 194–5.   [4] *Ibid.* p. 196.   [5] *Ibid.* p. 199.

have been very large. Wealth was concentrated in few hands and many of these were ecclesiastical corporations. Even in the first half of the sixteenth century the yearly average of probates at York was only 290 and of administrations only 50. The breaking-up of monastic estates and increasing activity in industry and commerce meant more wealth in more hands, so that the average yearly business in 1612–19 was 970 probates and 675 administrations, a rise of nearly five times in about seventy-five years. It is against this background that the story of the Exchequer Court in these years has to be placed. Before recounting that story, a brief description of ordinary testamentary procedure must be given.

PROBATE AND RURAL DEANS

There were two ways in which a will could be admitted to probate or an administration be granted. The method followed in a great majority of cases was by 'common form', undertaken by the executors named in the will or by the next-of-kin who took out an administration. In the event of a dispute arising concerning these matters, or when a dispute was thought to be in prospect, or in the probate of the will or administration of the estate of a very wealthy person, a longer and more unchallengeable method was used, known as probate 'by solemn form of law'. Administrations were granted by a similar procedure.

The extent of the diocese of York, together with the wild, mountainous, afforested and swampy nature of much of its area, had rendered it impracticable for every person requiring a probate or administration to journey to York in order to obtain it. There had thus grown up in the diocese a practice whereby they were granted in common form by the rural deans, and this system became so general in the diocese that even in York city itself the Dean of the Christianity of York performed this function.[1] The use of rural deans for these purposes was quite natural, for they were episcopal officers, removable at will and consequently easily disciplined, and they had each an apparitor through whom the orders of the commissary of the Exchequer could be effected. Indeed, so close was the attachment of rural deans to the work of the Exchequer, that it was the commissary who was responsible for their appointment.[2] Fortunately, there remains the evidence of the Rural Dean of Craven in 1564, describing how he granted a probate, and this is sufficiently interesting for it to be quoted in full.

[1] A similar situation produced a similar result in the diocese of Chester, see Wm. Dansey, *Horae Decanicae Rurales* (1835), II, 77 f.
[2] This is true in every patent to a commissary from the time of Archbishop Savage.

This examinate is the deane of Craven and is aucthorysyd by a comission directed from mr Johns [Walter Jones, Commissary] to Receyve witnesses or proves (*sic*) upon all wills and testamentes within his deanery and to approbate the same, spirituall mens willes having benefices or other spirituall promocion excepted, [and about Easter of the previous year, the executors of T. Talbot exhibited to him] in skipton in the dwelling house of mr middope in a parlour ther this schedule or testament annexed to this matter and now redd to hime at the tyme of his examinacion [i.e. attached to the articles in the cause about which he was giving evidence], and another testament wrytten in parchment agreeinge worde by worde with this same schedule, and he knoweth the same by reason this and the said parchment testament was then examined together by this examinate and mr laurence preston [one of the executors] and agreed in every poynte...[The Dean then read the will, those who had witnessed it being present, after which he] did then call the same iiij^{or} witnesses by their names and asked them yf they wolde be witnesses of the said will or no, and they answering sayd yea, whereupon this examinate did Commande John Cleveley his summoner to holde theme a booke, whereupon they all iiij laid their handes on the booke, and then this examinate did gyve them their othe in this manner following, this shalbe your othe that this will which you have now harde red is the trew will laste will and hole will of Thomas Talbot late departed, and that there is no other will maid by the said Thomas Talbot, neyther by worde nor writings sence this will was maid that you know of, so helpe you god and the holly contents of that booke, and thereupon they kissed the booke...the same was about two or three of the clocke in the afternoone.[1]

Two acts recorded in the Exchequer Court show the limits of the rural deans' authority. On 12 March 1606, Richard Gymney, Dean of Newark, was dismissed from his office because he had granted an administration of an estate exceeding the £40 limit specified in his commission.[2] His commission apparently had no such limit concerning probates, and also included the ability to grant tuitions (about which more will be said below). The powers of a dean at that time had been increased from the position thirty-five years before, when the Dean of Dickering was said to have granted a tuition without authority.[3] The increasing amount of testamentary business had evidently compelled a further devolution of the work of the Exchequer.

Though probates in common form usually sufficed, they could be challenged at any time during the next ten years. If, in the interval, a witness died there was no record of his evidence as the rural dean's examination was only *viva voce*; furthermore, if there was any doubt about the validity of a will it was better to have the commissary's opinion on it at once, rather than to risk having the fees for probate in common form wasted by a challenge in court.

[1] R.VII.G.1159, 1223. Talbot *c*. Arthington *et al*. I have inserted commas in this transcript.
[2] Further mention of him is made in the chapter on Nottingham; he was reappointed Rural Dean in 1617.
[3] A.B. 1570–72, fo. 142v.

The process for probate in solemn form was usually commenced by the executor and a citation was issued against all persons having interest in the estate—usually the person who would have the right to an administration if probate failed was specifically named—to be present at the proving of the will. At that time the will was exhibited in court and the witnesses were sworn; their examination was held in private by the court's examiner as was usual in church courts. If the will was opposed the cause proceeded in a normal manner with interrogatories being ministered to the witnesses by the party contesting, or allegations entered on his behalf to which the agent (as the plaintiff was called) might be required to reply and the proctor making them to prove. At the conclusion of the proceedings the judge pronounced on the validity of the will (or of a codicil), and it could not then be further challenged except by way of appeal.[1]

Administrations granted by rural deans could likewise be challenged in court by one or more claiming closer kin to the deceased than the person to whom the grant had been made, or even by one claiming equal kin and who wished to be made a co-administrator. Administrations could also be challenged by a person claiming to have a will or to be an executor. The Exchequer also granted administrations in solemn form of law, sometimes to next-of-kin who wished to make sure of an unchallengeable title, sometimes to creditors who wished to see an estate legally administered by the next-of-kin so that they could begin an action for recovery of the debt, or by themselves if the next-of-kin refused to act. Many of these causes were entitled 'to produce a will or take an administration', but the production of the will was known to be impossible and the first clause of the title was included merely for sake of form.

Guardians of minors were called 'tutors' in civil and ecclesiastical law. Often they were appointed in wills but failing such provision the next-of-kin was entitled to undertake the duty. Real estate, which operated under the rules of common law, had its own system of guardians. Land held by knight service rendered a minor liable to guardianship by his superior lord, and as the guardian did not have to account to his ward on the latter attaining his majority, it was a very valuable right. In the testamentary law administered by the church courts the tutor had to account to his pupil (as the ward was called), a more equitable system than common law. Even where knight service did not hold and the guardian had to account (as in lands held in socage), the common law courts were very ineffective for compelling the guardian to discharge his obligations.

Much of the work of the Exchequer both in and out of court was concerned with the conduct of executors and administrators. Strict account of their

---

[1] See H. Swinburne, *A Brief Treatise of Testaments and Last Wills* (1590), p. 224.

transactions had to be made, and they were required on taking up their duties to make a bond of sufficient amount to exhibit an inventory of the estate for which they were responsible, to deal faithfully and to submit their accounts. The Exchequer's task was increased because it was the custom of the Province of York—and the custom was the law—to specify the portions of an estate which should be inherited by a widow alone or by a widow with children, regardless of whether there was a will or not. An intestate's estate was divisible by certain well-established rules. The custom originated in Roman law, and in many respects the testamentary practice of the province followed that law.[1] The court therefore had to admit and support the claims of next-of-kin for their appropriate shares of the surplus available for distribution and sometimes to adjudicate on conflicting claims.

OFFICE OF RECEIVER-GENERAL

The Commissary of the Exchequer also acted as the receiver-general of the ecclesiastical dues of the see of York, and this function was described in a document concerning the removal of Miles Sandys from the registrarship of the Exchequer Court.[2] He collected all the ecclesiastical revenues of the see, and accounted for them to the archbishop's auditors. These revenues comprised the rents from appropriated rectories, pensions, procurations and synodals, and 2s. for every probate or administration. The collection of the procurations and synodals took place at the Easter and Michaelmas synods of the diocese; and, as the commissary had the right to appoint rural deans because they were his agents for probate business, so he also was given the place of president of the diocesan synods, presumably to facilitate the collection of the archbishop's dues. The seventeenth-century patents to the commissaryship granted those officers all the fees arising from their office, saving only to the archbishop the probate fees from wills of citizens of York and an annuity of £40 per annum.[3] Archbishop Savage's patent of appointment to the combined office commenced with the grant of authority to detect and punish ecclesiastical faults and crimes, a general provision not included in Elizabethan patents, where coercive power was limited to matters concerning testamentary business.[4] In default of any evidence about the activities of the commissary in the early sixteenth century, it may be assumed that coercive

---

[1] *Ibid.* p. 96, where the matter of the appointment of tutors is given as an example.

[2] Bishopthorpe MSS. bundle 24 (unlisted).

[3] In the fifteenth century this place was occupied by the vicar-general, who also collected the ecclesiastical dues; see patents granted in 1408 and 1480; Thompson, *op. cit.* pp. 190, 193. Archbishop Matthew's patents are in R.VII.P.4, pp. 32–5 and fos. 155 v.–158.

[4] E.g. that to John Rokeby, 1569, quoted by Dr Ritchie, *op. cit.* p. 19.

power was granted not so much to supplement or conflict with that of the vicar-general, but rather to enable the former to compel the payment of ecclesiastical dues.

DEVELOPMENT OF THE EXCHEQUER COURT IN THE SIXTEENTH CENTURY

If this supposition was true, and knowing what we do about the mingling of administrative and judicial business in medieval times, knowing also that the commissaryship and the function of receiver-general was a united office, we should expect to find the earliest Exchequer act book reflecting this state of affairs, and we are not disappointed. The act book covers the years 1548–55, and although time has dealt hardly with it, enough remains to enable an accurate picture to be made of the work of the Exchequer office.

During these years the Exchequer was certainly called a 'Court', and the commissary acted in a judicial capacity. Caveats were entered to prevent wills being proved without first calling the person entering the writ; citations were also entered in the book, especially those to persons opposing, or thought to be opposing probates in solemn form of law, and to show cause why administrations should not be granted; other citations concerned actions about alleged false inventories, or similar promoted causes against executors and administrators. The judicial acts in these causes were also entered, but very often not under court days, as was customary in other act books, but under each cause separately. They show that contested testamentary causes were few, and litigation was not protracted. Proctors were employed and witnesses examined, but no weekly session of the court was held, acts being made as convenience dictated. During the Michaelmas term 1554, nine causes entered the court, if the probate of two wills and the granting of administration of three estates in common form can properly be described as causes. The other business was three probates in solemn form and a renunciation of an executorship. While the number of causes, some of them uncontested, was as few as that, there was no incentive to establish anything like a regular court of law. Certain of the administrative acts of the commissary were also entered in the book, such as a citation *Quorum nomina* to the Rural Dean of Cleveland to cite all persons in that Deanery, being executors or next-of-kin, to appear personally or by deputy in the Exchequer at York on the tenth day after the issuing of the citation, or the next court day after that, to prove wills and undertake administrations.[1]

---

[1] Fo. 39 (4 Nov. 1552). This citation arouses some speculation about the place of the dean in the probate business of the time, but it is probably to be understood as an order to those who had not

The functions and powers of the commissary as receiver-general are well illustrated in the act book. Payment of ecclesiastical dues was enforced by the Exchequer Court. The commissary issued a citation *Quorum nomina* on 3 November 1552, to the rural deans of Ainsty and Otley to cite all rectors, vicars and lay rectors or their representatives to appear before him to pay all procurations and synodals due at the synods of that year and remaining unpaid. For those who refused to obey such citations the penalty was sequestration, and the commissary issued sequestrations to the local rural dean and his apparitor on several occasions during the years covered by this act book, so that the debt could be recovered.

This Exchequer act book, with its collection of court acts and orders, citations, caveats, and matters arising from the collection of the ecclesiastical revenues of the see of York, represented a day-to-day record of the business executed by the commissary in his office at the Exchequer. It is unfortunate that parts of many pages are missing, and that they cover so few years, for this period, from 1548 to 1555, was the closing chapter of the medieval epoch of the Exchequer's history.

The concluding years, 1553–5, of this earliest extant Exchequer act book, covered the period *sede vacante* after Archbishop Holgate. The work of the receiver-general was much less apparent in the next book, 1556–9, covering the commissaryship of Robert Johnson, LL.B., Archbishop Heath's nominee. Nevertheless, in 1556 he had one recalcitrant farmer of tithes before him for refusing to pay an ecclesiastical due.[1] One important development took place during his period of office. The number of contested probates and administrations and other causes connected therewith was probably noticeably increasing. In the Michaelmas term 1554, as has been stated above, there were only three probates in solemn form: in the corresponding term of 1558, eight such probates were entered in the act book. The rise in the number of such probates, and perhaps also in their complexity, found the Exchequer organization unfitted to deal with the litigation involved. Furthermore, Johnson had other duties[2] and was evidently increasingly unable to carry out judicial work. He engaged substitutes, especially William Rokeby, Commissary of the Consistory Court, and on 9 March 1558, deputed him to hear and determine all disputes concerning wills, *in loco Consistoriali Ebor.*, returning the proved wills, with fees, to the Exchequer Court for sealing and registering.

already undertaken those functions legally, to do so at once. There are no other similar citations recorded, and it may be that in the wild and isolated districts of Cleveland *de facto* rather than *de jure* was the ruling principle. For citations *Quorum nomina* see p. 181.

[1] Fo. 16 v.

[2] See *Alumni Cantab.* He was chancellor of the diocese of Worcester until 1558, and Headmaster of 'York School' *c.* 1557, etc.

Thereafter Johnson's name rarely appears in the act book and Rokeby undertook judicial duties, not only in the Consistory, but also simpler causes in the Exchequer itself. The Consistory had been accustomed to have testamentary causes before it. In 1548 it was deciding causes of disputed wills and even, on 14 March 1549, appointing a tutor, but the number of such causes was very small.

A similar situation continued during the commissaryship of Walter Jones. As has been described in Chapter 2, Jones was appointed by Archbishop Young to act as an assistant to the vicar-general, John Rokeby. He was concerned only to give general oversight to the Exchequer, his main duties lying elsewhere. For routine administration he employed John Bateman, Rural Dean of the Christianity of York, and the acts show that Jones himself appeared in the court infrequently. The business was increasing and becoming more varied. In the Michaelmas term 1564, for instance, there were introduced to the court eleven causes, eight being probates and administrations in solemn form of law, two concerning the granting of tuitions, and one a promoted cause against an executor. A few causes seem to have been lengthy ones, particularly that concerning the will of the Earl of Westmorland,[1] and in one Jones assigned an advocate to a defendant on his petition. The increase in business caused the court to institute regular weekly morning sessions for business of a judicial nature, in order to separate it conveniently from other routine tasks of administration. Yet the total number of causes remained small, despite the comparative increase. During the court sessions during the Michaelmas term of 1567, the number of causes before the court on any one day never exceeded five, and averaged about three. The summary or informal nature of the proceedings in the Exchequer at this date can be seen from the fact that it was possible for Bateman to assume control of a cause, turning it from a civil into a criminal cause, to interrogate the defendant personally in court, and to reserve further ordering of the matter to himself.[2]

By the time of Jones, or perhaps from the beginning of his commissaryship, the administrative acts of the court and of the receiver-general and his prosecutions were no longer entered in the act books. These became purely a record of judicial work, and the recovery of ecclesiastical dues was undertaken thenceforth by a civil suit (i.e. an instance cause) in the Consistory Court. The act book had become the act book of a court of law, not the record of the routine administration of the Exchequer office. The provision of a specified regular time for hearing causes had given to the Exchequer the appearance of a court of law not dissimilar from that of other courts. But as yet act book and judicial sessions were only a departmental organization of

[1] A.B. 1562–8, fos. 48, 53–7 v., 63.   [2] A.B 1562–8, fos. 68–9.

part of the Exchequer's work. Protracted and difficult causes were directed to the Consistory Court,[1] and the acts of that court show that a regular flow of probate and allied causes was being initiated in it, without reference to the Exchequer. So it was that the Consistory Court could reverse the grant of probate or administration by the commissary's deputy, a rural dean, without reference to the commissary himself.[2]

Walter Jones' commissaryship ended with the death of Archbishop Young. The next Primate, Grindal, first appointed John Rokeby to succeed him, but evidently as only a temporary expedient, until he had time to consider the position further. Rokeby was too old to carry out the extra duties for more than a short time. As permanent commissary and receiver-general Grindal appointed Richard Percy, and his patent was granted, for the first time in the history of the court, for life.[3] The innovation is the more notable for Grindal did not appoint his chancellor in this way, and it may be regarded as another step in the recognition of the commissary primarily as a judge, and only secondly as head of the archbishop's financial department. It is unfortunate that the lack of the relevant documentary material makes it impossible to trace the division of functions from the administrative as well as from the judicial standpoint.

There is an act book extant covering the opening part of Rokeby's short commissaryship and the first months of that of Percy (1570–2). Thereafter there is a long gap until 1591, making the reconstruction of events an exercise in probabilities. The evidence of the act book, so far as it goes, shows that Percy began by making no changes in existing practice. Rokeby had altered the judicial sessions from Wednesday morning to Friday afternoon, presumably to dovetail with his other judicial work, and the time was found so convenient that it remained until the Commonwealth. The acts performed by Rokeby and Percy in these sessions continued to be of a simple kind, many of the probates and administrations in solemn form being made without any opposition. Difficult and lengthy causes were still remitted to the Consistory Court.[4] The volume of judicial work transacted in the Exchequer

[1] Exchequer A.B. 1562–8, fos. 160, 173.

[2] E.g. the cause *re* will of Talbot, cited above. Tutors were also assigned by the Official Principal, see Consistory A.B., 19 Oct. 1564. One exception to the general rule was the cause concerning the probate of Christopher Estofte's alleged will, commenced in the Exchequer Court 18 Sept. 1566; it was contested, commissions were issued to examine witnesses in St Paul's Cathedral, London, the commissary and the court's actuary went themselves to the widow's home to take her evidence, finally an appeal against an interlocutory decree was made to the Court of Delegates and the cause disappeared from the acts after fourteen months of litigation.

[3] See the papers concerning the eviction of Miles Sandys from the commissaryship in Bishopthorpe MSS., bundle 24, unlisted.

[4] E.g. Consistory A.B., 8 Oct. 1575, office for proving will of Edward Preston, said to be remitted by the Exchequer Court of York. Similar remissions, 17 March 1576, 31 March 1576.

itself continued to increase gradually. In the Michaelmas term of 1571, the number of causes before the court at each judicial session varied from twelve to one, but averaged six to seven.

To the later observer, blessed with hindsight, it may appear obvious that the relationship between Exchequer and Consistory Court had to undergo some change. The work of the former in testamentary matters was expanding and the number of contested causes and those requiring judicial sentence was likewise increasing. It was sometimes impossible to determine at the outset whether a cause would require extensive litigation: a mistaken estimate would mean a transfer to the other court with consequent waste of time and expense. Speed was often vital in testamentary causes, so that an estate could be placed under proper administration as soon as possible and the rights of all interested persons safeguarded. The smaller list of causes and the greater facilities for dealing with testamentary business possessed by the Exchequer, meant that suits could be heard more expeditiously and effect given to sentences with greater rapidity than was possible in the Consistory Court. Most of all, however, there was needed one judge to interpret the law of the diocese in testamentary matters if uncertainty was not to result, and the question was whether this was to be the judge who heard the few important causes or the judge who supervised the bulk of testamentary business. Nevertheless some particular event or coincidence of events was required to disturb an established custom. The necessary stimulus was provided by the chancellorship of Robert Lougher (1577–85).

Lougher's other interests resulted in frequent absences from York during term, and the business of the Consistory Court consequently suffered.[1] The smooth flow of causes through the court was interrupted whilst his arrival was awaited to give interlocutory decrees and final sentences, and consequently important causes were delayed. The substitute usually present during Lougher's absences was Anthony Iveson, a vicar-choral of York Minster, and like most of that profession at the time, a non-graduate. In Lougher's early days as chancellor, Iveson was only responsible for routine acts in causes, but as he became more experienced and the congestion more acute, he was allowed to deliver judgments. The delay in the hearing of causes, together with having to endure a man of Iveson's status pronouncing sentence from the place where Rokeby had sat only a few years before, must

---

[1] He was away most of the Hilary term of 1579, from the beginning of October 1579 until 19 March 1580, all the Hilary term 1581, from the beginning of April until 16 June and during the Michaelmas term 1582 (excepting a fortnight in November). In 1583 he did not appear until 22 June, he was absent from 12 October 1584 until 4 March 1585, and from 26 March 1585 until his death. (Percy became chancellor 18 June 1585.) These were Lougher's more protracted absences after Archbishop Sandy's metropolitical visitation.

have aroused the indignation of the lawyers of York.[1] There was little they could do to alter the situation, but one step they were able to take.

During the first two or three years of Lougher's chancellorship, events proceeded normally. He was naturally away for a time in the years 1577–8 conducting Sandys' metropolitical visitation, and during this time Percy was one of the substitutes whom he employed.[2] As late as June 1579, a probate cause introduced into the Exchequer was remitted to the Consistory because of the litigation involved.[3] Four years later the situation had altered. A few days after one of his longest absences, Lougher made a pronouncement in open court in which he ordered all advocates and proctors not to prosecute in the Exchequer Court causes which by the statutes of the Consistory Court were to be prosecuted before the Official of that court or the vicar-general under penalty of suspension.[4] It is apparent, therefore, that during, and probably because of the chancellor's absences, the lawyers were taking causes to the Exchequer which before would normally have gone into the Consistory, and this must have happened with the encouragement of Percy.

Consequently it is possible to date the re-establishment of the Exchequer Court as a fully-fledged court of law to the years 1582–3. Percy's assumption of control of the full range of probate business was symbolized by the fact that he changed the custom of the diocese in one particular.[5] Lougher's threats had no effect and probate and allied causes continued to decrease in the Consistory until they disappeared altogether.[6] The lawyers' protest against the chancellor's conduct of business was successful, but it may be presumed that their action must have had the support of the archbishop, in order for it to have defied the warning of possible coercive measures by the chancellor. The accord existing between Sandys and Percy at this time can

[1] It is to be noted, however, that Iveson must have been a man of some competence and reliability. Lougher's predecessor as chancellor, John Gibson, was also commissary of the Dean and Chapter's Court. During Lougher's chancellorship, Gibson was often away from York and employed Iveson as his substitute (see R.As. 59 *passim*).

[2] Consistory A.B., 5 July 1578.

[3] *Ibid.* 18 June, office for proving the will of Sir John Constable, Kt.

[4] Consistory A.B., 27 June 1583. As there are no statutes of the Consistory Court extant, it is impossible to determine whether there was at this time a specific order regarding these causes, or whether Lougher was merely placing his own interpretation on some old statute.

[5] Four proctors in the Consistory Court deposed, 26 Oct. 1583, 'that by the stile and custome of the consistory and the courte of exchequer of york by the space of this twenty yeares last past and more, that (in every inventory or most of them, where calculacion of rights due to wief, children and deaths part) the funerall expenses hath beene taken and deducted furth of the deaths parte and not furthe of the whole goods untill of late viz. within this twelve months last past or thereabouts that it is now otherwise used in the said exchequer by the appointment of mr doctor Percy iudge there…' (Consistory A.B., Brake *alias* Ledell *c.* Murton). The 'deaths part' was the part of the estate which was freely disposable by the testator.

[6] The last was 22 April 1585, office for proving will of George Warde; this is the only such cause I have found after December 1584.

be gauged from the fact that upon Lougher's death, Percy was nominated to succeed him as chancellor.

Apparently unable to enforce his will upon the advocates and proctors, Lougher attempted to continue his jurisdiction over testamentary causes by means of legal ingenuity. To understand what happened it is necessary to examine first the position regarding appeals from the Exchequer Court. Everything points to the fact that during the Middle Ages such appeals went directly from York to Rome as was the case in the Consistory Court. The deduction is made, first from an appeal in Queen Mary's time to Cardinal Pole, Papal Legate,[1] secondly from the fact that appeals after her death went to the High Court of Delegates, the English substitute for the Pope's appellate jurisdiction. Consequently there was no appeal from one of the archbishop's courts to another. Of the two ways by which a probate in solemn form could be initiated, by direct process in the Exchequer or Consistory, or in protest against a probate in common form before a rural dean, the second could perhaps be regarded as an appeal from a judicial decision. Here was Lougher's opportunity.

During the long vacation following the chancellor's abortive attempt to coerce the advocates and proctors, an appeal was entered in the Chancery Court, before his substitute Iveson, by Robert Tempest, esquire. The nature of the cause was the proving of the will of Richard Tempest, esquire, and it had been promoted by Elizabeth Tempest against Robert. The appeal was against a decision by William Webster and Christopher Taylor, 'sub-delegates' or deputies of the commissary of the Exchequer—in fact, rural deans of Pontefract. The proctor who introduced the appeal was James Stock, erstwhile member of the staff of the principal registrar, who may reasonably be regarded as being Lougher's agent to introduce the action in that court. Iveson inhibited the judges *a quo* and the promoter of the original cause in the usual way, and ordered them to be cited to answer the party appellant.

The jurisdiction of the court was questioned when the proctor for Webster and Taylor answered the citation on 27 September 1583, before Lougher himself. He founded his case on two principles: first, that an appeal lay from a sub-delegate to the delegate from whom the sub-delegation was made; second, that there was an essential difference between proving in common form and proving in solemn form, and the sub-delegates only did the former. The inference from these two principles was that if the matter was one of appeal, the appeal lay to the commissary, but if that was not a valid argument, then it could be argued that it was not an appeal at all. Stock's reply to these

[1] Exchequer A.B. 1556–9, fo. 54, office for proving will of Wm. Turnell.

arguments ignored the second contention, and concentrated on the matter of appeal. It was, he said, not a matter of appealing from the sub-delegate (i.e. rural dean) to the delegate (i.e. the commissary) but to the person from whom the original delegation had been made, the archbishop—and hence to his vicar-general and official principal (i.e. the judge appointed to hear appeals to the archbishop). The commissary, argued Stock, had delegated all his power in a simple form of delegation to the sub-delegates, and therefore the appeal lay not to him but to the originator of his powers, the archbishop (and his vicar-general and official principal for him).

The argument was subtle, for a suit for probate in solemn form could result from the suitor's attempt to reverse a rural dean's common form probate. Although it had probably never been thought of as such, this type of suit might be regarded as an appeal. If Stock's reasoning was acted upon, the effect would have been to return these causes to the chancellor's court, only now in the guise of an appeal. There was an element of reasonableness in Stock's argument, for one could not normally appeal from a judge who had been delegated judicial powers (e.g. a chancellor or commissary) to the person who had delegated them (e.g. a bishop). One flaw in this line of thought was that the archbishop had delegated his probate jurisdiction to his commissary, so that the rural dean was ultimately a delegate of the archbishop himself. The other and more fundamental flaw was that the granting of common form probates was not a judicial, but an administrative action, and the act book unfortunately does not record any submission by Stock on this premise.[1]

It seems probable that the original promoter, Elizabeth Tempest, had meanwhile proved the will in solemn form before Percy, because on the same day as the above argument before Lougher took place Stock entered another appeal, this time against a judgment of the commissary in her favour. The appeal was admitted and an inhibition sent out and both appeals were continued for two weeks, by which time agreement had been reached between the parties. Although from the point of view of the historian it is regrettable that the litigation ended in this peaceful manner, it is significant that never again was an appeal of this kind brought into the Chancery Court. Exchequer causes remained in that court.

[1] Chancery A.B., 14 and 27 Sept. 1583. These considerations did not prevent the commissary from reversing a decision of a substitute when appealed to, without any objection by the proctor of the client who lost by this appeal (Stanhopp *c.* Law, in *re* estate of Katherine Hanson, Exchequer A.B. 27 March, 17 and 28 April 1629). The substitute's award had been badly worded and obviously needed rectifying, and this was done in the deputy registrar's house between 5 and 7 p.m. Strictly speaking, a substitute's decision bound the judge, but here equitable considerations over-rode the strict letter of the law. The act was *extra curiam* because the party had been excommunicated for not obeying the substitute's award, and courts would normally absolve as soon as a party appeared and submitted.

There is one other trace of the conflict of jurisdictions that deserves mention. The partial lapsing of the Exchequer's right to hear causes in the reign of Mary, and the concentrating of its work on the hearing of non-litigious probates and allied concerns, must have made it seem in some ways more a probate office than a court of law. When Percy sought to assert his right to determine causes, he must have had to meet objections that he had no competence to act as a judge. It is, therefore, interesting to observe that in the four extant act books of the period before the conflict, marginal annotations have been made in handwriting of the Elizabethan period. This annotator was interested in all references to the Exchequer as a court. The expression '*Curia Scaccarij*' was often noted, as also 'this Court', the 'judge of this Court', the 'style and constitutions of this Court', while the annotator was particularly happy to underline such manifestations of official power as proceedings *ex officio mero* in the earlier act books. Other acts of the judge in the Exchequer, before he had delegated his powers to the Consistory, must have delighted the annotator. He marked places where interrogatories were ministered to witnesses, evidence was published and sentence was delivered. The importance attached to the establishment of the Exchequer as a court of law by the annotator was not entirely confined to the conflict with the Consistory Court. If the annotator was Percy himself, he was aiming to secure another prize besides the Consistory probate causes, as will be described below when the jurisdiction of the Exchequer is considered.

The history of the Exchequer Court was, after 1585, an untroubled one, so far as the exercise of its functions was concerned, but there were two incidents affecting its judges which are worthy of record. The first related to Percy and Archbishop Sandys' propensity for intruding his young sons in the offices of his courts. Percy held his patent for life, but in 1585 Sandys granted another to him and Miles Sandys jointly, also for life. Percy never surrendered his original patent, but accepted the second, Miles never taking possession of the office until after his father's death when Percy retired. Apparently, however, he made some claim to it then, and an unnumbered MS. in the Bishopthorpe MSS. bundle 24 contains a legal opinion upon questions obviously framed with the intention of finding a legal loop-hole to render the joint patent null and void. The various points made in the document are hard to follow, as the situation which caused its production is unknown to us, and the actual wording is obscure in its meaning. The general impression is that the archbishop reserved to himself the 2*s.* fee payable on each probate and administration, but after his death Miles entered a claim to it. The attempt to render the patent void must therefore have been undertaken by Sandys' successor, Piers. Nevertheless, the latter in 1590 respected the grant to Miles for life by naming a new patent to him and Benet jointly, on Percy's retirement. Three years later, Miles was eventually removed when another patent was issued, to Benet and William Goodwin.[1]

HISTORY OF THE COURT IN THE SEVENTEENTH CENTURY

Benet, and after him Swinburne, continued the work of the court without any known incident, until the latter's death in 1623. The confusion which resulted from the granting of several patents, and the eventual emergence of Easdall as the working commissary have been described in Chapter 2. Easdall's subsequent appointment to the chancellorship of Durham caused him to hand over the working of the routine of the court to Wickham and Hodson, who were also helping him in the Consistory and Chancery. Eventually, in 1632, he gave up his other work in order to concentrate on his duties as Archbishop Neile's chancellor. The man appointed to succeed Easdall at the Exchequer was John Levett, LL.D., third son of Thomas, one of those who figured in the abortive patents of Archbishop Matthew in 1624. It may well have been that Neile was seeking to conciliate the landed gentry by this appointment, a class often alienated by the political and religious policies supported by him, rather than consulting primarily the interest of justice,[2] and it caused the second of the two incidents to be recorded.

Levett was an advocate of Doctors' Commons, and he clearly regarded his work at London as of first priority, although his commissaryship at York must have been valuable as his was the first patent to a sole holder of the office since the time of Walter Jones. There is no extant record of his activities until 1635, when acts of the court become available and show that Hodson was performing the routine duties of the judge, and that Levett himself only occasionally visited York. Hodson must have acquired some legal knowledge after his years in the High Commission and as Easdall's substitute, and with Levett's help from time to time, the business of the court must have been conducted in a passable, if not ideal, manner.

For some unknown reason Hodson retired from the court in 1637, and the following year Paul Glisson, LL.B., assumed his duties, and after some weeks when Levett appeared to give judgments, he assumed full control of all business. Glisson had only been admitted an advocate the previous year[3] and then only as a supernumerary, for he never practised. Despite his fellowship

[1] Chapter A.B., 10 April 1590 and 29 Nov. 1593. Goodwin, later Dean of Christ Church, Oxford, was a leading York preacher and pluralist.
[2] Patent of appointment in Institution Book 1632–68, p. 100.
[3] Consistory A.B., 1 Aug. 1637, see Appendix II.

at Trinity Hall, Cambridge,[1] he was evidently content to accept the small stipend which Levett would allow him, and risk unpopularity with the other ecclesiastical lawyers at York. These can hardly have accepted with equanimity the necessity of arguing causes involving the property of wealthy and important clients before an advocate of such little legal experience, and probably without the status of a permanent deputy such as Dodsworth had been for Benet.

Whether the initiative came from the lawyers or from the archbishop and his advisers, the latter determined to act. It may reasonably be supposed that Levett was first warned and refused to respond, before action was taken. The archbishop's first step was to call a cause before him, and take a purely formal act in it before returning it to the Exchequer. The action, although not unprecedented,[2] was certainly most unusual. At this time Levett had not been seen in York for four months, and the move may best be regarded as an intimation to him that he must alter his administration of the court.

The warning had no effect, Glisson continued to act as judge, and the gathering clouds of political and religious conflict probably diverted Neile's attention from the matter. So it was not until 14 May 1639, that he made another move. On that day he called two causes before him; in the one he made a formal act, in the other he pronounced judgment, Easdall, Mottershed and other advocates being present at Bishopthorpe for the occasion. Doubtless the chancellor had read the papers in the cause, produced on the archbishop's order, and had prepared the judgment himself. This time the earnest of Neile's determination produced its effect, and on 11 June Levett wrote a letter from London containing a new list of substitutes, with the name of George Stanhope first on the list. Stanhope, Precentor of York Minster, and a regular attender on the bench of the High Commission Court, was one of Neile's henchmen. He acted as judge until 1641, when he was succeeded by a senior advocate. Stanhope's father had been vicar-general of the Archbishop of Canterbury and chancellor of London diocese, and he himself had been a member of Gray's Inn before taking holy orders;[3] he was also an older and more mature man than Glisson.

The incident illustrates Neile's concern for the good administration of justice in his courts, as well as the result of how his concern to win the sympathy of the landed gentry led him to depart from that principle in making Levett's appointment. It also illustrates the difficulty of disciplining

---

[1] See *Alumni Cantab.*
[2] Exchequer A.B. 1548–55, fo. 46, cause heard by Archbishop Holgate. The fact that the archbishop had the power is distinctly specified in counsel's opinion on Miles Sandys' patent, Bishopthorpe MSS. bundle 24.
[3] *Alumni Cantab.*

a judge who held a patent for life. In the last resort the only action available was for the archbishop to threaten to take over the whole business of the court himself, for the ultimate responsibility for a church court lies with the ordinary from whom it derives its authority.

THE FOUNDING OF THE PREROGATIVE COURT

The increase in the work of the Exchequer Court and of its probate acts in common form, was achieved not only by the growing wealth of a larger number of persons, but also by an extension of jurisdiction. The medieval Exchequer, to judge from the pre-Elizabethan act books remaining to us, concerned itself only with probates within the diocese of York, excluding the peculiar jurisdictions. The probates granted during metropolitical visitations, when other jurisdictions in the province were inhibited, were a function of the Visitors then appointed, rather than of the Exchequer. It is unlikely that the number of medieval wills of persons with *bona notabilia* in more than one jurisdiction was very considerable. Where a person had goods or property lying within the two provinces of Canterbury and York at the time of his death, it was necessary for his executors or administrators to prove the will or take an administration in both provinces.[1] In such probate or administration the court at York was careful to limit its act to goods etc. 'within the jurisdiction of the Archbishop'. Where the deceased's property lay within both the archbishop's and a peculiar jurisdiction, it is likely that probate was granted in a similar manner, although only one late cause has been found where such action was recorded.[2]

There is little evidence in the acts of the Exchequer before 1572 that the court was concerned with provincial probate matters, and there is no reference to such a jurisdiction in the patents granted to the commissaries. The first reference to a cause concerning an extra-diocesan matter so far traced did not occur until 1565,[3] when the commissary assigned the same tutor as had been assigned when probate was granted in the Durham Consistory Court. It is not clear why this cause came into the Exchequer, but the annotator marked it as indicating prerogative jurisdiction. The second cause concerned a will where the deceased had lived in the diocese of Chester, and it had already been proved as far as property in the southern province was concerned; the will was then proved in solemn form in the Exchequer as far

---

[1] See Exchequer A.B., 1562–8, fo. 66.
[2] Exchequer A.B., 1570–2, fo. 215. The judge suspended a cause until a will should be proved in the peculiar court in which the deceased died, reserving to himself the granting of administration of the deceased's goods being within the archbishop's jurisdiction.
[3] A.B., 1562–8, fos. 100, 104.

as it related to property in the province of York.[1] Neither of these two causes, however, referred to the existence of *bona notabilia* in more than one jurisdiction, and the first clear reference to the existence of such goods (actually in the form *bona iura et credita*) did not occur, significantly, until the time of Percy's commissaryship.[2]

The absence of any jurisdiction by the Exchequer where the deceased had *bona notabilia* in more than one diocese or peculiar (the prerogative jurisdiction) in the acts of the court, is paralleled by its absence in the act books of probates and administrations.[3] There are various acts recorded where the deceased lived in the province of Canterbury, but references to persons who died elsewhere in the northern province, implying *bona notabilia* within that province, are very few. From 1514 to 1582 there were only five probates or administrations granted of persons noted as living outside the diocese, and one tuition was granted of children living in a diocesan peculiar.[4] Even these may have been explained by the fact that the deceased died within the court's jurisdiction, and therefore was subject to its control.[5]

The extreme paucity of the evidence for any prerogative jurisdiction before the time of Percy indicates that any such right was latent rather than patent. Yet by 1591, when the extant series of act books recommences after nearly twenty years hiatus, the prerogative jurisdiction was obviously established and working without any opposition. Its origin can be dated to the grant by Archbishop Sandys to Percy of the office of custodian and commissary of the Prerogative Court, the first such patent ever granted. It was dated 3 May 1577, which was only a few weeks after Sandys first arrived in York as primate. It seems more probable, therefore, that the initiative for the creation of the jurisdiction came from the archbishop, who was familiar with southern practice and might well have desired to see the same established at York.

Two things are notable about the patent.[6] First, that it set out a vague legal

---

[1] Exchequer A.B., 1562–8, fo. 133 v. This probate was, however, merely a tactical move in more protracted litigation. The will had been proved also at Chester, and an appeal was then lodged in the Consistory Court at York, and eventually the cause went to the Court of Delegates, see R.VII.G.1313 (Will of Sir Thos. Gravenour, Kt.).

[2] A.B., 1570–2, fo. 172, administration granted of goods of Lady Ellen Stanley of the diocese of Chester.

[3] Printed in the *Yorkshire Archaeological Society's Record Series*, various vols.

[4] 4 Feb. 1532, Wm. Northorpe 'late living in co. Northumberland' (administration); 10 June and 9 Sept. 1556, William, Lord Dacre and Thos. Lord Dacre, respectively of 'Kyrkeoswalde', diocese of Carlisle (administration); 16 April 1565, tuition of children of John Burland, Bugthorpe peculiar (entered with administrations), 14 Dec. 1565, John Peryse *alias* Butterfielde of Newcastle-on-Tyne (administration); 11 Sept. 1582, Thos. Ball of Chester (administration).

[5] See patent of Rokeby as commissary, quoted by Dr Ritchie, *op. cit.* p. 19, and for examples, p. 20.

[6] Register, vol. 31, fo. 59 v. It is quoted by Dr Ritchie, *op. cit.* pp. 21–2. Dr Ritchie is quite right in his suggestion (p. 22) that the patent indicated that the prerogative jurisdiction 'was a fairly

basis for jurisdiction, stating that it is 'notoriously known to belong solely and wholly to us and our successors, as much by the common law of this realm of England as by the Prerogative of our cathedral and metropolitical church of our Blessed Peter of York'. Secondly, that it gave the right to Percy to hear and determine all causes that might arise in the execution of the jurisdiction. Whether or not Sandys knew of the exact position at York, where the causes of the Exchequer went into Consistory when litigation occurred, may be doubted, as the issuing of the patent was one of his first acts, but its effect was to establish Percy as a judge in a court of law, a position he can hardly be said to have occupied before. It was perhaps this that urged him to assert, or reassert, the competence of the Exchequer as a court of law when the opportunity arose. Alternatively, it may have been Percy who urged Sandys, before he had had time to study the legal position, to create this office in order to extend the power and income of the Exchequer Court.

There is no record of any attempt to challenge the establishment of the prerogative jurisdiction at its first inception, and it is likely that if there had been such a challenge, some trace of it would have been found in the High Commission or Chancery Court acts. Prerogative probates were not at first in large numbers, and it was only in 1624 that a separate act book for registering them was thought necessary.[1] Before that date they were often entered in the York City act book. It is likely that the small number of probates at first attracted by the action of Sandys and Percy, together with the general utility of having to have only one probate or administration instead of two or more, encouraged general acceptance of the innovation. There was, in addition, the added advantage that causes begun in the Prerogative Court had only one possibility of appeal before them—to the Court of Delegates—while a probate in a diocesan court went to the Consistory Court at York on first appeal, before passing to the Delegates.

In the court records now extant there are only two instances before the Civil War when the prerogative jurisdiction was challenged in such a way that the archbishop had to take action to defend his rights. Neile found cause, about 1637, to prosecute the Chancellor of Durham and the registrar of the Allerton peculiar jurisdiction in the High Commission, and although the court acts for that date are missing, the articles containing the case against

recent development', but is wrong in his assumption (p. 20) that 'the court books...in this case are wanting'. Prerogative Court acts were entered in the same books as Exchequer acts, and no separate record was ever kept of them.

[1] In the precedent papers is a series of sewn folios which apparently were a contemporary record of prerogative acts covering May 1587 to June 1589, totalling forty-seven. The probates given here are also found in the ordinary series of acts in the York city deanery, but not the administrations (R.VII.PCC.37).

them remain.[1] The jurisdiction of the Prerogative Court was said to be founded on Canon XCII of 1603, and Thomas Burwell, the chancellor (who after the Commonwealth became Chancellor of York), was accused of neglecting to obey the canon generally, by not swearing executors and administrators to admit any *bona notabilia* over £5 as ordered by the canon. In particular he was charged with summoning two persons before the High Commission Court at Durham for contempt of his jurisdiction, although they had proved a will and taken an administration respectively, before the Prerogative Court at York.[2] A further article charged Burwell with not swearing executors and administrators to admit any *bona notabilia* of

divers and sundrye persons [who] have dyed within the said dioces of Duresme, whoe att the times of theire deathes respectivelye were owners or part owners respectivelye of divers shipps, barks, keeles, boats and other vessels, which att the times of theire deathes respectively were upon the sea or other Rivers within the high water marks and without the bounds or Corps of any Countye of the said dioces, and had divers goods and good debts oweinge unto them beyond the seas by reason wherof the probate of the wills of such partyes or the grantinge of the Administrations of theire goods belonged to the said Commissary Judge or Keeper of the Prerogative Court...

The article is worthy of note as illustrating how far the lawyers at York construed the extent of the prerogative jurisdiction.[3] The libel went on to record the fact that Burwell had been privately warned about his infringements, and that he had replied that he 'would answeere it and trye it with Doctor Levett', i.e. he was willing to make a legal action about the matter. The extant acts of the Court of High Commission when they recommence at Trinity term of 1638 make no mention of the prosecution.

The articles against the registrar of Allertonshire were based on the fact that two peculiars existed there, one belonging to the bishop, the other to the Dean and Chapter of Durham. A widow whose husband had *bona notabilia* in both peculiars took an administration of the estate in the Prerogative Court. Later, Thomas Bullock, the registrar of both peculiars, at the instigation of another, forced her to take out administrations in each of his courts, at what were alleged to be excessive fees. The last article of the libel alleged that Bullock knew that Burwell had been 'lately questioned in this Courte for contemning of' the prerogative administration, and that therefore Bullock's

---

[1] R.VII.P.L.138; part only of the articles against the registrar remains, inserted in those against the chancellor.

[2] The case against one, John Heighington, Mayor of Durham, is recorded in *Acts of the High Commission Court within the Diocese of Durham*, Surtees Society, XXXIV, 174. The other case, against Richard Milbourne, I have not been able to trace in that volume.

[3] The articles were written by Francis Parker, the head clerk of Mottershed's office.

own contempt was thereby aggravated. Presumably, the alleged contempt came to the notice of the authorities at York when the widow appealed to the Consistory Court against the compulsory administrations. The appeal was, however, agreed out of court.[1]

The comparatively small proportion of the Exchequer's ordinary business contributed by the prerogative jurisdiction can be estimated by the fact that while the yearly average of administrations granted in the seventeenth century was over 600, from 1628–34 the prerogative administrations were only 20–30 annually. The High Commission causes just noted may have been part of an attempt to enforce the prerogative jurisdiction more successfully, for the number rose from 35 in 1635 to 51 in 1636, remaining about that level for the next two years, before declining when the troubles began in 1639. It is worth noting, in addition, that the jurisdiction had become so respected that after the defeat of the royalist forces no less than 84 administrations were taken out in 1645, in 1649 there were 56.

NATURE OF LITIGATION IN THE EXCHEQUER

The type of cause coming before the Exchequer merits more than a passing glance because it was unparalleled in the majority of church courts in England. All courts heard causes of disputed wills and codicils, the refusal of administrators and executors to undertake their duties lawfully and refusal to produce inventories and accounts, the suppression of wills or impeding the execution of a will.[2] Owing to common law attacks the church courts had lost the power to hear actions challenging the accounts but not, apparently, inventories.[3] This was obviously of great concern to creditors and legatees, who had to find increasingly a remedy in the royal Chancery Court. The Exchequer Court at York, however, possessed a full power over accounts, and they could be, and were, challenged by creditors, legatees or the beneficiaries of an intestate estate.

The existence of such beneficiaries was due to the custom of the Province of York. Except in one or two areas of the Province of Canterbury (such as the City of London), when the administrator of an intestate estate had paid the debts there was no power to compel him to share out the remainder and he

[1] Consistory appeal: R.VII.H.2284; last reference to it in A.B. was 12 July 1638, Crosley *c*. Hutton, Bullock and Meed.

[2] This is a brief summary of the causes heard in the courts at Norwich, Sudbury and Ely, and generally agrees with the statements of T. F. T. Plucknett, *Concise History of the Common Law*, pp. 729, 741–3, and W. Holdsworth, *History of English Law*, I, 629.

[3] Plucknett appeared to think that what was true of accounts was also true of inventories. Few such challenges have been discovered, but two actions against inventories occurred at Norwich in 1623–4 (CON/11, fos. 179, 189).

normally retained the lot.[1] Similarly, following common law principles, over most of England there was no restriction on the ability of the testator to dispose of his estate at will. The custom of the Province of York, however, divided an estate into three equal portions: one went to the widow, one to the children and the third, the 'death's part', was alone freely disposable. Likewise an intestate estate was divided into two, the widow's and the children's portions. In this respect, too, the civil law tradition of the church courts at York was superior to common law, but its importance lay not only in its more equitable principles but also in the fact that, in order to make them effective, strict supervision of accounts was needed. It was for this reason that the Exchequer Court retained its power to supervise accounts, as well as to order the division of estates, and this power included the ability to compel co-executors and co-administrators to account to their fellow executors and administrators.

The fact that the common law allies of the Puritan propagandists were willing to deprive the Englishman of an equitable system of testamentary law by their attacks on the church courts, as they also deprived him of an equitable system of mercantile law by their attacks on the Admiralty Court, has never been sufficiently investigated by ecclesiastical historians. The latter have simply applauded the Puritan-minded common lawyers as being wonderful champions of English liberty against the tyranny of the Stuarts—although they had then to proceed to explain how these champions of liberty became involved in the Cromwellian dictatorship. The common lawyers were neither better nor worse than any other group of professional people in honestly confusing their particular interests with those of the country at large, and emphasizing whichever of those interests they thought would do them the greatest amount of good at any given time.

What is more remarkable is that they were never able to reduce the Province of York to the same position of impotence to which they had reduced her sister province. One clear reason for their inability was the existence of the Council in the North. It is unfortunate that Dr Reid, in her monograph on the Council, was so influenced by the generalizations of the legal historians as to think that effective control over testamentary matters had been lost by all church courts. She therefore assumed, without any supporting authority, that the Council was exercising this jurisdiction.[2] It is much more probable that the Council only exercised the common law jurisdiction in these matters,

---

[1] Apparently administrators sometimes voluntarily asked the judge to distribute an estate (Norwich Consistory A.B. ACT/45A, 13 July 1614, In re estate of Wm. Smith), but such actions were comparatively rare.

[2] *The King's Council in the North*, pp. 308–9.

that is over real estate, as did its sister Council in Wales.[1] The Chancery Court case of Holmes *c*. Crosthwaite and Wheath (1632), the papers of which are extant because the deceased was a beneficed clergyman, gives some indication of the state of affairs.[2] Holmes had married the widow of the deceased, and on her behalf had successfully recovered her widow's portion of the real estate before the Council, and her eldest son was at that time seeking to recover his child's portion there. The evidence shows that if the real estate was greater, the guardian was appointed by the Council: if the personal estate was greater, then the church court was responsible for his appointment. This evidence suggests that the Council and the Exchequer worked together according to certain well-established rules, administering the same law in their respective spheres. It may have been principally due to the testamentary litigation before the Council that it was provided with a civil lawyer on its bench of judges; but the Council was the real power behind the continued existence of the customary law of the province. After being abolished by the Long Parliament the Council was not re-established after the Restoration, and the church courts then proved unable by themselves to maintain their distinctive law.

The Council, of course, was staffed by common lawyers, and its close connection with the other lawyers in York, and its own conflicts with the common law courts in London, encouraged it to assist rather than impede the Exchequer Court. There was also another way in which the two courts worked in harmony. When an executor, administrator or tutor was admitted by a church court, he had to make a bond in favour of the ordinary for the faithful discharge of his duties. In the Exchequer, an aggrieved person, e.g. a beneficiary of an estate, could promote an action to compel the executor or administrator to make a new bond of a larger and more adequate sum, or could apply to the court for the handing over of the bond so that the suitor could recover it 'in the secular court'.[3] At this time the London common law courts were doing their best to make these bonds unenforceable,[4] so the secular court in question was most probably the Council in the North. The present writer's researches at Norwich have so far failed to uncover any action on bonds in the records of the courts preserved there.

One other reason why the Exchequer Court continued its work unchallenged was that it was generally acceptable. We have already commented on

[1] C. A. J. Skeel, *The Council in the Marches of Wales* (1904), pp. 154–7, 224, where there is also an account of how this Council was defeated in its conflict with the Prerogative Court of Canterbury.
[2] R.VII.H.1951.
[3] R.VII.PD.270 is a receipt by a son for a bond given by two men (evidently administrators) for a payment of a son's portion, ten years after it had been made.
[4] Holdsworth, *op. cit.* (4th ed.) III, 558.

the fact that at Norwich the apparitors were encouraged to discover persons who had failed to take lawful administrations of estates (usually widows), or executors who had neglected to prove wills.[1] The separation of powers at York between chancellor and commissary gave the former no incentive to seek out such omissions (although they were sometimes presented at visitations), while the latter acted as a civil court, rarely instituting proceedings *ex officio mero*. The Exchequer, therefore, would not have created opposition or unpopularity by a rigorous enforcement of the letter of the law.

Before concluding this chapter, it is appropriate to take a brief glance at the volume of business transacted in the court and the fees charged. It has been observed that Exchequer litigation was small until the time of Percy. The absence of documentary evidence during his commissaryship prevents a statistical examination of the growth of business resulting from the changes he initiated. Table 10, therefore, simply offers a comparison of a year in late Elizabethan times, after Percy's work had been completed, with a year before the troubles began with the First Bishops' War.

TABLE 10

Exchequer litigation 1592–3 and 1637–8

Type of cause	1592–3	1637–8
Concerning probates	29	77 (12)
Concerning administrations	62	71 (14)
Concerning tuitions	2	10 (3)
Concerning bonds	10	6 (0)
Concerning accounts and distribution of estates	19	48 (14)
	122 (4)	212 (43)

The figures in brackets refer to prerogative causes included in the totals.

Causes of this nature are not strictly comparable with those in the other York courts, so that the only worthwhile comparison is between the two years themselves. The main items accounting for the rise in the number of causes were probate in solemn form (up from 9 to 31), to compel the next-of-kin or others to take out an administration if they could not prove a will (up from 12 to 38), to compel production and examination of accounts (up from

[1] Above, p. 23. The traditional form of action in the Exchequer was '*Officium domini promotum...*' as in the case of privately promoted disciplinary suits in the Chancery. Soon after Swinburne took control of the Exchequer he changed the style to '*Officium juducis promotum...*' (from 23 Nov. 1605). The change may possibly have been to emphasize the civil nature of the proceedings in the Exchequer. *Ex officio mero* actions were occasionally undertaken (four in the Michaelmas Term 1605), but they were exceptional.

6 to 17), and to secure distribution of an estate (up from 1 to 15). The rise in the amount of court business was largely due to a greater proportion of estates being involved in court orders ($8\frac{1}{2}$ per cent in 1592–3, 16 per cent in 1637–8), but as many of the probates and administrations in solemn form were uncontested, as were the monitions to compel probate, the rise in truly litigious estates was not so great as the figures indicate. As an example, in the Michaelmas Term 1605 only four probates in solemn form were contested out of eighteen in court. The result was that actions were often speedily decided, and out of fifty-seven entering the court in that term only seven remained unconcluded at its close. The quick dispatch of business and the close control exercised over estates made the Exchequer Court one whose efficiency it would be hard to fault. The only drawback to its working was that its coercive power was limited to excommunication. In some cases this sentence was effective, for an excommunicate had no legal standing and was thereby debarred from further interfering with an estate, but it was more cumbersome as a device for recovering cash or goods. It was probably for this reason that the practice of suing for breach of the conditions of the bond was adopted.

FEES

There are two tables of fees giving the amounts charged in mid-Elizabethan times, the one printed by Conset at the end of his *Practice of the Spiritual Courts* (dated 13 Eliz. I), the other a late seventeenth-century copy in the York archives (in use during the first eighteen years of Elizabeth's reign).[1] Both agree that the ordinary fees for probates and administrations were charged according to the statute of Henry VIII,[2] but Conset shows that, in addition, prerogative business was charged 1s. extra 'for founding the Prerogative Jurisdiction', and that if business was done through the local rural dean he was entitled to an additional fee of 6s. 8d. The MS. copy adds that the rural dean's apparitor received 6d. where the estate was £5 to £40 and 8d. where it was over £40. As the rural dean only paid 10s. 4d. fees for his commission, it is obvious that the office was one of considerable profit, particularly in heavily populated areas.[3] Other fees were similar to, or less than those in the southern province. For example, a certificate that an executor or administrator had rendered his accounts cost from 10s. to 23s. 4d. (according

---

[1] R.VII.PO.135.

[2] Above, p. 24. This was apparently true. The probate A.Bs. show three fees being returned by rural deans in the early seventeenth century, 6d., 3s. 6d., 5s.

[3] It may be noted that at the time when the rural deans lost their disciplinary functions, their testamentary work was increasing by leaps and bounds and must have more than compensated for any loss in income.

111

to the total sum involved) in the Prerogative Court of Canterbury and the Consistory Court of London, while at York a standard fee of 11s. 4d. was charged. The appointment of a tutor or guardian at York cost 10s. 8d. in fees, at London it was 13s. 4d. These fees were also charged at York and London respectively for a commission to prove a will, etc.[1] The other fees show little significant difference, except that an excommunication and absolution cost 2s. 7d. at York, 3s. at London and 4s. in the Canterbury Prerogative Court.

The history of the Exchequer Court in these years shows (1) how the administrative duties of the receiver-general of ecclesiastical dues was separated from the testamentary administration; (2) how the litigation involved in testamentary administration was at first farmed out to the Consistory Court and then recovered; (3) how the prerogative jurisdiction of the northern archbishop was created almost out of nothing; (4) the inconvenience of appointing as judges of the courts at York men such as Lougher and Levett whose main interests were in the south, and how the York lawyers took objection to being treated like an archdeaconry court; (5) how the custom of the province of York was more akin to civil law than the testamentary law of southern England, and how it was fully applied despite the inability of church courts in the south to do the same; and (6) how much indebted the Exchequer was to the Council in the North for protection from outside attack. After the dissolution of the Council, Parliament was compelled eventually to enact the Statute of Distributions (1670) to compel distribution of intestate estates and the checking of accounts, but widows and children could not claim maintenance, if cut out of a will, until the twentieth century.

Additional Note (1)

Since these chapters were written, Dr W. J. Jones' *The Elizabethan Court of Chancery* (1967) has been published. This book shows how that the royal Chancery usually supported the jurisdiction of the church courts, as in matters of tithe, probate and matrimony. Yet it was always careful to retain suits which extended beyond the bounds of a simple ecclesiastical cause. It was because suits involving legacies were so often bound up with more complex matters and common law issues that it gradually seems to have assumed a jurisdiction for the simple recovery of legacies which must have harmed the business of the church courts. This matter of legacies was, however, an exception to its usual reference of ecclesiastical causes to ecclesiastical judges.

[1] Table of Fees, Prerogative Court of Canterbury *temp.* Elizabeth I, R.VII.PO.25; that for the Consistory Court of London, R.VII.PO.80.

The church courts were unable to go beyond certain set limits, and this was really the cause of their stagnation and decline. Litigation gradually became more and more involved, and increasingly outside the capacity of the church courts. Dr Jones illuminates this theme in chapter xi, and it would appear that it was this fact, rather than the battle of prohibitions which has hitherto caught the eye of historians, which eventually reduced the church courts to insignificance.

Dr Jones still views testamentary litigation as it existed in the Province of Canterbury, with the relatively feeble powers of the church courts there, and shows how the Chancery was able to deal with the accuracy of executors' and administrators' accounts. The Exchequer Court of York, as we have seen, exercised exactly the same powers. Study will have to be made of the royal Exchequer court before full knowledge can be had of the secular courts' testamentary activities, and it will be very revealing to discover how many of their cases came from the northern province.

Additional Note (2)

The argument on pp. 96–102 depends on the assumption that York lawyers rebelled against absentee southern judges who made infrequent appearances and failed to provide satisfactory substitutes. Mainwaring functioned at Richmond through substitutes, as did Eden in the Sudbury Commissary Court, and it was the only method by which smaller courts could have experienced judges. But arrangements for substitutes needed to be satisfactory, and in at least one other case action had to be taken against a judge who failed to make them. The Archdeacon of Berkshire (John Ryves LL.B.) presided in his own consistory in Oxford on 15 May, 1639, and after the session was over publicly refused to recognize any longer the acts of his Official (Charles Tooker LL.D.). He ordered a proctor to hand over the seal of the Officiality, but the proctor refused to do so until he had written to Tooker in London. The archdeacon apparently referred the matter to the Court of Delegates, among whose records the relevant A.B. now remains (P.R.O., DEL/8/61). An obvious reason for the archdeacon's action was Tooker's failure, for upwards of two years, to provide a proper substitute. The proctors, all graduates, took it in turn to adjudicate on the formal stages of each others' causes. Despite this merry-go-round the court did good business, averaging 58 new causes a year in the three years 1637–9.

4

VISITATIONS

The activities of bishop and archdeacon in their capacity of Visitor of their respective jurisdictions are the best known of their administrative and judicial functions, for visitations continue to be held to this day, and the grumblings of churchwardens about the fees which they are then called upon to pay still maintain an ancient tradition of their office. In this chapter the rights of the Archbishops of York to make official visitations will be described —together with the way in which they were effected—the visitations of the three Yorkshire archdeacons, the law which they all administered and the procedures used in certain typical visitations.

DIOCESAN AND PROVINCIAL VISITATIONS

The Archbishops of York had a right to visit their diocese in every fourth year, and to visit their province upon their accession to the see. During these times all inferior jurisdictions were inhibited, and the cognizance of all ecclesiastical causes, whether of instance or of office, belonged to the archbishop. If an archbishop died shortly after concluding a diocesan visitation, his successor could still hold his metropolitical visitation as soon as he liked after his accession, so that the diocese was sometimes visited within two years of a previous visitation by the archbishop.

The act books of visitation courts held in the diocese are not extant before 1567, but from that date the series is complete except for those held in 1611 and 1630.[1] In some of the Elizabethan books care was taken to enter all the formal acts of the visitation, but thereafter only the proceedings against persons presented were recorded. Some of the acts in court were only entered in an abbreviated form; when the numbers of contumacious persons became large, the actuary very often omitted recording in each case that the offender had been thrice called in court, had not appeared, been excommunicated and that the sentence had been ordered to be read in his parish church. Sometimes

---

[1] The acts for 1604 and 1640 are only partially complete.

only 'Ex' was entered in the margin, or 'Emt' showing that it had been sent to the parish to be denounced in service time, very often no entry at all was made.

The visitation began with a formal opening in York Minster. Archbishop Sandys in 1578 robed in the Treasurer's House (home of the widow of Archbishop Young), and came in full procession with the Dean and Canons to his throne in the Minster. The Earl of Huntingdon, Lord President of the Council of the North, and many gentlemen and others were present in the congregation. The Litany and other prayers were sung by the vicars-choral, followed by the hymn 'Come, Holy Ghost' in which all the clergy and people joined. A sermon was then preached on the text Matthew xxi, 12–13 ('My house is a house of prayer and ye have made it a den of thieves'). After this the congregation left, and Sandys proceeded to the Chapter House for the visitation of the Dean and Chapter.[1]

The visitation of the diocese sometimes began in York with the rural deaneries of York City and New Ainsty. In 1578, the assembled clergy, schoolmasters and churchwardens of those deaneries heard a sermon by Matthew Hutton, then Dean of York, followed by the Archbishop's Charge. The churchwardens were then sworn into their office, and directed to attend Hugh Askew, 'keeper of the articles', to receive a copy for each parish and to hand in their replies to the chancellor before Monday after Low Sunday. The delay given to them to consider what presentments to make must have promoted evasion and corruption, for at his next visitation Sandys provided that the apparitor-general should be present with the articles, and that the churchwardens should then attend persons appointed for the purpose, who would examine them and then write their answers to the articles.[2] Whether this more rigorous examination was maintained may be doubted. The considerable increase in presentments in 1632 over the number for 1627 was probably due to the fact that the system of examination was then re-introduced after having lapsed.[3] As a considerable effort was being made by Sandys to improve the standard of theological education among his clergy and schoolmasters, they were examined by his chaplains in 1578, whilst the churchwardens were being sworn.[4]

The clergy, churchwardens and schoolmasters who were called to the visitation were cited by the appropriate archdeacon under a direction given to him by the archbishop. Consequently, either he, his Official or his registrar or their deputy, was present at the visitation to certify that the citations had

[1] R.VI.A.6., fo. 1. [2] *Ibid.* fo. 137.
[3] Further consideration of this point is made in the chapter on Nottingham.
[4] R.VI.A.6., fo. 3. The clergy were also examined in 1582, doubtless to see how their education had progressed, *ibid.* fo. 137.

been issued.[1] After the presentments had been made by the churchwardens, citations were issued to the apparitor of each rural dean to summon to the visitation court each person who had been presented, so he attended at each such court to certify that the citations had been executed,[2] and to act as court usher.

The visitation was conducted by Commissioners appointed by the archbishop for the purpose. Sometimes he accompanied them and was present at several or all of the places where the visitation was held. A typical schedule for the Visitors is the one for 1594[3] shown in Table 11.

TABLE 11

Itinerary for 1594 diocesan visitation

Place	Deaneries	Date
Southwell	Nottingham and Bingham	Wednesday, 24 April
Southwell	Chapter of Southwell	Thursday, 25 April
Southwell	Retford	Friday, 26 April
Southwell	Newark and Southwell peculiar	Saturday, 27 April
Doncaster	Doncaster	Monday, 29 April
Pontefract	Pontefract	Tuesday, 30 April
Helmsley	Cleveland and Allertonshire peculiar	Tuesday, 7 May
Helmsley	Ryedale	Wednesday, 8 May
Beverley	Hull and Holderness	Tuesday, 14 May
Beverley	Harthill and Beverley and Howdenshire peculiar	Wednesday, 15 May
Malton	Buckrose and Dickering	Friday, 17 May
Ripon	Craven and Otley and Ripon jurisdiction	Wednesday, 22 May
York	York City and Ainsty	Friday, 24 May
York	Bulmer	Saturday, 25 May

The chancellor was always included in the commission to hold a visitation, and he usually was the sole judge in the subsequent correction court. In early Elizabethan days, however, correction courts were often attended by one or more clerical commissioners, but Sandys' chancellor conducted the courts by himself, and this became the usual practice.

As the chancellor had spent the Easter vacation travelling about the diocese as commissioner for the visitation, he was probably loath to repeat the process later to hold the correction courts, particularly as until the beginning of August he was occupied with the litigation in his courts at York. Consequently, until 1586, all persons presented at the diocesan visitations, from however remote a parish, were compelled to attend at York. There is no reason to suppose that this was anything but a continuation of the medieval

[1] E.g. R.VI.A.4, fo. 4.   [2] E.g. R.VI.A.6. fo. 212.
[3] Register, vol. 31, fo. 68 v.

practice, but the greater numbers of persons presented under the Reformed moral and ecclesiastical discipline of the Elizabethan Church, necessitated an improvement of the administration of these disciplinary courts.[1] In 1586, perhaps as an experiment, the offenders in the Rural Deanery of Doncaster were called to a court held in Doncaster church, and in every visitation thereafter the correction court went on circuit. As an illustration of the circuit system, the first correction court held in each deanery in 1619 is shown in Table 12.[2]

TABLE 12

Itinerary for correction courts 1619

Date	Place	Deaneries, etc.
Wednesday, 30 June	Hull	Hull and Holderness
Thursday, 1 July	Beverley	Harthill, Beverley, Howdenshire
Saturday, 3 July	Settrington	Buckrose and Dickering
Monday, 5 July	Helmsley	Cleveland and Allertonshire
Tuesday, 6 July	Helmsley	Ryedale
Thursday, 8 July	Sutton-on-Forest	Bulmer
Monday, 19 July	York	York City
Tuesday, 20 July	Tadcaster	Ainsty
Saturday, 24 July	Skipton	Craven
Monday, 26 July	Bradford	Pontefract (part)
Wednesday, 28 July	Wakefield	Pontefract (part)
Friday, 30 July	Rotherham	Doncaster (part)
Saturday, 31 July	Doncaster	Doncaster (part)
Monday, 2 August	East Retford	Retford
Wednesday, 4 August	Southwell	Newark and Southwell
Friday, 6 August	Nottingham	Nottingham and Bingham

As it was usual to hold the visitation in the Easter vacation, so the first correction court followed during July and August.

At the correction court certain orders were given by the judge to clergy and churchwardens, and punishments awarded to convicted offenders. After 1596 a second correction court made a circuit, though smaller than the first, to receive certificates that its commands had been obeyed. In 1615 these second courts were held on 2 September at Otley, 14 September at Beverley, 16 September at Malton, 5 October at Pontefract and 7 October at Southwell. The places chosen for the holding of courts varied slightly from year to year,

[1] The increase in number of presentments can be judged by the number of entries under the Deanery of Craven: 1571, 64; 1575, 72; 1582, 85; 1586, 116; 1590, 173. Many of these entries contained the names of more than one person.
[2] R.VI.A.19.

but most of these centres were fixed ones. Settrington was chosen by Dodsworth as a centre because it was his home, more often Scarborough was used; the Deanery of Cleveland occasionally had a court at Thirsk or Whitby and offenders in Bulmer normally were cited to York.

One arrangement made to deal with offenders is worthy of comment. The most important town in Yorkshire at this time, outside of York itself, was Hull. The visitation records always show a few presentments from the town but nothing in proportion to the size of the place. The explanation seems to lie in a private arrangement made with the town. There is a record that in 1599 Archbishop Hutton and the mayor agreed that commissioners should be appointed—the mayor, an alderman and two preachers of the Word of God—to examine immoral persons and drunkards according to ecclesiastical law, keeping proper records, and sending those found guilty to York for punishment by the chancellor. The reason was that 'the poorer and baser sorts of the people...cannot be convened hither [*sc.* to York] for their punishment and reformation without travel and charges which they are not well able to perform and undergo'.[1] The arrangement was made at a time when Hutton was opening the Chancery Court to disciplinary presentments, and may not have been permanent. Nevertheless it may have developed, and by the association of the civic authorities ensured a higher standard of obedience. Some such a permanent court, or a working arrangement with the justices, must have been made to explain the paucity of presentments.

The evidence of the correction courts also suggests a measure of local action, presumably before the secular court, in one of the largest parishes in the diocese, Sheffield. In 1590, 17 persons were presented by the churchwardens; by 1619 this had grown to 46, and in the archdeacon's visitation of 1635, there were 35 (inclusive of previously excommunicate persons and recusants). During 1635 the chancellor proceeded against the Puritanism of the parish, and his efforts at re-establishing the Church's discipline were so successful that in the diocesan visitation of 1636, no less than 147 offenders were presented, and, in addition, 32 previously excommunicate persons. In a Puritan area such as this, offences were unlikely to go unnoticed, and it can reasonably be assumed that known offenders averaged the numbers presented in 1636, but that most of them had been previously brought before the local justices.[2]

Since during the visitations all rights of archidiaconal and peculiar courts

---

[1] John Tickhill, *History of Kingston-upon-Hull* (1796), pp. 266 f. Dr P. Collinson records a similar arrangement at Northampton in 1571 which he regards as a Geneva-type consistory. (*Elizabethan Puritan Movement*, 1967, p. 142.)

[2] The archidiaconal visitation of 1635, Sheffield Presentment Bill, in R.VII.H.2087.

were inhibited, all causes usually heard in them were heard either in the Consistory or Chancery Courts (as courts of the chancellor who acted as commissary of the visitation) or, where important courts were functioning, the judge of those courts acted as a deputy of the chancellor. Thus it was that probates of wills and administrations of estates in peculiars were granted by the chancellor during inhibitions, not by the commissary of the Exchequer.[1]

The Elizabethan Archbishops of York apparently had difficulty in extending their visitations to some, at least, of the peculiars. In 1575 Archbishop Grindal only visited five of them and in two cases where offenders belonged to other jurisdictions the commissaries, Gibson and Percy, dismissed them.[2] Even then Gibson had to suspend the registrar of one of the peculiars visited from his office of proctor for infringing the inhibition, and its commissary was made to acknowledge the archbishop's jurisdiction in open court.[3] Archbishop Sandys, however, visited all peculiars, and the only resistance subsequently noted was in 1604, when the two incumbents and the churchwardens of the parishes and chapelries of the Laughton peculiar refused to attend the visitation.[4] In the next diocesan visitation the churchwardens attended the commissaries, but the Vicar of Laughton ignored the inhibition, and also held his own court; but unfortunately, although he answered a citation to appear at the archbishop's correction court, the proceedings were not recorded.[5] Sufficient action must have been taken against him to compel him to submit, for there is no later record of any contempt.

Documentation of the archbishop's provincial visitations of the two remoter dioceses, Carlisle and Durham, is scarce. The only evidence at York for a visitation of Durham relates to the famous incident in 1577 when Dean Whittingham withstood Archbishop Sandys' attempt to visit the Chapter of Durham. The procedure used by the archbishop was to depute the Bishop of Durham, Barnes, to be his commissary in that diocese. The bishop then issued an act of surrogation to two of the archbishop's chaplains to do the

[1] Some of these are entered in the correction court books, e.g. R.VI.A.19, fos. 375 v.–376; R.VI.A.20, fo. 361 v.

[2] R.VI.A.4, fos. 95 v., 158 v. The peculiars visited were: the Dean and Chapter's, the Chapter of Southwell's, Allertonshire, Howdenshire and the (now dissolved) Treasurer of York's (R.VI.A.5, fo. 3 v.).

[3] Consistory A.B., 13 June 1575. The Registrar submitted and the suspension was removed on 30 June. The peculiar was that of the dissolved Treasurership.

[4] 1604 correction court act book, known as High Commission A.B.20, fo. 66 v. The actuary after noting the contempt recorded, 'These of Lawghton and Harmesworth (Handsworth) are verie contemptuous, some course must nedes be taken against them (so that) my L. Archb: may not loose his iurisdiction. They have in former times bene something disobedient but never utterlie Refused to appear in anie Archiepiscopal visitacion before this tyme.' The Vicar of Laughton, Robert Gifford, was a nonconformist Puritan, and so had a personal interest in keeping the archbishop's authority out of his parish.

[5] R.VI.B.3, fo. 65. For his nonconformity he was remitted to the Prebendary of Laughton.

work, which they then proceeded to carry out. The only resistance they encountered was that of the Dean and Chapter.[1]

If an archbishop ever repeated the process, he probably used local commissaries as he did in the diocese of Carlisle. The documents concerning the visitation of the latter diocese in 1577 and 1592 are entered in the archbishop's register, and seem to repeat a familiar and unopposed pattern.[2] A commission was issued to the Chancellor of the diocese of Carlisle, a canon of York and another of Carlisle to visit the diocese in 1592, and all three undertook the duty. It may be supposed that they, or the chancellor by himself, acted as judge at the correction courts, so that the records of the latter were retained at Carlisle, and that this accounts for the total lack of such records at York, except those for the year 1693. The York authorities sent the registrar or his deputy to accompany the visitors, so that a correct return of visitation fees was made to the archbishop and his officers.

The visitation of the diocese of Chester lying in and to the west of the Pennines presented some problems to the administration at York. In 1590, when there were two chancellors, Benet made a circuit through the archdeaconries of Cleveland and the East Riding in August, and the West Riding (less the deanery of Craven) in October, apparently leaving the remainder to Gibson. The latter began work in his home county of Cheshire in September (leaving the second courts to the rural deans), but was apparently interrupted. The consequence of this interruption was that Swinburne was sent to Skipton-in-Craven in November to hold courts for that deanery, Westmorland and Lancashire. To attempt to cover such a large area from one centre could only have been an improvisation in an emergency, so in May 1591 he went on circuit to Skipton, Kendal (for Westmorland) and Lancaster with greater success in securing attendance.

At the next provincial visitation the chancellors shared both dioceses. They held courts for the whole of Yorkshire at York in July and August 1594. Gibson toured Cheshire, Lancashire, and as far as Kendal in September 1595, while Benet operated in the Yorkshire part of the Chester diocese in October. Gibson left the receipt of certificates and other action to local clergymen at Manchester, Preston and Lancaster. Benet divided such action

---

[1] Register, vol. 31, fos. 24–5, 27–36 v. The Dean and Chapter won their case by a judgment of the Court of Delegates, 4 Dec. 1588 (*Parliamentary Accounts and Papers*, vol. 57, 1867–8, p. 109). There was a separate conflict concerning jurisdiction in the diocese of Durham *sede vacante* which the Dean and Chapter lost by a judgment of the same Court, 3 Dec. 1590—an exemplification of which was entered in the Archbishop's Register, vol. 31, fo. 264 v. Bishop Howson, however, contested Archbishop Harsnett's visitation in 1630: the articles of his appeal to the delegates are at the West Suffolk Record Office (Archdeaconry of Sudbury MSS.), E 14/11/3, fo. 177.

[2] Vol. 31, fo. 23 (1577), fos. 62–3 (1592). The 1592 visitation dates, places and officials' names were also recorded in R.VI.A.10, fos. 34–6 v., when they had performed their duty.

between the Rector of Richmond, and himself at York. On an average, the 1595 organization produced less impressive results, in terms of percentage of offenders who were obedient to court orders. The two deaneries of Kendal and Lonsdale showed a drop from 37·75 in 1590 to 32·75 in 1595; and there was a much more pronounced decline in the Frodsham and Nantwich deaneries from 54·3 to 36·8, apparently as a result of refusing to use rural deans, and making all offenders from Cheshire go to Manchester.

There is a gap in extant records of provincial visitations of Chester, recording administrative details, which extends to Easdall's visitation of 1633–4. The chancellor and two other visitors held the visitation and gave their instructions in August 1633. Easdall presided over correction courts in November when he covered the whole diocese, except the three Yorkshire deaneries which had to wait until February. He adopted the usual practice of referring further action to rural deans or other local clergymen, but so few certified obedience to these agents that he took stronger measures. He issued large numbers of new citations to contumacious persons ordering them to attend court, or else to be 'signified' to the secular authority for arrest by the sheriff's officers.[1] The advocate, Giles Burton, was sent on circuit in December 1634 to round up the absentees. The device was successful, for not only did many come to hand in their certificates, but no less than 328 persons who had ignored Easdall's first courts now came forward to obey orders. The administration at York, however, could not keep sending substitutes on circuit, and those who had to attend again were ordered to come to Borough-bridge on the Great North Road on 12 February 1635. Needless to say, although some came from Cheshire, Lancashire and Westmorland, many failed to do so.

The provincial visitations of the diocese of Chester give the impression of the York administration endeavouring to attempt something which they could only imperfectly achieve. So much of that diocese was no further away than parts of their own that the York officials succumbed to the temptation to visit it themselves rather than by deputy. Sometimes, however, local authorities took advantage of the presence of a superior power to try and enlist its help. For instance, at Kendal in 1633 the churchwardens presented thirty-eight who had defaulted on their church rates, some as far back as 1622—defaulters who included a baronet, two knights and an assortment of esquires and gentlemen. Efficient churchwardens never looked to Easdall in vain.[2]

[1] Significavits are only marked in large numbers in the acts of the Yorkshire part of the diocese but it is most probable that they were issued generally to secure the good attendance before Burton.

[2] Chester visitation acts are: 1578–9, R.VI.A.7. and 8; 1590, R.VI.A.11 and 12; 1595, R.VI.A.14 and 15; 1630, R.VI.A.22; 1633, R.VI.A.23. The accounts for Archbishop Matthew's primary

The Church under the Law

ARCHDEACONRY VISITATIONS

The...Archdeacons in Yorkshire have not Contentious Jurisdiction. They have only power of holding Visitations and Correction Courts, which are held at some places in the Archdeaconry at a proper Distance of time after the Visitation: Where they correct those who have been presented, if they may be dealt with in a summary way, But if the case is such as require a formal proceeding at law: It is referr'd to your Grace's Consistory.[1]

These remarks of Chancellor Audley to the Archbishop in 1724 well describe the archdeacons' jurisdiction as it existed before the Civil War. Only five act books are extant from this period but they are sufficient to show that the annual visitation was the limit of the archdeacons' activities to detect offenders, and that they held the necessary correction courts afterwards.[2] The powers of these courts to enforce repairs to churches and chancels and other monetary payments was diminished by the fact that where a ratepayer or lay rector denied liability, it was necessary for the churchwardens or others to institute formal proceedings in the diocesan courts. At the time Mottershed was Official of the Archdeacon of the East Riding such a cause was transferred to the Chancery Court, with the innuendo that the ratepayers had deliberately sought to evade their responsibilities by procuring an advocate's opinion that they were not liable to repair a vestry. Mottershed himself acted as advocate for the aggrieved incumbent, who feared that he might find himself left with the responsibility.[3]

The archdeacons' courts went on circuit after the annual visitations. That of the Archdeacon of York followed a similar itinerary to the one already outlined as used by the diocesan Visitors. Table 13 shows where courts were held in 1598.

Table 14 shows that the Cleveland circuit in 1634 was much more adventurous than its diocesan equivalent, penetrating into the north of the archdeaconry.

After the first circuit a second was apparently made, but the subsequent activities of the courts during the year are hard to trace. In 1613, for instance,

visitation in 1607 (R.VII.PCC.80) show that he made a profit from it of £58. 5s. 11d. Income from the diocese of York was £143. 11s. 11d. and from the remainder of the province £118. 13s. 10d. The expenses of the visitation commissioners in the province were £52. 7s. 5d. The archbishop visited the diocese in person, costing in Yorkshire £92. 4s. 2d., and in Nottinghamshire £58. 7s. 7d.
[1] Bishopthorpe MSS. 28/67.
[2] York, 1598 and 1613; Cleveland, 1632, 1634, and 1640 and part of 1641 (bound as one).
[3] R.VII.H.2115, office promoted Corbet (Rector of Patrington) c. Thornley and Ranson (churchwardens of Patrington), 1636. The churchwardens were alleged that they 'well knowinge that the judge articulate (Mottershed) had not cognizance of causes at the instance of parties...did de facto cunningly procure an opinion in writinge, thereby to gitt yourselves out of the Archidiaconall Court...' This was after they had been ordered to repair the vestry.

TABLE 13

Itinerary for correction courts: Archdeaconry of York 1598

Date	Place	Deanery
28 May	York	York City
1 June	Otley	Old Ainsty
2 June	Skipton	Craven
19 June	Darfield	Doncaster (part)
20 June	Doncaster	Doncaster (part)
21 June	Pontefract	Pontefract (part)
28 June	Wetherby	New Ainsty
3 August	Huddersfield	Pontefract (part)

TABLE 14

Itinerary for correction courts: Archdeaconry of Cleveland 1634

Date	Place	Deanery
4 August	Sheriff Hutton	Bulmer (eastern part)
5 August	Kirkbymoorside	Ryedale
7 August	Guisborough	Cleveland (eastern part)
8 August	Stokesley	Cleveland (western part)
9 August	Thirsk	Bulmer (western part)

after the initial court at Skipton in the archdeaconry of York, 3 June, there were apparently others there 3 and 30 August and one at Tadcaster 9 November.[1]

The Officials and registrars of the archdeacons made some attempt to carry out their duties efficiently. There was evidently an unofficial liaison between the various courts, for at the end of the Cleveland act book for 1632, the registrar wrote various notes about offenders who had moved out of his jurisdiction, and whose names and offences he had to transmit to other registrars. The lack of records prevents us from gaining more than a few glimpses of archidiaconal administration. The Archdeaconry of York had a long spell under the advocate Mainwaring as Official, and no trace of a clerical Official at this period has been found. Administering a large and populous archdeaconry from one corner—York—must have presented severe problems. Only one clue as to how they were overcome is revealed in the acts remaining. In many instances persons presented did not attend court, but their penances were sent to them. This procedure seems to have been effective, and it supports the impression given by a study of church disciplinary

[1] See acts under Keighley and Heptonstall.

courts, that it was the trouble and inconvenience of attending them, rather than contempt for them, which prevented some persons from being amenable to ecclesiastical discipline.

The 1632–4 acts of the Archdeaconry of Cleveland show that it had a clergyman as Official—Timothy Thurscross, Rector of Kirkbymoorside. As far as it was possible to be in the centre of this archdeaconry, Kirkbymoorside was the best place to live. His registrar, however, lived in York, and although it was legally wrong for the Official to act without his registrar, it is clear that he did so act, and sent a record of what he had done to York. For those in the archdeaconry who lived nearer York one of the vicars-choral of the Minster would perform any necessary function in the registrar's office. This system seems to have been well-established, for Thurscross' predecessor at Kirkbymoorside had also been Official.[1] The figures given below, p. 208, show that the efficiency of these two archidiaconal administrations was good, better than that of the diocesan visitations. In Cleveland there were two peculiarities worth noting. Thurscross was a Puritan, and in many cases he did not at first excommunicate for contempt—a practice the Puritans criticized—but only issued suspensions *ab ingressu ecclesiae*, and only excommunicated when this warning proved ineffective. This process did not reduce the efficiency of his court. The second feature was that here, almost alone of the acts investigated in this study, alongside the usual paupers was marked an occasional *dives*. One such, at least, who did not attend court, was forced to do so by threat of the issue of the writ *de excommunicato capiendo*.[2]

There are no court acts for this period of the Archdeaconry of the East Riding. For some time Thomas Bell, Rector of Beeford, was Official until he was supplanted by Mottershed. Beeford was centrally placed in the east of the archdeaconry, and he probably operated much as did the Cleveland Officials. The evidence in one cause describes how he absolved a contumacious person and issued a penance privately in his house at Beeford, without his registrar being present (and received 3s. 10d. fee for the absolution).[3] He may be presumed to have used a vicar-choral and his registrar to carry out duties on the other side of the archdeaconry.

Bell's registrar was Robert Claphamson, a proctor, who wrote two letters to John Cosin in 1625 and 1626 shortly after the latter had become Arch-

---

[1] William Denton. See *North Riding Quarter Sessions Records*, II, 171–3, 182, 201; and High Commission, A.B., 30 July 1616, where Denton was ordered to hand over the books of presentments to his registrar. Denton later became Rector of Langton and resigned Kirkbymoorside and the Officiality. The High Commission acts for 4 Sept. 1634 tell the story of how two pursuivants sent to arrest him were lured away from the rectory to the church at Langton, while Denton made his escape.

[2] R.VI.C.26, Deanery of Bulmer, parish of Sowerby.

[3] R.VII.H.2357, 2358 (1631), Hodgson c. Nicholson.

deacon of the East Riding.[1] He was apparently an incorrigible pessimist, saying that he had 'been much troubled with the perverse conditions of the laity in these latter days, and I may well say in these profane times and also some of the Clergy', and much more in a similar strain. His chief concern came from impropriations. The owners were often southerners, sometimes one rectory had several lay owners who each lived in different ecclesiastical jurisdictions, and sometimes the owner was the Crown, who had freed its agents from any responsibility. Consequently, curates were provided who were often ill-paid, and when they sought to augment their pittances by performing clandestine marriages and were found out, the Official was hard put to know what to do. He suspended some, but that merely deprived the parishioners of pastoral care. Furthermore, chancels were falling down, and little could be done to force the lay rectors to restore them.[2] An Official of an archdeacon was effective against minor malefactors, but when confronted by such a situation he was almost powerless. Only ceaseless vigilance by the diocesan authorities could prevent lay rectors from ignoring their responsibilities. Claphamson's tale of woe to Cosin was an indication of the malaise which had overtaken diocesan administration by the end of Matthew's primacy: the stern hand and keen attention to duty of Neile and his officers were required to prevent the rot spreading, and must have been welcomed by many conscientious Christians such as the registrar.

Neile's drive for church restoration and strict conformity to the canons and also to the royal injunctions concerning preachers, was reflected in the activity shown by the archdeacons' courts. Each year, in December, each archdeacon and his Official were required to make a report to the archbishop on the state of their respective jurisdictions, on which he based a report to the king on the condition of his diocese.[3] Two examples of these archidiaconal reports are extant. The one for York for the year 1635 recorded that at the Easter visitation all the clergy had been warned to observe the royal injunctions concerning preachers and lecturers, and churchwardens were ordered to present infringements; church repair and adornment was progressing satisfactorily and it was hoped to complete it by the end of the following year. The archdeacon's court had been busily engaged in enforcing the regulations about churches, and supervising the work required.[4]

[1] Surtees Society, *Cosin Correspondence*, I, 80–2, 93–4.
[2] Claphamson added that the chancellor had sequestrated some rectories, but that there had been no improvement. At least the chancellor's activities noted here show that Dodsworth was more active than our other records suggest.
[3] *Cal. State Papers Dom.* 1633–4, pp. 443 f.; 1635–6, pp. 198 f.; 1636–7, pp. 409–11; 1638–9, pp. 430 f.
[4] Bishopthorpe MSS. bundle 1, unlisted.

The work of reconstructing and repairing churches and supervising the provision of the canonical ornaments, books, furnishings and utensils, was enforced by the archdeacons' courts, or at least those of which Mottershed was Official, by the use of commissioners. Two or three clergy were empowered to inspect churches in their area, with power to require the necessary production of keys, and to make a list of the defects which they found. These lists were then forwarded to the Official who used them as a basis for his instructions to the appropriate churchwardens.[1] Other activities of Mottershed were reflected in orders to the minister and churchwardens of a parish not to allow non-parishioners to attend their church,[2] a monition to the minister and churchwardens of Holy Trinity, Hull, to enforce bowing at the name of Jesus,[3] and a commission to five persons to view a chancel, and, with the aid of workmen, survey the required repairs.[4] In Cleveland, the correction acts make little reference to any suppression of nonconformity and nothing is known about what happened there concerning churches, for defects and orders concerning them were kept in a special 'booke of defects in vieweing Churches'.[5]

The only copy of the articles issued to churchwardens before the Civil War and still at York is one for the Archdeaconry of York, 1635. The interest of this is that it repeats, almost word for word, all the articles issued by the archbishop which were applicable to an archdeacon's jurisdiction.[6] Whether Neile had his articles adopted in the other archdeaconries is a matter for speculation, but it must have helped his administration considerably if all the courts had uniform articles and were directing their efforts towards the attainment of the same objectives. One of the features of ecclesiastical administration at the time was that after the archbishop had conducted a diocesan visitation and discovered what was wrong, the execution of his subsequent orders had to be left for the next three years to the archdeacons'

---

[1] A copy of such a commission by Mottershed, R.VII.P.A.96. A rough draft of Mottershed's report on his archdeaconry, R.VI.A.39/16, showed, *inter alia*, that in 1639 over £155 had been spent on fifty-three churches in four deaneries, indicating that the period of reconstruction was coming to an end.

[2] R.VII.P.A.23, draft, parish of 'Ev.'.   [3] R.VII.P.A.5, draft.

[4] R.VII.P.A.92, draft, issued in his capacity as commissary of the Dean and Chapter.

[5] Mentioned under Edston, in Cleveland 1634. These 'views' had some previous history, at least in this archdeaconry. In 1614 the registrar's clerk, giving evidence on an article in a case which alleged excessive fee-taking, deposed that 'he hath heard some grudginge by churchwardens and others within the said Archdeaconry against the officiall and register thereof for taking of fees at the viewe of Churches and Chappells last' (Edmundson *c*. Bell, R.VII.H.1171). Because direct documentary evidence is lacking, it cannot be assumed that the administration of Archbishop Matthew did nothing to keep churches in good repair.

[6] Contained in the file of the office *c*. the churchwardens of Sheffield, R.VII.H.2087. I have not seen a copy of Neile's articles for York, but I have based my comparison on those he used at Winchester, 1628. (*Royal Commission on Ritual Report*, 1868, pp. 502–6.)

courts. In the chapter on Nottinghamshire, where alone there remains a continuous series of archdeacon's records for this period, some notice will be taken of the effects of this circumstance.

The Nottinghamshire records also direct our attention to one feature which it is most convenient to mention here. It is quite apparent from them that there was a reorganization and enlargement of the archdeacon's visitation in that archdeaconry immediately after Archbishop Grindal's primary visitation. The question that poses itself is whether or not the increased number of cases presented to that archdeacon's court represented a drive for increased efficiency in detecting offenders. What happened in the one archdeaconry was likely to have occurred in all, if, as seems probable, it resulted from a mandate issued by the archbishop.

The answer that the records suggest is that what happened was not so much an intensification of ecclesiastical discipline, but rather a transference of its exercise from rural deans to archdeacons. In 1604 the *Puritan's Defence of the Admonition* averred,

In Cheshire, Lancashire, Yorkshire, Richmundshire and other northern parts, there be many whole deanries exempted from the bishops' jurisdiction, wherein the deans and their substitutes have not only the probates of wills and graunting of administrations, but also cognizance of ecclesiastical crimes, with power to use the ecclesiastical censures. Yea, and this authority of the execution of ecclesiastical censures have those deans, either long since, by some papal priviledges obteined, or els by long use prescribed against the bishops.[1]

It is likely that by that date the situation thus described was already past history in Yorkshire, and the fact that by then the deans' powers of enforcing ecclesiastical discipline had been reduced shows that they were not exempted from episcopal control by any immutable privilege. In this respect their activities in probate business were on a different footing from their disciplinary functions.

During the vacancy of the see after the death of Archbishop Young, the Dean and Chapter issued a commission to the rural deans of the diocese to grant probates and to exercise ecclesiastical discipline within their respective deaneries,[2] and there is no reason to suppose that this was anything more than the continuing of their normal commissions which had lapsed on the archbishop's death. At this time, therefore, the exercise of ecclesiastical discipline was part of the rural deans' duties. The acts of the diocesan visitations show that in early Elizabethan times they were the usual officials before whom the average offender against the Church's laws was tried.[3]

[1] Quoted by Dansey, *op. cit.* II, 79.　　　[2] Register, vol. 30, fo. 58 v.
[3] R.VI.A.2, fo. 61 v., commission to R.D. of Retford and Laneham to impose a penance; R.VI.A.3a, fos. 31 v. ff., several commissions to R.D. of Holderness to hear purgations, receive evidence, etc.;

References to cases before or referred to archdeacons were almost entirely absent, the more serious presentments being remitted to the High Commission. After 1596, however, it is equally difficult to discover any mention of rural deans, and it may reasonably be assumed that their place in the administration of ecclesiastical discipline had by that time been so completely swallowed up by the archdeacons' visitations, that they had ceased to have any practical function therewith.

During the first three decades of this period the function of the rural dean became restricted to his testamentary duties, not so much by any formal edict abolishing his powers to correct offenders, but by the creation of a system of archdeacons' visitations which gradually attracted to itself all presentments of offenders. The evidence of the acts for the visitation of the Archdeaconry of York in 1598—the earliest archdeacon's acts in Yorkshire now extant—shows that by then these visitations were producing a large number of presentments, and the evidence at Nottingham equally confirms that from Grindal's time onwards the archdeacons' courts were functioning so fully that there could have been little disciplinary business left for rural deans. From the administrative aspect the change was a considerable improvement, for it was much easier for an archbishop to control his diocese through four archdeaconries than through a multiplicity of rural deans' courts. Legally, the archdeacon's Official acted only in the presence of his registrar, while it is doubtful whether rural deans did so and thus their actions were open to challenge.

DISCIPLINARY LAW

It is appropriate here to include a consideration of the law which the disciplinary courts administered. The law governing causes of instance and testamentary causes, as also that concerning immorality and similar offences, was the medieval canon law, amended in some particulars by subsequent

fos. 81 v. ff. R.D. of Ainsty certified an accused had already done penance, ordered to hear a case, letters testimonial under his seal produced to prove a purgation; fos. 102 v.–117 v., 5 cases referred to R.D. of Craven; R.VI.A.4, fos. 40 ff., 3 cases referred to R.D. of Craven; fos. 78 ff., 5 cases referred to R.D. of Doncaster; fo. 148, a man who had previously confessed to the R.D. of Holderness retracted confession before the archbishop's Visitors, and 3 cases referred to this R.D. at that time by the Visitors; fos. 161–87, 6 cases referred to R.D. of Pontefract; R.VI.A.6, fos. 66–74 and 203–11, 6 cases referred to R.D. of Holderness; R.VI.A.9, fo. 120, 1 case referred to R.D. of Cleveland; fo. 118 v., ditto; fo. 132, 2 persons presented for not performing penance ordered by R.D. of Beverley; R.VI.A.10, fo. 133 v., case referred to R.D. of Holderness; fo. 153, punishment of an offender referred to R.D. of Ryedale; R.VI.A.13, fo. 139 v., 2 persons dismissed on receipt of 'a certificate' from R.D. of Cleveland; R.VI.A.16, fos. 166 r. and v., 3 cases referred to R.D. of Ryedale. This list is not exhaustive. R.VII.G.3258 (office *c.* Elithorpe *et al.*, 1576) contains an Information to the High Commission by the Rural Dean of Beverley and Harthill of three persons presented to him who had been contumacious.

parliamentary legislation.[1] However, the needs of the Reformation had produced many new administrative regulations, culminating in the canons of 1603[2] and the enforcement of them was principally the task of the diocesan and archidiaconal visitation courts.

Elizabethan ecclesiastical administration was based on the Injunctions issued by the queen in 1559 which had to be read quarterly in each church, and of which each parish had to possess a copy.[3] The early years of her reign, coinciding with the primacy of Archbishop Young, saw little attempt to apply them in detail in the diocese. All the authorities could do was to examine clergy and schoolmasters, removing those disloyal to the Reformed Church of England, to secure that churches were stripped of the more obvious signs of medieval religious observances, and to ensure that the Book of Common Prayer was used. It was left to Archbishop Grindal to issue a series of Injunctions[4] based on those of the queen, which he sought to enforce in detail, and these were followed by others of Archbishop Sandys.[5] They derived their authority partly from the Queen's Injunctions which were administered as if they had been the law of the land, and partly from the archbishops' own powers as Ordinary to order churches in such manner as they thought fitting.

The extent to which the courts were executors of the royal will was shown clearly by their treatment of the canons of 1597 and of 1603. The former were passed by the Convocation of Canterbury and were thereupon confirmed by the queen and ordered by her to be enforced in both provinces,[6] and this was duly carried out at York.[7] The same course of events occurred in 1604, with Archbishop Hutton obeying the royal command to act upon the canons,[8] but this time the Convocation of York objected, secured a royal

---

[1] For a discussion of the general principles governing the law which the church courts administered at this period, see *The Canon Law of the Church of England* (The Report of the Archbishops' Commission on Canon Law, 1947), chapter IV.

[2] These canons are sometimes inaccurately cited by modern writers as the canons of *1604*, but at the time they were always described as the canons 'of the synod held at London A.D. 1603'. In 1763 the Bishop of Carlisle wrote to Archbishop Drummond about the matter, and the latter replied that they had always been known as the canons of 1603, and he thought it best and safest that they should continue so to be called (Bishopthorpe MSS. bundle 28, no. 15).

[3] E. Cardwell, *Documentary Annals*, I, 178–209.

[4] *Report of the Royal Commission on Ritual* (1868), pp. 411–15.

[5] *Ibid.* pp. 421 ff.

[6] Cardwell, *Documentary Annals*, I, 161.

[7] Cf. the institution of an assessor to pronounce excommunications, referred to above, and the enforcement in the visitation of 1600 (R.VI.B.2) of the canon *De registris in ecclesiis salvae custodiae committendis*, where it was ordered that the minister should read the register in church. The requirement, designed to ensure accuracy, was not repeated in 1603, and was then allowed to lapse.

[8] In April and May 1605 he deprived those who refused to subscribe to the three articles of Canon XXXVI, cf. Chancery A.B.

licence to consider them, and passed them on 19 March 1606.[1] The action of Convocation, however, was purely a matter for its own prestige, and had no influence on the archbishop's courts, which were already executing the new canons. It was on royal authority only that James I issued his *Directions Concerning Preachers* in 1622, and although there remains little evidence that they were ever acted upon at York, yet Charles I's similar orders in 1633 were enforced by Archbishop Neile. There is no doubt that the Supreme Governor of the Church of England could be the sole fountain of ecclesiastical law by his mere decree.

As far as matters within their own purview were concerned, the archbishops were arbiters of what they judged to be right. Grindal, for instance, to ensure that the reading of Morning and Evening Prayer was audible to the congregation, ordered that a reading-place should be made in 'the body of the church', excepting only the smallest churches where the minister was allowed to remain in his traditional place in the chancel.[2] Neile, however, in pursuance of his policy of conservatism and restoration of medieval order wherever practicable, ordered the minister to return to the chancel, and the reading-place in the nave to be abolished.[3] A similar change was made in the placing of the Communion Table. Elizabeth's Injunctions had decreed that it should be placed where the altar had formerly been, except during the Communion Service, when it was to be 'so placed in good sort within the chancel, as whereby the minister may be conveniently heard of the communicants...and the communicants also more conveniently, and in more number communicate with the said minister'. Neile, fortified by the judgment in the St Gregory-by-Paul's case,[4] caused the Communion Table to be railed and the communicants to come to the rails when they communicated.[5] The extent to which he had to issue directions to enforce the alteration reflected the manner in which the earlier Injunctions had been obeyed.

The discretion exercised by the archbishops in using their inherent

---

[1] Convocation A.B.

[2] *Ritual Report* (1868), p. 413.

[3] In some of the schedules in the Chancery A.Bs., there was no reference to the reading place, in others there was a monition to repair it without reference to its position, but at Hickleton (12 June 1635), Thorne (16 June 1635), Stillingfleet (19 June 1635), Ilkley (7 July 1637), Appleton-le-Street (10 February 1636/7) and Slingsby (10 February 1636/7) there were specific commands to remove it from where it was and to provide a place in the chancel for the minister when he read prayers. At Walkington (27 July 1638) the reading-place in the nave was ordered to be removed without any direction about a new one. It is clear from these examples, in churches which were not small, that Neile was reversing Grindal's order where it had been obeyed.

[4] Cardwell, *Documentary Annals*, II, 185–7.

[5] The railing of the tables was a recurrent theme in the schedules, see also the chapter on Nottinghamshire.

authority as ordinaries was continued when they administered statute or canon law. A good example was the attitude adopted to the requirement in the Act of Uniformity, 1559, that

all and every person...shall diligently and faithfully, having no lawful or reasonable excuse to be absent, endeavour themselves to resort to their parish church or chapel accustomed, or upon reasonable let thereof, to some usual place where common prayer and such service of God shall be used in such time of let, upon every Sunday...and...holy days.

What was to be allowed as a 'reasonable let' whereby a parishioner was to be allowed to go to another church? The thirty-third of the Queen's Injunctions of 1559 interpreted this as meaning, 'except it be by the occasion of some extraordinary sermon in some parish of the same town'. In the diocese of York an even more lenient interpretation of the exception was admitted for many decades, whereby those who wished to go elsewhere to hear any sermon were permitted to do so, provided that there was not one in their own church.[1] The interpretation was changed by Archbishop Harsnett in 1630[2] and after him by Neile who made parishioners attend their own churches without any exception.[3]

A similar latitude was followed when interpreting the canons of 1603. The Injunctions of 1559, followed by Grindal's own orders and Canon xv, had ordered the reading of the Litany on Wednesdays and Fridays, but until Neile's primacy the visitation courts had been content if it was read on those days only in Lent.[4] A similar course was taken with catechizing, ordered by Canon LIX. Certain orders of the canons were not enforced until Neile's primacy, notably that contained in Canon XIV concerning the reading of Common Prayer on the Eves of Sundays and Holy Days. Even this archbishop, keen to enforce the letter of the law, could on occasion neglect a canon altogether. Canon LXXXVI ordered archdeacons and judges of peculiar jurisdictions to survey all churches within their authority every three years and certify the defects to the High Commissioners, whereupon the latter were to secure that due reparation was made. The canon was never obeyed. The commissions to view churches issued by Mottershed approximated to

[1] R.VI.A.19, fos. 202 v.–203, 357 v. These presentments, and some more on fo. 75, prove that in 1619 enquiry was made in the visitation articles concerning persons not going to their own parish churches. In the city of York arrangements were made to allow citizens to hear sermons at the Minster on Sundays (R.VI.A.6, fos. 12 r. and v.).   [2] See chapter on Nottingham.

[3] One of the articles against the churchwardens of Rowley (1635) was that they permitted a loft to exist, erected to allow strangers to hear sermons (R.VII.H.2106). Cf. R.VII.P.A.23 mentioned above.

[4] R.VI.A.19, fo. 366 v. and R.VI.A.21, fo. 200 v.—the canonical requirement was, however, mentioned in Archbishop Matthew's visitation articles: cf. the articles against Oldfield in R.VII.H.1710. There is in this episode a distinct warning not to rely on visitation articles alone as a guide to church practice.

fulfilling the first part of the requirement, but he enforced repairs on his own authority as Official, the High Commission never entered into the proceedings. Another canonical requirement never enforced by any archbishop was that commanding one person from each household to attend the reading of the Litany on Wednesdays and Fridays. A few unfortunate extremist Puritans were required by Neile to read Morning and Evening Prayer daily, demonstrating that such reading was lawfully necessary, yet even he had to tolerate the negligence of the majority of his clergy in this particular.

One of the canons hitherto infrequently enforced, but to which Neile secured conformity, was LVIII where it was commanded that a minister should wear the hood of his degree when saying public prayers or ministering the sacraments or other rites of the Church. The canon specified that a surplice should be provided at the cost of the parish, but no mention was made of who was responsible for providing the hood. In the diocesan visitations, defaulting clergymen were presented for the deficiency and were ordered by Easdall to provide a hood and wear it. In the Archdeaconry of Nottingham, during Mottershed's administration, churchwardens were presented, or presented themselves, for the deficiency and were ordered to provide the article. When they objected, saying that they thought the minister should provide his own hood, they were overruled.[1] It is difficult to find a better example of the degree of liberty of interpretation given to the canons by the ecclesiastical judges, than such a difference of principle in the administration of a single diocese by two such eminent lawyers as the Chancellor of York and the Advocate-general in the North.

The difference in attitude to the canons, as also to the rubrics of the Book of Common Prayer which were then regarded as legally binding, between Archbishops Matthew and Neile has been amply illustrated in the examples given above. It is worth emphasizing, however, that the former's toleration of nonconformity was a matter of distinct policy and not due to inefficiency. Where a nonconformist stubbornly refused to obey the canons and Book of Common Prayer, and Matthew was unable to convince him of the error of his ways, it was the clergyman who won the struggle.[2] Perhaps the most

---

[1] Archdeaconry of Nottingham MSS., A. 44, 29 Oct. 1635, churchwardens of Winthorpe. The nearest approach to such an idea in the diocesan visitation was at Welbury in 1632, where the churchwardens presented themselves for the lack of a hood; they were ordered to provide one 'and be at halfe the charge...yf the rest of the inhabitants would give consent'. This was a unique case in these acts, but clearly the parish's contribution was purely voluntary (R.VI.B.4, fo. 411).

[2] The most notable case was that of Thomas Toller, Vicar of Sheffield, for whose career see my *Puritans and the Church Courts in the Diocese of York : 1560–1642*, p. 285.

famous case of the archbishop's attitude to canon law in this connection was his collation of Alexander Cooke to the Vicarage of Leeds. Cooke, who was deprived of the Vicarage of Louth, Lincolnshire, in 1604 for refusing to subscribe to the three articles of Canon XXXVI,[1] was collated on 17 January 1615,[2] but reference to the subscription book used by the archbishop shows only a significant space, equal in length to one subscription, in the place where Cooke should have subscribed. Search through the book has failed to reveal any subsequent subscription, and it was hardly to be expected that a man of his standing and views would change his principles.

Cooke's case illustrated Matthew's church policy, but the latitude shown to the Puritan did not mean that he was reluctant to use his inherent authority where necessary. One unexpected sphere where this was exercised was in what appear to be grants of monopoloy for certain specialist tasks concerning the repair and decoration of churches. In 1620 he issued a licence to two men each from York and Nottingham to paint texts of scripture on church walls and to paint royal arms for churches, and inhibiting all others from doing so. The licence was renewed in 1622 and 1626. In the same year (1620) he issued other licences to a York man to do plumbing repairs throughout the diocese (i.e. any repairs involving lead), and in 1622 to three York men similarly to repair clocks and chimes.[3] These last two licences 'nominate, authorize and commend' the licensee to perform these functions, but contained no reference to the inhibition of others. Yet it would seem that such was their practical effect, and there may have been others of which no record remains. One other was certainly to another York citizen, to mend organs. A letter written to the mayor and aldermen of Hull on the point is worth quoting:

This bearer John Raper being a man of knowne qualitie and skill for the making of Musicall Instruments and well approved of...hath a graunt from me under my hand and Archiepiscopall Seale to make and repaire Organes in all Churches within my Diocesse, where in former tymes they have been used. [Such an organ existed at Hull]...most of the parishoners in places where the said John Raper hath tendered his service, doe showe themselves willing and well affected to give way thereunto, onely some few which doe hinder his proceedings, as I am informed, which seemeth to mee verie strange (especially if it be by any of my Clergie) whoe above all others ought to accomodate themselves to such my dissynes with such respect, as that which is by mee their Ordinary intended, should be by them and others entertayned and furtherd...[He hoped this delay would not happen at Hull, and their organ would be restored forthwith]. 20 January 1623.

A further letter was sent by the archbishop to the same effect (now lost), and in June of the same year yet another was written. This last complains of

---

[1] Lincoln Record Soc. XXIII, pp. cv–cvi, 370.　　　[2] Institution Book.
[3] R.VII.P.4, 130–3 and 143.

having no reply to his two previous letters, asks for a report, and orders that they and their minister should announce his will in the matter and make a voluntary collection for the project.[1] The exact outcome of the matter is unknown, but, as Neile's chancellor made no order about the organ (as he did at Sheffield), something may have been done. It would appear that the licensees used their licences to make churchwardens employ them where they detected defects, but the importance of Hull made Raper arm himself with a special letter of introduction. If this was so, Matthew was trying to improve his churches through the private initiatives of the licensees, short-circuiting the visitation procedures. Yet in so doing he was making a novel use of his powers as ordinary.

VISITATION PROCEDURE AND FEES

The purpose of this section is to describe the working of visitation courts and to make some comment on visitation and court fees. It is based on the records of the visitations of certain deaneries in selected years, and the results of these visitations are further analysed in Chapter 6.

When the circuit system became fully developed, the formal work of both the visitors and the courts was undertaken in the parish church of the chosen centre in the morning. After adjournment for lunch, routine work was conducted by the registrar in a temporary office. Very often the latter was in a room at the inn where the lunch was taken. At visitations routine work principally included receiving the presentments from the churchwardens who had officiated during the previous twelve months and swearing in their successors, and receiving fees from the clergy and churchwardens. The visitation fees in the diocese of Norwich appear to have been 1s. 8d., together with a charge of 1s. if the churchwardens used a clerk of the court to write their presentment bills for them,[2] and the Nottingham archdeaconry table of fees also suggests a total of 1s. 8d., but in fact parishes there paid 2s.[3] The same fee was paid by Holy Trinity, Goodramgate, York, in both archdeaconry (of York) and diocesan visitations.[4]

A fee of this size cannot be regarded as excessive, but it was not the only charge which the churchwardens had to bear. One of the features of a visitation was the dinner when the bishop or archdeacon, his officers, the clergy and churchwardens sat down together. The present writer is of the opinion that these social functions had their own valuable part to play in the life of the

---

[1] Hull Civic Archives, L 192 and L 202.   [2] *Registrum Vagum*, I, 171; FCB/1 fo. 19.
[3] Fees in (York) R.VI.P.O.30; receipts in (Notts.) CL 175 and other call lists.
[4] Figures for this parish are taken from the churchwardens' accounts, R.XII.Y/HTG, 12.

Church, and did something to offset the formality of the business transacted, but they undoubtedly added to the cost of the occasion.[1] In a city like York, where the majority of the churchwardens were prosperous citizens, the dinner was an expensive meal. In the parish of Holy Trinity, Goodramgate, the churchwardens in the 1620s were leading merchants and made no charge on the parish, but in the 1630s their successors claimed 10s. (on an average) for their four dinners. In the country, entertainment was on a less lavish scale. The Nottinghamshire parish of Upton in 1616 spent on five dinners (the minister's was included) only 4s. 2d., and in 1636–8 (inclusive) 5s.[2] The dinner was probably regarded as one of the perquisites of the office, in the same way as men working on the church and bell-ringers were provided with ale at the parish's expense. At Upton, 5s. to 7s. a year in the early part of the seventeenth century, and 10s. in the 1630s was charged to the parish for bread and ale in Rogation week at the 'beating of the bounds', so presumably the parishioners did not grudge the 5s. on the visitation dinners. It is only by making such comparisons as these that the fees can be kept in proper perspective.[3]

At the correction courts in the church a roll call of those due to attend was made, and where a person had not been cited personally by the apparitor an order for a new citation was made. This second citation was regarded as effective, even if not served personally, if it was nailed to the person's door or that of his parish church. Formal orders and dismissals were also made before lunch. In the afternoon the offenders attended to receive their penances, those absolved to receive their absolutions, and sometimes late arrivals appeared and had their cases adjudicated. This practice explains why 'not extracted' is sometimes written against a case where a penance had been ordered: the offender had thought better of his submission and had gone home without his schedule. The most amusing account of an incident at this stage of the court's work was given after the Civil War by the nonconformist minister, Oliver Heywood. After describing the formal business in Halifax church, one day in 1664, he related how the court adjourned to the 'checker Chamber' of the Star Inn. Heywood was at that moment at home, praying fervently that God would bring down the church courts, when the floor of the inn room collapsed and the registrar and others landed in the cellar upsetting some of the beer. The incident gave Heywood 'extraordinary assis-

[1] The other valuable feature of a visitation was that the clergy had to listen to a sermon preached by someone other than themselves.
[2] Upton churchwardens' accounts, transcribed by W. A. James (unpublished).
[3] Very often fees and dinners were confused in parish accounts—only the totals being entered. At Wragby (*Wragby Registers*, Yorkshire Parish Register Society, pp. 31–43) this was so, and the totals vary from 6s. 6d. (1606) to 13s. 7d. (1619). An ordinary dinner cost 4d. to 6d.

tance and inlargement in prayer'.[1] Such use of inns is rarely mentioned in the records.[2]

Churchwardens, like clergy, were sometimes themselves cited to court, either to answer for some neglect of duty or for some defect in the church or furnishings. When so cited, they normally had to pay the court fees. At Upton the summons for the lack of a bible of the largest volume involved a fee of 1s. 2d. to extend the time within which it had to be provided (1614). Four years later the churchwardens lost their parish register and paid 5s., and the following year 2s. 6d. was debited to the accounts when a church-warden was excommunicated (probably for not attending a visitation). The church porch of Upton was responsible for 4s. fees in 1627, but the repairs then executed were not satisfactory and cost 8s. in 1632 for further appearances and for the summons. The most expensive year, however, was 1635, probably at the time when Archbishop Neile's church restoration schemes eventually reached the parish, for no less than 15s. had to be paid. Averaged over the years, however, the sums spent in such fees were negligible.

These churchwardens' accounts give a clue to something which is not explicit in the court records themselves. Scattered through the accounts are small items, usually not more than 2s., headed 'Paid at the Chapter Court', or to that effect (Upton was in the peculiar of the Chapter of Southwell Minster), and not followed by an extraordinary expenditure on ornaments or repairs. These expenses were evidently of the same nature as those of Wragby in the West Riding, which in many years itemizes not only expenses at the visitations but also at the correction court (varying from 4d. to 6s. 9d.). The inference is that when the churchwardens made a presentment of offenders, they sometimes had to attend the correction court to give evidence, if required, on the grounds for their charge, or the poverty of the accused.[3] These expenses were part of the necessary cost of the system, but they should be distinguished both from visitation fees proper and from costs of cases involving the churchwardens directly.[4]

An example of how the circuit system developed was the deanery of Doncaster. An experimental local court was held in the town in 1586, and local courts became established in the diocese in 1590 at diocesan visitations. Even then the court officers took a leisurely view of their duties and the

---

[1] *Diaries, etc.* ed. J. H. Turner (1882), I, 191.
[2] E.g. *Acts of the Durham High Commission*, p. 10.
[3] For remission of fees in cases of poverty see below, pp. 228–34.
[4] In a case such as that at Hatfield, Doncaster Deanery 1590 (R.VI.A.10, fo. 219 v.), it is clear that both churchwardens and minister were present. Thomas Ricard owed 10s. to the churchwardens for burials in church. His servant attended with a certificate that it had been paid, 'and so muche both the minister and churchwarens dyd affyrme'. Another man, ordered to pay his church rate, at once paid it in court to one of the churchwardens of his parish.

correction court at Doncaster was six months after the Easter visitation. With an annual presentment, this meant that the average offence was a year old when it came to court. At this time late attenders had to go to York, and were often dealt with by one of the vicars-choral who acted as substitutes for the chancellor. Having to travel to York cannot have encouraged absentees from the original court to seek absolution, neither can it have made the returning of certificates of the performance of court orders easy. This apparent lack of concern for the inability of many to travel, thus making difficult the return of certificates, was a feature of Elizabethan diocesan visitations in York, and probably accounts for the high contumacy rate in some places.

By 1619 the circuit system had become fully developed. Sessions were held in both the west and east of the deanery, at Rotherham and Doncaster respectively, at the end of July. A second court for certificates and late offenders was held at Doncaster on 9 October, although those living nearer Pontefract were allowed to attend at the second court held there. Later acts at York were always ordered personally by Chancellor Dodsworth, confirming the impression derived from the acts of other courts that he maintained daily supervision of his office, unlike the Elizabethan chancellors whose real interests lay in a much wider field than the courts at York.

The 1619 acts provide evidence of three other aspects of church discipline.

(1) Matrimonial: in the Doncaster Deanery acts for 1590 there were no presentments for pre-nuptial immorality, and such presentments only gradually began to flow in during that decade. The 1619 acts show that in the Dodsworth period a commonly successful defence to the accusation was that conception occurred only after a contract of marriage had been made. Yet the Archdeaconry of York acts for 1613 show that that court did not accept such a defence and exacted the full rigour of public penance. The Cleveland Archdeaconry acts for 1632 and 1634 also fail to record pre-contract defence, but such offenders were more leniently punished by simply having to make a private confession before the minister and churchwardens, or in their ordinary clothes and not in a white sheet. The diocesan acts from the time of Easdall (1627 onwards) show many fewer defences of pre-contract, suggesting that such contracts were beginning to die out. Easdall sometimes accepted it as a full defence or awarded a modified form of penance.[1]

(2) Penances: the acts of 1590 and 1619 usually detail the places where penances were to be performed. Most sexual offenders had to appear

[1] E.g. R.VI.A.24 (1637), fo. 171, declaration before minister and churchwardens; fo. 188, dismissed. In the Cleveland Archdeaconry visitation acts of 1632, there is a single case of alleged pre-contract: there parties were ordered to make a declaration before the minister and churchwardens (R.VI.C.26, not foliated).

twice, once in each of the parish churches of the couple concerned, or if both came from the same parish, then on two successive Sundays. Sometimes a penance in a market-place was substituted for one in church or imposed as an additional punishment. Multiple penances of this type were also usual in the archdeaconry courts. The 1633 visitation actuary did not enter the details of the penance, so it is impossible to detect whether such severity was maintained, but it appears also to have been normal practice in the Norwich diocese. There were two types of penance, the full penance, bare-headed, bare-legged, bare-footed, dressed in a white sheet and with a white rod in hand, standing on a form or platform in church, and made after the second lesson at Morning Prayer. The other penance, or 'making a declaration of his (or her) offence' as it was sometimes called, consisted in reciting the approved schedule of contrition for the offence and promise of amendment, but in ordinary clothes. The York courts were generally stricter than those in the Norwich diocese, if the 1627 visitation of the latter is typical. The northern practice was to enforce penance on drunkards, swearers and similar offenders, while at Norwich they often escaped with an admonition—as did non-attenders at church and non-communicants. At York the latter had to return a certificate that they had mended their ways.

(3) Commutation: the general impression from records and contemporary literature is that the practice of commuting penances for a money payment became more frequent during Elizabeth's reign, and at the same time came under increasing attack from the Puritan opposition. This criticism was effective, and from the turn of the century the practice was much more restricted. There was not a single instance of commutation in the Doncaster deanery in 1590, but in one case where a man claimed to be dispensed by the archdeacon for his offence (presumably implying a commutation), the chancellor over-rode it and ordered penance.[1] Perhaps his action was a presage of what was to come, for the eventual solution was to reserve to the archbishop personally the awarding of commutations in the Yorkshire part of the diocese.[2] The acts of 1619 show one of the concomitants of commutation—lay influence. A man from Wath-on-Dearne admitted immorality and was ordered penance in two churches. He asked for commutation and was told to pay 13s. 4d. to the poor of the two parishes; his penance was reduced to the making of declarations of his offence. In the margin is the significant entry 'Lady Sheffield'.[3] The other case of lay influence in this deanery in the

---

[1] R.VI.A.10, fo. 219.   [2] For Nottinghamshire see pp. 175–8.

[3] R.VI.A.19, fo. 143 v. Those involved in court proceedings often sought the help of important persons to influence a judge in their favour: see a discussion of the subject in W. J. Jones, *The Elizabethan Court of Chancery*, pp. 328–36, and below, pp. 228–9.

same year concerned a man from Tickhill who had committed adultery with his servant. He failed to purge himself and admitted his guilt.[1] The chancellor ordered penance in two churches and Doncaster market place. He eventually certified only one penance performed in church, but he was dismissed on this alone at the petition of Sir John Jackson, Kt.[2] The 1623 visitation records contain a few more instances of the former of these two types of reduction of punishment. While in the whole of the diocese the archbishop only authorized the commutation of two offences presented at that visitation (for £15 and £20), there were several remissions of one of the two penances upon payment of 10s. to 20s. to the poor of the parish.[3] Commutations in the Norwich diocese were slightly more frequent, five being allowed in the diocesan visitation of 1633, but this was out of a total of 262 presentments for immorality. No commutation or partial remissions have been noticed in the acts of Archbishop Neile's visitations, and this is what might be expected from his stricter discipline.

The visitation of 1632–3 was chiefly notable for showing up Neile's problems and methods. First, it was the visitation of an old man in a hurry (he was seventy when appointed to York). He was not enthroned in time to hold his primary visitation at Easter 1632, and being unwilling to wait until the next year, he took the unprecedented step of holding it at Michaelmas. For the court officials this was undoubtedly an unpopular move because it reduced by half the number of ordinary cases coming before the correction court, on the fees of which they depended for their 'bread and butter' income.[4] The apparitors' department would have been particularly affected, as the apparitors would have to cover the same mileage serving but half the number of citations, and therefore receiving but half their expected income. It is no wonder that there were signs of unrest in the apparitor-general's office at this time.[5] The visitation was held at Doncaster on the last day of October 1632, but Easdall could only afford time to hold one correction court for the deanery instead of the usual two—at Rotherham on 13 March 1633. Not only did he have insufficient time to hold a session at Doncaster but he failed to hold a second court at all, the subsequent business being transacted at York

[1] Purgations were often successful, but instances such as this show that they were by no means a formality.
[2] R.VI.A.19, fo. 139.
[3] Such remissions were usually in the less serious cases, such as where the persons subsequently married, e.g. R.VI.A.20, fo. 24 v. In Cleveland Archdeaconry 1632 (R.VI.C.26), the commutations were of a pauper for 40s., and of five who had buried an excommunicate recusant in a churchyard, for 26s. 8d.; in 1634 (R.VI.C.27) there were two in one case, for an unspecified sum.
[4] The lower courts were inhibited for about the usual period, however, so that perquisites from testamentary and other non-correction business were the same—from 17 July 1632–28 Feb. 1633 (Nottingham A 39).
[5] Above, p. 59.

on Chancery Court days. Nevertheless, Easdall attended to it personally, it was not left to substitutes.

Secondly, there was a considerable tightening up of the presentment system. The churchwardens of seventeen parishes were charged with neglecting to make true presentments—in every case the deficiency relating either to the defaults of their minister or themselves. As some of these failures were detailed, e.g. for not reading the Litany on Wednesdays and Fridays 'except in Lent', or occasional, such as for neglecting to beat the bounds of the parish, it is likely that direct questioning had revealed the facts, and it was not the work of some detective agency (such as apparitors) hastily sent round the parishes. In all cases the churchwardens were simply admonished on this charge but had to pay their fees.

Thirdly, the visitation revealed, and checked, the nonconformist practices which had been allowed to grow unmolested in Puritan parishes, particularly the disuse of the surplice and the substitution of psalms for canticles at Morning and Evening Prayer. The extent to which nonconformity had grown under Archbishop Matthew cannot be known exactly, for the first blow against it was struck by Archbishop Harsnett, the records of whose visitation of the diocese of York have not survived. His acts in the diocese of Chester in 1630 make clear that his visitors uncovered much of the Puritanism of Lancashire and Cheshire, and that he had no compunction in interdicting those of the parochial chapels which had become, in effect, nonconformist conventicles and which refused to conform. It may be assumed that he took similar severe measures in his own diocese, so that Neile's task was of the nature of a follow-up. The 1632–3 visitation saw the beginning of the constructive part of Neile's policy, the restoration and improvement of churches.[1]

Fourthly, Neile's primary visitation uncovered many clandestine marriages in this part of the diocese.[2] One of the recurring offences before the High Commission at York was that of clergymen who had performed these illegal ceremonies.[3] Those who had been thus married (usually without banns or licence, or not in a church, or both) were lightly treated by Easdall. One couple was ordered to appear in the Chancery Court for formal prosecution but most of the remainder were declared to be *ipso facto* excommunicate and, on payment of fees, were absolved. The fees charged ranged from 5s. to 16s. per husband and wife, and as 5s. was the normal fee per person for simple dismissal, these were not extortionate. In a few cases, however, the accused

---

[1] For further description of this policy and its enforcement, see my *Puritans and the Church Courts*, ch. 4. Acts of Archbishop Harsnett's visitation of the Diocese of Chester are in R.VI.A.22.

[2] For statistics see below, p. 219.

[3] For statistics see my *Puritans and the Church Courts*, pp. 216–17.

did not pay their fees and so remained under sentence of excommunication. There was little the court could do as clandestine marriages, once performed, were legal, but it would be interesting to know why those concerned were not made to perform penance.

Fifthly, in no case did Easdall refer presentments to local clergymen or to the rural dean for investigation or decision. This practice, common in Elizabethan days when the powers of rural deans in matters of discipline were still in a state of flux, had continued on a reduced scale. Dodsworth, on occasion, referred doubtful matters to be investigated by a local clergyman and ordered him to award a penance if he thought it appropriate.

The subject of fees charged at correction courts was, and is, one which leads to much confusion. A modern writer, for instance, when exemplifying excessive fees charged by church courts, quotes the case of a man who had to pay 13s. 4d. for a certificate of discharge in addition to other fees. When the same writer wishes to prove that excommunication had little effect, he is able to quote persons who could have had an absolution for 1s.[1] Table 15 is derived from official tables, and from the record of sums actually received and entered in the act books. Where the latter differ from the former, the sums actually charged have been recorded in the Table.

The highest charges during most of the period were to be found in the diocese of York. The North had been a very poor area, and at the beginning of Elizabeth's reign the fact was reflected in the very low level of fees. The scale went up considerably during the reign and thereafter was stabilized at a rate which persisted until the Civil War. A rise in fees in the archdeaconries also took place, and the only puzzling feature was that in the Archdeaconry of Nottingham, in the decade before the Civil War, some system operated whereby some offenders only paid half-fees for their appearance and dismissal.

A little light on the actual charging of fees was thrown by the unusual cause of Edmundson *c.* Bell.[2] Thomas Bell, Rector of Felixkirk, had an altercation with Thomas Edmundson, the registrar, on the subject of fees at an Archdeaconry of Cleveland correction court at Thirsk in 1614. During the course of the dispute Bell called the registrar a usurer, for which he was sued for defamation in the Consistory Court. One witness was Robert Lupton, then Edmundson's clerk, who later succeeded him as registrar of the Dean and Chapter. He deposed that in the Cleveland archdeaconry the only fees taken were those normally charged by archdeacons' registrars in the diocese—

---

[1] C. Hill, *Society and Puritanism in Pre-Revolutionary England*, pp. 309, 370. These instances are doubtless accurate, but too much can be made of isolated examples taken out of their context.
[2] R.VII.H.1171.

which indicates that there was a standard table of fees, so the East Riding fees may be assumed to be those used throughout the diocese. The only exception which he admitted was that where a party purging himself was 'of good habilitie' he was charged 2s. and each compurgator 1s. (the East Riding table gives the registrar's fee in these cases as 4d. and 2d.), 'yet yf the partie was pore then les was taken'. Here is evidence for a two-fold scale of fees—one for the rich and the other for the poor—which may explain discrepancies in fees charged in other instances, such as that at Nottingham.

TABLE 15

Fees charged at correction courts[1]

Court	Year	Appearance and dismissal	Excommunication and absolution	Penance
Diocese of York	*c.* 1560	8d.	2d.–6d.	1s. 6d.
	1570	1s. 0d.	1s. 11d.	?
	1590	5s. 0d.	3s. 0d.	3s. 0d.
	1633	5s. 0d.	3s. 0d.	3s. 0d.
Archdeaconry of Nottingham	*c.* 1570	1s. 0d.	?	?
	c. 1590	2s. 4d.	?	?
	1633	4s. 8d. or 2s. 4d.	2s. 8d.	1s. 6d.
Archdeaconry of the East Riding	1623	1s. 4d.	2s. 2d.	1s. 6d.
	1633	2s. 4d.	3s. 8d.	3s. 0d.
Diocese of Norwich	1559–1640	1s. 4d.	6d. (if charged)	nil (apparently)
Diocese of Ely	1619	1s. 5d.	4s. 6d.	1s. 0d. (if charged)
Archdeaconry of Taunton	1623	4d.	1s. 6d. (if charged)	not charged
Archdeaconry of Suffolk	*c.* 1603	9d.	?	6s. 8d.

The attempts of the Archbishops of Canterbury, particularly Whitgift, to keep down the fees in the southern province seem to have been successful.

[1] Sources. York Diocese: act books, especially R.VI.A.11, fo. 115, and, for period immediately before the Civil War, R.VI.A.39/38.

Archdeaconry of Nottingham: act books, and table in R.VI.P.O.30.

Archdeaconry of East Riding: table of 1623, corrected by Mottershed's clerk, Francis Parker, R.VII.P.O.28 and 29, *c.* 1633.

Diocese of Norwich: act books, table in *Registrum Vagum*, I, 171 and FCB/1, fo. 19.

Diocese of Ely: act book for 1619, in Cambridge University Library, Ely Diocesan Records, B/2/37, and compare table of fees for first 18 years of reign of Elizabeth I in F5/52, fos. 220 v.–222.

Archdeaconry of Taunton: Act Book, Somerset Record Society, vol. 43 (1928).

Archdeaconry of Suffolk: *Registrum Vagum*, I, 73–5. The Archdeaconry of Cleveland fee for dismissal in *c.* 1530 was also 9d. ('Office Book', fo. 18 v.), which suggests that these very low fees were all the unchanged medieval scale.

The Norwich scale never varied throughout our period, and it seems that little attempt was made to charge for excommunications and penances. The only device adopted by the chancellors of Norwich for raising money was to charge the standard fee for each offence for which a person was presented, so he sometimes found himself paying double or treble fees. The Ely scale was substantially the same as that of Norwich, except that a high impost was levied for excommunication. The Archdeaconry of Taunton (in Somerset) scale was very low. Probably the 4*d*. fee was paid entirely to the registrar, and the clergyman who acted as judge (not described as an Official) may well have acted in a voluntary capacity: both he and his archdeacon were Puritans.[1]

After these preliminary remarks, some comment is needed to explain the differences and also the increases, or lack of them. Underlying all increases at this time was a general inflation in the monetary system, but there were certain other features of the ecclesiastical administration itself which explain much. These all produced various complications and local peculiarities.

(1) Growth of the visitation system: examination of churchwardens' accounts shows that in pre-Elizabethan times there was no regular and systematic visitation such as has been described in this chapter. In the dioceses of York and Chester most of the work of summary correction of faults was done, presumably very cheaply, by rural deans. Centralized administration costs more than local justice. The big increase in fees in 1590 coincided with the introduction of the circuit system. If the court officials had to peregrinate the diocese, somebody had to pay their expenses.

(2) Laicization: the increase in fees in 1590 also coincided with the realization that there would never again be clerical chancellors. Gibson, through court influence, managed to hold on to some of his ecclesiastical preferments, but Benet never received any. Mottershed the layman, who took over from the pluralist clergyman Bell, raised the fees in the East Riding, and in his new scale the Official benefited more than the registrar.

(3) Influence of probate business: the fees of both diocesan and archidiaconal officers were higher in Yorkshire than in the south. This may have been due in part to the orders of Archbishops of Canterbury (those of York being able to escape the scrutiny of the Church's critics). It is more likely to be due to the fact that in the south distances of circuits (and therefore expenses) were less, and particularly to the fact that the normal diocesan chancellor had a probate jurisdiction. To this extent the Chancellor of York relied more on correction court fees than did his southern equivalents.

The effect of these factors was even more important to the local commis-

[1] Francis Gough, B.D., Vicar of Winsford, was described as 'Surrogate of the Archdeacon' (Samuel Ward, D.D.).

saries. When they went on circuit they conducted probate business, litigation between parties and correction courts. When the Yorkshire Officials went on circuit they had to rely on the profits of their correction courts only.

(4) Parish-population ratio: in the south there were usually large numbers of parishes, each with comparatively small populations. This was particularly true of East Anglia. By comparison, in Yorkshire there were many large parishes, and even allowing for semi-independent chapelries with their own churchwardens the result was to produce fewer churches in relation to the population. The consequence was that the visitors in the south received more in parochial visitation fees in relation to the population than did the visitors in Yorkshire, and so again were less dependent on correction court fees.

(5) Differentials: the Chancellor of the diocese of York was a very important official in the northern capital, and he had a considerable position to maintain. He therefore expected to receive more in fees from a correction case than did a more lowly archdeacon's Official—and so he did, 2s. compared with 1s. to 1s. 4d. The Chancellor of York probably expected also to make more from his office than did a normal diocesan chancellor. The Chancellorship of Ely was only a part-time office.

(6) Swings and roundabouts: comparison of fees is a subject which needs to be treated with caution. The correction court fees in the Table would need to be compared with the full range of court fees in each court for a complete assessment to be made. The Table correctly shows that a person admonished in the diocese of York had to pay more heavily for his appearance than an East Anglian offender similarly warned. It was of little benefit to him that a clergyman requiring an induction in the Archdeaconry of Suffolk had to pay 22s. fees, but in the Archdeaconries of Nottingham and the East Riding only 11s. 8d. Yet such differences have to be taken into account if a true picture of the rewards of the legal officers is to be made. In the Archdeaconry of Suffolk the lesser offender paid at rock-bottom rates—9d. for an admonishment—but if he performed a penance he had to pay 6s. 8d., while in the East Riding only 2s. 10d. was charged under the old scale for this punishment, and 5s. 4s. under Mottershed's revision. The difficulties of comparison are enhanced because the items are not always specified in the same way in different tables, and because of differences in court practices. The Norwich visitors, according to the fees recorded in the act books, seem to have rarely charged for excommunications and penances. They likewise infrequently charged if a special commission had to be issued to receive the oath of an executor or administrator who could not travel to the local office to make it. The Suffolk archdeaconry acts are lost, but the fee books show that the registrar there nearly always charged the fee to which he was entitled for

these commissions. The facts make this subject one on which it is unwise to pronounce speedy judgments.

(7) Comparisons: it would be useful to make comparisons between the fees charged in secular and church courts. Quarter Sessions were the secular equivalent of the correction courts, and in the West Riding the fees paid to the Clerk of the Peace in 1623 were 2s. for each appearance, 2s. for each dismissal or binding over to keep the peace, 4s. for binding over to be of good behaviour or dismissal from being bound over in this way.[1] The Council in the North, answering criticisms by justices, stated that it only charged 2s. for binding over (in total), while Quarter Sessions charged 7s. for binding over, and this fee was payable at each sessions so long as the person continued bound.[2] The Council in the North does not appear to have raised its fees in the course of time, and so became cheaper than other courts, but not much cheaper than the archdeaconry fee for admonishment (the ecclesiastical equivalent of binding over). The diocesan admonishment fee of 5s. does not seem much different from Quarter Sessions' charges.

How these fees compared with contemporary values is another problem, and here remissions on account of poverty have to be taken into account. The standard of living varied much more between classes than it does today, and many people depended much less on money than they do today. A North Riding carpenter in the pre-Civil War decade received 1s. a day, and this may be taken as a standard measure.[3] The diocesan correction court scale would therefore have cost an offender about a week's wages (allowing for a day off to attend court) if he was admonished, or nearly two weeks' wages if he had to perform penance. These were very considerable sums, but most offenders fortunately were tried by archdeacons' courts which were appreciably cheaper. In the diocese of Norwich court fees were hardly a burden, but the rate of contumacy there was not appreciably different from that in York, suggesting that the fee scale was not in itself the main barrier to obedience of church courts.

It may be not entirely cynical to suggest that, despite the low level of fees in the East Anglian courts, those charged in the North more nearly represented what church lawyers would have liked to have seen throughout the country. Low fees were not necessarily an advantage, particularly in a period such as this. They increased the temptations to extortion, minor accusations and unnecessary litigation. The low fees charged for correction business in

[1] *West Riding Quarter Sessions Records*, II, 403 (Yorks. Arch. Soc. Rec. Series LIV, A.D. 1915).
[2] R. R. Reid, *The King's Council in the North*, p. 337.
[3] Deposition of witnessess in R. VII.H.2125 (A.D. 1635). A. Dent in *The Dalesman*, vol. 29, no. 2 (May 1967), p. 123, quotes from a Yorkshire farmer's MSS. to show that in 1641 a farm foreman was paid 70s. to 80s., a skilled man 45s. 6d. to 55s. and a boy 20s. p.a.

the Norwich diocese went hand-in-hand with the apparitors' detections of widows who had not taken out legal administrations of their husbands' estates.

Church discipline was part of Reformed religion. Puritan and Anglican would administer it differently, but up to the time of the Civil War few in authority questioned the need for its existence. The booming nature of business done by church courts—probate, administration and litigation—helped to produce naturally the circuits and frequent courts of the local commissaries, judges, registrars and their dependants, whose principal occupation it was. A similar development will be shown in the next chapter to have taken place in Nottinghamshire. Discipline in Yorkshire evolved in a different way. The powers of the rural deans were suppressed, but the archdeacons had neither litigation, licence nor probate business to sustain frequent courts or circuits. Furthermore, their legal officers were either clergymen resident in their benefices or lawyers who were tied to York in term time. Thus completely different systems of discipline were produced within one diocese: the simple annual visitation in the Yorkshire archdeaconries, the frequent circuit courts with a continuous inflow of presentments in Nottinghamshire.

5

THE ARCHDEACONRY OF NOTTINGHAM

The Archdeaconry of Nottingham existed as a semi-independent jurisdiction, a status doubtless achieved basically because of the county's distance from the see city. The Yorkshire archdeaconries all abutted on York, but on the map Nottinghamshire looks rather like a sausage being dangled by one end from the main part of the diocese. Its physical separation from Yorkshire was recognized by the fact that its clergy had a synod of their own which met at Southwell. This synod probably provided the archbishop with his chief means of contact with the county between diocesan visitations, but the fact that he had a residence and estates there also made it easy for him to visit the county at other times, as for instance on his journeys to London and back.

The interest of studying this archdeaconry lies not only in the fact that it had an entirely distinct consistory and correction court and administration, but also in the fact that it has a well-preserved set of records of this period. From these archives we gain some insight into the way that the smaller administrations worked, as well as being able to fill in the details of some of the changes on a large scale already noticed.

THE ARCHIDIACONATE OF JOHN LOWTH (1565–90)

The history of the archdeaconry in Elizabethan times is so involved with the personal history of its archdeacon, that some account must be given of the latter. Shortly after John Foxe had published his *Acts and Monuments*, Lowth wrote to the author about his troubles under Queen Mary, hoping that they would be printed in a later edition.[1] From this account we learn that John was the youngest son of Edmund Lowth, esquire, of Sawtry, Huntingdonshire, born in 1519. The father was on bad terms with the monks of the abbey there, and John was fully persuaded that the monastic tenants who attacked and killed his father when he was but three years old had been

---

[1] Printed by J. G. Nichols, *Narratives of the Days of the Reformation* (Camden Society, 1859), pp. 1–59.

10-2

TABLE 16

The Archdeaconry of Nottingham

Archbishop	Archdeacon	Official	Deputy Official	Registrar	Deputy Registrar
		Before		Before	
		1554 Robert Cressy		1565 John Lee	
1561 Thomas Young	1565 John Lowth			1568 Thomas Lowth	
				1569 William Newman	
1570 Edmund Grindal		1571 or 2 Robert Green			
		1574 or 5 John Hacker		1574 John Martiall	
1577 Edwin Sandys		1577 Zachariah Babington		1577 Humphrey Lowth	
		1581 Thomas Wethered			
		1581 Richard Byrdsall			
		1583 Simon Parratt			
		1583 Thomas Petty			
		1585 Remegius Booth and Petty			
1589 John Piers		1589 Christopher Diggles			
		1589 Petty (restored)			
	1590 John King	1591 Miles Leigh		1591 Thomas Wilmot	1590 John Martiall
1595 Matthew Hutton				1596 Matthew Weeks	
			1599 Michael Purefey		
		1600 Michael Purefey			
		1601 Nicholas Langford	1601 Thomas Petty		1602 John Tibberd
			1604 Michael Purefey		
1606 Toby Matthew					
	1611 Joseph Hall				
					1625 Edward Copinger
					1626 Hatfield Reckles
			1627 William Greaves		
	1628 Richard Baylie				1628 Edward Farmery
1629 Samuel Harsnett				1629 Carr Coventry	1629 John Coombe
1632 Richard Neile	1635–42 William Robinson	1635 Edward Mottershed	jointly { 1635 Robert Malham 1635 Christopher Fielding 1636 Edmund Laycock		
1641 John Williams		1641–74 Edward Lake	1641 Robert Malham (alone)	1638–67 John Coombe	

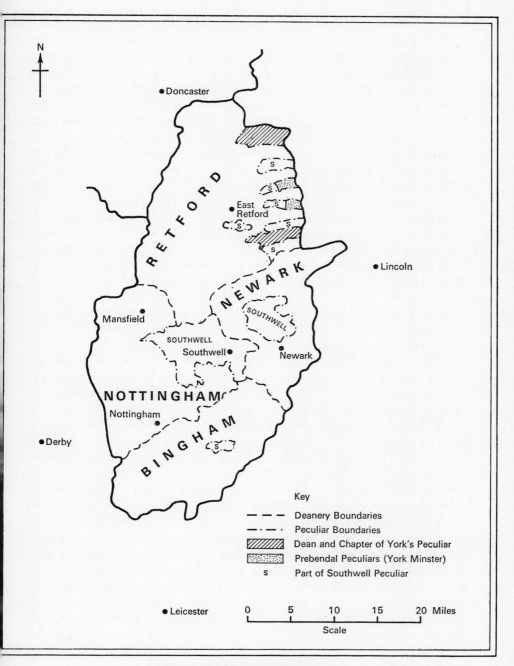

N

• Doncaster

R E T F O R D

• East
Retford

S

S

S

S

S

• Lincoln

N E W A R K

SOUTHWELL

• Mansfield

SOUTHWELL

Southwell •

• Newark

N O T T I N G H A M

Nottingham •

• Derby

B I N G H A M

S

Key

– – – Deanery Boundaries

– · – · Peculiar Boundaries

▨ Dean and Chapter of York's Peculiar

▦ Prebendal Peculiars (York Minster)

S Part of Southwell Peculiar

• Leicester

| 0 | 5 | 10 | 15 | 20 Miles |

Scale

Map 2.   Archdeaconry of Nottingham

149

incited to perform the deed by the monks themselves. This would, at least, have made suitable material for Foxe's readers. What they would not have known, as Lowth himself may not have known, was that his father was not only an enemy of the regular orders (as a good Protestant should have been) but had also driven his rector out of the parish so that he was too frightened to return.[1] Lowth entered Winchester at the age of fifteen and it was there that he first became acquainted with Protestant literature, and became a friend of John Philpot (later Archdeacon of Winchester and a Protestant martyr). From Winchester Lowth went to New College, Oxford, proceeding B.A. in 1540, and after five years as a fellow of his college, he matriculated fellow-commoner at Corpus Christi, Cambridge. The reason for the move was his appointment as tutor to the eldest son of Sir Richard Southwell (a member of the Privy Council and Master of the Ordnance), who was a student at that college. With him Lowth made a further migration to Lincoln's Inn and it was during this period that he narrowly escaped detection and punishment as a heretic. Even then, however, he had the benefit of the patronage of an influential man and became Vicar of Louth, Lincolnshire (1549), and of Chew Magna (Somerset) in 1553. About this time his legal studies reached the stage where he was able to proceed LL.B., although no record of the grant of the degree remains.

There is a complete lack of information about Lowth's activities during Mary's reign, but it is not unlikely that he retired to his Somerset benefice, for on the accession of Elizabeth he at once emerged into the public life of the West country. He acted as surrogate of the Chancellor of the diocese of Bristol from 1559 until he became Chancellor of the diocese of Gloucester in November 1562, and added to these active duties the less onerous burdens of canonries at Lincoln (1560) and Lichfield (1561).[2] It was one of the more remarkable features of his life that Lowth managed to acquire so much ecclesiastical preferment without proceeding further than the diaconate, but the time came when it was necessary for him to take priest's orders. Later on, as will be recounted, he lost his letters of orders, and to prove his ordination depositions were taken from witnesses which described the circumstances.[3] About 1561 Lowth was rector and prebendary of Dinder, a place very close to Wells, and resided there, being also chaplain to the bishop (Gilbert Berkeley) and a great friend of Dr Cotterell, the bishop's chancellor. The latter, indeed, gave him a priest's cap on the eve of his ordination. A vicar-choral testified that after that event Lowth 'remained in Wells and about Wells...by the space of 2 or 3 years and preached there as well in the

---

[1] Lincoln visitation acts, quoted by M. Bowker, *Journal of Ecclesiastical History*, xv, i, 44.
[2] *Alumni Cantab.* [3] (York) R.VII.P.1, pp. 1003–8.

cathedrall churche as in other places very well and with good commendacions'
(another vicar-choral put the duration as one year). It seems likely, therefore,
that Lowth remained at Wells until his appointment as Chancellor of
Gloucester, a post for which he was fitted both by his religious opinions and
his legal knowledge.

There is a reasonable clue as to how Lowth came to be Archdeacon of
Nottingham. We have noticed that Archbishop Young appointed Walter
Jones to be his vicar-general, to assist Rokeby, and that as Mrs Young was
Jones' executor or administrator, there was a close connection between the
two. Among his preferments, Jones counted the Sub-deanery of Gloucester,
and it may well have been that through his influence he secured the Archdeaconry for Lowth. Jones was also a canon of Southwell, and he seems to
have worked well with Lowth in the administration of Nottinghamshire. The
appointment was a fortunate one for Lowth as he was inhibited from performing his duties as chancellor in 1565,[1] and the following year travelled
north. His first home was in Nottingham, but after he had been removed from
his vicarage there in 1572, he lived at Hardwick Hall, one of the residences of
the famous Bess of Hardwick. When he became Rector of Hawton in 1574,
he took up residence in his parish, later moved to another of his benefices,
Gotham, and by 1585 he had settled at Keyworth and remained there until
his death.[2]

Lowth's policy as an administrator was the one that might have been
expected from a man of his views. He did very little, as far as one can tell
from the records, until the strong reforming activity of Archbishop Grindal
enabled him to take over all disciplinary power, relieve the rural deans of
their corrective functions, and bring the archdeaconry up to the standard of
the archbishop's Injunctions and of the Book of Common Prayer. A stricter
observance of Sunday was enforced, sabbath games were forbidden, drunkards, swearers and similar disreputable persons began to be brought to
court.

The new archdeacon's first disappointment must have been his failure to
secure the benefice of St Mary's, Nottingham. To have become vicar of this
fine church would have increased his personal standing and given him access
to the most influential pulpit in the town. Lowth was instituted to the vicarage
on 2 March 1568 on the presentation of the Queen and enjoyed it undisturbed
until 1572. On 1 February that year William Underne sued Lowth for
possession in the Chancery Court at York with a presentation dated only a

[1] F. D. Price in the *Church Quarterly Review*, April–June 1939, p. 96.
[2] Various references are scattered through the archdeaconry acts, e.g. A1, 26 March 1573 (Hardwick
Hall); A2, 8 Aug. 1577 (Hawton); A3, 27 Feb. 1579 (Gotham); and a patent of 2 October 1585 in
acts for 16 Oct. (Keyworth).

month previously (4 January). It may be presumed that Underne had found some technicality which rendered the original presentation invalid and had been cunning enough to secure a new grant to himself. Lowth was already having trouble with Underne, who had been charged in the archdeacon's court with impeding Elias Okeden (Ogden) in his possession of the vicarage of Greasley.[1] The trouble-maker was eventually excommunicated by Lowth,[2] but as the sentence was pronounced after the commencement of the cause at York it was suspended by the chancellor. The archdeacon must have been conscious of the weakness of his position, because he seems to have made little effort to defend himself except by procrastination. Eventually Underne appeared at York on 24 July in answer to an order by the archbishop, and for the first time produced the actual deed of presentation. The chancellor refused to act on it and deferred sentence until 31 August. In the meantime Lowth made an attempt to produce legal arguments in his favour (1 August), but later he gave way and Underne was instituted on 4 October. The new vicar was apparently an unsatisfactory man, and when the archdeacon began fresh proceedings against him in the following year, the prosecution was interrupted because the vicar had been incarcerated in Nottingham prison.[3]

The affair of Underne, however, was only a pin-prick as compared with Lowth's quarrel with Archbishop Grindal, which proved the decisive check to his career. At the time of Grindal's appointment to the archbishopric in 1570, Lowth was in a position of considerable power in his archdeaconry. His own court had not yet acquired the monopoly of criminal prosecutions which it later achieved, but it dealt with the more serious offences, and if any proved recalcitrant Lowth had a reserve of power at his disposal. There remains a single document to show that about this time the archdeacon and Walter Jones were the regular members of a branch of the High Commission Court of the province of York, meeting from time to time in St Mary's, Nottingham, and using the archdeacon's registrar as their actuary.[4] The document contains the acts of the proceedings against a single defendant, together with the evidence of witnesses, so there is no means of telling the volume of business transacted, but the only apparent limit on the power of these commissioners was the fact that they were able to proceed summarily, lacking proctors or advocates able to plead before them. On Grindal's accession, therefore, Lowth was at the height of his career; he had amassed four prebends, an archdeaconry and two benefices—one of considerable importance; he had his own court which had a jurisdiction concurrent with

[1] A1, 1 July 1570.
[2] 26 April 1572 (see Chancery A.B. 2 May 1572).
[3] A1, 26 Feb. 1573.   [4] York, R.VII.G.1545.

that of the archbishop, and he had a local High Commission Court at his disposal.

The first hint of trouble came after Grindal's primary Visitation, when Lowth was charged in the Chancery Court of York with granting sequestrations, and the licences to marry which clergymen were required to obtain from their bishop by the Injunctions of 1559. He made no attempt to defend the latter action, but the former he maintained was part of his right as archdeacon. Nevertheless, he was inhibited from issuing sequestrations until he had proved his contention.[1] These jurisdictional disputes occurred from time to time where ecclesiastical powers sought to extend their sway or tried to defend themselves against encroachments from outside, and should not be taken too seriously. The vital quarrel which shortly broke out, however, was one in which Lowth appears to have acted foolishly.

One of Grindal's attempted reforms was to institute an examination of clergymen presented to him for institution. Thus on 29 August 1572 James Stevenson was examined in Latin and New Testament when he appeared with a presentation to the rectory of Hawton near Newark made by Francis Mollineaux, esquire. Unfortunately, he failed to satisfy the examiner and a letter was sent to the patron willing him to present another and better minister.[2] Mollineaux refused to comply and brought an action in the secular court against Grindal. Eventually the suit was decided for the plaintiff, the incumbent who had meanwhile been collated by the archbishop was deprived by the Archbishop of Canterbury on the court's order,[3] and Mollineaux was free to present his own nominee. The surprising feature of the incident was that this nominee was none other than Lowth himself. One can only suppose that he had been annoyed by having to surrender St Mary's, Nottingham, and sought some other preferment to compensate himself, while he was not concerned if he offended Grindal who had been seeking to restrict his powers. Lowth was instituted on 12 August 1574 by the Archbishop of Canterbury, pursuant to the order of the secular court,[4] and fifteen days later Grindal relaxed the sequestration.[5] The subsequent court acts show that Lowth had added insult to injury by himself issuing a sequestration of the vacant benefice.

The archbishop decided that the time for action had arrived. On 24 September 1574 Lowth constituted a proctor to represent him in actions in the Chancery Court, but he was unduly optimistic. He was actually called before the High Commissioners at York on 19 October, together with

[1] Chancery A.B., 1 Feb. 1572.
[2] Institution Book 1572–1619, fo. 10 (York).
[3] *Ibid.* fo. 57 v. (21 June 1574).
[4] *Ibid.* fo. 61 v.
[5] Chancery A.B., 23 Aug. 1574.

Mollineaux, his wife and servant, and Richard Morley, Rector of Teversall. The cases against them were not recorded in detail, but may be deduced from the acts. First, there was the accusation that Lowth, Mollineaux and Luke Leake, his servant, had violated the archbishop's sequestration of Hawton; this prosecution was later remitted to the Chancery Court and eventually terminated by prohibition from the secular court.[1] Next, there was the general right Lowth claimed of issuing sequestrations; he was compelled to produce his 'book of acts' for the last two years,[2] apparently so that the Commissioners could have evidence of those which he had granted; no further information is available of any further act on this particular item. Thirdly, there was an action against Mrs Mollineaux and Morley for suspicion of adultery, which dragged on until Morley purged himself before three commissioners at Nottingham on 1 June 1575.[3] Lastly, there were two distinct personal charges against Lowth. Somehow Grindal came to suspect that there was something deficient in the archdeacon's ordination, and he was ordered to produce his letters of orders.

Unfortunately, the archdeacon had mislaid his letters of priest's orders and was only able to show those of his deacon's orders, which, he argued, were sufficient to enable him to hold an ecclesiastical benefice. The case rested there until the further charge against him was investigated. It seems that this new prosecution began on 22 January 1575 when Lowth was summoned before a special session of the High Commissioners; a week later the prosecution's proctor put into court as evidence a letter written and signed by Lowth, and on 3 February he was committed to prison in York Castle for writing a slanderous letter against the Commissioners. Writing to the Archbishop of Canterbury on 4 March, Grindal reported that Lowth had compared the proceedings of the High Commission with those of the Spanish Inquisition.[4] The prisoner was released after a short imprisonment of eleven days, but was confined to the city until further order.

The release was perhaps prompted by the fact that Grindal believed he had an even better weapon at hand with which to attack Lowth, a belief which inspired the order to show his letters of priest's orders. The archbishop was thereby reviving his previous charge, for if it could be substantiated, Lowth might be deprived of all his preferments. In his letter to the Archbishop of Canterbury, Grindal stated that he believed it would be proved

[1] Chancery A.B., 22 Feb. 1575.
[2] High Commission A.B., 19 Oct. 1574 (York).
[3] In the archdeacon's court, 25 Sept. 1593 (A7), Morley admitted adultery within the last three years with his servant. Penance commuted for £6. 13s. 4d., three-quarters of the yearly value of his living temp. Henry VIII.
[4] *Remains of Archbishop Grindal* (Parker Soc.), p. 353.

that Lowth had never been ordained a priest, although he had acted as one for fifteen or sixteen years, and asked that if Lowth petitioned for a pardon either to the Queen or to the archbishop, the latter would use his influence to see that it was not granted. Archbishop Parker replied later in the same month, saying that he would refuse any application, 'nor yet to favour the suit that might be made unto me out of Carlisle etc.'.[1] This last reference must be to something contained in a previous letter by Grindal, the import of which we do not know. The archdeacon's reaction to the Commissioners' enquiries about his orders was to send his registrar to Wells, where he collected witnesses and had sworn depositions made before the chancellor of that diocese. A former porter of the bishop's palace and a gentleman usher testified that they had seen Lowth ordained with one Lyde but did not know to what order, a resident of Dinder testified that Lowth had lived there for six months and acted as a priest, and two vicars-choral described how Lowth had been ordained and afterwards dressed and acted as a priest, being one of the bishop's household at that time. The evidence was exhibited to the Commissioners on 14 March and must have given a severe check to Grindal's hopes of uncovering an imposture. Thirteen days later Lowth was given licence to leave York with an order to attend again on 8 October, and when he then appeared he was able at last to produce his letters of priest's orders.[2] Grindal's translation to Canterbury took effect in the following February and the prosecution of Lowth was abandoned.[3] The result of all the proceedings was that neither the archdeacon nor his friends were convicted of any offence, but there is no doubt that they prevented Lowth from obtaining any further preferment. Indeed, it appears that Grindal's translation came only just in time to save Lowth, for whatever lack of success followed the prosecutions, he executed a deed of resignation of his archdeaconry and vicarage of Hawton in November 1575, probably because of pressure applied to him, but on hearing of Grindal's move revoked the resignations in January.[4] In the diocesan visitation of 1575, the archbishop had been still probing for a weak point in Lowth's armour, as evidenced by the record that his registrar showed the Visitors the accounts of the commutations of penance granted in the archdeacon's court.[5]

The advent of the new archbishop, Edwin Sandys, relieved Lowth of one source of worry. The new diocesan chancellor, Robert Lougher, significantly had the formal reading of his appointment in a room in Mrs Young's house not, as customary, in open court, one of the witnesses being Walter Jones.[6]

---

[1] *Correspondence of Archbishop Parker* (Parker Soc.), p. 474.
[2] High Commission A.B. 1574–6, fo. 234.   [3] *Ibid.*, 15 July 1576.
[4] Archbishop's Register, vol. 31, fo. 6.   [5] York. R.VI.A.4, fo. 15 v.
[6] Chancery A.B., 22 May 1577.

In the following year the chancellor issued a formal permission to Lowth's Official to issue sequestrations and marriage licences, so that the jurisdictional dispute between the two authorities was ended for the time being.[1]

It is probable that the quarrel with Grindal caused Lowth to be demoted from two places of authority within his own archdeaconry. Of the first there is no evidence, but it can hardly be expected that he would have been allowed to retain the powers of the High Commission at his disposal, and the fact that there is no further record of a separate branch working in the archdeaconry is an indication, perhaps, that it was abolished by Grindal. The second of Lowth's demotions has more positive evidence. In 1572–3 there appears in acts of the archdeacon's court certain references to the synod of the clergy held at Southwell. Thus the penalty for the contempt by a clergyman in not answering a citation to court was held over until the next synod, and two clergymen who had failed to provide quarterly sermons were ordered to certify at the next synod that they had mended their ways. These orders presuppose some connection between the archdeacon and the synod, but from mid-1573 until 1577 there are no similar references in the acts. It is probable that Lowth had previously used the synod for such purposes by arrangement with Jones, who, as Commissary of the Exchequer and Receiver-general, formally presided at the synods of the diocese. He may even have deputed Lowth to act for him. Jones died early in 1577 and was succeeded by Percy, who was doubtless fully employed at York and who would also depute the presidency. That Lowth acted in this capacity seems proved by the fact that after Grindal's departure from York disciplinary offences connected with the Southwell Synod begin to appear in the acts of the archdeacon's court. On 24 October of that year the Vicar of Worksop was cited before the Official and absolved from a suspension passed upon him at the synod for something he had said there, and on 9 November the Rector of Costock was absolved from a suspension awarded against him because of his absence from the synod.[2] More significant still, because of the fact that the synod had its own registrar and act books, is an entry in the court acts for 8 October 1584 recording the suspension of the Vicar of Farringdon for absence from the synod held that day.[3]

The fact that Lowth's peaceful tenancy of the presidency of the synod was due to the friendly terms existing between Sandys and himself was shown by the way in which he was replaced after the archbishop's death. The first synod to be affected by the change was that of Easter 1588, and on 14 September following four clergymen were called before the archdeacon; one appeared and it was put to him:

---

[1] Register, vol. 31, fo. 51 v.   [2] A2.   [3] A3.

that he and others dyd usurpe or take upon them his [i.e. the archdeacon's] Jurisdiccion viz. in sytting at Southwell at soundrey tymes, in the Synod there, usurping or taking upon them the Judiciall Seate and proceedings apperteyning to the same Synod which was contrarey to their due obedyence towardes hym and more then of right they ought to do.

To which it was replied by the accused:

that he dyd sytt there by authorytye geven unto hym and others from Mr Doctor Pearcy, saying that yf they dyd anythyng contrarey to right they are very sorey for yt and would be lothe to doe any thynge hereafter which should be preiudiciall to his Jurisdiccion.[1]

Despite this reasonable reply, they were pronounced contumacious but the award of a penalty was deferred for thirteen days. On that day the prosecution was adjourned *sine die* owing to a letter sent to Lowth by the Dean of York (acting for the Chapter, *sede vacante*). Any further proceedings in the matter took place outside the courts, but Lowth continued until his death to maintain his right, as is shown in the last patent which he issued to his Official in which that officer was empowered to attend the Southwell Synod and punish all absentees.[2] It is very difficult to see any legal basis for Lowth's pretensions in the matter, only a desire on his part to secure greater rights for the archdeacon, making him less dependent on the archbishop. A similar tendency may be seen in the patent just mentioned, where the Official is also referred to as the 'vicar-general' of the archdeacon, a description—like the reference to powers at the Southwell Synod—peculiar to this patent and not repeated in subsequent ones. A vicar-general was properly a deputy of the bishop, and there can be little doubt that Lowth tried to exercise as much of the episcopal jurisdiction as he could. There is no evidence that other archdeacons or their Officials tried to obtain authority over the Southwell Synod, and, as we shall see, the fact that Dodsworth ordered offenders with whom he was dealing in diocesan visitations to attend there, shows that under Archbishop Matthew the diocesan officers were keeping firm control of the synod.

OFFICIALS AND REGISTRARS

Something of the standing of the court and its place in society, as well as an understanding of who worked it, can be gained by an examination of the careers of the two most important officials, the judge and registrar. The troubles which afflicted the life of Lowth were reflected in troubles with his officials. Various allegations were made that he sold patents of the officiality,

---

[1] *Ibid.*

[2] A5: the patent is recorded on a sheet of paper pinned to the acts for 30 Sept. 1589.

but it is impossible to determine whether venality was the root cause of what happened. As a former diocesan chancellor, Lowth could himself have acted as his own Official, for the work involved must have seemed a spare-time occupation after the management of a diocese. This probably was the real motivating force behind his actions: as his connection with the synod indicates, he wanted to be supreme authority in his own jurisdiction.

The Official whom Lowth found in office upon his arrival in Nottinghamshire was Robert Cressy, a canonist of the old school of lawyers, who had weathered the storms which had swept the Church since he first became an incumbent in 1533. He had been appointed Official before 1554, and was rewarded for his conformity to the Elizabethan settlement by the gift of prebends at Southwell and Lincoln. In 1567 he also became Auditor (or judge) of the court of the Southwell peculiar jurisdiction, twenty-eight parishes, most of them in the immediate vicinity of Southwell, in the heart of Nottinghamshire. That he was regarded by the authorities as a reliable man is demonstrated not only by these appointments, but also by the fact that he was nominated later by Archbishop Grindal to act as judge in the visitation courts of the 1575 episcopal visitation of the archdeaconry, and by Archbishop Sandys for the same purpose in 1578. Cressy was, however, part of the established order of things in the district, an older man than Lowth, and perhaps not quite so enthusiastic for reformation. The archdeacon did not quarrel with him immediately, but dismissed him in 1571, on the eve of changes in the administration. Following his primary visitation, Grindal had given a sign of his approval to Cressy by appointing him to a second prebend at Southwell. It is typical of the bad relations which existed between the archdeacon and his superior, that Lowth chose this moment to dismiss Cressy. The latter appealed to the archbishop, and the Chancery acts for 19 May record a reference of the case to Grindal for his personal decision, but the judgment was not entered in the acts.

Some indication of the type of man Lowth really sought as an Official is found in his first appointment. Richard Green, a non-graduate, was a local clergyman, and in the two years during which he performed the duties he sat in court only four times. This may have been due to the fact that Lowth thought it best to guide the changes himself, but was more likely occasioned by his desire to do things personally—to be seen to be in control of the archdeaconry, rather than simply as a power in the background.

The changes in the administration of discipline initiated after Grindal's primary visitation have been noted above.[1] They consisted largely in the removal of the ordinary jurisdiction from rural deans and its concentration

[1] P. 127.

in the hands of archdeacon and archbishop, and the enforcement of obedience to the detailed regulations which were promulgated in the archbishop's Injunctions of 1571. The records of the Nottingham correction court begin in 1565. At that time the court sat in St Mary's, Nottingham, at irregular intervals of two to four weeks. The number of cases was small, usually less than ten per session; for example, on 1 April 1570 nine cases were before the court, eight of them being for immorality. During the succeeding twelve months the following prosecutions were commenced: immorality, 16; non-payment of rates, 9; absence from church, 1; vicar who did not read service at proper times, 1; churchwardens, for repairs to a churchyard wall, 1; total, 28. The cases came in gradually, and there was no concentration such as was produced by a visitation. Yet archdeacon's visitations were being held, for there was one in 1566, and it is possible that routine cases and less serious charges were referred to the rural deans.[1] Indeed, the use of rural deans may have been the reason, at least in the north of England, for the apparent decline in the effectiveness of the archdeacon's visitations during the later Middle Ages.[2]

It is for this reason that the change which came over the archdeacon's correction court after 1571 may or may not have indicated a strengthening of discipline, as it is not known how much discipline the rural deans exercised. The change came in September 1572, for on the twenty-fifth of that month no less than fifty-two cases were down for hearing, instead of the six or seven that had been usual earlier that year. Presentments increased until in 1579 there were fifty-four from the Retford Deanery alone at the Easter visitation. The effect must have been gradually to extinguish the rural dean's jurisdiction in disciplinary matters.

During the period of the extension of the court's activity, Lowth personally acted as judge. He moved the court sessions from Nottingham to Mansfield, which was close to Hardwick Hall where he was living. About 1575 he left Hardwick for Gotham, and the sessions were held at Newark nearby. In this year a diocesan visitation was held, and at its conclusion Lowth appointed (probably at the archbishop's direction) a legally qualified Official, John Hacker, LL.B., aged at that time about twenty-seven. Hacker only remained for two years before being promoted to be Official of the Archdeacon of Derby, but he parted with Lowth on good terms, and worked as a proctor in the court for the next eighteen years. He was succeeded by another young man, Zachary Babington, M.A., twenty-eight years old, a

[1] A1, 11 May 1566, the Vicar of Arnold ordered to answer a presentment against him at the last archdeacon's visitation; 11 May 1574, the Rural Dean of Retford was still holding a correction court.

[2] A. H. Thompson, *The English Clergy*, pp. 61 f.

member of a family which had extensive connections in Leicestershire and Nottinghamshire. It will be as well at this stage to consider the functions and importance of the Official of Nottingham.

The Official had the full powers of the archdeacon, which in Nottingham included the control of the administration of the archdeaconry as it was exercised through the granting of licences and faculties, of the discipline of clergy and laity, and sat as judge in the consistory court. He was subject to the directions of the archbishop (or his chancellor) and of the archdeacon himself. Medieval archdeacons had been notable absentees, and this was as much a practice in Elizabethan days as it had been previously; Lowth was an exception to this rule. If an archdeacon lived in his archdeaconry, his Official had little discretion over administrative matters if his master wished to issue directions on a day-to-day basis himself. The standing of the Official within the legal profession can best be gauged by its financial rewards. As the office existed in 1565, with only a small amount of disciplinary business, the income from fees must have been very modest, so that it was only a part-time occupation. The routine work would have been done by the registrar, and Cressy need not have attended at Nottingham more than once a week or once a fortnight to attend court and make decisions on matters referred to him by the registrar.

When the court work increased, the income and expenses must have increased with it. It is possible to make a rough estimate of the value of the office towards the end of Lowth's archidiaconate. Two non-professional witnesses estimated respectively that over a period of thirty months a claimant for the post had lost £80 and 100 marks, while Hacker and the registrar both testified that the sum was £40.[1] Unfortunately, the position was complicated by the fact that for nine months there had been a diocesan visitation, which would have eliminated all fees from correction courts, and during the whole period the claimant was himself receiving the fees for the Retford Deanery. Allowing for these factors, as accurately as possible, it seems unlikely that the total emoluments of the Official exceeded £23 per annum. Such a stipend was receivable by the headmaster of a country grammar school, and was reasonable for a country clergyman, and may be equated with about £1,100 per annum today. The office, therefore, was worth possessing, but compared with the rewards obtainable in the legal profession, or in the upper circles of the clergy, it was a very minor post. Such reasoning is confirmed by the comparative youth of both Hacker and Babington: both used the office as a stepping-stone to higher things, in the case of Babington to the chancellorship of the diocese of Coventry and Lichfield after four years at Nottingham.

[1] Public Record Office, Chancery Proceedings, Petty *v.* Booth (C.21. P39/5).

The exact status of Hacker in society is difficult to determine. He was apparently a clergyman, for there was no complaint over his excommunications, as there was over those of his lay successor, and after his resignation he was for some years Rural Dean of Newark. In 1588 he described himself as a gentleman living at Kirkby Woodhouse, Nottinghamshire (when witnessing in the case just mentioned) and gave his opinion that one party was unfit to be an Official because he was a layman. Yet Hacker himself apparently was unbeneficed. It is likely that Babington was the first Official who devoted the major part of his time to his duties in this office, and it may have been because of his efficiency that he aroused an opposition which took exception to the fact that he pronounced excommunications himself.[1] In the first year of his office he held correction courts at Nottingham, Mansfield, Retford and Newark, thus establishing a precedent which later became standard practice.

The incentive to go on circuit may have been derived from a combination of influences. First, the fact that the rural deans had been in the habit of holding local courts. There would be local objections to poor offenders having to travel further than the distance to which they had been accustomed. Secondly, the combined facts that the court officers were not bound to attend frequent sessions of other courts—which gave them time for regular circuits—and that they were more dependent on church court fees for their income, prompted them to suit the convenience of those who had to attend. Thirdly, the knowledge that frequent circuits were becoming standard practice elsewhere in the country. It will be shown below that the frequency of the circuits varied from time to time, that the court could never make up its mind whether Mansfield deserved a court or not, and that sessions at Newark gradually declined in frequency. The reason for this variation was that the court had no routine office work, such as probate business, which made regular visits otherwise necessary. Nevertheless, it seems that the probate business transacted by rural deans at Nottingham passed through the registrar's office, for there remains a document of 1595–6 recording the probates and administrations granted by the rural deans of Nottingham and Bingham, written in the hand of the registrar's clerk.[2] There is thus a possibility that it was customary in Nottinghamshire for the registrar to attend the rural deans when they did their business.[3]

Babington married Lowth's daughter, Thomasin, and the fact that both he and Hacker remained on good terms with the archdeacon shows that the

[1] Above, p. 64, and (York) R.VII.P.1, p. 721.   [2] LB219.
[3] There is some confirmation of this idea in the eighteenth-century archdeaconry records which contain accounts of all four rural deans (AC 85), and in a letter from the Official to the archbishop's registrar in 1756 referring to the engrossing of wills in the Nottingham office (AC 100). Registrars' accounts for this business, 1756–72, are in AC 87.

latter was not altogether an unreasonable man. The Official was ordained about 1581 and left for the diocese of Coventry and Lichfield. From that year to the end of his life, Lowth succeeded in reducing the officiality of the archdeaconry into chaos by a succession of grants of its patent, the reason for which it is impossible to determine. The results may be briefly summarized:

(1) Babington was succeeded by a clergyman, Thomas Wethered, Auditor of the Southwell peculiar court. March–November 1561.

(2) Richard Byrdsall, 1581. Otherwise unknown; never appeared in person, but only by Babington acting as his deputy.

(3) Simon Parratt, non-graduate, Rector of Eastleach Martin, diocese of Gloucester, 1583. His father-in-law was James Fermer of Rowthorne, Derbyshire, yeoman.

(4) Thomas Petty. Non-graduate. Living at Hault Hucknall, Derbyshire, in August 1583, when granted the patent. Fermer alleged he was the 'cheef mean' whereby Petty secured the office.

(5) Babington (despite sometimes appearing as deputy for Byrdsall) alleged he had a patent granted in April 1583. Apparently this patent was not valid until he had compounded with Parratt (who had a patent for life).

(6) Remegius Booth, M.A., 1585. At that time he was Fellow of Gonville and Caius College, Cambridge, and involved in the disputes which then racked the College.

(7) Christopher Diggles, LL.B. Rector of Partney, Lincolnshire, 1589 (joint patent with Booth).

During Byrdsall's term of office the courts were usually held by Richard Gymney, a non-graduate (ordained at Chester 1572–3), who was first noted in the court acts in October 1576, but did not become beneficed until 1578. He was evidently attached to Lowth's household, for he wrote 'payd to my mayster viijs. iiijd.' and similar sums,[1] and he received a gratuity and his board and lodging for his work.[2] He reappeared during the following years when emergencies arose and Lowth could not himself sit in court.

The various patents produced a variety of suits, not in the archbishop's Chancery, as Cressy had attempted, but in the royal Chancery. Parratt brought one which came to an inconclusive end and had no practical effect.[3] Babington sued Lowth, Gymney and Petty for maliciously destroying his patent and issuing another to Petty. He either dropped the suit or lost it.[4]

[1] Scattered through A3, especially 1586–7.
[2] A3, 26 April 1583, 'geven to Sir Rychard for his payns ijs 6d'.
[3] A3, 9 Jan. 1587, Parratt produced a royal writ in court and ordered Lowth to desist from hearing causes. Lowth ignored him and nothing more was heard of him. No trace of the case can be found in the Chancery files in the P.R.O.
[4] P.R.O., Chancery Proceedings Series 2, C 3 bundle 204/100.

Petty sued Booth in Chancery for usurping his patent (which he admitted losing). The suit was begun in January 1586, evidence was given in April 1588, and judgment was given in his favour in October 1589.[1] At the time the evidence was given the patent was in the hands of Parratt's lawyer in London, which might suggest that Petty was compounding with the former Official as Babington had failed to do.

It will not be profitable to attempt to sort out this muddled series of events. Only a few considerations need comment. The first is the energy of Petty. As a non-graduate he was ill-equipped to enter the legal and ecclesiastical world. Babington described him as a man 'on the make':

being a person thoughe peradventure of sufficient abilitie by himselfe or friends to bye an office of greater profitte than the said officialshipe, yet a man altogether insufficient to be a judge in causes of such weighte as dailie arise and happen in the course of the said official, being in truthe a person merelie ignorant in the canon and civile lawes, never graduated in any Arte crepte latelie into the ministrie for lack of more sufficient meane, since preferred as it is thought not without some corruption into a poore vicarage, and nowe from thence moved by the rich rewards or promise of rewards to a judiciall seate.

His activities as a judge tend to confirm this impression. Babington, after his initial experiment with sessions in market towns, had abandoned it for weekly or, occasionally, fortnightly courts in Nottingham. His successors maintained frequent courts, and occasionally went out of Nottingham, but it was Petty who fully established the circuit system as a permanent feature of the court's work. Table 17 gives the correction court sessions held after the Easter visitation of 1584.

During the period of his suit with Booth an agreement was made whereby Petty presided at the courts held at Retford, and thereby maintained his interest in its business as well as its efficiency. Petty's temperament was revealed by the fact that it was not until Lowth had personally installed Booth in the judge's seat in court that he ceased to sit there, and he afterwards several times challenged Booth in court.[2] Booth alleged that Petty had been the subject of complaints to Lowth because of alleged bribery 'and other synister dealinges'. One may suppose that Petty's vigour would indeed be the subject of complaint, but the real reason for his dismissal cannot be known. Petty had satisfied the archbishop's examiners and received a preacher's licence; he also acted for some time as permanent deputy to the absentee Official in the seventeenth century, and held correction courts for Archbishop Matthew in 1607. Archbishop Hutton appointed him to a

[1] P.R.O., Chancery Proceedings, P2/23; C 21. P 39/5.
[2] See Petty's bill of complaint in Petty *v.* Booth.

TABLE 17

Correction court sessions held after Easter Visitation of 1584

Nottingham	Retford	Newark	Mansfield
10 May	11 May	25 May	30 April
23 May	29 May	17 June	30 or 31 May (date missing)
1 June	15 June	8 July	16 July
20 June	6 July	22 July	23 July
4 July	20 July	12 August	30 July
18 July	3 August	2 September	3 September
5 September	15 August	16 September	10 September
19 September	29 August	30 September	17 September
3 October	12 September	14 October	1 October
13 October	26 September	4 November	10 December
31 October	10 October	18 November	
14 November	2 November	2 December	
28 November	16 November	16 December	
	26 November		
	12 December		
	23 December		

prebend at Southwell in 1603. It is unlikely, therefore, that however he obtained the office, he was altogether unworthy of it, but was an example of a poor man making the most of his opportunities in a minor appointment.

Booth was not a good choice to replace Petty. Lowth and Gymney did his work until he resigned his fellowship and came to Nottingham. A year was enough to prove that Lowth had made a mistake, and complaint was made of bribery to a Judge of Assize at Nottingham. Hacker himself testified to paying money to Booth over and above the ordinary fees, and the registrar acknowledged that complaints had been made to him about money exacted by the Official.[1] It may have been due to these complaints that Lowth was forced to dismiss him, and appoint a legally qualified clergyman, Christopher Diggles. By the device of a joint patent to Booth and Diggles, Lowth evidently hoped to avoid another legal action. Diggles was probably officially recommended to Lowth because he was also entrusted with the diocesan visitation of 1590; he carried on until a new Official was appointed in 1591.

Lowth and his succession of Officials had achieved the establishment of the

[1] Evidence in Petty *v.* Booth. Besides his troubles at Cambridge, Booth was in debt throughout his life, see Chancery Proceedings 1596–1616, bundle 260/4. For debts due to the registrar see A3, 19 Feb., 14 March 1588. He and his brother were presented for not attending Holy Communion: he was dismissed when Lowth remembered seeing him receive it one Holy Day (A3, 6 June 1589).

centralization of discipline in the archdeacon's court, the establishment of the Elizabethan Church settlement, a system of frequent courts in the leading market towns of the archdeaconry and, one suspects, a lack of public esteem for the court itself. The credit for the constructive work achieved by Lowth's administration must in some measure go to the registrars. The first vacancy in this office after Lowth's appointment was filled by a relative, Thomas Lowth. He was either too young or too incompetent.[1] The extension of the court's activities took place under William Newman (1569–*c*. 1574) and John Martiall (*c*. 1575–6). Lowth dismissed the latter to make way for another relative, Humphrey, to whom must go the credit for maintaining the court in working order during the decade after 1580 when there was chaos in the officiality. Martiall appealed against his dismissal to the Consistory Court, but a settlement was apparently reached whereby he was given a place in the office of the principal registrar at York.[2] When he returned to his native county in 1589 to become registrar of the Southwell peculiar, he must have been the most experienced church lawyer in the district. He became deputy registrar of the archdeaconry in 1591.

Lowth was succeeded as archdeacon by John King, a Buckinghamshire man, and a graduate of Oxford. He appointed Miles Leigh, B.C.L., as his Official; Leigh being probably the son of the man of the same name who was registrar of the archdeaconries of Oxford and Berkshire.[3] Leigh had entered Oxford in 1558 as an undergraduate, so by 1591 he was a man in middle-age, very different from the young men who had succeeded Cressy. In order to obtain the services of a lawyer of this calibre, much needed as such a man was to restore the court's prestige, it was necessary to resort to pluralism. Leigh lived at Southwell, which suggests that he succeeded Diggles as Auditor of the peculiar court,[4] and he had the perhaps unique distinction for a layman of being a rural dean.[5] This last appointment was evidently made through the influence of King to secure a sufficient income for his Official through the increased amount of fees which he would collect. Leigh retired to Oxford early in 1599 and died in 1601. He left as his deputy Michael Purefey, who succeeded him in December 1600, but perhaps only as a 'place-warmer', for he resigned after less than a year and was succeeded by another Oxford man,

---

[1] He gradually ceased to attend court during 1569, and when he was there the names of one or two additional witnesses were included in the court acts.

[2] Consistory A.B. (York), 7 Feb. 1577. His distinctive handwriting first appeared in the acts of this court in May 1577.

[3] E. C. Brinkworth in *The Archdeacon's Court 1584* (Oxford Record Soc. vol. XXIII, 1942), ix. and P 283, fo. iv.

[4] Diggles is known to be Auditor in 1591 through a reference in (York) R.VII.P.1, p. 969.

[5] LB 218. He was joint rural dean of the Deaneries of Nottingham and Bingham with a clergyman.

Nicholas Langford, M.A.[1] The appointment may indicate that the increased stability in the court had increased the Official's income, for Langford was an absentee and worked through deputies who presumably only received part of the fees. The first deputy was Petty, who was succeeded in 1604 by the returned Purefey.

One observation that may be made about this administration is that it was very local. A village tucked away in the fold of a Pennine valley might well regard the centralized administration at York as being remote from its problems, as indeed it was. But the Officials of Nottingham all lived on the spot, and the circuit system encouraged them to travel around their jurisdiction. This local tradition was continued by Purefey and his successor. Purefey was not the type of ecclesiastical judge usually painted in Puritan propaganda. It is true that he very probably learned his law in York, where his uncle was first counsel and then a legal member of the Council of the North, but that was in the time of the 'Puritan' Lord President, the Earl of Huntingdon, who was his friend. In the year after his uncle's death, Michael Purefey came to Nottingham.[2] He was a member of a Puritan-sympathizing family of landed gentry, and although he took action against the Separatists, mere nonconformity was lightly regarded. He was so established in the life of the city and county that he was elected as a Member of Parliament for Nottingham in 1621, and as a proctor in Convocation in the following Parliament.[3] What other work he did is not known. After his death in 1627, it was necessary to revert to a clerical judge, William Greaves, B.D. His legal knowledge before becoming a judge was probably slight, but he had the advantage of good local connections. His father was alderman and coroner of Nottingham and married the sister of the town clerk. William's brother, Robert, eventually succeeded to the town clerkship. As the town clerks were also clerks of the peace, i.e. registrars of the Borough Sessions, this close link was very useful in dealing with recalcitrant sinners.[4] The local connections of the court were doubtless one of its strongest assets in a world which was becoming more hostile to church courts generally, and enabled it to do things which would have aroused much opposition elsewhere.

Humphrey Lowth was displaced as registrar when Archdeacon Lowth

[1] A Mathew Langford of Oxford is referred to in the Precedent Book (P 283) containing Oxford court forms, now in the Nottingham archdeaconry archives. Nicholas is described as 'of Worcestershire, gentleman'; he was proctor of the University in 1600.

[2] For Humphrey Purefey see R. R. Reid, *Council of the North*, p. 251 n.; J. Nichol, *History of Leicestershire*, IV, 602.

[3] *Nottingham Borough Records*, IV, 373, 375; A 33, 3 Feb. 1624.

[4] Greaves was Rector of Brailsford, Derbyshire, 1607, and Nuthall, Nottinghamshire, 1612. Fellow of Corpus Christi, Cambridge, 1603–13. Died 1646. For the action of Borough Sessions at this time see p. 225.

died, but he was provided with a similar post at Derby.¹ He was succeeded in 1591 by Thomas Wilmot of Bishopthorpe, either Archbishop Piers' legal secretary or one of his staff. The appointment was in the nature of a reward for services, and Wilmot acted through Martiall as his deputy. After Piers' death, Wilmot was followed by Matthew Weeks who lived and worked in the county until 1602.² Nothing more is heard of Weeks after 1602, and he acted by a deputy, John Tibberd.

Tibberd's connection with the court began in 1595 or earlier and lasted until his death in 1639. He was the nephew of Martiall, and presumably was apprenticed to him in the registrar's office.³ This employment was carried on with Weeks, and beginning in December 1599 he gradually assumed responsibility for the work of the court. From 1602 until 1625 he performed all the duties of registrar, although as his prosperity grew he employed clerks to enter the court acts. As a typical country lawyer, it will be worth pausing for a moment to describe what is known about Tibberd.

Shortly before he assumed the duties of deputy registrar, on 23 November 1601, he married Amie Richardson in St Mary's, Nottingham, and set up his first home in Angel Row, being about twenty-eight years old.⁴ When he began to collect the archdeacon's procurations and synodals, he started a rough account book in which he also made a variety of entries on other matters. He was due to collect each year nearly £60 and one wonders if it was with some of this money, paid in some time before it was due to be accounted for, that he took to money-lending.⁵ He noted down the sums he lent from 1610 to 1621, but never mentioned any interest due, and marked off the items as he was repaid. Most of the sums were small, from ten to twenty shillings, on occasion half-a-crown to an apparitor. In 1613, he made three consecutive loans of £5 each; from April to October 1612 he lent £21. What seems humorous to the modern reader are the items where he took a security in pawn, e.g. 'Lent to goodwife Paule uppon one coverlet the collors are red and yellow—vj shillings'; or a more intellectual pawn, 'Lent to Mr Phippes uppon a booke called Greenhams workes until Lammas daie nexte—iij s. 4d.'

---

¹ There is a loose sheet in A3, Dec. 1586, which is concerned with the 1590 visitation of the Archdeaconry of Derby signed by Lowth as registrar.
² His name appears scrawled across the first folio of the Consistory A.B. for 1569, which might indicate a connection with York.
³ A41, 18 Jan. 1621, Tibberd acknowledged a receipt from 'my Cosin Martiall for this Courte'. This Martiall was John junior, a proctor in the court at that date. If he was the elder Martiall's son, then John senior was Tibberd's uncle.
⁴ In evidence in July 1602 he said he was twenty-nine—(York) R.VII.H.124.
⁵ AC 83. Edmundson *c*. Bell (York, R.VII.H.1171) shows that the registrar of the Archdeaconry of Cleveland, who was also the registrar of the Dean and Chapter of York, was an active money-lender. He usually charged the 10 per cent interest allowed at that time (1614).

Mrs Phippes was in difficulties in the same year (1617), when she borrowed twenty-four shillings on security of one pair of 'flaxen' sheets, one holland sheet, one 'diaper towell' and one tablecloth. The loans were for comparatively short periods, even for two weeks, and reflect an age when there was no banking system as we know it. A similar reflection is given in a list of bonds for money lent by persons other than Tibberd in 1612—presumably witnessed or held by him for the interested parties. These bonds are for substantial sums, e.g. £44 lent by Purefey to Edward Copinger of Hexgrave and William Cartwrighte of Edingley, gentlemen, and quite outside the scope of the lawyer's modest dealings.

In these years, 1611–13, we are surprised to discover Tibberd dealing in timber. There are a number of entries showing receipts from sales of timber, his timber yard being at the 'Chapel Bar'. The timber was apparently bought in wholesale, e.g. 'Memorandum that the sixte of June 1612 I paide to Patricke Cope and — Daye for all such wood as I have already boughte and for tenne other trees to be chosen by my brother out of those which are unsolde weavers excepted the sume of Eighte pounds nyne shillings and tenne pence'. It is difficult to know if Tibberd maintained such activities, of which we are only given glimpses for a few years in each account, for the whole of his life. His affairs, and his family, appeared to have grown and prospered. In an inventory of the goods in his house made in 1612, he refers to 'the new chamber', probably one built by him. In the next year he moved house,[1] and entered the 'Expenses at my coming into Bridlesmith gate since the first of September 1613', but it had to be substantially repaired in 1614. From payments made in these years, we learn that his household staff consisted of one manservant and two maidservants. In 1615, John received in cash for six months' service, 5s.; and Marie, 3s.; Anne's payment was not entered. The following year 'Dorothie' agreed to serve him for twelve months for the princely sum (comparatively) of 26s. 8d., but this lady was doubtless 'my Cosin Dorothie Wood' to whom he had lent one piece of gold (a crown) and sold 16 lbs feathers for 5s. 10d. in 1610.

Besides timber interests, the Tibberd household smacks of the farmhouse. In the 1612 inventory are mentioned a milk house and a cheese press, but there are no references to the cost of fodder or cows. For the years 1618–22 there are accounts of his farming of a four-acre and a two-acre field, which was done, as we should say, by an agricultural contractor. The four-acre, in 1619:

Imprimis xvij strikes of seed barley   xlijs. vjd.
For ploughinge, sowinge and dressing of the same four acres   xxs.

[1] 'vulgariter vocat the signe of the Talbot' (A23 (iii) 1 April 1615).

Some of the barley was sold for malting purposes to his wife and (1619–20) to his father. The home-brewing had apparently always been done—as was common at the time—for in the 1612 inventory he listed three hogsheads and five barrels, one new hogshead having been bought during his time at Angel Row for 3s. The agricultural side of Tibberd's life later took a new twist, described in another series of entries: 'The charges that I have binne at in gettinge in my parte of Nottingham and Sneton tithes which I took of Mr Palmer the second daye of August 1620', together with a record of his sales from the tithe barn. These accounts show that he not only had the tithes carted from the fields, but also had the corn winnowed and threshed, so that it was sold to the millers or other buyers ready to be used.

The note of household goods bought 'since comminge into Bridlesmith gate' ends in 1618. There is an entry: 'The charges of my buildinge made uppon the olde stable in anno 1620', which suggests that Tibberd had moved house again and was making suitable alterations; he had certainly moved about this time for he recorded 'The Charges of palinge the garden at my howse in the lowe pavement' in 1627. There is no hint of any subsequent move. His prosperity had apparently reached its summit for in 1625 he resigned from his office as deputy registrar, no longer needing its income. He had also reached the age of fifty-two, and the prospect of riding off to Retford or Newark for court sessions must have lost its appeal. From now onwards, Tibberd's connection with the court was as a proctor. His abstract book of the causes in which he appeared shows that he usually had about twelve in hand at any one time,[1] not very many by the standards of busy courts, but which should have brought in about £20 per annum in fees, a useful supplement to his other income. He also practised in the Southwell peculiar court, but references to this are very few.[2]

We have noted with some surprise the lawyer turned timber merchant and corn-dealer, but the last facet of Tibberd's career is no less unusual. In March 1634, he was ordained deacon by the Bishop of Coventry and Lichfield, and appeared under St Mary's, Nottingham, at all visitations until his death in 1639.[3] The reason for this accession to the ranks of the clergy is clear from a document certifying that in 1637 he had denounced two excommunications in the chapel of Sneinton,[4] evidently he read service there on Sundays and holy days. It would not be inconceivable that, as the tithe-owner, he was responsible for finding a curate to do this duty and it was cheaper to do it himself than to employ someone else. Being only a chapel, it did not need the services of a priest.

[1] A 43.
[2] E.g. A precedent, 11 March 1633/4, in P 285.
[3] CL 166.
[4] E 185.

The account book shows us little of Tibberd's private life. The entry, 'Memorandum that the firste of August 1612 I receaved of Mr Littlefeere for the teachinge of his sonne William for one weeke—xijd', should not be taken as indicating another part-time activity, it is quite exceptional. Yet he did enter various rules of arithmetic, for division, the rule of three and others, which might have been useful to a pedagogue. More interesting are his astrological tables, 'A table to show what Planet ruleth everye houre of the daye which is from the Sunne risinge to Sunne settinge', 'A table showinge what sign the mone is in and shall be for ever and also what parte of manes bodye everye signe dothe governe with the infirmities thereto', and a variety of others.

There is little information about Tibberd's official duties. Besides the accounts of his receipts and payments on behalf of the archdeacon, there are small sums received and payments made for the Rector of St Nicholas, Nottingham, 1612, a few reckonings with an apparitor, and a considerable number of receipts of sums collected by apparitors in response to briefs. The appeals for the French Protestants were well supported, bringing in £27. 7s. Ordinary appeals, for fire-damaged churches, necessitous clergymen and the like, were nearer the £2 total. The apparitors each received a gratuity of half-a-crown for their trouble in collecting the money, but Tibberd's office seems otherwise to have made no deduction for expenses.

Edward Copinger, notary public, acted as actuary at one session of the court in February 1624, but from September of that year until the following June, he was actuary at many sessions, especially those held out of Nottingham. He was apparently acting as Tibberd's deputy, and some of their financial settlements were entered in Tibberd's account book. The break came in June 1625, when Copinger became full-time deputy registrar. One cannot say whether he was the same man who owed money to Purefey, as noted in the bond mentioned above,[1] or a relation, but his untidiness suggests a lack of business sense. From July 1626 to September 1628, the deputy registrar was Hatfield Reckles. The earliest mention of Reckles noticed is in Tibberd's account book, when he witnessed a debt bond in 1612 suggesting that he was then an apprenticed clerk in the registrar's office. He was a local lawyer who had begun to practise as a proctor three years before he took over the registry, and he soon built up a successful practice in the court. His knowledge of church law was sufficient to enable him to become registrar to the Chapter of Southwell in 1631, at the same time as he continued his work as a proctor in the archdeacon's court. The state of the court records during his period as actuary are even worse than in Copinger's time, and can only be described as the by-product of a very busy life. That Purefey felt under some obligation to him, is indicated by the fact that of all the court officials he was the only one to receive a legacy in Purefey's will (£5).

It is unlikely that Reckles ever intended to do the work permanently, and one of the unknown features of the situation is the reason for the inability of any local lawyer to continue the tradition of Tibberd and Martiall. If Reckles was prepared to act for the Southwell Chapter as their registrar, to the extent of burgling the records from his predecessor's house,[1] why was he not prepared to undertake the more profitable post? One can only suppose that court duties in different parts of the county did not appeal to him on the terms offered. All this time there is no mention of the registrar himself—it may have been that through some physical handicap he was unable to act. It is most likely that his occupation of the office ended in September 1628 when Edward Farmerie took over from Reckles. Farmerie's acts were kept in the manner of visitation acts elsewhere, and not in the way usual at Nottingham. It may well be that he was a lawyer sent by the new registrar to perform the duties until a suitable permanent deputy was provided.

The new registrar was Carr Coventry—'of London' we learn from the registration of his patent with the Dean and Chapter—but as he did not bother to register it until 1630, it is impossible to be sure when he was appointed. Farmerie was succeeded by John Coombe in the spring of 1629, Coventry making a short visit in September–October of that year. It is worth noting that Coventry had a local connection in the person of his nephew Thomas Benson, Rector of Carlton-in-Lindrick, Prebendary of York and Southwell and chaplain to the archbishop.[2] Coombe's appointment was a success. He was an efficient actuary and administrator, and was promoted to be registrar himself in 1638, living long enough to revive the court and ecclesiastical administration after the Civil War.

The feature of the court's history from the death of Lowth to that of Purefey was the gradual association of a group of clergymen with its work. The canons of 1585 required, and those of 1597 re-enacted, that a clergyman should be associated with a lay ecclesiastical judge in matters of excommunication for contumacy, and should pronounce such a sentence at the order of the judge.[3] Booth, probably learning from Babington's troubles, appears to have had a clerical assistant, Henry Collinson, for he is often mentioned in the acts. Miles Leigh, the next lay Official, acted in accordance with the canons, and from his first court, 21 July 1591, he used a clergyman to read

[1] Chancery A.B., 22 June 1632.
[2] See letter from Benson to Coventry, quoted below, p. 184.
[3] Cardwell, *Synodalia*, I, 144, 155, and above, p. 64.

and sign sentences of excommunication and to pronounce absolutions. At first any clergyman who happened to be present was used for the task, but increasingly the work devolved upon a few regular attenders. For instance, Richard Gymney, Lowth's associate, was often used, but after a time his place was taken by Charles Aynsworth, Rector of Bulwell, near Nottingham, and jointly Rural Dean with Leigh of Nottingham and Bingham. After 1614 Robert Malham, Rector of St Nicholas, Nottingham, shared the work of that court with Aynsworth. At Retford, Stephen Coe, Rector of Ordsall, George Turvin, Rector of East Retford, and Thomas Bishop, Rector of West Retford, were the most usual clerical assistants. At Newark, Gymney usually attended court.

When the practice first began, a note was often made in the act of the case recording who had pronounced the excommunication or absolution, but from about 1615 onwards the clergymen concerned had become so familiar with court procedure that they were elevated to the bench itself, and their names were entered with Purefey's in the heading to the acts of each session. It must have been left to the clergymen themselves to decide who should attend any particular session, as the scribe who prepared the act book used to leave a blank space after Purefey's name in which the name of the assistant could be inserted on the day. Occasionally two clergymen would attend and both would sit with Purefey. The assistants, or course, had to attend consistory as well as correction courts, and when they began to sit with Purefey in the latter they also took their place on the bench in consistory courts. It would appear, however, that Purefey did not entirely rely on their legal ability, for, during his only lengthy period of absence—to attend Parliament in 1621— he provided as a substitute a surrogate who had rarely attended court before. This man, Francis Withington, Rector of West Bridgford, sat with Purefey's assistants in the usual way, although they were not essential to the work of the court when a clergyman presided.[1] It may have been thought to have added to the impressiveness of the court to have more than one man on the bench, and to make it look more like justices at Quarter Sessions, but the practical effect was to bring it closer to the Puritan ideal. The arrangement ended with the death of Purefey, for Greaves needed and used no clerical associates. He occasionally had the assistance of Bishop as a substitute for himself at Retford, but generally he acted in person.

[1] The sums paid for his expenses and his dinner were entered in Tibberd's account book.

THE JURISDICTION OF THE ARCHDEACON

Having now discussed the personal side of the archdeacon's administration, we must next examine their powers which it exercised. The archdeaconry comprised the whole of the county of Nottingham less thirty-six parishes, most of which were in the Southwell peculiar, and plus one parish and parts of two others in Yorkshire. Within these limits the consistory court of the archdeacon had concurrent jurisdiction with the archbishop's consistory court at York. In addition the Official issued all manner of ecclesiastical licences and also sequestrations to benefices.

The earliest record of the issue of a sequestration at Nottingham so far discovered was one by Cressy in 1560,[1] granted in his own name, and we may presume that he was issuing marriage licences at the same time. The peaceful exercise of these rights by the archdeacon was challenged by Archbishop Grindal in 1572 during the course of his quarrel with Lowth. This quarrel involved a prosecution of Lowth in the Chancery Court at York for issuing sequestrations and marriage licences without authority; he maintained that the right pertained to his office and was given time to prove it.[2] No further reference was made in the Chancery acts to the case, although a subsequent order of the High Commissioners that he should hand over 'his book of acts' suggests that watch was still being kept on his activities.

Lowth's happier relationship with Archbishop Sandys is illustrated by an agreement with the authorities at York which largely conceded his position. He was given power to grant sequestrations and marriage licences, on condition that he returned an appropriate record of them to the diocesan registry.[3] The Chancellor of York, however, refused to recognize the inherent right of the archdeacon, and gave his commission only during pleasure, and then direct to the Official. The exact terms under which this commission was given were not recorded, and the only information on the subject comes from after the Civil War. Correspondence between the registrar and Official in 1666 reveals that the court had gained the exclusive right to issue licences in the archdeaconry in return for a fixed sum paid to York as a composition.[4] The terms of the composition were set down by Archdeacon Marsden in 1727:

(1) The chancellor can grant licences in the Archdeaconry of Nottingham, as the Official also can.

(2) But for £10 paid yearly by the Official to the chancellor, and £10 by the register, he agrees that the licences in the Archdeaconry of Nottingham be granted only by the Official of Nottingham.

---

[1] (York) R.VII.P.1, p. 87.   [2] York, Chancery A.B., 1 Feb. 1571/2.
[3] York, Register, vol. 31, fo. 51.   [4] MISC.254, Coombe to Lake, 3 April.

(3) In the year when the archbishop visits, the archdeacon is inhibited for several (maybe six) months, the Official and register use (*sic*) to pay the Chancellor £15 apiece.

(4) This composition appears to be time out of mind.[1]

It is most probable that the terms here stated were agreed in Elizabethan times, following the disputes between Lowth and the authorities in York. John Martiall, when he was deputy registrar 1590–6, was careful to enter in his acts of the court all the sequestrations and licences granted,[2] and these entries clearly show that these documents were issued in the archdeacon's name. The patent granted to Diggles as Official in 1590 by Archdeacon King,[3] the archbishop's former chaplain, contained power to grant sequestrations and licences, thus demonstrating that it was not only Lowth who believed he had this inherent right.

If, however, the chancellor surrendered completely his right to issue sequestrations, it is hard to understand why he issued one to James Piercy in 1624. He obtained a sequestration to North Collingham from the chancellor in 1624, but on arrival found an archdeacon's sequestrator in possession. He adopted various ruses to gain admittance to the pulpit, which caused him to be cited to the archdeacon's court. When he did not attend he was excommunicated,[4] and his claim to the sequestration was ignored on his subsequent appearance, order being given for his signification to the secular power for his contempt in remaining excommunicate. He threatened to appeal to York but there is no record that he ever did so.[5] The calm manner with which the Nottingham court simply ignored Piercy's claim probably implies that whatever the right of the chancellor, in practice he would not issue a sequestration in normal circumstances, and without informing the Official.

In the eighteenth century there is plenty of evidence to show that the Official issued the full range of ecclesiastical licences—curate's, schoolmaster's and parish clerk's.[6] Evidence for the pre-Commonwealth period is much more scanty, but occasional references indicate that they were also issued then, and demonstrates the long-established nature of the custom or the

[1] Archdeacon Marsden's Pocket Books, v, 17. This MS. is in the possession of Mr K. S. S. Train, Secretary of The Thoroton Society of Nottinghamshire, to whom I am indebted for allowing me to consult it.

[2] E.g. A6, pp. 698–9.   [3] A6, 14 Oct. 1590.

[4] A 41, 25 June, 8 and 22 July.

[5] PB 326 contains presentments describing his activities; the upshot was that Piercy and two supporters were each fined 10s. at Quarter Sessions for disturbances in church. (H. H. Copnall, *Nottinghamshire County Records*, p. 33.)

[6] Fees for these licences are entered in the accounts, e.g. AC 86 and 100. Licences issued to parish clerks and schoolmasters were entered in A 80 and 82, covering the latter half of the century. The fee for the licensing of curates was in the normal table of fees—e.g. that for 1728 in the uncalendared MSS.

right.[1] One necessity before the Civil War, particularly in the reign of Elizabeth, was the licensing of lay readers, and this was also undertaken by the Official.[2]

The special position of the court at Nottingham was recognized in another way. The diocesan officials always closely scrutinized the commutation of any penance for a money payment by a lower court. In 1575 the registrars of the Yorkshire archdeaconries were summoned before the chancellor and given orders that they were not to commute penances without authorization by the archbishop or himself.[3] No such episcopal control was exercised over the Nottingham archdeaconry, although it is unlikely that the Official was allowed to grant commutations at his discretion. The court acts under 18 February 1592 recorded that the archdeacon had given his permission to his Official to allow six commutations, which shows that, at least at this period, these grants were fully investigated.[4] It is for this reason that 'there is no instance of money offered for commutation of penance being refused'.[5] Arrangements had to be made out-of-court, the scale of payment fixed, and necessary permission obtained, before the offender offered his money in court. It was because of the labour and the expense of making these arrangements that court officers were sometimes allowed a share of the payment.[6] It was a condition of commutation that the fact of the guilt of the offender and the commutation should be published publicly in church, though this may sometimes have been omitted in practice. In the latter event, the many critics of the practice had some justification for their complaints. In 1591 the congregation at Newark was dissatisfied with the punishment of a fornicatrix, and the judge ordered that the court's order should be published on each of the succeeding two Sundays in Newark church,[7] evidently to make good a previous neglect.

Despite control from above, the Nottingham court in Elizabethan times made fairly frequent use of commutation, but this must be seen in the context of the much greater use which it made of monetary penalties than

---

[1] On one occasion the Official confirmed the election of a parish clerk and admitted him to office (A 7, 13 June 1592). Nicholas Oldham was admitted to the curacy of Nuthall (A 6, 7 Oct. 1591); John Noble to that of East Retford in 1643 (Misc. 281). Fees for licensing to a cure of souls are included in a list of the time of Mottershed (York, R.VII.P.O.30).

[2] A 6, 11 Nov. 1590, 1 March 1590/1, etc. These licences were strictly *tolerations* to read divine service, catechize and bury the dead, but cost the same as a curate's licence, 2s. 8d.

[3] York, Chancery A.B., 12 Nov.
[4] A 6.

[5] C. Hill, *Society and Puritanism in Pre-Revolutionary England*, pp. 364–5.

[6] E.g. the penances of Richard Sherborne, Esq. and Eleanor Gregson were commuted in 1623 for £150. (York, R.VI.A.20, fo. 75 v.) Of this sum Dodsworth and the High Commission's pursuivant each received £10, other court officers £3, and the remainder was given to charitable purposes, of which £30 was spent in Sherborne's own parish.

[7] A 6, 1 June.

seems common elsewhere at the time.[1] A full investigation of commutations has not been undertaken, but the court did not confine them to the rich. For instance, after the chancellor had ordered a public declaration of an offence (fighting in church) at the visitation of 1596, the Official commuted it to a payment of 6s. 8d.[2] An unbeneficed clergyman who admitted adultery escaped with a payment of £3.[3] The sums collected by the court were expended on a variety of subjects, some of which were noted in the court acts. Table 18, which is not exhaustive, gives some indication of how the money was spent.

TABLE 18

Payments from commutations

		£	s.	d.
1592	Paving Bar Lane at Southwell	5	19	10
	Paving at Retford	3	0	0
	Paving at Retford (Market Place)	5	0	0
	Paving at Nottingham (Free Lane)	13	6	4
	To poor scholars at Oxford (*via* the Archdeacon)	6	0	0
	Half cost of repairing organ, Southwell Minster	2	0	0
	Repairs of Orston Church	4	10	0
1593	Paving Bar Lane at Southwell	10	0	0
	To a poor clergyman	1	0	0
	To the poor of Nottingham in time of plague	3	6	8
	Special grant to apparitor		6	8
	Special grant to Martiall		8	8
	To a poor sick man		2	6
	Costs of defence of action in Star Chamber against the Official and other court officers	10	6	8
1594	To the poor of Nottingham in time of plague	3	6	8
	Paving streets in Newark	3	6	8
1595	Repairs and improvements to Southwell Grammar School	4	14	3
1602	20 buckets in St Mary's, Nottingham, for fire-fighting	not stated		
1604	'Pious uses' in St Mary's parish	1	0	0

These entries gradually became less, probably because Weeks and Tibberd did not register administrative acts so thoroughly as their predecessor

[1] E.g. A 3, 13 Oct. 1578, £2 to the poor for usury; 7 March 1579, 3s. 4d. for harbouring an adultress, 2s. for not presenting her; 3 Nov. 1579, 6d. each, three men for mocking the catechism; 22 Feb. 1583, Rector of Winthorpe, 10s. for performing an illegal marriage. There are many other instances. The court undertook the enforcement of quarterly sermons by fining the incumbents an amount equivalent to what the omitted sermons would have cost in fees to the preacher. All fines were given to the poor. [2] A 11, 7 May 1597.
[3] A 7, 19 June 1592. Similar conclusions can be drawn from E. R. C. Brinkworth's *The Laudian Church in Buckinghamshire* in the *University of Birmingham Historical Journal*, v, 1 (1955), 35-7. Commutations in the Buckingham Archdeaconry Court varied from £25 to £3, in one case to a man described as a 'yeoman'. There were also small payments of 3s. 4d. and 2s. The system of commutation included the middle as well as the upper classes.

Martiall, and also because pecuniary penalties declined generally in the court and fewer commutations were granted though the practice never entirely died out.[1]

The troubles of the court, and particularly in this matter of commutation, may be read in the Star Chamber case, the bills of which are mentioned in Table 18. Robert Smyth of Laxton was cited to the archdeacon's court in 1591 for suspicion of incontinency with a woman who named him as the father of her child. He did not attend two sessions and was excommunicated. He was summoned before two justices and a bastardy order was made against him, and he was fined one mark for the use of the poor. Peter Roos, one of the Justices, was his master, evidently his landlord for Smyth is described as a yeoman. He approached Martiall, the deputy registrar, about a commutation, saying that he had the support of Roos. Later, Roos himself approached Martiall. It is clear that Leigh and Martiall were in a dilemma. Leigh had only very recently become Official, and both men knew the reputation which the court had latterly attached to itself in the days of Lowth. Martiall told Smyth that he would have to have the permission of the archdeacon who 'was scrupulous and not running the corrupt course that others did before him'. The pressure of local society, however, must have borne hard on a single, unimportant judge like Leigh. He had to work with it because its influence could be useful to his court, so he replied to Roos that if Smyth would go through the necessary formalities—absolution, sentence of penance, plea for commutation—then Roos' request would be granted, and Roos himself could fix the sum which Smyth should pay. Smyth duly appeared and was absolved (and paid 4s. 10d. fees, to judge 2s., to registrar 1s. 10d., to apparitor 1s.), but brought no note from Roos. Leigh therefore continued the cause *in statu quo* for five months until he gave up hope of hearing from Roos, and as Smyth did not appear again he was eventually excommunicated once more.[2]

The second excommunication was never returned to court with the denunciation in Laxton church duly certified. Leigh in evidence expressed the opinion that it had been retained by Roos or under his orders, an opinion which was probably based on fact as it was the apparitor's job to keep a check on these matters. One may presume that Roos was behind the Star

---

[1] This seems to have been the practice throughout the country. In the 1633 Visitation of the Norwich diocese only four commutations in cases of sexual immorality are recorded in the very full acts.

[2] P.R.O. Star Chamber, 5/S63/17. No judgment in the case is preserved. The fact that the court had to pay costs does not prove that Smyth won. Evidence was taken on commission at Southwell, and Smyth may not have had the means to pay the heavy costs of the case if he had lost. Certainly, the case did not alter the practice of the court in any way. A 6, p. 731, contains the registrar's note recording the archdeacon's consent to the commutation of Smyth.

Chamber case, and that it was brought because he intended to show Leigh that he could not treat one of his dependants in that way. It is true that Smyth claimed that he had been approached (he did not say by whom or where) to commute his penance, but his evidence is vague compared with that of Leigh and Martiall. Smyth also made vague and general accusations of corruption against the court officers,[1] including misappropriation of commutations. In the event, he was two or three years too late to establish his point. There are no detailed accounts of commutation income, so it is impossible to prove that none of it went astray, but Martiall's act books give the impression of one who was trying to keep a full and honest record of payments out of this money.

Smyth admitted in evidence that the sum of £5 to £10 had been discussed as appropriate for his commutation. This being so, Leigh and Martiall were probably correct when they alleged that it was with the connivance of a friend that Roos had let Smyth escape with a fine of 13s. 4d. when the latter came before them in their capacity as Justices of the Peace. It was by no means only the church courts that were open to improper influence.

In an age when a man's credit and reputation were regarded as being of the utmost importance, and when the hierarchical nature of society gave added value to these attributes, the humiliation of a public penance was a much greater punishment the higher one went up the social scale. It was for this reason that the practice of commutation provided a safety valve enabling the church system of discipline to operate in a society where it was practically impossible for a member of the gentry and nobility to sacrifice his prestige by performing public penance. The restriction of commutation, which occurred from about the turn of the century, came at about the same time as increasing numbers were claiming the status of gentry (which included using their influence on behalf of hangers-on). Men like Roos only tolerated church discipline because it had the power of the government behind it. They were the first to rejoice when they could do without it, and take all discipline into their own hands as justices.

THE CORRECTION COURT

The Elizabethan Officials followed contemporary progressive administrations and developed the circuit system. Taken together with an efficient method of gathering presentments at frequent intervals, their organization was far ahead of secular attempts to punish and correct criminals. At this time the

[1] Including Gymney, who had pronounced the second excommunication, for abuses with probate fees in his capacity as rural dean of Newark.

Justices of the Peace were not able to try offenders at Petty Sessions, and the methods used at Quarter Sessions were so cumbersome that a period of seven to ten months normally elapsed between the detection of the crime and its punishment.[1] The church court procedure in Nottinghamshire ensured that this period was no longer than four months, and instances will be given where almost instant action was taken. As in all church court matters the limiting factor was not the organization employed but the fact that the ultimate sanction in most cases remained excommunication.

Sufficient stress has previously been laid on the interaction of the different branches of ecclesiastical administration, suggesting that the developed circuit system needed a greater volume of business than that provided merely by correction work. The Commissary of the Norwich Archdeaconry made a monthly circuit of his jurisdiction, and in 1625–6 he only had about twenty-five civil causes before him at any one time. It is clear that in the County of Norfolk most of the consistory work went directly to the bishop's court. The commissaries, however, had a considerable volume of probate administration to sustain them. The Commissary of the Sudbury Archdeaconry was particularly fortunate because he had a large consistory business in addition to his other activities. The number of parishes in the Sudbury Archdeaconry was only one-third greater than that in the Archdeaconry of Nottingham, yet it attracted twice the number of consistory causes. The Sudbury court was particularly bad in securing obedience to its orders, and its disciplinary work seems to have suffered also in its level of detection. The 1633 presentments for Sudbury were only about the same as those in the Nottingham Archdeaconry in 1636, despite the larger size of the former. It might also be that the greater reliance of the Nottingham court on criminal work induced them to have a more efficient system of detection. As the Nottingham court had no probate work and only a moderate amount of consistory work to sustain it, its financial basis must be sought in its revenue from licences and sequestrations. It is for this reason that Grindal's attack on this source of revenue was of vital importance to Archdeacon Lowth. If Grindal had been successful Lowth's administration (still subsisting on the old scale of correction court fees) would have been crippled.

The Official received a fixed payment of £4 per annum and his fees.[2] The £4 was evidently in consideration of supervising the Easter visitation, for which the Official received no direct fee from the parishes. The rise of the circuit system prompted a demand for more frequent presentments than once a year. In Elizabethan times it seemed natural to ask for them quarterly,

---

[1] H. H. Copnall, *Nottinghamshire County Records*, pp. 12, 23.
[2] (York) R.VII.G.2172, copy of Parratt's patent of the office.

the same frequency as for the Justices' Sessions.[1] Quarterly presentments have been detected in Nottinghamshire[2] and their production was enforced.[3] Following strong criticisms of such enforcement, Canon CXVI of 1603 allowed compulsion only at an Easter and a Michaelmas visitation. In Nottinghamshire there was no change as a result of the canon until after the diocesan visitation of 1619 (suggesting archiepiscopal direction). A Michaelmas visitation was then established, although the collecting of presentments at other times of the year continued on a voluntary basis. For this visitation the Official was granted a fixed payment of £3. 10s.,[4] and the parishes were charged 1s. each compared with 2s. at Easter.[5]

Archbishop Whitgift's reforms included an attempt to ensure that offenders were properly presented by churchwardens, not merely cited on the information of apparitors. The Norwich court included in the apparitors' oath an affirmation that they would conceal no offence but inform the churchwardens of it so that proper presentment might be made.[6] In other words, apparitors had to continue to act as detectives, but had to work through the proper channels. It may be that there is here the clue to the two different formulae in the Nottingham disciplinary acts. Those presented in the normal way on the presentment bills were entered as 'A.B. of X. presented for...', but Martiall and Tibberd used another form in addition, 'suspected for...', while Coombe called it 'notorious for...' It may be that these were offences which had been detected by apparitors, but about which the churchwardens were sufficiently uncertain to present them as established facts, so the persons concerned were reported as being implicated.

There are, however, certain folios filed with the Retford Deanery presentments for 1625 and 1626 which arouse suspicions.[7] They are unheaded and unsigned but may reliably be assigned to the apparitor, and consist simply of lists of offenders and their alleged crimes. There are the usual ones commencing 'we present A.B. of X. for...', and are obviously the inter-visitation presentments collected by the apparitor which have been noticed flowing into the courts. Other entries begin 'X. There is one A.B. of the same who

[1] E.g. 'for writing every verdict at the generals [*i.e.* at the general visitation at Easter] and quarter courts in the Archdeaconry of Suffolk 2d' (*Registrum Vagum*, I, 75).

[2] By Mr R. G. Riley in his M.A. thesis 'The Ecclesiastical Control of Parochial Life in the Nottingham Archdeaconry 1590–1610, as Illustrated by the Causes of Office'.

[3] E.g. a prosecution of churchwardens on 3 Feb. 1585 for not returning presentments seems to be too long after the Easter visitation to refer to it.

[4] No contemporary record of this payment is extant, but the two payments of £4 and £3. 10s. were being paid in the eighteenth century, and it may be presumed that the second sum was fixed when the Michaelmas visitation was established (AC 85).

[5] The fees are marked in the various Call Lists. The Upton churchwardens' accounts show that the second visitation was also established in the Southwell peculiar in the same year.

[6] *Registrum Vagum*, I, 31, 43.   [7] PB 339.

hath...', and these sometimes specifically state that the churchwardens have not presented the person. Here perhaps are the 'notorious' offences of the act books, and it is more than likely that such folios were once more numerous, but not being official documents were not normally filed like the official presentments.[1]

A letter from Robert Baguley, the apparitor of the Newark Deanery, to Coombe in 1636 shows the method of detection working rather differently. Instead of returning a list of offences in the way done in the Retford case, and citations to court being prepared from it, Baguley asked that citations be sent direct to him,

...if there be any more courts after this I would have you to put in Rowland Bilbie of the parish of Kellam and leave a blank for the woman for fornication and Richard Robinson and Priscilley his wife of Farndon and Henry Heptinstall and Alice Johnson of Newark into the process upon a fame of fornication.[2]

It can hardly be doubted from the form in which the request was made that these offences were discovered by Baguley's own activity. One of the sources of the apparitor's information was most probably the clergy themselves. The following letter found its way into the presentment bill file,[3] although it was addressed to an apparitor, many others doubtless never being filed:

To his very Frend (*sic*) Thomas Dennyson Apparitor at East Retford geve these. Thomas Dennyson: I would as you have desired me, to cyte Dvyd Rychardson and Elyzabeth Lilyman, both single persons that have lyved longe in Lound incontinently, very offensive and suspitiouslye in Wm. Settles house, and never come at churche, as alsoe Margerye Gyll a common Scolde and a greate Swearer and blasphemer of gods holy name as I heare of more, I wyll certifye you, for their good not of any malyce, and the example of manye, I would have you some holy daye to come to our Church for I cannot make them accompanye me these dayes. thus hartely Farewell.   January 6. 1599.
                                        Your Frend assuredly
                                        James Brewster

Brewster had evidently discussed the first case with the apparitor previously, but, what is more interesting, he evidently thought that the official's presence on a holy day would encourage church attendance. This could only have been true if the apparitor had power to initiate court action in some way.

In Elizabethan times the court used a citation called a *Quorum nomina*, as is evidenced in the suit by Smyth against Leigh.[4] A debased form of this citation was sometimes used (not shown to have existed at Nottingham)

---

[1] The practice of citations on the apparitor's sole motion was forbidden in the visitation of 1578 (R.VI.A.6, fo. 104), and by Canon CXXXVIII of 1603.
[2] PB 328: letter dated 20 Feb. 1636, on the Michaelmas 1635 files.
[3] PB 292.   [4] Above, p. 177.

which enabled the apparitor to add the names of those whom he wished to cite as occasion arose. Smyth alleged that this was what had happened in his case (his was a 'notorious' crime), but it was denied by the registrar and apparitor. These citations were made illegal by Canon CXX of 1603, and after that time all names had to be entered by the registrar before delivery to the apparitor—hence Baguley's letter quoted above.

The court did not only receive information from presentments and its apparitors. Information came into the registrar's office from unofficial sources, and it was one of the duties of apparitors to investigate it. For instance Tibberd, in a note in his act book under 19 November 1608, remembers that he has to tell the apparitor to 'inquire whether Wm. Caute of Bramcote be maried or not and whether the fame is not that he was in bed with her whome he intendeth to marrie'. Occasional jottings relating to persons and offences suggest similar oral information which had to be investigated. It is clear that the court did make an attempt to sift information, and that it had good ground for proceedings before they were taken. Where proceedings were begun by presentment, courts still took care to establish the facts. We have noticed previously that churchwardens attended correction courts[1] and sometimes clergymen or others would represent parishioners or send letters to court. There is an interesting instruction among those given to the registrar of the Archdeaconry of Suffolk in 1664, in which he is ordered to consult with apparitors about those cited on presentment before the court session began.[2] These instructions appear to be a set of 'judge's rules' for the newly re-established court after over two decades of disuse, and presumably represented traditional pre-Civil War practice. Such pieces of evidence suggest that the courts did their best, within the framework of their system, to administer justice to the best of their ability. The evidence also demonstrates the essential place in the system occupied by the apparitor.

The existence of an Official and registrar who were continually concerned with administration, frequent sessions of the court, and apparitors who were both policemen and detectives, enabled a close supervision to be exercised over the archdeaconry and in particular over the churchwardens. This was evident in the troubled days of 1604–8 when Separatism was being evolved out of Puritanism. The churchwardens of the Puritan parish of Babworth admitted that they lacked a surplice and the latest edition of the Book of Common Prayer, but had not presented it.[3] Someone, perhaps an apparitor, took the names of all those from other parishes who attended a sermon by a

[1] Above, p. 136.
[2] East Suffolk Record Office, Ipswich, *Liber Actorum in Causis Officij 1664.*
[3] A 24. 9 Feb. 1604–5.

deprived clergyman at Sturton on Whitsunday 1605—they were in court before the end of the week.[1] A drive against unlicensed preachers undertaken in 1607 seems to have closed the pulpits to Separatists. Churchwardens were sometimes accused of not presenting defects, e.g. those of Car Colston, where an admission was made that the churchyard wall was dilapidated. The unfortunate churchwarden who attended court was then confronted with his presentment bill where no such defect was mentioned, and admonished.[2] The churchwardens of Arnold had a like experience in 1623, involving a surplice, and other instances could be cited.[3]

The administration was very well informed about conditions in the archdeaconry and could easily take action when action was needed. The gaiety of the summer Sundays of 1618 was followed by the appearance in the autumn court sessions of morris dancers; in the autumn of 1619 it was the turn of Sunday golfers. A different situation was revealed in 1623, where at the Michaelmas visitation a question was asked concerning those who resorted to the 'Stroaking Boy' of Wysall. As a result a score of persons were presented who admitted the charge. This boy apparently effected cures by stroking. At the same time, Robert Shawe, formerly of Trowell, now of Bramcote, was presented 'for consulting with a wizard'.[4] It must have been felt by many clergy that the situation was out-of-hand, and needed stern action to prevent the powers of the boy becoming too well known and used. What is remarkable, compared with contemporary witch-hunts and the like, is that no action was taken either against the boy himself or his parents.

The fact that churchwardens, once elected, were compelled to serve and could not resign, and the practice in some parishes of appointing these and other parochial officials by rota among the principal parishioners, resulted in some instances of churchwardens who were negligent in their duties. Such negligence might have been derived from a distaste for disturbing their neighbours by rigorous enforcement of the law. Some clergymen likewise preferred to let sleeping dogs lie, but others did their best to keep the churchwardens to their task. For them, the church court was the obvious lever to motivate reluctant churchwardens. Two examples may be given. The first of these comes from a letter written by the Vicar of Orston in 1628 in which he pleaded the case of a parishioner.[5] He went on to ask the registrar's

---

[1] See my *Puritans and the Church Courts*, p. 152.
[2] Although this confrontation was not recorded in other instances, the cases against the churchwardens of Sandby, Clayworth and Walesby at the same time (A 14, 17 Dec. 1605–21 Jan. 1605/6) were probably of a similar nature.
[3] A 33, 26 July 1623 (Arnold); e.g. A 6, 16 Dec. 1590, churchwardens of Headon.
[4] See especially A 33, 8 and 22 Nov., and PB 297 for Oct. and Nov. 1623.
[5] Below, p. 221.

help to have Orston churchyard fenced, so that it could be kept as consecrated ground and not resemble a common. He refused to assess responsibility, but begged the registrar to 'reform this abuse and terrifie, if not punish, the delinquents'. A citation against the churchwardens was immediately issued, and, within ten days of the letter being written, one of them appeared in court. The amount of repairs needed cannot have been great, for a fortnight later the vicar certified that they had been completed. The court was not always obeyed with such alacrity, but there can be no doubt of its general effectiveness.

The second example of clerical initiative came from Thomas Benson, Rector of Carlton-in-Lindrick, uncle of the absentee registrar, Carr Coventry, in a letter written in 1630:[1]

On Whitsonday last wee had a Communion in Carlton Church: Richard Huit our Churchwarden provided wyne, (yf I shall rather call it wyne, than dreggs) when I came to give it to the Communicants, both my conscience and stomac did ryse against it; from one bottle yssued somwhat into the chalice, which I was faine to take out with my knyfe. From another, somewhat lyke a cobbwebbs, From a third cupp, somwhat lyke a hogg-louse, yf not a spyder. I called him before the Clarke and some other in Communion tyme, and showed him his impious abuse of the holy Sacrament, and the parishoners. He hath beene a most crosse felow, all his tyme.

I desyre you to move Mr Official (to whom I wish my respect (*sic*) maye be presented) to call him to answere this at Nottingham, by a proces *ex officio*; or yf you thinke it more fitt, in a cause of instance at my sute, of which cause I entreate you to take care, and the proctor whom you will appoint for me, shall have his fees truly payd. Pray let me hare from you, as sone as may be).[2]

The letter was written on the third of June and the delinquent churchwarden was in court on the sixth of July. The rector's letter was treated as a present-ment to which 'Huit' replied, 'that he did get the bottles clean washed and that he is very sorry that such things happened to be in the wine and sub-mitted himself'.[3] He was ordered to acknowledge his fault before Benson and the other churchwardens on the next Sunday after Morning Prayer and to certify on 27 July. He was evidently not so submissive outside court as inside, but he eventually produced the certificate on 16 September. Benson was one of the 'upper class' clergy, as witnessed by his willingness to pay the bill for an official prosecution, but even his position did not enable him to deal with his 'crosse felow' without the assistance of the court.

Both these examples are taken from the pre-Laudian period in the arch-deaconry's history. The Laudian Church is sometimes credited with initiating a new drive against desecration of consecrated buildings and

[1] PB 340.   [2] PB 340.   [3] A 40.

grounds, and other abuses in church services. It may have dealt more hardly with offenders, and sought to separate the sacred from the secular by expelling the common ploughs and schools from churches, but many of the cases it unearthed were no novelties, they had appeared before in the courts. What the Laudian regime would have done in the Benson case would have been to make the offending bottles unnecessary by ordering the purchase of a canonical flagon, together with a prosecution of Huit for not presenting the lack of one. To this extent the Laudian officials secured a tighter discipline.

A word may be said here about the apparitors themselves. There was the usual allocation of one for each deanery, but that for the Deanery of Nottingham was sometimes called the apparitor-general. They needed to have the quality of probity, and during the whole period under review only one doubtful incident occurred in the records—the sudden abandonment of his post by John Richardson in 1627 after a tenure of only three years.[1] Several had long and presumably honourable terms of office.[2] Their constant employment by the local court on both criminal and consistory work and, presumably, their attendance on rural deans for testamentary matters, must have secured for them a sufficient regular income to reduce considerably any attractions of bribery or corruption.

DIOCESAN VISITATIONS

The diocesan visitations provided unwelcome interruptions to the normal routine of the Nottingham court. The period of inhibition could evidently extend to a whole year, the longest cessation of the correction court was from 10 February 1582 to 8 January 1583[3] and the shortest from the end of May to 9 July 1636. Usually there was at least six months during which the Official was unable to hold his correction court, but after the establishment of a Michaelmas visitation the routine was observed whereby the Visitors held one (usually at Easter) and the Official the other one in the year. The Consistory Court continued to function normally, with the registrar as deputy for the archbishop's registrar. The Official was sometimes deputed to hear causes in the Consistory Court, unless a local person had been appointed to act in both correction and instance causes. This latter arrangement prevailed usually in the seventeenth century. The result was that the Official

---

[1] A 37, 1 Dec.

[2] From references in the acts Thomas Denison functioned 1590–9 (inclusive); Robert Greaves 1612–22 or after; Richard Wightman 1617–28; Robert Baguley 1628–40; George Malin 1606–22 or after. William Crane, apparitor-general during the short time Lowth was Vicar of St Mary's, Nottingham, was parish clerk of the church (York, R.VII.G.1461). Malin described himself in his will (1625) as a yeoman.   [3] A 3.

and registrar lost a considerable percentage of their court fees for at least half
the year, for the composition concerning licences presumably did not extend
to normal court fees. If anything was calculated to induce corruption and
inefficiency, the system of inhibition served the purpose best, for it was
obviously in the interests of the local officials to hold up business until they
could receive the benefit of full fees, and to extort as much as they could in
the full years to last them over the lean. They must have been very disappointed when an archbishop died or was translated soon after having completed a visitation, for they knew that his successor would hold another
shortly—e.g. 1594 and 1596, 1604 and 1607, 1627, 1629 and 1632. The best
time for the court was under Archbishop Piers (one of whose legal staff was
registrar), for the Official and registrar were appointed to act as deputies
during visitations, and the courts continued to function normally (1590,
1594). Chancellor Benet held one session of correction courts at each of three
centres in Nottinghamshire, but left the remainder of the work to the Official,
so there was no interruption in the holding of sessions. Likewise in 1607 the
local clergyman (Petty) appointed as deputy continued the court on circuit
in the normal way, simply replacing Purefey.[1]

The archbishop sometimes attended the visitation in person, as did Sandys
in 1582, when he both preached and gave his charge, and Matthew in 1607
when he preached at both Nottingham and Southwell centres. The chancellor was the principal official deputed to visit, and in Elizabethan days it
was customary for him to be accompanied by canons either of York or
Southwell. The latter were employed to examine clergy and schoolmasters
as to their learning and conformity. The centres which they used were the
normal ones of Retford, Southwell and Nottingham, except in 1590 and 1594
when all were summoned to Southwell on successive days, and in 1582 when
Newark replaced Retford. The object of the visitations was to bring the whole
of the diocese immediately under the eye of the bishop and to ensure that all
was well. Archbishop Young did something to introduce Reformed standards
of furnishings, vestments and liturgy into the churches and to root out clergy
and schoolmasters who would not conform. Archbishop Grindal improved
the discipline and practice of the church by enforcing conformity to his
Injunctions.[2] Archbishops from Piers to Matthew had the same task, each of
whom had his own methods. Harsnett particularly sought to restrain
parishioners from sermon-tasting at churches other than their own. Neile's
aims were of the type denominated 'Laudian'. Offences against their orders

---

[1] The 1590 acts are in A 6, for 1594 in A 8, for 1596 in A 10, for 1607 in A 24. Acts for 1567, 1600,
1619, 1623 and 1636–7 are at York. Other diocesan visitation records 1567–1640 are not extant.
[2] *Remains of Archbishop Grindal* (Parker Society, 1843), pp. 123–44, 154–5.

and routine offences were presented in the normal way and sentenced at correction courts. Only Piers apparently had confidence that the Official would act in such manner as he required, or it may be that the officials at York were always somewhat jealous of a rival court at Nottingham and sought to limit it wherever possible.

The judges of the correction courts, as far as they are known, are shown in Table 19.

TABLE 19

Judges of correction courts at diocesan visitations

1567	The Bishop Suffragan of Nottingham, Chancellor Rokeby, Walter Jones (vicar-general). Courts at York, August–September, with one at Southwell by Jones, 15 September.
1571	The co-chancellors and other clergymen.
1575	Jones, Cressy, two canons of York.
1578	Cressy.
1582 and 1586.	No records.
1590	Diggles. Normal archdeaconry court routine.
1594	Leigh. Normal archdeaconry court routine.
1596	Benet at first sessions. Later actions left to Leigh. Courts at Nottingham, Retford and Southwell, October. Thereafter normal court routine.
1600	John Cooper (Auditor of Southwell Peculiar Court). Courts at Southwell, August; 9 Oct. Southwell (probably Dodsworth).
1604	No records.
1607	Petty. Normal archdeaconry court routine.
1611	No records.
1615	John Brook, D.D., for Dodsworth. Courts at Retford, Nottingham and Southwell, June.
1619	Dodsworth. Three centres, August. Second court at Southwell, 7 Oct. Local courts by Wharton at Nottingham and Feilding at Retford.
1623	Dodsworth. Three centres. Second court at Southwell in October.
1627	No records.
1629	Withington—no records.
1632–3	Withington—no records.
1636	Easdall (second courts by Kemp). Three centres. September–October 1637.

It will be seen that in Dodsworth's time the second courts (to receive certificates of penances, deal with late attenders, etc.) were held at the time of the Michaelmas Synod of the clergy, which Dodsworth presumably attended, and which was a convenient time (for the clergy, at least) to hold a court. Any other business which came in later from offenders presented at the diocesan visitation, was presumably transacted by the local clergyman deputed by the chancellor to act for him, and then the record sent to York. Considerably more inconvenience must have attended presentment at a diocesan visitation than at an archdeacon's, where the court circuits were handier for the offender.

The system whereby the archbishops controlled their diocese by bringing the normal courts to a halt each fourth year, and substituting their own, was unwieldy. The mass of common offenders might with advantage have been left to their own local courts. There would not then have been the anomaly whereby the equivalent of a High Court judge took over Petty Sessions from time to time. The explanation lies in the system of fees rather than in any wish on the part of the archbishops to prevent the growth of independent jurisdictions, for the archbishops could in any case have asserted their power by reserving administrative and any other major cases to themselves. The visitations provided a valuable perquisite to chancellor and registrar which more than compensated for the extra work involved. The fact that their fortune was someone else's loss did not worry them. The only local officials who did not suffer from diocesan visitations were the apparitors—they were employed equally by whoever was holding a visitation, and no one took a cut from their fees.

THE NOTTINGHAM CONSISTORY COURT

The existence of a Consistory Court at Nottingham apparently owed its origin to the tradition of an Official resident in the archdeaconry. In the remainder of the diocese there was a centralization of the administrative machinery at York, and, as business had to be brought there, it was naturally taken at once to the diocesan court. The Official and registrar at Nottingham derived a modest income from consistory business, but the advantages which it gave them were not primarily financial. First, their control over the administration of the archdeaconry was greater because they could prosecute by means other than simple summary procedure. The benefits of formal prosecution were not only in the greater expenses to which the offender made himself liable, but also in the court's ability to collect evidence under oath. As complaints by private individuals against clergy, churchwardens and others would be usually made, in the first instance, to the Official, he had a greater degree of control over the discipline of his archdeaconry, and was able to decide whether or not to prosecute, to deliver a simple unofficial warning or to allow a private prosecution. These responsibilities in the remainder of the diocese appear to have devolved upon the chancellor (through his control of the Chancery Court) rather than upon the Officials. The second advantage was that rate-payers could not avoid paying their dues, when presented to the archdeacon, by raising a legal quibble as they did in Yorkshire. The Official could aid the churchwardens to cite such persons quickly into his consistory, while at York the formal procedures and full lists of the consistory made the process much more costly and time-consuming.

Other advantages of having a consistory at Nottingham were to the litigants themselves rather than to the court officials. The need to have local proctors experienced in civil and ecclesiastical law produced a small number of lawyers, resident in or nearby Nottingham, who specialized in the work of the church courts. These men could give all the advice needed in most cases, without having to send the prospective litigant to York to see a proctor there. If litigation ensued, the parties and their witnesses did not have to travel far from home to attend court: it was both cheaper and more convenient to go to Nottingham rather than York, particularly as travelling was so hard for aged, infirm and poor persons.

The Consistory Court at York had concurrent jurisdiction with that at Nottingham and heard appeals from the latter. The York court also had the advantage of more learned and experienced lawyers; consequently important causes were often taken direct to York to reduce the expense of a possible appeal, and to obtain better legal advice from the beginning. Many defamation causes, however, could just as well be heard at Nottingham as they involved no legal complexities, and many of the tithe causes brought there did not concern complicated rights but were rather in the nature of actions for debt. For this reason, an appreciable proportion of causes were settled out of court—e.g. seven in the Michaelmas term 1634, fourteen in the same term 1636. The usefulness of the local court can be gauged by the fact that the local nobility and gentry initiated suits in it, and also by the occasional very full file of papers in a cause which remains in the archives. If a tithe cause was going to involve the collection of much evidence, it was probably as convenient to begin it at Nottingham, as to take it to York and then have to request a local commission to collect the evidence. Provided the local proctors had expert advice in framing the articles on which the cause was based, and in making the interrogatories to witnesses, it could more conveniently, and probably at less expense, be commenced locally. The only exception to this rule was in the case of testamentary business (other than recovery of legacies), which from the beginning of the seventeenth century was normally sent to York.[1]

It was by this convenience, rather than by cut price fees, that the Nottingham court was able to compete with York. The York registry lacks a table of consistory fees of this period, but a table, alleged to date from the time of Henry VIII, was printed in the Ecclesiastical Courts Commission Report, 1832.[2] The scale there given differs little from the Nottingham fees, except

---

[1] Exceptions, heard at Nottingham, included: accounts of an executor (A 41) 29 Oct. 1624; unlawfully acting as executor (A 41) 25 Sept. 1634, (A 46) 6 Nov. 1639. It was a common contemporary practice for many suits to be initiated which were later settled before judgment (W. J. Jones, *The Elizabethan Court of Chancery*, pp. 286, 306).

[2] Pp. 519–20, and see p. 116, no. 25 and p. 119, no. 87.

for the fees to the court actuary. The latter may have been added in the early seventeenth century,[1] and slightly increased the expense of the York consistory. The suitor at Nottingham was also able to economize by not employing an advocate.

It is impossible to compare all the fees in different courts, but a representative selection is given in Table 20.

(1) Archbishop Whitgift's standard fees, 1597, established as a maximum in all courts by Canon CXXXV of 1603.[2] There were slight variations in the fees he allowed in his provincial courts, for instance, a fixed fee for copy of evidence, and a high fee for the sentence, 20s. judge, 6s. 8d. registrar, 1s. apparitor,[3] compared with the usual total of 10s. to 11s. There is another standard table of fees, that supplied as being normal in commissary courts to Charles I's Commission on Fees in 1630.[4] The latter scale of charges did not show any great advance over those of Archbishop Whitgift—citations had increased by 10d., but the judge and registrar were 1s. each lower for a sentence.

(2) The Norwich Consistory Court fees were higher than Whitgift's table for certain items, but on average a suitor would not have had to pay more for any given cause. The fact that Norwich retained its pre-1597 scale shows that Canon CXXXV was not obeyed to the letter, although its spirit was observed because the fees were not subsequently increased.

(3) The Nottingham fees were slightly cheaper than Whitgift's scale.[5]

(4) The High Commission scale was appreciably higher than that of the ordinary courts, and was probably modelled on the High Court or Star Chamber scale.[6]

(5) The vice-admirals' courts were regional secular courts comparable with consistory courts. Their fees were also similar, except that they were more heavily weighted in favour of the judge. The vice-admiral had to employ a lawyer to act for him, so that the judge's fee was on a scale to support two persons.[7]

The impression given is that there was a general level of fees considered applicable to church courts, and within that range there were local variations. The only significant exception was the fee on sentence to the provincial officers of Canterbury, a fee not given to those at York, who had to be content with the usual diocesan scale. There was considerable contemporary criticism of fees, which resulted in Archbishop Whitgift's attempt to fix them, and later in Charles I's Commission. Professor G. E. Aylmer summarizes the

---

[1] Above, p. 58. [2] R.VII.P.O.18. [3] R.VII.P.O.26.
[4] R.VII.P.O.19 [5] R.VII.P.O.30. [6] R.VII.P.O.27.
[7] P.R.O., HCA 50/1, fos. 238–9.

TABLE 20

Comparison of fees for certain items in civil suits

Item	Archbishop Whitgift's Standard Fees			Norwich Consistory Court			Archdeaconry of Nottingham Consistory Court			Canterbury High Commission Court		Vice-Admirals' Courts		
	Judge	Registrar	Apparitor	Judge	Registrar	Apparitor	Judge	Registrar	Apparitor			Judge	Registrar	Marshall
	s. d.	*s. d.*		*s. d.*	*s. d.*		*s. d.*	*s. d.*		*s. d.*		*s. d.*	*s. d.*	
Citation	5	5	2*d.* per mile	4	8	1*s.* and 1*s.* for over 10 miles	3	5	2*d.* and 2*d.* per mile. (1*d.* per mile in summer.)	3 4		2 0	1 0	1*s.* and 2*d.* per mile.
Copy of libel	—	By length	—	—	—[1]	—	—	1 6 or more	—	6 8 (more or less)		—	2 0 or less	—
Examination of a party to a suit	9	9	—	9	9	4*d.*	6	6	—	2 0	Total fees	1 0	6	—
Examination of the first witness	9	9	—	9	9	4*d.*	6	6	—	2 0[4]		1 0	6	—
Examination of other witnesses	4½	4½	—	6	6	—	6	6	—	2 0[4]		6	3	—
Copy of answers of a party	—	By[2] length	—	—	9	—	—	6	—	2 0		—	1 0	—
Copy of answers of a witness	—	By[3] length	—	—	6	—	—	6	—	2 0		—	8	—
Sentence	6 0	6 0	1*s.* 4*d.*	6 8	3 4	6*d.*	6 0	3 0	1*s.* 0*d.*	30 0		6 0	2 0	2*s.* 0*d.*
Proctor's fee for writing libel		5*s.* 0*d.*		3*s.* 4*d.*–6*s.* 8*d.* depending on nature of cause				3*s.*4*d.*		Not given			3*s.* 4*d.*	

[1] No fee given in this diocese. Perhaps libels exchanged by proctors.

[2] In 1631 given as 1*s.*

[3] In 1631 given as 8*d.*

[4] The same fee was charged in the royal Chancery Court (W. J. Jones, *The Elizabethan Court of Chancery*, p. 142 n.).

situation by saying that the civil law courts and the Councils in the North and Wales had a better reputation than the common law courts and the royal Chancery.[1] The Nottingham court had a minimum of overhead expenses and could operate profitably on fees which were only slightly lower than a diocesan consistory.

The consistory court, unlike the correction court, kept legal terms. The number of sessions varied over the years and according to the amount of business. In the heyday of Babington and Petty, when the court was actively attracting business, thirty sessions a year were not uncommon, but in the seventeenth century it settled down to a normal average of twenty. The fortnightly or three-weekly courts seem to compare unfavourably with York, where the Consistory was held twice weekly, but as causes there were normally advanced about one stage in a fortnight, there was little extra delay at Nottingham. We have already noted that the Consistory Court of Norwich had only thirteen sessions in a year, while that at Bury St Edmunds averaged seventeen to eighteen.[2] The Nottingham court was therefore as active as a normal church court. The only feature of the consistory sessions which is unusual is the practice begun by Petty, and continued with less regularity by Purefey and Greaves, of hearing causes at Retford. The judge and the registrar had to travel there for correction courts, and it was convenient to examine the parties and witnesses in causes from the north of the county near their homes. This area was much nearer to York than the south of the county and therefore the advantage of using the local court was less strong unless it worked also in north Nottinghamshire.

The small number of causes heard, compared with diocesan courts, resulted in larger fluctuations of business, particularly within each category of cause. Table 21 gives some indication of the litigation brought before the court. As in other church courts, tithe and defamation causes provided most of the business. In the years reviewed in the Table, tithe causes varied from six to twenty-four in one year, but the number is occasionally exaggerated by a tithe collector commencing several actions at once. So it was that in a year near the top of the list in tithe causes, 1610–11, almost all the eleven causes initiated on 21 June and 5 July were by one plaintiff. At York, these multiple summonses were often bracketed together and counted as one cause. The number of defamation causes varied between twelve and thirty-seven. The Table shows that the fluctuations in these types of causes often balanced each

[1] *The King's Servants* (1961), ch. 4 and especially pp. 244–5.
[2] The information about the court of the Commissary of the Archdeaconry of Sudbury given in this section is derived from an act book of his court which was held at Bury St Edmunds, 9 Jan. 1621 –6 Aug. 1622, now kept with the Norwich Episcopal Records (ACT/52), and one at the West Suffolk Record Office, Bury St Edmunds, (Acc. 909/6) 1634–9.

other, but in a year where there was a high number of both types (e.g. 1610–11) the work of the court was considerable. Table 21 also shows the decline which has been noticed at York during the late 1620s, but the explanation here is probably connected with the difficulties in the registrar's office at that time. The total of twenty-nine causes in the whole year 1627–8 compares with twenty-two in the Michaelmas term alone three years before, when the court was working normally. An indication of the use made of the court for official prosecutions in the Laudian period is clearly shown under the year 1637–8, when there were no less than thirty-seven *ex officio mero* causes. At this time, too, ordinary instance causes had revived in number, fifty-three in 1636 (1 May) to 1637 (30 April), not shown in the Table, and sixty-one in 1637–8. As late as 1639, thirty-nine instance causes were introduced in the Michaelmas term alone. The relatively small number of causes in the court resulted in some types not occurring in any one year. A good example was pew suits which do not figure in the Table at all, yet three such causes have been noted, one promoted by no less a person than the Countess of Devonshire.[1]

Table 22 gives for comparison the details of two years' work of the Sudbury Commissary Court sitting at Bury St Edmunds. The number of parishes in its jurisdiction was one-third more than that of Nottingham, and its population was probably proportionately greater. Yet the number of causes heard was about twice as great, a fact which reflected the comparative lack of attraction of the diocesan court at Norwich for those in West Suffolk. Because of the volume of business the court was able to employ a notable civilian Dr Eden, as judge, and three out of four of its proctors were graduates in law. Its legal standing was therefore similar to a diocesan court, and it enjoyed the further advantage that appeals from it could be made directly to the provincial courts of Canterbury, thus giving it the same status as a diocesan court. The comparison with the Nottingham court is useful because it explains why the latter either had to employ the young or the undistinguished, and why its proctors were usually local lawyers who had not graduated in law.

A list of proctors is given in Appendix IV. The nominal establishment was four, but in practice a smaller number usually secured most of the causes. In mid-Elizabethan times two graduates, Hacker and Charnock, shared most of the work. After them there was no other graduate until Saunders, who was perhaps attracted by the revival of business in the 1630s. Martiall, Tibberd and Reckles, who all were specialists in church law, had good practices, as did

---

[1] A 30, 13 Oct. 1621, Stringer *c.* Burton; A 41, 23 Sept. 1624, Hart *c.* Smyth; A 38, 15 Jan. 1629, Christine, Countess of Devonshire *c.* Osborne *et al.*

TABLE 21

Causes commenced in the Consistory Court at Nottingham

Legal year	Suits between parties. Instance causes												Disciplinary			Grand total
	Tithe	Defamation	Testamentary Not legacy	Testamentary Legacy	Matrimonial	Dilapidations	Churchwardens' and Sequestrators' accounts	Recovery of Proctors' fees	Mortuary	Church rates	Other and not stated	Total instance	Official prosecutions	Private prosecutions	Total disciplinary	
1577-8	13	12	7	—	4	2	1	—	1	—	1	41	—	3	3	44
1587-8	6	17	—	3	5	1	—	—	—	—	—	32	—	1	1	33
1597-8	14	27	4[3]	1	2	—	—	—	—	—	1	49	—	2	2	51
1606-7[1]	6	37	—	3	1	1	—	—	—	—	—	49	1	—	1	50
1608-9	9	25	—	1	1	—	1	—	—	—	—	37	3	1	4	41
1610-11[2]	22	31	—	4	3	—	1	—	—	—	2	62	—	2	2	64
1617-8	15	19	1	1	3	—	—	—	1	—	—	40	1	3	4	44
1627-8	5	16	—	2	—	—	—	2	—	1	1[4]	27	1	1	2	29
1637-8	24	31	—	4	—	—	—	1	—	—	1	61	37	7	44	105

TABLE 22

Causes commenced in the Consistory Court at Bury St Edmunds

Legal year	Suits between parties. Instance causes												Disciplinary			Grand total
	Tithe	Defamation	Testamentary Not legacy	Testamentary Legacy	Matrimonial	Dilapidations	Churchwardens' and Sequestrators' accounts	Recovery of Proctors' fees	Mortuary	Church rates	Other and not stated	Total instance	Official prosecutions	Private prosecutions	Total disciplinary	
1621-2	36	65	7	4	2	—	—	7	—	—	—	121	—	2	2	123
1635-6	24	28	15	6	—	2	1	8	—	—	—	84	4	15	19	103

1 1 Mar.–28 Feb.
2 1 Apr.–31 Mar.
3 One cause by delegation from the Exchequer Court.
4 'Business of justifying a presentment', probably church rates.

Charnock who was probably registrar of the church court at Derby. After Reckles resigned the registrarship in 1628, he shared with Tibberd almost all the causes until Saunders' admission in 1637. These lawyers probably all practised in the Southwell peculiar court, but it is evident that the amount of ecclesiastical business available in the locality really justified only two, or at the most three, lawyers specializing in it.

Besides these leading lawyers, there were a few others who appeared less often. Even before Archdeacon Lowth's death, his general stand-in, Richard Gymney, acted as a proctor, and after the retirement of Hacker and Charnock he developed a medium-sized practice, for a time sharing many of the causes with Brandereth. His practice was taken over *en bloc* by Reckles in 1623— one of the few instances of such a transfer. Under canon law the clergy were not allowed to practise for money, but Gymney certainly took fees, and so the other clergy who practised occasionally may have done the same.

The items for which a proctor was allowed to charge varied between York and Nottingham, so a direct comparison between their level of fees is not possible. The York proctor, at 5s. a term, could earn £1 per annum in a cause. The Nottingham proctor, at 2s. 6d. per court sitting, could earn £2. 10s. per annum in the same way in an average year of twenty sessions, but he could not charge for attending witnesses at examination, being present at informations and other duties which brought his York brother extra fees.

THE LAUDIAN PERIOD

The years immediately before the Civil War witnessed a variety of changes in the administration of the archdeaconry. Some of these produced conditions which were typical of the country generally wherever Laudian bishops were in control. The most significant change in Nottinghamshire itself was in the way in which the detailed administration was brought directly under the control of York. Previous archbishops had issued their instructions which had been obeyed by the Officials as they thought best, but nothing new happened in the archdeaconry after the close of Archbishop Neile's primary visitation in March 1633. Although the deputy Official, Greaves, was ejected from his Derbyshire living by Parliament in 1645 for scandalous life and neglect of cure indicating that he was not a Puritan, he did nothing to implement Neile's policy and therefore had to be removed. Neile secured the resignation of the Official, Langford, which at once terminated Greaves' authority,[1] and had him replaced by Mottershed in 1635.

[1] York, R.VII.P.M.132, form of a proxy to Mottershed, Francis Parker and another by Langford to present his resignation to Archdeacon Baylie at Oxford; in the hand of Neile's secretary, Liveley.

TABLE 23

Sessions of the Correction Court, 1620

Nottingham	Retford	Newark	Mansfield
15 January A	8 February PB	24 April	18 January A
29 January MW	21 April Archdeacon	Archdeacon P	2 March A
12 February PA	(and visitation)	(and visitation)	21 March A
26 February PA	16 May PB	17 May PG	30 May PA
11 March PA	20 June B	31 May PG	3 October PA
18 March W	11 July PB		7 November PA
1 April AW	19 September B		
19 April Archdeacon	24 October PB		
(and visitation)	28 November B		
29 April PA	12 December PB		
*13 May PA			
*27 May PA			
17 June AM			
1 July AMW			
15 July PA			
29 July PA			
16 September A			
23 September A			
7 October PA			
21 October PA			
4 November PA			
18 November PA			
2 December A			
16 December A			

*   Combined consistory and correction court.
P= Purefey.
A= Charles Aynsworth, Rector of Bulwell, Rural Dean.
B= Thomas Bishop, Rector of Babworth and E. Retford.
G= Richard Gymney, Rector of Stoke, Rural Dean of Newark.
M= Robert Malham, Rector of St Nicholas, Nottingham.
W= Francis Withington, Rector of W. Bridgford.

Mottershed's appointment indicates the importance attached by Neile to the work to be done in the county. There were competent surrogates who could have acted, such as Francis Withington, who was commissioner for the visitation in 1629 and 1632, and who was subsequently imprisoned by Parliament. Alternatively, a young advocate from among those encouraged by Neile to work at York, could have been sent to gain experience. Mottershed was not only Neile's most reliable administrator after his chancellor, but was already fully employed as Advocate-general, Admiralty judge, Official of the East Riding and with his private practice. He did not trust the local clergy

TABLE 24

Sessions of the Correction Court 1631–2, William Greaves, judge

Nottingham	Retford	Newark	Mansfield
7 May	24 May	25 May	12 May
21 May	14 June	22 June	
11 June	5 July	28 September	
17 June	19 July		
25 June	25 October		
9 July	(Bishop judge)		
*16 July	15 November		
23 July	(Bishop judge)		
24 September	13 December		
8 October	7 February		
*15 October	(Bishop judge)		
22 October	6 March		
5 November			
(Malham judge)			
*12 November			
19 November			
3 December			
†10 December			
15 December			
21 January			
*28 January			
4 February			
†18 February			
†3 March			
17 March			

    * Newark Deanery cases only.   † Including Newark Deanery cases.

very far, and it was not until 1638 that he even allowed them to sentence routine cases. He always reserved administrative decisions to himself, although he had perforce to allow the local clergy to receive certificates of the completion of his orders. These clergy, who sat in court in his absence, were Malham, one of Purefey's assistants, and Laycock (Vicar of St Mary's Nottingham, a Laudian who was evidently preferred to Malham but was not always resident) at Nottingham, while at Retford the rural dean, Feilding, replaced Bishop, a man with Puritan sympathies. Mottershed himself could not always attend Visitations, but had to send Giles Burton, a York advocate, or a reliable Yorkshire clergyman, and was represented by Francis Parker, his chief clerk.

Tables 23–5 show the working of the court under Purefey, Greaves and

TABLE 25

Sessions of the Correction Court, 1638

Nottingham	Retford	Newark	Mansfield
20 January L (1)(2)(3)	23 January F	14 March S	22 February MS
3 February T(1)(2)	4 April Mott	10 April Mott	7 June L
20 February MS(2)	1 September Mott	21 August Mott	
17 March M(1)(2)	3 September Mott	5 September Mott	
6 April Mott(1)	9 October F	5 December A	
7 April Mott(2)	11 December F		
26 May L(1)(2)			
23 June M(1)			
25 August Mott(2)			
27 August Mott(1)			
8 September Mott(1)(2)			
3 November M(3)			
1 December M(1)			
8 December M(2)			

A = George Allsopp, R. of S. Collingham.
F = Christopher Feilding.
L = Edmund Laycock.
M = Robert Malham.
Mott = Edward Mottershed.
S = George Saunders, LL.B., proctor.
T = Robert Theobalds, M.A., R. of Colwick.

(1) Cases from Nottingham Deanery.
(2) Cases from Bingham Deanery.
(3) Cases from Newark Deanery.

Mottershed. The year 1638 represents the year of the latter's maximum effort to enforce the Laudian policy in the archdeaconry. He was present both at the Easter visitation and at the end of August when he held the Michaelmas visitation.

The smooth flow of business was held up, awaiting the arrival of the Official, and the large number of administrative cases must have considerably strained the resources of the registrar's office. During these years the Consistory Court functioned normally, usually with Malham as judge although Laycock sometimes presided.

One feature which distinguished the administration at this period was in its relationship with churchwardens. Previously they were allowed to hand in their own presentment bills—and many oddly sized pieces of paper remain on the files—or, if they wished, to make use of the services of the registrar's clerk. Mottershed made the use of an official provided by himself compulsory. The churchwardens had henceforth to be actually examined on the visitation articles, a process designed to elicit more information and to give less excuse if they were subsequently detected to have omitted something. Tibberd,

Reckles, Parker, Coombe, or even, on one occasion, Baguley the apparitor, were used to conduct these examinations. Increasing attempts were made to bring pressure on churchwardens by means of formal prosecutions for omissions to present known offenders, as well as by increasing the number of formal prosecutions of offenders themselves in the consistory court. Considerable success was achieved in producing outward conformity, and in repairing and bringing churches up to standard. But the decreasing number of presentments is a marked feature of the bills from 1639 onwards. Mottershed's pressure met increasing resistance.

As usual in the court, presentments were supplemented by private information about the conditions of churches. A scrap of paper preserved on the Retford presentment bill file for Easter 1635[1] contained information about five churches but was general in nature, with detailed remarks only about Sturton church, having the appearance of the notes made by an apparitor. There are no signs that commissions to view were made at that time, when Mottershed first visited the archdeaconry, but they were certainly contemplated. Tibberd wrote such a commission in which he entered the year 1635 in the date, leaving the day and month blank. The first notice of 'viewing' of churches was contained in the Michaelmas presentments for 1638,[2] where the parishes of Thorpe, Stoke, Kelham, Girton and North Clifton had been inspected. In addition, on the same file, is a letter from the Vicar of Marnham to Coombe, in which he indicated that Laycock had inspected the church. The churchwardens of Kelham, however, concluded their bill ' . . . And more saveinge the defects whereof Mr Official hath alreadie taken notice and given order to be amended they have not to present'. Words such as these suggest personal intervention by Mottershed and the impression is confirmed when the 'view' of Kelham is traced. Bound into the act book A45 (1637–9) are several folios concerning cases heard by Mottershed at East Retford and Newark, 3 and 5 September 1638. All the cases concerned the churchwardens, rectors or farmers of rectories of seventeen parishes. A list of requirements was written out, and underneath an act *ex officio mero* against previous churchwardens for not presenting their respective deficiencies. The handwriting was Parker's; the folios were not originally part of the registrar's book and were ignored in his numbering of the folios. The various offending churchwardens who appeared were either excommunicated, absolved and dismissed the following day (which cost them 7s. 6d. in fees) or were dismissed with an admonition (costing only 4s. 8d.).[3] Inspections by the Official himself as well

---

[1] PB 341. [2] Newark Deanery PB 328.
[3] The schedules are printed in Thoroton Soc. Trans. XXXI, 129 ff. The Retford Deanery parishes were probably viewed (except for West Retford) on a journey leaving the Great North Road at

as prosecutions of defaulting churchwardens may have been intended to galvanize other churchwardens to do their duty. It was evidently intended to continue viewing churches in 1639, and a schedule derived from such an inspection of Kilvington church (unsigned) is preserved.[1] The commission originally drawn up by Tibberd in 1635 was redated 21 May 1639, and intended for George Alsopp, Rector of South Collingham (one of the Newark surrogates) and George Darker, Rector of Elston, but it was never issued.[2]

The inference from the evidence remaining is that the system of viewing churches was not used extensively in the archdeaconry, and that such inspections as were made were confined to the Retford and Newark Deaneries. The main burden of effecting changes was laid therefore on the court itself, working through visitation presentments and court orders, and their enforcement. The first concern was for the repair of the actual structure of the churches, and then for their re-equipment in an orderly and seemly manner. That Archbishop Neile was very proud of his efforts in these matters may be gathered by the care he took to collect the totals of sums expended on churches, and to send them with his annual reports to the King.[3] The figures which the examiners collected from churchwardens were written down on the presentment bills and show that in some cases considerable amounts were spent.[4] The average amount is perhaps a more reliable guide to the general activity, and on the forty-eight churches of the Retford Deanery the average sum spent in 1635 was £7. 15s.; in 1636, £9. 8s.; in 1637, £10; and in 1639, £3. 18s. There are no comparable figures for the years before Mottershed's time but the averages suggest that a greater expenditure was usual in all churches during his period of office than was normal. If the expenditures for 1638, when the activity was at its highest, were available, the totals would have been even more remarkable. It is likely that in the five years 1635-9 the average parish in the deanery spent about £40 on its church in fabric repairs and improvements, and on the provision of church furniture and ornaments. The act books of the court reflect the expenditure, a majority of the orders

Bawtry and making an eastwards semi-circle, rejoining it at Tuxford. The Newark Deanery churches were visited in a short journey to Girton, and by inspections of the churches nearest to Newark town.

[1] PB 328, Newark Deanery, Michaelmas 1639 file.

[2] MISC 257. That it was never used is proved by the fact that the names of the churches to be viewed were never entered on the document, although the commission specified that they were to be written in a list below the main text. Its terms are similar to those printed in my *Puritans and the Church Courts*, pp. 218 f.

[3] *Cal.State Papers Dom.* 1635-6, p. 199. £6,562 spent in archdeaconries of York, East Riding and Nottingham.

[4] For further details see my article, 'The Restoration of Nottinghamshire Churches, 1635-40' in the *Transactions of the Thoroton Society of Nottinghamshire* (1961), pp. 57-93, which contains the orders for each church and the sums expended on them.

issued being certified as completed. In the remainder of the cases the lack of a notice of a certificate indicated probably that it had been submitted out of court. In a few cases churchwardens were excommunicated for not obeying orders. The churchwardens of four parishes remained under that sentence without submitting themselves, but even in these cases activity can usually be noted.[1]

Two specific requirements of Archbishop Neile were the provision of a hood in each parish for its minister, and the railing of the holy table in the east end of each chancel. The former was enforced at his primary Visitation, and similarly by Mottershed. It is, therefore, a commentary on the system, that the archdeacon's Visitations in December 1636 and Easter and Michaelmas 1637 between them discovered thirty-five parishes still lacking hoods, about one-fifth of the total—despite two episcopal (1632–3, 1636) and the archidiaconal Visitations. Nevertheless, the efforts of 1637 and 1638 had their result; the Michaelmas presentments of 1639 had little to say on the subjects which interested Mottershed. His thoroughness, combined with prosecutions in the Consistory Court, had had their effect. Yet even so, one is forced to speculate how complete even Mottershed's enquiry was. At the Michaelmas Visitation, 8 September 1638,[2] the churchwardens of Arnold returned *omnia bene*. On the same file is a sheet of paper recording these observations:

Arnoll.
The seates in the Chauncell are over high and not Chauncell wise and have lockes and keyes.
The Chauncell floor is not even paved especially the step into it.
The Communion table is not sufficient.
All the seates from the Cross Ile to the Chauncell and in the 2 side quiers are ununiforme and over high.
The Iles are not even paved.
There are divers tresles seates and formes sett in the Iles.
There is much rubbish in the lower part of the church.
There wants a poor mans box.
The font wants a decent Cover.
The Church porch is not even paved butt full of holes.
The Minister is not to teach schoole in the Church.

The discrepancy between this schedule, accepted by the court as a basis for action,[3] and the churchwardens' own ideas about the sufficiency of their

---

[1] Thus the chapelwardens of Barnston (Langar parish) were excommunicated on 26 April 1639, but in that year £10 was spent on the chapel, a large sum for a hamlet. The Lyndby churchwardens for 1638 were excommunicated, but a certificate of completion was introduced in 1639. The churchwardens of Harworth were given an order 26 Aug. 1639 and excommunicated 21 Jan. 1640 but in 1639 they had spent £13, 10s. on their church.

[2] PB 303. [3] A 45, 27 Aug. 1638.

church is apparent, and indicates that even Mottershed could not produce an entirely reliable visitation enquiry.[1]

The principal business of the court, however, was the administration of justice and ecclesiastical discipline. Mottershed's methods disrupted the well-tried and long-established system of frequent courts held on circuit. The holding-over of business from the Easter Visitation until the end of August, for Mottershed's convenience, resulted in cases from the Michaelmas Visitation not being cited until December or January. The efficiency of the court was therefore seriously prejudiced, and in 1638 the Official was compelled to allow the surrogates to hear routine cases in June and July, and in 1639 to hear them shortly after the Easter Visitation. The administration of criminal justice was further hampered because presentments made during the diocesan Visitation of 1636 were not brought to court for nearly eighteen months. Easdall did not arrive until September 1637.

Mottershed was elected a proctor in Convocation to the Short Parliament with Francis Withington,[2] but too much should not be read into these appointments which were usually to conduct only the formal work of the Northern Convocation. However, it is interesting to note that the two representatives to the Long Parliament's Convocation were moderate men unconnected with the administration, one indeed, an opponent of Mottershed's orders.[3] The opposition, reflected in the churchwardens' growing lack of co-operation, soon took a practical turn. In the days of Diggles and Leigh, who had lived at Southwell, the court had been held in Newark church, but in 1597 Leigh had taken it back to Nottingham and gone to live there himself. From that time onwards it had been held regularly in St Peter's church.[4] In the days when the court was maintaining orthodox Puritanism, St Peter's had become a Puritan parish. Chancellor Easdall and Mottershed between them reduced it to conformity, but it bided its time. The Official died early in 1641. In the summer of that year the Long Parliament abolished the coercive power of the bishops, and on 28 September the door of St Peter's was barred

---

[1] A similar list of 'Defects observed in the Church of Kilvington not presented by the Churchwardens' was made following the Michaelmas visitation of 1639 (PB 328). Again the presentment bill reads *omnia bene*. The *Petition to Parliament from the County of Nottingham* (1641) objected to 'fining parishes excessively (without limit) for not altering of seats, painting of Churches, or buying of Ornaments, etc. at their pleasure (though unnecessarie) and so forcing them to extreme and needlesse charge therein'; and also 'for signing bills of presentments by some Clarke of their owne, which otherwise they refuse to take' (p. 4).

[2] A 47, 31 March 1640.

[3] *Ibid.*, 20 Oct. 1640. Thos. Savage, Rector of Sutton Bonington St Michael, and John Moseley, Vicar of Newark. For Moseley see my *Puritans and the Church Courts*, pp. 196, 309.

[4] Charles Deering in 1751 recorded that the court was held at the west end of the south aisle, but 'formerly' it had been in the chapel of All Saints in the north aisle (*An Historical Account of Nottingham*, p. 102).

in the face of the court officials. Malham retired to his own church and maintained the forms of the court, although it was not long before people realized that there was no point in their attending it. Visitations were held as late as Easter 1642 at Nottingham and Easter 1643 at the more royalist Newark and Retford.[1] The Laudians had won a legal battle, but they lost the war. They lost it simply because they did not recognize the limitations of law and the enforcement of law in spiritual affairs. The attempt to maintain the medieval concept of canon law had failed, and no body of Christians benefited more from the subsequent freedom of the spirit than the Anglican Church herself.

[1] CL 166, 169, 175.

6

CHURCH DISCIPLINE

This concludes the description of the church courts in the diocese of York, but one question clearly remains to be answered. How effective was the administration of church discipline? The general impression is that for the normal business of private litigation between parties the consistory courts provided an effective service to litigants. It is true that many parties were excommunicated for non-appearance on first being cited, but then many were also absolved shortly afterwards.[1] The activities of the visitation courts lend themselves to more exact statistical analysis, although the figures produce certain difficulties of interpretation. Despite these uncertainties, the results given in the following tables are full of interest.

Table 26 gives a breakdown of diocesan visitations in York and Norwich in typical years. It has been designed to show the proportion of persons presented for offences who were amenable to church discipline, and also to illustrate the large-scale nature of disciplinary cases. In order to avoid distorting the results, certain adjustments have to be made. First, the number of those who died before their cases came to court has been eliminated. Next are shown two classes which need to be distinguished from the mass of the accused. Persons who previously had been excommunicated for contempt of court obviously should not be counted again when estimating contumacy, while most of those presented as Roman Catholics had also been previously excommunicated. It is quite clear that visitations were not regarded as an effective means of dealing with recusants. Very few of them ever attended court and excommunication for contempt was the only sentence the court could pronounce. If necessary, the High Commission took further action. They present a special problem when analyzing the effectiveness of the

---

[1] In Norwich Consistory Court, 1635–6, there were thirty-two cheap absolutions at 3*d*. or 6*d*. each: these were cases where letters of excommunication had not yet been issued for denunciation in the parish concerned. Other parties waited until their excommunications had been publicized before attending. In that year there were no writs to Chancery for the arrest of obstinate excommunicates. The royal Chancery Court had similar problems of securing appearances by defendants (W. J. Jones, *The Elizabethan Court of Chancery*, pp. 229–30).

TABLE 26

Effectiveness of church discipline. An analysis of two diocesan visitations

Result of court action	Diocese of York, 1623					Diocese of Norwich, 1627				
	Archdeaconry of				Total for diocese	Archdeaconry of				Total for diocese
	York	East Riding	Cleveland	Nottingham		Norwich	Norfolk	Suffolk	Sudbury	
Dead before case came to court	13	4	2	5	24	3	5	12	5	25
Previously excommunicated and presented as such	313	33	55	17	418	17	18	27	17	79
Recusants	323	259	522	107	1211	45	60	34	132	271
Attended: dismissed, admonished, obeyed court order	374	243	111	167	895	360	376	227	93	1056
Attended late: dismissed, admonished, obeyed court order	63	73	21	8	165	48	53	35	52	188
Total attending	437	316	132	175	1060	408	429	262	145	1244
Percentage attending (ignoring first three categories above)	31.4	41.6	20	43.75	33	46	44	43.5	35	43
No entry (presumably non-attenders)	859	98	502	187	1646	13	206	50	62	331
Non-attenders marked as excommunicated	23	298	6	1	328	437	231	206	174	1048
Attended: did not obey orders	6	4	—	42	52	21	24	2	13	60
Total contumacious (ignoring first three categories above)	888	400	508	230	2026	471	461	258	249	1439
Record of case not completed	75	41	19	42	177	13	90	86	20	209
Total (ignoring first three categories above)	1400	757	659	405	3221	892	980	666	414	2892
GRAND TOTAL	2049	1053	1238	534	4874	957	1063	679	568	3267

courts, but the view has been taken here that as they repudiated the jurisdiction of the Church, it is better to ignore them when computing the courts' effectiveness. The necessity for isolating them statistically, however, is well illustrated by the figures for the two dioceses. There was such a large recusant remnant in the North that failure to exclude them would considerably unbalance calculations in the dioceses of York and Chester, while their effect on the statistics for Norwich would be marginal. Occasionally, obstinate excommunicates and recusants did attend court, and where they were amenable to its orders they have been shown under this category, but the total numbers are so few as not to warrant separate treatment in analysis.

Where a presented person attended court a record of his attendance was made, and therefore the figures given under this heading may be regarded as accurate. It is possible that when a person obeyed a court order and arrived with (or sent in) a certificate of performance, the certificate was filed, but the actuary forgot to enter it in the court acts. Such lapses might account for the relatively large numbers (fifty-three) in the Doncaster Deanery in 1590 who took the trouble to attend, but failed to obey orders.[1] Unfortunately, there is little firm evidence to support such a suggestion in the great majority of cases. Indeed, what evidence there is points the other way. At the 1623 visitation Dodsworth re-cited all those presented in 1619 for major offences who still remained contumacious—765 in the whole diocese. As a result it was discovered that two certificates and one dismissal of a cause had not been entered in the 1619 acts, not a very considerable proportion. This does not, of course, prove that the entries in 1590 were as well kept as those in later times, but it does rule out any argument from silence unsupported by other evidence.

It is because these entries appear to be generally reliable that they have been used as a basis for estimating the effectiveness of church discipline. The percentages show the proportion of those presented who attended court and obeyed any orders given to them, ignoring those who were dead, previously contumacious or recusants. The figures should probably be about 1–2 per cent higher, because it is likely that where the record of the case was left incomplete, action was sometimes dropped or concluded in another court or out of court, e.g. in the case of a clergyman before the bishop privately. The percentages show that two out of four archdeaconries in the York diocese and three out of four in the Norwich diocese record a level of 42–46 per cent

---

[1] A more probable explanation is that the chancellor in this year still expected certificates of performance of orders and late-attenders to go to York: the circuit system for second courts had not yet begun. The 1623 figures probably reflect the provision of this amenity. Where the actuary has neglected to record certificates, this can be detected by a complete lack of such records over a whole deanery, e.g. Furness Deanery, 1590 (R.VI.A.II, fos. 51–5).

which may be regarded as about the national average. The Deanery of Frodsham (Cheshire) recorded a percentage of 62 in 1633 but this was due to certain exceptional features, which will be mentioned below, while the Somerset Deaneries of Crewkerne and Dunster in 1623 had one of 52, which is nearer normal.

The diocesan figures show three archdeaconries with appreciable below-average percentages—York, Cleveland and Sudbury. The latter was just as bad in 1633 as in 1627 to judge by the Deanery of Sudbury (see Table 31 for percentages in immorality presentments for 1633), and the fact that it was further away from the diocesan centre at Norwich than the other archdeaconries cannot in itself explain the difference. There was an efficient commissary court in the archdeaconry, and much of the area was no further away from the centres at which the visitation courts were held than were parts of the Archdeaconry of Suffolk. Again, the area was very much under Puritan influence, but this was common to the whole of the county of Suffolk in particular, and East Anglia generally. The problem must be left unresolved as no correction court records of the commissary court are extant to provide a cross-check.

TABLE 27

Archdeaconry of York by deaneries 1623

Deanery	Attended	Contumacious	Percentage attended
Christianity (York City)	12	60	20
New Ainsty	96	160	37½
Old Ainsty and Craven	110	213	39
Pontefract	110	309	26
Doncaster	109	221	33½
Total	437	963	31⅓

It will be noticed that the five archdeaconries returning approximately the same percentages were all closely-settled agricultural districts. The Archdeaconry of York, however, contained large urban populations (including that of the City of York) and industrial areas (the Leeds–Halifax part of the West Riding in particular). A breakdown by deaneries makes the situation even clearer—again ignoring dead, obstinate excommunicates and recusants. The Deanery of Pontefract included the large industrial parish of Halifax, which was a notorious 'black spot' for disobedience to the church courts, while the Deanery of Doncaster contained the Sheffield industrial area, and other relatively well-populated areas around Rotherham and Doncaster. Nevertheless, the figures reflect the lack of energy with which diocesan visitations generally were conducted, for as late as 1637 the efficient Easdall secured obedience in the parish of Halifax itself by 37 per cent out of 328 persons cited. The most conspicuous lack of success, and one which is most difficult to explain, is that for York City itself. The records themselves contain no hint as to any solution, but it is possible that the cases were simply referred to the city authorities or settled out of court, particularly the many presentments for non-payment of small sums of church rates.

The Archdeaconry of Cleveland, the other bad offender, was a difficult one to adminster. The whole of the central area of Cleveland is occupied by the North Yorkshire moors, so that there is no natural focus from which a court could operate. The situation was made more difficult by the large recusant population, which created spheres of influence inimical to the church administration. The diocesan visitation in 1623 began its courts for the archdeaconry on the coast at Scarborough, moved north to Whitby, returned around the southern flank of the moors to Helmsley, and concluded at Thirsk in the west of the archdeaconry. Yet all certificates of the performance of court orders had to be handed in and late-attenders had to report to one court held at Malton on the southern boundary, many miles from the greater part of the archdeaconry.

The loss of most of the pre-1662 archdeaconry records has prevented any extensive checking of the efficiency of diocesan against archdeaconry visitations; yet what can be done suggests that the latter were much more effective. The York City efficiency of 20 per cent in 1623 compared with an efficiency of 47 per cent in 1598 and 61 per cent in 1613 in archdeaconry visitations. For the same years in the Craven Deanery the figures were 39 per cent (and 43 in the diocesan visitation of 1619) compared with 62·5 and 47 per cent in the archdeaconry visitations. This 47 per cent in 1613 would have been nearly 60 per cent too, if it had not been for a list of eighty-one non-communicants at Mitton, of whom only eight attended court. If this list was really a list of recusants, which seems likely, the apparent decline in the court's effectiveness can be easily rectified. Table 33 shows similar divergencies in the time of Archbishop Neile in the Archdeaconry of Cleveland, with the archdeaconry efficiency running at a rate of over 25 per cent greater than the diocesan visitation of the same area.

The good results from Cleveland may be explained by an active Official living in the centre of his archdeaconry and adopting a vigorous policy.[1] The fact that the archdeaconry level of fees was about half the diocesan scale may

[1] See p. 124.

also have been a small contributing factor,[1] but probably the major influence was that each archdeaconry administration had a continuing control over the area and had a much smaller number of cases, so that it was able to devote a more detailed attention to each one.

The next comparison of figures to be made is between two visitations of the diocese of Chester, in 1595 and 1633 (see Tables 28–9). The Yorkshire part of that diocese seems to have been very much like the remainder of the county, with pockets of recusancy and Puritanism but no particular problems of church discipline. The Consistory Court at Richmond, for many years in the seventeenth century presided over by Mainwaring, kept these areas under control. Across the Pennines the situation was more complicated, for in the middle of the diocese lay the problem county of Lancashire. The tables show, particularly that for 1633, something of the large extent of recusancy, and it was only by the fortunate chance that Henry, fourth Earl of Derby (succeeded 1573, died 1593) had been a strong supporter of the Elizabethan settlement that Anglicanism had made any headway against the Roman Catholic gentry. After the Queen, the reigning Earl of Derby was the most powerful person in the county. The principal means whereby some parts of Lancashire became Anglican was Puritan preaching, so the county became split between the recusant–Puritan extremes to a much greater extent than the remainder of the diocese, or even Yorkshire. The result of these influences was that Anglican discipline in Lancashire was extremely weak.

The actual records of the visitation are similar in form to those of diocesan visitations of the same years. The Elizabethan acts contain few records of excommunications, hence the column headed 'No entry' implies such a sentence. This conclusion is confirmed because the acts of a case where a person appeared late simply begin with his absolution. The heading 'Entry not completed' normally refers to cases where the person presented failed to certify obedience to a court order, but again his excommunication went unrecorded. These acts show a comparatively large number of persons who neglected to certify in this way, as do those for the diocese of York at the time, and pose the question whether the court actuary kept them up-to-date. These certificates had to be returned at one or two courts, and it is difficult to see why the actuary should happen to record a few of his list in each deanery and not all of them. For this reason it is better to assume that he did record each certificate, and the large numbers of persons who initially attended court, but refused to certify the performance of their penance or other court order, has to be taken at its face value.

The 1595 figures do not show a very good level of obedience to church

---

[1] Above, pp. 142–4.

TABLE 28

Diocese of Chester, 1595. Analysis of acts in provincial visitation

County and Deanery	Obeyed court			Probably disobedient			Died while case pending	Miscellaneous	Recusants	Percentage obeyed (ignoring last three columns)
	Dismissed or admonished	Certified obedience to court orders	Total	No entry in acts of case	Entry not completed	Total				
Yorkshire										
Boroughbridge	11	—	11	16	6	22	—	—	171	57·6
Catterick	65	13	78	30	16	46	—	—	18	
Richmond	66	12	78	44	11	55	2	1	123	
Westmorland										
Kendal	37	2	39	67	26	93	—	—	—	29·5
Lancashire										
Lonsdale*	31	2	33	39	17	56	1	—	5	31·2
Amunderness	61	4	65	158	44	202	2	—	83	
Blackburn	16	12	28	82	29	111	1	1	77	
Furness	15	3	18	13	12	25	1	1	2	
Leyland	17	8	25	30	21	51	—	—	27	
Manchester	49	12	61	162	66	228	1	—	7	
Warrington	36	2	38	84	50	134	1	—	190	
Cheshire										
Bangor	1	—	1	12	—	12	—	—	16	27·9
Chester	18	—	18	48	33	81	—	—	5	
Frodsham	18	9	27	25	13	38	—	1	1	
Macclesfield	13	4	17	32	15	47	—	2	—	
Malpas	8	—	8	15	3	18	—	—	9	
Middlewich	15	5	20	25	16	41	—	—	—	
Nantwich	28	1	29	53	6	59	—	1	1	
Wirral	6	—	6	16	14	30	—	—	1	
Total	511¹	89	600	951	398	1349	8	6	736	30·8

* Partly also in Yorkshire and Westmorland.
¹ Of these 25 attended late.
Additionally, 52 previously excommunicated persons were re-presented.
Total presentments (less previously excommunicated and recusants): 1963.

TABLE 29

Diocese of Chester, 1633. Analysis of acts in provincial visitation

County and deanery	Obeyed court			Excommunicated			Died while case pending	No entry or case not completed	Recusants	Percentage obeyed (ignoring died and recusants)
	Dismissed or admonished	Certified obedience to court orders	Total	Never attended	Disobeyed court orders	Total				
Yorkshire										
Boroughbridge	53	11	64	30	12	42	1	7	105	56·6
Catterick	80	29	109	105	11	116	1	21	144	
Richmond	168¹	38	206	77	12	89	4	9	313	
Westmorland										
Kendal	119	62	181	146	20	166	3	11	215	50·5
Cumberland										
Copeland	99	72	171	63	4	67	3	35	30	62·6
Lancashire										
Lonsdale*	33	49	82	63	10	73	2	8	132	37·4
Amunderness	96	43	139	282	19	301	1	20	1392	
Blackburn	86	34	120	176	24	200	—		218	
Furness	74	30	104	63	17	80	1	6	35	
Leyland	23	20	43	43	14	57	1	2	740	
Manchester	130	109	239	352	76	428	4	13	38	
Warrington	73	40	113	189	18	207	2	5	1918	
Cheshire										
Bangor	18	7	25	11	6	17	—	—	43	56·8
Chester	103	34	137	61	23	84	1	8	16	
Frodsham	181	86	267	109	40	149	6	9	24	
Macclesfield	85	22	107	45	17	62	—	2	1	
Malpas	26	13	39	22	6	28	2	—	29	
Middlewich	94	40	134	91	50	141	5	5	21	
Nantwich	79	24	103	105	16	121	3	2	95	
Wirral	41	27	68	11	9	20	2	4	33	
Total	1661²	790³	2451	2044	404	2448	42	167	5544	48·3

* Partly also in Yorkshire and Westmorland.
¹ Including 87 from one parish.
² Including 293 late attenders.

³ Including 35 late attenders.
   Additionally 118 previously excommunicated persons were re-presented (81 of which from Manchester Deanery), and there were 25 miscellaneous results of cases not tabulated above.
   Total presentments (less previously excommunicated and recusants): 5,123.

discipline outside of the Yorkshire part of the diocese, indeed in a sample of two deaneries in Westmorland the proportion of obedient persons dropped by 5 per cent and two deaneries in Cheshire by $17\frac{1}{2}$ per cent compared with five years before.[1] Easdall's efficiency in 1633, therefore, did little more than restore the figures to what they had been in 1590, but the magnitude of this achievement is to be judged from the attendant circumstances that church discipline had been under continual pressure from opponents during the period, and that the number of offenders had increased so considerably. It is unfortunate that the records of the 1630 visitation of Chester (undertaken when Easdall was not giving his full attention to his duties at York) only record the first act taken in court, and so its efficiency cannot be compared with his personally supervized visitation three years later.

The 1630 acts confirm, however, those for 1633 in one important particular—the vast increase in the number of presentments. The total in 1595 was 1,963 and it had grown by 1633 to 4,762 (adjusted to allow for the fact that the Copeland Deanery acts in 1593 are not extant), an increase of 143 per cent. A small proportion of the increase was due to the greater number of churchwardens and clergy before the court in 1633, but if the figures for the Frodsham Deanery are a guide (Table 30), the 1630 acts show that all classes of presentments contributed to the general increase over the years—particularly the main item, sexual immorality. If large blocks of presentments from two parishes in 1633 are ignored, the figures for this deanery in the two years are almost identical.

Church discipline in this diocese, therefore, did not suffer any decline over the years, but rather improved as a much larger number of offenders were detected; although it might be argued that the discipline had failed as far as offences had increased. The court mechanism itself had not grown less efficient, but rather improved—in 1595 only 15 per cent of attenders were given orders which required certification of obedience: in 1633 the percentage was 32. Of these, the percentage who obeyed in 1595 was 19, in 1633, 66.

General reflection on all these different figures suggests that the efficiency of church discipline varied according to time, place and circumstances. In a normal rural area, not unduly troubled by recusancy, nonconformity or idle court officers, over half the persons cited attended and performed any court order given. There were always some who died, fled, were otherwise dealt with, or had proceedings against them stayed, so that the registrars could probably account for about two-thirds of those cited. Urban areas and certain rural areas where church courts were not respected broke up the even pattern of church discipline. Some of the reasons for these exceptional areas can be

---

[1] Above, p. 121.

guessed readily enough, others are more difficult to assess. The internal histories of diocesan administrations also need study, as do their effectiveness as compared with archidiaconal or commissary courts. There were certain general features relevant to church discipline, but no part of the country was free from a variety of individual circumstances which can only be discovered by particular research.

Some of these particular features are suggested by the tables of statistics for individual deaneries. In Yorkshire, the Deanery of Doncaster has been chosen as a norm because of its size and varied character. The figures for 1590 in Table 30 reflect the beginnings of the circuit system at diocesan visitations in Yorkshire. The percentage of attendances shows how much had to be done to make diocesan visitations effective. The 1619 figures show the effect of church discipline when it had been firmly established and with a second circuit for certificates and late-attenders. By this time the courts were always held at both Doncaster and Rotherham, and efficiency had improved. Archbishop Neile's primary visitation was held at Michaelmas 1632 after an archidiaconal visitation at Easter, consequently non-administrative presentments were much fewer than in previous years, but ordinary discipline, as reflected in cases of sexual immorality, had changed little since 1619. A detailed analysis of the returns for 1636–7 has not been made, but a simple check shows that the Neile administration had not begun to lose its grip by that date. Entries recording obedience to the court (ignoring recusants, etc.) were 53·6 per cent, disobedience 40·4, miscellaneous (not completed, etc.) 6. The result is the more impressive because the number of persons represented in these percentages was 588, by far the largest ever to be presented at a diocesan visitation in the deanery. The system of presentment may consequently be regarded as also being in full working order at this time.

The analysis of the Frodsham Deanery indicates what was happening in a typical Cheshire deanery. The number of presentments showed a dramatic rise, even allowing for the block of seventy-three presentments from one parish for non-attendance at catechism. But the fact that nearly all these attended court helped to make the contumacy rate better than normal, as may be judged from Table 31. The general improvement in this diocese came about more by the raising of the level of the worst deaneries to the average, rather than by general, all-round improvement.

The Deanery of Sudbury has been selected because it returned the largest number of presentments of any deanery in the Norwich diocese—a diocese of small deaneries. It was probably typical of its area, the Suffolk–Essex border, but the diocesan statistics show that it was in the part of the diocese where discipline was least effective. The disparity with the remainder of the diocese

TABLE 30
Results of court action in selected deaneries

	Doncaster			Frodsham		Sudbury		Crewkerne and Dunster
	1590	1619	1633	1590	1633	1593	1633	1623
Against clergy:								
Admonished or dismissed	8	1	7	3	2	13	9	3
Ordered to amend: obeyed	—	—	13	1	13	6	2	4
disobeyed	4	2	8	—	—	3	—	2
No record of end of case, dead, etc.	5	1	7	3	3	10	4	5
Against churchwardens:								
Admonished or dismissed	2	3	19	1	2	—	14	3
Ordered to amend: obeyed	3	1	8	3	7	10	2	4
disobeyed	1	—	6[1]	—	2	4	—	—
No record of end of case, etc.	—	—	4	—	5	4	—	1
Against other laymen:								
Admonished or dismissed	35	102	59	20	145	20	39	19
Performed penance or obeyed other orders	18	54	29	22	46	5	3	10
Appeared late: obeyed	9	31	21	4	52	35	6	15
disobeyed	8	9	6	—	10	2	—	—
Disobeyed orders given at first hearing	45	27	31	3	28	4	—	2
Never appeared	136	176	169	20	122	36	93	111
No record of end of case, dead, absconded, etc.	12	9	20	17	18	2	31	7
	286	416	407	97	455	154	203	186
Net figures after deducting recusants and obstinate excommunicates	263	358	316	94	427	144	136	108
Percentage of attenders, based on net figures	27·3	53·5	47·3	58	58·7	62	55·5	53·7

[1] Represents twenty-two individuals.

214

TABLE 31

Results of presentments for sexual immorality

	County of Norfolk 1633	Doncaster			Frodsham		Sudbury		Crewkerne and Dunster 1623
		1590	1619	1633	1590	1633	1593	1633	
Performed penance	55	15	51	20	21	22	5	5	1[1]
Never attended court, or appeared but disobeyed court orders	133	104	111	48	15	44	22	23	17
Absconded	19	2	1	—	—	1	—	2	—
Dismissed or purged themselves	37	14	41	13	14	13	3	1	11
Dead before court held	2	1	1	3	—	1	—	1	1
Record of case not completed in court acts	16[2]	5	1	6	5	—	3	4	—
Total	262	141	206	90	55	81	33	36	30
Percentage of total represented by contumacious persons (sexually immoral)	58·5	75	54	53	27	54	67	67	57
Percentage of contumacious persons in all offences	—	66	43·5	41	21·5	31	34	19[3]	34

[1] Seven of those dismissed had previously been punished in the ordinary correction court, so the effective total of penances is eight.
[2] Of these, six were in Bridewell.
[3] The value of this figure is much reduced by the high percentage of cases where the record is incomplete. The true figure is probably about thirty-eight.

215

is illustrated in Table 31 where the contumacy percentage of 67 is contrasted with 58·5 for the two Norfolk archdeaconries in cases of sexual immorality.

Lastly, an analysis is given of two deaneries in the Archdeaconry of Taunton, 1623, derived from a transcript of a visitation act book made by the late Claude Jenkins.[1] The attendance record in these deaneries was almost exactly the same as in Doncaster in 1619, but in some other respects this archdeaconry contained certain notable contrasts with the other areas surveyed as will be shown below.

It is to be expected that the effect of church discipline would be different on different classes of persons. It would be possible to break down results into separate categories for each type of offence. For our purpose it has been thought sufficient to separate the general results in Table 30 into clergy, churchwardens and laity, and to provide in Table 31 a breakdown of results for the most serious type of offence—sexual immorality.

It should be axiomatic that clergy and churchwardens were more amenable to discipline than laymen, but Table 30 shows that this was not always true. The Deanery of Doncaster provides an example of clergy who appear to be undisciplined. While the incomplete entries here may sometimes be taken as references of the case to the archbishop, as in presentments for nonconformity, the fact that as many as eight were suspended in 1633 for small offences (usually failure to read service on Wednesdays and Fridays or Eves of Sundays and Holy Days) shows that the court's censures were not always respected. Where a curate changed his curacy the suspension only took effect if he committed a new offence and it was renewed: where an incumbent discharged his duties by a curate he was unaffected by the sentence. In other areas clergy were more generally obedient. The large number of unfinished cases in Sudbury in 1593 was due to reference (recorded in the acts) of nonconformity to the bishop.

The record of churchwardens was also usually good. The only substantial opposition was to Neile's requirements, probably as a matter of principle. The five churchwardens of the large town of Doncaster (nearly 6,000 acres) were excommunicated for refusing to certify that they had perambulated the parish boundary in Rogation week, doubtless thinking that it was too much to ask of eminent (and probably portly) citizens of an important town. Those of Darfield (five) and Kirk Smeaton (two) were in parishes where uniform seating and paved floors were required, while those of Fishlake (four) refused to attend for not presenting their aged vicar for nonconformity. Only two parishes had recalcitrant churchwardens who apparently were contumacious simply because they refused to undertake normal repairs to their churches.

---

[1] Somerset Record Society, vol. 43 (1928).

Where a deanery had a high parish/population ratio, and the visitors were engaged in some particular campaign of enforcement, the obedience of clergy and churchwardens helps to make attendance statistics look healthier than if there had been few parishes. Comparison of the figures for Frodsham (23 parishes, 427 offenders) and Sudbury (49 parishes, 136 offenders) in 1633 demonstrates this clearly. The twenty-four obedient clergy and church-wardens of Frodsham represent 5·7 per cent of the total amenable to discipline, while the twenty-seven of Sudbury represent 27 per cent of the total for that deanery. This is not an unnecessary complexity, but simply illustrates the difficulty of using visitation statistics in a meaningful way.

Some help towards their interpretation is given by Table 31, where the results of presentments for sexual immorality are set out. These figures eliminate complications such as those described in the last paragraph, and if the Sudbury 1633 contumacy percentage is read as indicated in the note, produce interesting data. In these cases the church courts were dealing with all classes of the population, but in numbers the majority were probably of the poorer parts of society, so it is clear that only 40–50 per cent of the general population were amenable to discipline. The Sudbury Deanery was a particularly bad area, as shown in the Table, and the 1627 visitation pro-duced an even worse result—out of forty-two presentments of this type not one person performed penance. In effect, church discipline over this class of offender had broken down in this area, or perhaps it would be truer to say, had never been established. Here the importance of comparative figures is indicated, for the 1593 visitation was no more effective than the one of 1633. For other areas the percentages show, as might be expected, that the con-tumacies for this offence were greater in proportion than those for all offences. In the Table the Doncaster and Frodsham results for 1590 stand out in marked contrast, probably in part due to the fact that the Yorkshire deanery had to return certificates to York, while the Cheshire deanery was supervised on the spot by the local dean. The 1619 and 1633 figures suggest that by the second, third and fourth decades of the seventeenth century an equilibrium had been reached in each area, the effect of church discipline varying only marginally from year to year.

The analysis of offences in Table 32 shows the main types of presentment. Sexual offences predominated throughout the period (by 1636 the Doncaster deanery figure reached 315), and by comparison other varieties of offences connected with evil living (drunkenness, evil language, 'scolding' and Sabbath-breaking) were comparatively few. The Laudian regime is usually noted for a more lenient attitude to Sunday, allowing certain pastimes as mentioned in the Book of Sports, but the effect of its enforcement of church discipline resulted in more presentments for Sabbath-breaking than usual. Similarly, in the Province of York, outside York City itself, little was done to tighten up effectively the observance of Holy Days, although this again is usually thought to be a major Laudian objective. The category of usury has been shown to indicate that, although an occasional presentment of this nature was made, it was a rarity. The only cases came from an area of considerable Puritan influence, but in each case those involved claimed that they took no more interest than allowed by law (10 per cent) and were dismissed.[1]

Table 32 shows the effect of certain campaigns of enforcement by diocesan authorities, and, in the footnotes, of certain parochial campaigns. Some of the latter reflect a local situation the complexities of which we are ignorant, and the results varied. For instance, the thirty-six who at Doncaster had not paid their church rates denied liability, and the churchwardens were told that their only remedy was a civil suit in the Consistory Court. Most of those who had failed in their duty to send children or servants to catechism at Great Budworth in 1633 attended court, and were admonished on promise of amendment. How much improvement resulted in practice is a matter for speculation.

It must have been difficult to know when to use the weapon of presentment against those who openly flouted the laws against Sabbath-breaking. The effect of presentment was too often simply to turn a Sabbath-breaker into an excommunicate, a process which did little good to anyone. It is for this reason that one suspects that church attendance, particularly on summer afternoons, was much less than the 100 per cent of fit persons envisaged by law. In 1633, 24 out of 30 Sabbath-breakers in the Doncaster Deanery, 12 out of 42 in Frodsham, and 19 out of 31 in Sudbury became obstinate excommunicants as a result of presentment. Yet it is apparent that not all Sabbath-breakers were presented, for it was physically impossible for the churches in the parish of Sheffield to hold all the parishioners, yet the numbers presented for non-attendance in 1619 and 1633 were one each year. Three examples of parish campaigns for enforcement may be given. In the parish of Nantwich (Cheshire) in 1595 thirty-five persons were presented, twenty-four of whom were for Sabbath-breaking. Of the latter, five were ordered penance, two were ordered to pay 12*d*. to the poor and dismissed, and three were admonished on promise of amendment; fourteen remained in contempt of court. The Puritan parish of Leeds in 1623 presented thirty-eight persons for Sabbath-breaking, non-attendance at church and non-communicating. Of

---

[1] Recurring cases can be found in the Nottingham Archdeaconry Court throughout the reign of Elizabeth, and also in the High Commission particularly under Archbishop Sandys. The rate was 8 per cent after 1624.

TABLE 32

Analysis of presentments

Type of presentment	YORKSHIRE Deanery of Doncaster (75 parishes)			CHESHIRE Deanery of Frodsham (23 parishes)			SUFFOLK Deanery of Sudbury (49 parishes)		SOMERSET Deaneries of Crewkerne and Dunster (83 parishes)
	1590	1619	1633	1590	1630	1633	1593	1633	1623
Defects in churches—responsibility of churchwardens	3	—	17	4	3	14	17[1]	1	6
Defects in churches—responsibility of lay rectors	3	3	6	5	—	8	1	1	2
Defects in performance of services by the clergy	2	—	18	1	—	8	2	5[2]	7
Nonconformity of clergy	3	2	11	3	13	7	25	2	1
Other clerical faults	12	2	6	3	9	3	5	8	5
Faults of churchwardens	3	4	20	1	13	2	1	15[3]	1
Faults of parish clerks	—	—	—	—	—	2	—	—	3
Lay nonconformity	—	5	5	—	29	20	1	10	—
Recusancy	11	33	78	1	38	27	10	43	16
Non-attendance at church	31	8	30	4	15	42	—	31	18
Non-attendance at Holy Communion	20	11	3	1	19	8	35	7	4
Working, playing games, drinking in service time, Sundays	—	8	22	—	9	26	2	—	18
Working, playing games, drinking in service time, Holy Days	—	1	2	—	1	1	—	—	—
Disturbance in church and churchyard	5	15	15	5	11	16	4	3	4
Not attending, or enforcing attendance at, catechism	—	4	—	—	2	77[4]	1	1	—
Abuse of clergy or churchwardens	—	8	3	—	—	3	1	1	—
Drunkenness, cursing, blasphemy	7	—	3	—	12	24	3	1	1
Common scold	4	3	7	—	—	6	—	—	—
Sexual immorality	141	206	90	55	106	81	33	36	30
Not cohabiting with husband or wife	13	4	6	9	—	12	1	1	3
Illegal or clandestine marriage	—	5	30	3	—	6	—	—	—
Usury	—	—	—	1	—	10	—	—	—
Non-payment of church dues	12	51[5]	6	1	32	37[6]	—	7	1
Obstinately excommunicate	12	25	13	2	14	1	33	24	62
Miscellaneous	4	18	16	3	14	14	14	8	4
Total	286	416	407	97	340	455	154	203	186

[1] Nine for lack of Protestant books only (e.g. Jewel's *Apology*).

[2] Weekday services, but no real increase from 1593 for many nonconformists in that year also presented for neglecting weekday services. Where a person was presented for more than one offence, only the most serious has been counted.

[3] Twelve for lacking terrier of glebe only.

[4] Seventy-three from Great Budworth.

[5] Thirty-six from Doncaster parish.

[6] All from Frodsham parish.

these, twelve were admonished, one failed to certify that he communicated, and the remainder ignored the court altogether.[1] Despite the fact that these presentments reveal that the churchwardens were doing their duty by searching the parish for those who preferred the ale-houses to church services, church discipline in the parish was weak all round. Of thirty-one persons presented in that year for sexual immorality, four were excused because of precontract, and only five of the remaining twenty-seven performed their penances. Finally, a more extreme case may be mentioned, that of the parish of Middleton Tyas, near Richmond, where in 1633 no less than eighty-seven persons were presented for being negligent in coming to church on Sunday afternoons. Only nine appeared in person and the remainder were excommunicated, but the curate later saw the chancellor and all were dismissed. The curate must also have passed round the hat before he set out because he was able to hand over 18s. to the registrar which was accepted as fees for the whole number—at about 2½d. each probably a record low fee for dismissal. But who had benefited by this procedure (other than the recipients of the fees)?[2]

The figures in the various tables in this chapter can be used to demonstrate both the effect and the ineffectiveness of the punishment of excommunication. Many persons simply ignored it, but it did succeed in making others obey the citation or orders given to them. It is difficult to know whether there were any practical disabilities from the sentence other than certain legal ones. Most excommunicates would not mind being barred from church and sacrament, a few simply fled to London, Ireland or some other place where the sentence would have no effect. Their relatives might get into trouble for trying to bury them in consecrated ground.[3] Sometimes a dying person would

---

[1] R.VI.A.20, fos. 26 v.–33.

[2] The Vicar of Felixkirk reported in the Cleveland Archdeaconry visitation 1634 'that they never have above fower persons att evening prayers, and none att evening prayers upon holly dayes'. The judge evidently sent some unrecorded general monition to the parish and respited the case until the vicar 'certifye whether there be reformacion or not' (R.VI.C.27, p. 50). At the same visitation Henry Ayscough, Rector of Dunnington, charged in February 1634 with not reading the Book of Sports, presented four men 'for that contrary to the King's Declaration concerning lawful sports to be used upon Sunday, the 29th June last past they did ioyne them selves with a great number of other parrishes [*sic*] and begunn may games and merrie dances before any divine service in the forenoone of that day continueing the said sports until the Evening and useing in them unlawfull weapons such as are guns, spears, swords and the like'; the court saw that three out of four performed penance, but the effect of these penances on a congregation probably sprinkled with others who had similarly offended must have been minimal (*ibid.* p. 213).

[3] The most extraordinary case was at Thornton where some people buried an excommunicate woman at night. Some men later unearthed the coffin and reburied her simply in her shroud. The pigs (which wandered at will through Tudor and Stuart villages) rooted her up and began to chew the shroud when some others rescued her, recovered the coffin and again reburied her. The original people were punished in the court of the Dean of York's peculiar; no proceedings were taken against the others (R.VI.C.27, p. 126).

send to court and secure his absolution so that he might be buried in the churchyard, but these are exceptional cases. The average contumacious person lived and died excommunicate. If he was poor, the legal disabilities would weigh lightly on him, and the only pressures which would induce him to seek absolution were the persuasions of the minister or of his employers. In a rural area where the squire reigned supreme the latter force might be considerable, but not all country parishes had squires. One letter written to the archdeacon's registrar at Nottingham shows how excommunication was a very practical punishment, by depriving a woman of the assistance of midwives:

I have received a writt of Excommunication against Marie Bell (my parishioner) and I dare not stay it without warrantie from your Court. Will you be pleased to be certified, that she waites her everie houre, and not able to travaile halfe a mile out of the towne. Let mee intreat so much favour of you (if it may bee) as to reverse that which is done, or els to absolve her againe, that she be not deprived of womens helpe, which now shee is like to stand in need of. I hope you will pittie a woman in her case, and not to show the high (*sic*) of your power and rigour of Law...

If there had been any rigorous enforcement of such medical ostracism of excommunicates, somewhere some midwife would have been presented for an infringement of the law, but no such case has yet come to light.[1] The suggestion created by the lack of presentments of this nature is that the social effects of excommunication depended very much on popular opinion. Immorality was generally regarded as a serious offence, and a respectable midwife might quite well not wish to attend Mary Bell while she was in trouble with the courts and her offence had not been purged by public penance. If Mary Bell had been sentenced because of (say) a presentment for sleeping in church, it is difficult to believe that a midwife would have refused her services.

Presentments for consorting with excommunicate persons were very rare. An occasional clergyman was presented for conducting a service with an excommunicate in the congregation—his usual defence was that he was unaware that the person in question was under the sentence.[2] A person who had had a child in fornication found it difficult to secure shelter except at home, for anyone who took her in was liable to be presented for it. Such a harbourer of an immoral person could only secure his freedom from censure by pro-

---

[1] Nottingham PB 314, Easter 1628. Women in such a case, who had not confessed the name of the father of the child, were often forced to do so when in labour, and a midwife could be called to testify on such a matter (R.VI.A.24, fo. 170).

[2] E.g. A 11, 19 Dec. 1601 (Nottingham). This discipline was usually enforced, e.g. Wm. Bosvile, gentleman, an excommunicate, came into church and the minister had to stop the service at Kirkby Underdale in 1635 (R.VI.A.24, fo. 287).

ducing the defaulter in court, or showing good cause why he was unable to do so. Thus a relative who gave house to a woman in such a case was very rarely charged with consorting with an excommunicate, because he would be normally charged with harbouring an immoral person. Elsewhere the charge of consorting was apparently sometimes made. The Chancellor of the diocese of Peterborough sentenced persons accused of it, and some cases have been discovered in the records of the Archdeaconry of Buckingham.[1] Despite these cases, the general impression of the court acts is that consorting with excommunicates was not normally the subject of prosecutions in the church courts.

It was the very size of the problem of contumacy that defeated any solution. Theoretically, the church authorities could have sued out the writ *de excommunicato capiendo*, and eventually the sheriff would have arrested the offender and kept him in prison until he submitted. In practice, the time and money which would have had to be consumed was prohibitive. Each writ needed to be sued for individually, and the cost in fees to the secular courts would have been at least 30s., as well as fees to apparitors and the legal officers of the church courts themselves. Many of the excommunicates concerned could not have afforded the fees in addition to the charges for absolution and other costs.[2] Nevertheless on occasion, perhaps as a warning to others in serious cases and particularly of rich men, or if someone had offered to pay the costs, such writs were taken out by the authorities.[3]

If a person remained contumacious there were three alternatives open to the authorities:

(1) The use of the High Commission. Normally, serious offences were referred directly to the Commissioners at York, either by the person being handed over to their pursuivant by the visitation court judge,[4] or by the judge

---

[1] The complaint against the chancellor shows that it was an isolated occurrence, for he replied, 'the lawe warrants this proceeding, and in the particular complayned of, the excommunicate person was a notorious whoremaister, and a Recusant' (John Lambe to the King, quoted by Notestein, Relf and Simpson, *Commons Debates 1621*, VII, 607). E. R. C. Brinkworth, 'The Laudian Church in Buckinghamshire', in *University of Birmingham Historical Journal*, V, no. 1 (1955), 34, n. 23. Two presentments of men harbouring excommunicate women were made in the Manchester Deanery in the 1633 provincial visitation, and one of a woman for the same in the Archdeaconry of Cleveland, 1634, but they were extremely rare in the north.

[2] Pre-Civil War MS versions of Francis Clerke's *Praxis* (e.g. that in the Chapter Library at York) have a chapter (26) which lists the secular fees. A list of all fees, from first citation, through excommunication, arrest and final absolution, totalled £4. 3s. 4d. (Bury St Edmunds, W. Suffolk Record Office, Sudbury Archdeaconry Records, E.14/11/4 fo. 2).

[3] York: R.VI.B.2, fo. 125a; R.VI.A.10, fo. 167 v. Notts.: A 15, 4 June 1606; in (York) R.VII.P.1, p. 811 is a transcript of a certificate of a man from Scrooby, presented for suspicion of immorality and excommunicated, arrested under the writ, who had successfully purged himself and been dismissed, A.D. 1595.

[4] E.g. R.VI.A.11, fo. 117, Edward Shawcross, curate of Weverham. Among a long list of accusations is one of teaching birth control to unmarried persons.

applying to the Commissioners to issue a warrant of arrest. Such action was only taken in exceptional circumstances, but did ensure that offenders in the worst cases did not escape punishment.[1] In Archbishop Neile's time the York Commissioners took over from their southern counterparts the device of Letters of Assistance, whereby the judges at visitation courts could use their apparitors or local constables to make an arrest and secure a bond that the accused would appear before the Commissioners. Little reference to the Commissioners' assistance to ordinary courts has been found other than in such cases, but there are extant the papers in the High Commission case of the office *c*. Coates which indicate the way Neile's officers called such assistance to their aid.[2] Coates was presented for drunkenness in the provincial visitation of 1633 and was ordered to acknowledge his offence in church. He failed to certify at the second court, but attended when Easdall's substitute held a third court in December 1634—or rather he attended at the registrar's temporary office in the afternoon. The exact nature of the business is not specified—Coates may well have had a certificate—but he refused to pay the fees, saying that he would rather pay them to any alewife than to the court's officers. The judge-substitute thereupon had him arrested, by virtue of Letters of Assistance, and committed to the parish constable until he entered bond for his appearance at York. Coates protested that 'the constables were for the king only, but this commitment was for the bishop', and consequently they had no authority over him, for the bishop had nothing but his consistory. However, Coates made the trans-Pennine journey from his home in Cumberland to York in March 1635 and submitted. (He may by then have been in custody, as he had been ordered to attend in January.) Coates' original contempt may reflect a growing opposition to the church courts, or it may have been an isolated occurrence. What is not in doubt is his surprise at the result of his words. He was evidently not a pauper, and was sufficiently literate at least to sign his name. It was necessary to discipline such a man even more than an illiterate pauper. Action of this nature by the High Commissioners must have done something to induce more outward respect for the ordinary church courts in the years before the Civil War.

(2) If the offender escaped the church courts he might fall into the hands of Justices of the Peace. When Chancellor Gibson retired from judicial office and settled down as a country gentleman he became one of the most active justices in the North Riding, and in the North and West Ridings clergymen were also appointed as justices. In Somerset, the Bishop of Bath and Wells

---

[1] E.g. R.VI.A.3a, fo. 210 v.; R.VI.A.18, fo. 184a; R.VI.A.20, fo. 183 v.; R.VI.A.21, fos. 70 and v., 78 v., 80.
[2] R.VII.H.2025.

and some of the cathedral clergy were often on the bench at Quarter Sessions in Wells, and the diocesan chancellor was one of the most active justices in the time of James I. In Lancashire, the civilian, Robert Parkinson, was an active justice, and the Bishop of Chester was also a justice but did not sit on the bench. Such men doubtless did their best to see that offenders were brought to book and stirred up their fellow justices to enforce the moral law. In other areas, however, no direct connection between Church and Quarter Sessions can be observed. The first clerical justices in Nottinghamshire were not appointed until 1796, the year in which the archdeaconry court gave up disciplinary work. Some towns maintained links with the church courts, as has been detected at Nottingham and at St Albans.[1]

All justices had to take notice of sexual immorality, for they had to do their best to secure affiliation orders or, in the last resort, decide which parish had to maintain a fatherless child. Under 18 Elizabeth I c. 3 justices were empowered to punish such offenders by whipping, and by 7 and 8 James I c. 4 to send the woman to a House of Correction for a year. Such punishments were regularly used. Lancashire justices often whipped both offenders, naked to the waist, and put them in the stocks. Somerset justices usually ordered the woman to be whipped—often 'until her back be bloody'—less usually the man. West Riding and Nottinghamshire justices also ordered whipping, the stocks or even penance in church. The printed records of the North Riding justices make little mention of such punishments, but there is reason for thinking that they were just as severe. Church presentments from that area reveal a man fined £5 for this offence, two women who had served their terms in the House of Correction, and a widow who had been 'sore whipped by the Justices'.[2]

The difference between the treatment of male and female offenders was not primarily due to the partiality of a male bench. Most men were involved, apparently, simply on the accusation of the woman. The justices would accept this evidence (unless it could be disproved) as the basis for an affiliation order but, except perhaps in Lancashire, refused to order corporal punishment on this evidence alone. Such commendable reluctance had one

---

[1] For Nottingham see above, p. 166. For St Albans see R. Peters, *Oculus Episcopi*, p. 74. Such links apparently also existed at Cambridge, see C. W. Dugmore and C. Duggan (eds.), *Studies in Church History*, I, 182 n. 6. Quarter Sessions records are: *North Riding Quarter Sessions Records* (North Riding Record Society), vol. I (1605–12) contains a calendar of all items: succeeding volumes only extracts. *West Riding Quarter Sessions*, I (1598–1602) and II (1611–42) in Yorks. Arch. Record Series, vols. III and LIV. *Quarter Sessions Records for the County of Somerset, 1607–25*. Somerset Record Soc. vol. XXIII. (Lancashire) *Quarter Sessions Rolls 1590–1606*, Chetham Soc, vol. 77 (N.S.). H. H. Copnall, *Nottinghamshire County Records—Notes and Extracts: Seventeenth Century*.

[2] R.VI.A.24, fos. 311, 405 v. (1637); R.VI.C.27, p. 98 (1634).

very interesting result, at least in some areas. Many times, in the reign of James I, the Somerset justices made an order in this form: the woman to be stripped to the waist and whipped about the market, but as there is no certain ground or vehement presumption to inflict the like on the reputed father he is to be left to the judgment of the ordinary. In practice this meant that the churchwardens had to present him and, if he denied the offence, he would be made to purge himself. The Lancashire justices on occasion simply ordered purgation if a man was to escape an affiliation order. Purgation in the church courts was often condemned because it compelled a man to swear to his own innocence, and it was finally abolished at the Restoration,[1] yet justices found it a convenient procedure to establish guilt or innocence when their own procedures were unable to cope with the situation. Some offenders were not punished by the justices, sometimes because they had already performed the penance ordered by a church court, at other times no reason was given but presumably it was the same. This being so, it is surprising that so many refused to do penance, which was surely a lesser punishment than whipping.

Justices punished many more 'ecclesiastical' crimes or offences than sexual immorality. As they controlled licences for common ale-houses, they were particularly concerned to punish those who infringed the terms of their licences by opening their ale-houses during service time. Despite spot checks by churchwardens, the number of offending ale-house keepers was considerable, and justices had an ultimate sanction which was considerably more effective than that of the church courts—the power to revoke licences. Most justices punished other Sabbath-breaking infringements. In the decade before the Civil War the Nottingham town bench fined persons who drank or played cards instead of going to church, 10s.; habitual absentees were fined the statutory 1s. a Sunday in a lump sum at the end of a quarter. Lancashire justices—whose prohibition of Sunday games in 1616 provoked the royal Declaration on Sports in 1617, repeated for the whole country in 1618— were severe on Sunday games-players. Their basic premise that such merriment led to immorality was echoed by the Somerset bench when, in 1617, it ordered a reputed father and the mother of a bastard to be whipped 'till their bodies shall be bloody', and two fiddles to be played before them 'in regard to make known their lewdness in begetting the said base child upon the Sabbath day coming from dancing'.[2] The North Riding justices faced similar problems, particularly the tendency to put merriment before church attendance on warm summer afternoons. One ale-house keeper in that Riding

[1] 13 Charles II, St. I, c. 12, sect. 4. The *ex officio* oath was also finally abolished by this section.
[2] Somerset *Quarter Sessions Records*, p. 211.

organized drinking and dancing (with music by pipes and drummers) which drew crowds of one hundred persons on two Sundays in June 1606, and a person who used the churchyard for a game during Sunday afternoon service was whipped. Nottinghamshire justices likewise dealt with non-church-goers and non-communicants by fine, and also had many present-ments for disorders on Sundays.

Other offences of an ecclesiastical nature which were punished by justices were sorcery and fortune-telling (penance in church in the North Riding), drunkenness (fined up to £1), disturbances in church and churchyard, non-payment of church rates, common scolds (by the ducking stool), scandal (penance in church, by Somerset justices), recusancy and non-conformity. There were few offenders who could escape punishment either by church court or quarter sessions, except by absconding. The justices seem to have had as little effective answer to the absconder as the church courts, but the total effect of their actions must await further investigation of their criminal court rolls for much published Quarter Sessions material has been confined to their administrative orders. The most effective church court so far discovered was that of the Ely diocese where 77 per cent of persons presented were amenable to court order in 1619. In that diocese the bishop was the secular lord and appointed his own justices. His church court held Quarter Sessions to complement his secular court and the offender had a simple choice of frying-pan or fire.[1]

(3) The last alternative open to the church courts was simply to allow a contumacious person to remain excommunicate, and the figures provided in the Tables, showing the effect of visitations, indicate the extent to which this was done.

Where a person was marked as excommunicated, or there was a blank entry, and he subsequently appeared at another court session, he was always first absolved. Yet it is impossible to believe that all sentences were expected to take effect. The case of Alderman Matthew Topham of York is a good example. He figured among a list of persons owing a church rate in the 1623 visitation; his debt was 1s. The entry is blank, normally denoting non-attendance and excommunication, but in the following year he was elected Lord Mayor and subsequently gave evidence (in a prosecution of Puritans) as to what happened in church. Against this can be set the evidence of the Frodsham Deanery in 1590, where the local dean, left by the chancellor to deal with the cases, certified to York at the end of his acts that the persons concerned had either done their penance or their excommunication had been publicly denounced. It is probably right to regard York City as an exception,

---

[1] Cambridge University Library, Ely Diocesan Records, B/2/37.

for such cases could easily be handed over to the city authorities or dealt with informally.

The total who were officially excommunicated in 1623, allowing for a large proportion of the 'record of case not completed' category, was about 2,100 and in the Norwich diocese in 1627 and 1633, about 1,600 each year. Even if allowance is made for cases such as Topham's and the greater efficiency of archdeaconry visitations, the annual York figures must have been at least 1,500. These two factors, however, do not seem to have been present to the same extent in the Norwich diocese, and its total must have been much the same as for the northern diocese, although both totals were probably less at an earlier date. It will be observed that the number of 418 persons reported as obstinate excommunicates in York in 1623 (Table 26) bears no relation to the figures just cited. Further proof of its inadequacy is shown by the citation in that year of 765 persons who were contumacious in the previous diocesan visitation in 1619, having been presented for the most serious offences (sexual immorality and illegal marriage were the great majority). Clearly church-wardens did not often bother to present the same excommunicates visitation after visitation; it would simply have wasted everybody's time in serving useless citations. A similar conservative estimate for the diocese of Chester (Table 29) about the same period, would suggest that something like 2,000 excommunications a year were being issued (ignoring the Cumberland deanery of Copeland).

These three dioceses together cover 23·8 per cent of the area of England and Wales. The population of England and Wales at the time was about five and a half millions, but as there were large, sparsely populated areas in Norfolk, Suffolk, Yorkshire and Westmorland, and allowing for the concentration of population in the London area, it is doubtful whether more than one million people lived in the three dioceses. A very conservative estimate would be that a person lived ten years after excommunication, but allowing this as reasonable, there would be about 50,000 hardened excommunicates at any one time in the area, 5 per cent of the total population. It is doubtful whether other members of the families of these persons took their religious obligations at all seriously, so (allowing two members of a family for every excommunicate) there would be about 15 per cent of the population in the excommunicate classes—a seam of irreligious people lying below the greater mass of nominal Christians. While these figures cannot claim complete accuracy, they are not pure guesswork, and they serve to illustrate the pastoral problems which faced the parochial clergy. The not infrequent appearances in court of the latter on behalf of their parishioners indicate that these problems were realized and often tackled.

15-2

The truth is, the church discipline by itself had little compulsive effect on the poorer classes. Excommunication hardly touched them and the Church had no power to use the physical methods employed by Quarter Sessions on the poor—whipping, the pillory and stocks. Thus the 'paupers' were given what amounted to preferential treatment by the church courts. The most obvious way was over payment of fees. Those in the Norwich diocese were only 1*s*. 4*d*., but in the Sudbury Deanery in 1593, four persons were totally excused, six paid half-fees and seven paid 1*s*. In the Frodsham Deanery in 1590 seven were excused, and in Nantwich ten were excused and three paid in part; in 1633, twenty-three were excused in Frodsham and twenty-eight paid half-fees. Fees were not marked in the acts for the Doncaster Deanery in 1590, but two persons are noted as excused; in 1619, ten were excused, while fifteen owed their fees but were not punished for non-payment; in 1633, sixteen were totally excused and eleven were allowed to pay in part. No paupers were noted in Somerset but this was hardly surprising for the fees collected were normally only 4*d*.

Finally, two examples may be given from Nottinghamshire. The man involved with Mary Bell performed penance but was himself excommunicated for non-payment of fees. Two months later he attended court, presumably with a certificate of his lack of means, was absolved and discharged *gratis* as a pauper.[1] On another occasion a vicar wrote to the registrar on behalf of a man who, after excommunication, had repaired the part of the churchyard wall for which he was responsible. The man's trouble was that he only had 3*s*. or 4*s*. which he had borrowed, and could not pay the fees in full. The vicar begged the registrar to accept this sum, otherwise the man would have to remain under sentence. At the foot of the letter the registrar noted that the man was absolved the same day (he had probably brought the letter with him), but no word as to whether the borrowed money was accepted.[2] With evidence of this nature before us, it is impossible to accept at its face value the complaint of the *Petition presented to the Parliament from the County of Nottingham* (1641) that absolution was refused to the poor who had no money to pay their fees.[3]

The courts were also prepared to adjust their procedure to reduce expense for the poor, sometimes to such an extent that a pauper could escape on his bare denial on oath. The judge at Frodsham in 1590 remitted three cases for local examination because of poverty, and this was a usual practice at diocesan visitations. The process of purgation involved much expense: the fees for the examination of compurgators and sentence were the same as for witnesses and

---

[1] Thomas Key, A 37, 12 and 26 July, 27 Sept. 1628. For Mary Bell, above p. 221.
[2] PB 328, Michaelmas 1638 file. E. Warren of Marnham to Coombe, 27 Nov.
[3] Quoted by Hill, *Society and Puritanism* 364.

sentence in the Consistory Court, and in addition the accused was expected to pay the travelling and other expenses of the witnesses when they came to court. Consequently the poor were sometimes allowed to purge themselves on their own oath alone.[1] Appeals were not only addressed to registrars. One of the features of the age was the amount of detailed work on small personal matters conducted by the men at the head of the various branches of the administration, and the Church was no exception to this. Where someone who knew the archbishop thought that archiepiscopal intervention was the best way to secure his wishes, he evidently had no hesitation in writing direct to the archbishop on behalf of paupers. In April 1622 a husband and wife, presented as far back as 1619 for standing excommunicate for three years, were absolved *gratis* on the archbishop's order. They neither appeared personally nor were punished by the chancellor.[2]

Typical of the petitions addressed to court is a letter to the Chancellor of Norwich, preserved among the 1633 visitation court acts. It was written by the minister of Blythburgh in Suffolk, and also signed by five parishioners. John Sallowes and his wife had been presented at that visitation for incontinency before marriage, together with four others who had been caught drinking in service time. The correction court was held at Bungay, only thirteen miles away, but none of them attended and eventually the minister received the excommunications to denounce in church. Thereupon the minister wrote lamenting the poverty of the times, unemployment and high prices, and the poverty of the excommunicates. He then went on to say that, except for Sallowes and his wife, they had all recently been dismissed in the commissary court—rather an impertinence, for the diocesan visitation had been held at Easter and the local visitations at the following Michaelmas. Sallowes' poverty was likewise described, with the addendum that he had been recently chosen as parish clerk, an office which he could not now fill. As a result of the letter all were absolved and discharged *gratis*. Sallowes and his wife were not even required to do their penance.[3] The evidence examined

---

[1] One instance in Sudbury Deanery, 1593; another at Doncaster, 1633. Two persons denied immorality, a person present said he believed them to be innocent, the judge dismissed them 'by reason of poverty'—R.VI.A.24, fo. 432 v. (Retford, 1637). In the latter case the husband and wife were allowed purgation on their own oaths as paupers, and were absolved free of costs, although they did not attend until November 1638. A husband and wife cited in 1619 in the Doncaster Deanery did not appear; re-cited in 1623, the husband had died and the wife was simply dismissed *gratis* as a pauper. Another example of purgation on the accused's own oath is in R.VI.A.19, fo. 121 v., where poverty is not noted but may be suspected.

[2] R.VI.A.19, fo. 177. A similar case, R.VI.A.20, fo. 57 v.

[3] In the acts for Sudbury in 1627 is a similar case of a drunkard who was excommunicated for contumacy. After a letter from the churchwardens he was absolved and a written monition was sent to him, but fees of 1s. were entered as paid. The clergy's efforts on behalf of paupers were not always rewarded. At Wentworth (Doncaster 1619) two persons presented for immorality were

leads to the conclusion that partial or total remissions of fees and adjustments of procedure on account of poverty were an accepted feature of the church courts, so that, making allowance for occasional harsh judges, everything was done to make it possible for the poor to prove their innocence, carry out court orders or to obtain their absolutions.

A summary of many points raised, and a monument to church discipline in England, is provided by the figures collected in Table 33. The Neile administration's attempt to reinvigorate the visitation system reached its apogee in the diocesan visitation of 1636 and the subsequent correction courts of 1637. The pressure on churchwardens to present all crimes of ecclesiastical cognizance, and to be more vigorous in detecting them, resulted in an increase in presentments from 3,250 in 1623 to 5,100 (in round figures, ignoring those previously excommunicated and recusants). The vigorous use of all means of coercion of offenders produced conformity to the courts' orders at the rate of three out of every five persons, instead of one out of every three. In microcosm, the parish of Leeds which, in 1623 had presented 85 persons and saw 5 penances performed, in 1636 presented 139 persons of whom 26 performed penance and 5 obeyed other orders; in all, 30 per cent of those presented in 1623 were amenable to church discipline, while in 1636 the number of offenders had increased by 63·5 per cent and those of them amenable to church discipline had become 47 per cent. It is impossible to say how far these figures (satisfactory from the point of view of the church authorities) reflected a real increase in the number of offenders, and how far a more efficient system of detection. At least, churchwardens in town parishes and other refractory areas could take heart that there was some point in taking the trouble to perform their duties efficiently. We shall now look at some of these figures in more detail.

First, the record of the correction courts themselves. The number of presentments made it necessary to employ two registrars instead of one, and they kept a reasonably full report of the proceedings. In the 'entry incomplete' column in the Table are included cases which have no ending entered and where no act was done (and this stated), those respited or transferred to another court (usually Chancery), and where there was no entry. Most of the latter must be accounted contumacious, as elsewhere when there is no entry, on the assumption that the registrars simply forgot to enter the excommunication. There are various instances where a note of absolution was entered with no previous record of excommunication.[1] For this reason three-quarters of

excommunicated for contumacy. They both succeeded in obtaining the services of curates to go to York to secure their absolutions on promise of performing penance, but neither of them fulfilled their undertakings.   [1] E.g. R.VI.A.24, fos. 54 v., 57, 58 r. and v.

TABLE 33

Analysis of the York diocesan visitation of 1636–7 and the Cleveland Archdeaconry visitations of 1632 and 1634

Archdeaconry	Obeyed court					Excommunicated			Entry incomplete	Fled	Died	Sequestrations	Miscellaneous[1]	Total presentments	Percentage obedient	Previously presented	Recusants	Excused fees (no. of cases)	
	Dismissed or admonished	Performed penance	Obeyed other court orders	Purgations	Total	Never attended	Disobeyed court orders	Total										In whole	In part
Nottingham	200 (7)	66 (9)	30 (2)	3	299 (18)	153	83	236	61	11	6	—	3	616	52·5	10	80	17	10
York	616 (167)	560 (160)	57 (27)	19	1252 (354)	1015	105	1120	199	16	35	10	7	2639	50·6	112	509	57	36
East Riding	277 (40)	175 (48)	55 (39)	3	510 (127)	217	51	268	27	4	7	8	12	836	70·1	36	408	24	9
Cleveland	305 (84)	119 (67)	35 (15)	1	460 (166)	384	47	431	64	9	13	8	18	1003	50·0	18	1034	30	21
Diocese, 1637	1398 (298)	920 (284)	177 (83)	26	2521 (665)	1769[2]	286	2055	351	40	61	26	40	5094	59·4	176	2031	128	76
Cleveland, 1632	165 (39)	112 (25)	—	4	281 (64)	140	28	168	26	12	3	—	1	491	76·7	26	?[3]	13	4
Cleveland, 1634	271 (38)	120 (19)	2	7	400 (57)	5	8	13	104	13	17	—	—	547	78·9	18	718	40	1

Figures in brackets denote number of total in column who attended or obeyed after excommunication.

Percentage obedient calculated on total of obedient, excommunicated and entry incomplete only. 25 per cent of incomplete entries assumed obedient, except in Cleveland, 1634, where only 10 per cent so assumed.

Diocesan figures for Cleveland include peculiars of Allertonshire, Howdenshire and part of the peculiar of the Dean of York.

[1] Includes suspended clergy and schoolmasters, and those ordered to be attached for appearance before High Commissioners.

[2] Includes twelve who attended but excommunicated for non-payment of fees.

[3] Certain parishes with long lists were not entered in the A.B.

231

TABLE 34

Itinerary for correction courts 1627

Deanery	Date	Place
York	11 July	York
Doncaster	30 July	Doncaster
Doncaster	31 July	Rotherham
Pontefract	2 August	Wakefield
Pontefract	4 August	Halifax
Craven	7 August	Skipton
Old Ainsty	9 August	Otley
New Ainsty	11 August	Tadcaster
Hull and Holderness	14 August	Hull
Harthill and Beverley	15 August	Beverley
Buckrose and Dickering	17 August	Kilham
Ryedale	18 August	Malton
Cleveland	20 August	Helmsley
Bulmer	21 August	Sheriff Hutton
(No record of the visitation of Nottinghamshire)		

the number of incomplete entries have been assumed to be contumacious when estimating the effectiveness of the court, and the remaining one-quarter counted as 'obedient'.

The visitation was held at Easter 1636, as is proved by the lack of Easter visitation records in the Archdeaconry of Nottingham, where the next visitation was not held until 1 December. The correction courts were not held until 1637, and this can most plausibly be ascribed to the congestion of business in the York administration. Table 34 shows that when Easdall had a free hand—at his first visitation in 1627—all the courts were held during the July and August following Easter, in an orderly sequence, and at many centres.

Easdall's courts for the 1636 visitation were held in 1637 as shown in Table 35.

The fact that these courts were held a year or more after the original presentments had been made underlines the success achieved by Easdall in his drive for increased efficiency. He had no greater resources at his command than Dodsworth had in 1623, yet he was able to use his powers to much greater effect. This Laudian efficiency has misled the older generation of historians into believing that the Laudians were reviving an outworn medieval relic. Thus G. M. Trevelyan could write:

The Church courts, which had for a hundred years been cowed by fear of the emancipated laity and the prospect of further confiscations, were inspired once

TABLE 35

Itinerary for correction courts 1637

Deanery	Date	Place
Bulmer	14 March	York
York	7 or 17 March	York
New Ainsty (no record: acts follow immediately after York and were probably as for York Deanery)		
Harthill and Beverley, part of Dickering	28 March	Beverley
Hull and Holderness	29 March	Beverley
Ryedale and part of Dickering	31 March	Malton
Cleveland	17 April	Thirsk
(Two advocates acted as substitutes for Easdall)		
Buckrose	19 April	York
Craven and Old Ainsty	15 May	Skipton
(Some folios are headed 'Bradford' and a court may have been held there: at least one act was done at Otley on 16 May)		
Pontefract (no heading, but courts held at this time)		
Doncaster	19 and 20 May	Rotherham
Retford	8 September	East Retford
Nottingham and Bingham	12 September	Nottingham
Newark	14 September	Southwell

more with a conceit of their authority and traditions...The Church courts still retained the power to punish sin. In the last two centuries of Catholicism this jurisdiction had been odious and venal; under the Tudors the terrified clergy had let it fall into abeyance; and now a few honest men tried to revive what no large body of people were willing again to tolerate.[1]

Easdall's problem was, in part, not only to produce greater efficiency generally, but to inject more effort into diocesan visitations in particular. It has been suggested that archdeaconry visitations were appreciably more effective than those held by the archbishop,[2] and this is confirmed by the Cleveland archdeaconry figures given in Table 33. This archdeaconry was favourably situated at this time in having a resident archdeacon in its northern part (Henry Thurscross, Rector of Stokesley), and his son Timothy as Official and resident in the centre of the archdeaconry (Vicar of Kirkby Moorside), both Puritans, with the registrar convenient for the south-west of the archdeaconry at York. The Cleveland administration was, before Neile's primary visitation at Michaelmas 1632, securing obedience from three-quarters of those whom it cited, and although it may have been exceptional, it teaches us to beware of using expressions such as 'Laudian efficiency' too

[1] *England Under The Stuarts* (16th ed. 1933), p. 175.
[2] Above, p. 208.

233

loosely. A keen, Puritan court, operating with the support of the justices, could overcome the drawbacks of the large recusant minority in part of the area. The 'emancipated laity' and the 'unterrified clergy' combined to punish sin without the promptings of either Laud or Neile or the help of their 'few honest men'.

The number of persons who defied Easdall and remained excommunicate was about 2,300 (allowing for a percentage of the incomplete entries), showing that many persons were still prepared to ignore church discipline. Figures have been given to show the numbers of those who had to be excommunicated before they would comply with a citation or court order, about a fifth of minor offenders, but about a third where a court order had to be obeyed. The number of penances performed was considerable, but as many of these were husband and wife the actual number of cases was smaller than the number of individuals. Husband and wife, presented for the same offences, were regarded as one case by the registrar, and charged one fee. Court orders, either administrative in nature or to produce certificates of church attendance or communicating, were relatively few if allowance is made for many orders to churchwardens to provide copies of parish registers.[1] All the worst offenders who remained contumacious were re-cited at the diocesan visitation of 1640, and a sprinkling of these persons then sought absolution. The last recorded absolution was granted in 1643.

The last two columns show the number of cases (man and wife counting as one case) where remissions of fees were granted in whole or in part, in almost all cases to persons marked as paupers. As a result of these appearances *in forma pauperis* (as the Cleveland Archdeaconry acts call them), 289 persons or about one person in nine was relieved of the payment of court fees either totally or in some part. (The Cleveland Archdeaconry, averaged over two years, had a similar proportion of paupers.) The court did issue some excommunications for non-payment of fees, but only twelve persons obstinately refused to pay. These statistics would seem to show that fee-collecting was not one of the major problems of correction courts in the diocese, and that relief of the poor offender was given within reasonable limits.

Easdall held a diocesan visitation in 1640, but under great difficulties, and his efforts in 1636–7 represented the summit both of his achievement and of that of church discipline in the diocese for all time. Whether these results represent a typical picture of the Laudian era is something which must await further investigation. Certain conclusions about this survey of church discipline generally can, however, be briefly stated.

---

[1] A copy of the entry for each year should have been handed in at the Easter visitation. This seems to have been the first time the chancellor required them in the course of his diocesan visitation.

Church discipline

First, church discipline must be related to the total discipline exercised over private morals throughout the country during this period, including that enforced by state courts. Such discipline was generally thought to be necessary and the Church was considered the appropriate organ to enforce it, but the local Borough and Quarter Sessions also operated in the same way according to circumstances. Secondly, the effect of church discipline was to remove appreciable numbers of the population from effective membership of the Church by excommunication. It must have been accepted that the exercise of church discipline would have this effect, and that only a small proportion of obstinate excommunicates could be won back to a desire for church membership and absolution. Thirdly, the weight of court fees has been very much exaggerated in historical writing. There was always remission in whole or in part where circumstances warranted it, together with special treatment to enable paupers to fulfil the law's requirements in the cheapest possible way. Fourthly, the organization and efficiency of a court were usually reflected in the degree of obedience to its orders. Fifthly, the church courts being administrative organs of government policy in ecclesiastical matters, as well as the authority for administering moral discipline, inevitably suffered from attacks by opponents of both these aspects of their work. It is extremely difficult to separate genuine abuses from propaganda attacks, and it may never be possible to make this distinction with complete confidence on the available evidence. The number of persons who wished to see the abolition of moral discipline by the community was at that period very small.

Additional Note

The use of the church courts by Justices of the Peace to resolve their more difficult problems (above, p. 225) is illustrated by the action of William Lambarde. Lambarde, barrister, bencher of Lincoln's Inn and author of the standard work for J.P.s, *Eirenarcha* (1582), was a Justice for Kent. On 24 December, 1583, he and a civilian J.P. ordered an immoral woman to be whipped and sent to the house of correction, '. . . but as touching the reputed father, we left the decision thereof to the ecclesiastical trial, for that she confessed herself to have been carnally known of many men'. (Quoted by J. H. Gleason, *The Justice of the Peace in England 1558–1640*, 1969, p. 12.) Such a reference, by a Justice of Lambarde's standing, may be taken as typical, and does not suggest that the Justices (in Elizabethan days, at least) were unduly influenced by Puritan propaganda against the church courts.

CONCLUSION

THE ABOLITION OF THE YORK LEGAL TRADITION

In 1830 Granville Venables Vernon, Chancellor of the diocese of York since 1818, gave evidence before the Ecclesiastical Courts Commission. He was asked, 'What peculiarities of practice are there in the court at York?' He replied,

There were some, but I have one by one disposed of them. Our court is particularly circumstanced with reference to its practice, which I found no authority for, except oral and traditional evidence among its practitioners. I found there some advocates and proctors who had practised in it for a period of forty or fifty years, and they were in possession, or considered themselves so, of the practice of the Court; and when I was proceeding upon what I knew to be the law in Doctors' Commons, the advocates constantly met me with objections that this had never been the practice of this court; and for a time, if I found their statement authenticated by such other testimony as I could derive through the proctors, I yielded to it; but by degrees as I began to find my own ground stronger, and their memory perhaps weaker, I began to announce, that in future cases I should adopt the practice of Doctors' Commons; and having given that notice, I think I can now safely say that I have assimilated in almost every material point the practice of the court to that of Doctors' Commons.[1]

In these measured words, uttered with appropriate self-satisfaction, Vernon recorded his single-handed extinction of a legal tradition which the Reformation, the Stuart bureaucracy, the Puritan revolutionaries and all other disturbances in the even flow of history had alike failed to extinguish. It is true that the northern High Commission at first had been organized on the methods traditional at York, and the Laudians had made it conform with London practice, but this was a royal court, not part of the archbishop's prerogative, and there is no evidence to show that the Laudians either tried or desired to produce uniformity in the ordinary church courts. Nevertheless, there has always been a tendency to treat the Church in England as a unified whole, and the establishment of a national Church at the Reformation has allowed this process to gather momentum. The Church of post-Reformation England operated under a national system of law in which provincial variations had no place (whatever the theoretical powers of the Convocation of

[1] *Report* (1832), p. 119.

York). The mid-nineteenth-century reforms, which confined church jurisdiction to purely ecclesiastical concerns and abolished the practice of civil law, finally buried existing provincial traditions. Yet arguments for provincial organization are still heard. A Welsh province has been created, and many voices have been raised to support 'regionalism' in Church as well as in State. Chancellor Vernon's assumption that the practice to which he was accustomed in London was somehow 'right', and York's customs 'wrong' and so to be changed, is the very attitude of mind which provides 'provincials' with a reasonable argument for asserting their local autonomy within the wider framework of a national Church.

The York tradition, as discovered by Chancellor Vernon, was by no means confined to peculiarities of law and practice. His evidence revealed something the court records themselves could never tell us. He discovered that in matters of probate, if the registrar had any doubts about the validity of a will he consulted the chancellor—who for many years had also been commissary of the Exchequer. If the chancellor rejected the will his decision was usually accepted by the person submitting it, but it was open to the latter to prove it in open court if he could. Vernon continued this practice (although he lost fees by it) because it was so useful. He told the Ecclesiastical Courts Commission:

There is something of the same kind prevailing in the whole of the practice of our court, and certainly within my observation most usefully, yet in the eyes of a lawyer most very irregularly. I should say that the great utility of my position is rather that of an arbitrator than of a Judge, and I find, more particularly in matters that relate to the clergy and churchwardens, between the churchwardens and the parish, and between the clergy and the parishioners, by stopping the cause at the outset, the parties agreeing, not by any formal document, but by desiring to have my opinion on the case.[1]

And he proceeded to describe how cases that would have been long and costly and perpetuated a feud, had been stopped by an agreement to accept his decision. The legal peculiarities of the York church courts antedated the Commonwealth period, and it would be interesting to know whether this tradition of free legal aid, and of arbitration rather than the more expensive mode of litigation, also antedated it. Considering the tendency towards inflexibility which administration displayed in the eighteenth century, there is something to be said for tracing its origins further back.

Two observations may be made on the method of administration which Vernon inherited. The first is that it would be difficult for a common lawyer to adapt himself to it as Vernon had done. Vernon obviously found it unusual,

[1] *Ibid.*

even in church courts, but he realized its practical utility. The civil law tradition was less bound by precedent and more open to adaptation than the common law tradition. The second is that by acting as an arbitrator in disputes, rather than as a judge, he was performing a pastoral function in reconciling Christians in dispute, rather than simply pronouncing judicially on the rights or wrongs of the matter. To this we shall return.

THE LAICIZATION OF CHURCH ADMINISTRATION

An important feature of church administration during this period was the way in which it gradually came under lay control. An immediate result was an increase in fees, but there were others of greater significance. Lay judges tended to become independent of the bishops and clergy. The medieval judge who was a clergyman saw things from the inside of the clerical organization of the Church, and was part of it. The layman had an outsider's viewpoint and his own professional standards. In the period under review the cathedral clergy at York and local clergymen at Nottingham were still associated with the administration of the High Commission, church discipline and even judicial office itself. Clerical chancellors, Officials and commissaries also existed elsewhere, but they were increasingly in a minority. The lay chancellors of Norwich only used clergymen for very minor duties, such as the probate of uncontested wills, and at the beginning of the seventeenth century only one out of four commissaries in the diocese was in holy orders. The real divide came, however, with the abolition of the practice of civil law in the mid-nineteenth century. The common law judges who succeeded the civilians brought a different outlook to the working of the church courts and a legal training hardly in sympathy with the canon law–civil law tradition.

It is because the common law judge has come to exercise an independent position in the British constitution that common lawyers have fitted uneasily into the church system. Modern chancellors see themselves acting independently of their bishop, as a secular judge is independent of monarch, executive and legislature.[1] It is easy to forget that the modern chancellor acts almost always in his capacity as the bishop's vicar-general, and, as we have seen, the bishops of the sixteenth and seventeenth centuries knew the function of a vicar was that of a deputy and were always prepared to act themselves if the need arose. Faculty jurisdiction, which comprises the greater part of the modern chancellor's work, has evolved from a bishop's pastoral oversight of the churches in his diocese. If a bishop can alienate a part of his

[1] E.g. E. Garth Moore, *An Introduction to English Canon Law* (1967), pp. 130–2.

pastoral duties to a vicar-general who is then only responsible for his decisions to a superior judge (on appeal), then the whole episcopal system falls to the ground. The right ordering of churches and burial grounds is a pastoral responsibility of the bishop, and in exercising it on his behalf the vicar-general is fulfilling a pastoral task and his practice should take this into account. This tradition of independence was only possible because of the change to life patents in Elizabethan days. Dean Hutton rightly objected to Archbishop Sandys' grant of a patent for life to his chancellor as being hurtful to his successors. No longer could a bishop (or an archdeacon) appoint his own man to head his administration unless a vacancy occurred. Beneficed canonists had not objected to patents during pleasure because they were secure for life in their benefices. Career laymen also wanted security and a patent for life was their security. The system seems generally to have worked well but the stories of Levett at the Exchequer and of the early seventeenth-century Norwich chancellors indicate the difficulties which could arise—both in maintaining standards and over a conflict of aims in administration.

CIVIL LAW AND COMMON LAW

The church records themselves suggest directly little of the conflict of the lawyers and their courts, except for the occasional prohibition from the secular courts of a case in the church courts; but the fact that the church administration was staffed by civil lawyers had certain effects on the history of the Church in England.

First, civil law and common law reflected the two political philosophies current in England at the time. The one saw the source of law in the King-in-Parliament, the other in the monarch alone. Common lawyers generally supported the former, civilians the latter. Thomas Ridley, in his *View of the Civile and Ecclesiastical Law* (1607), said clearly that the king's will is law. He is to be obeyed in all things, except those contrary to the law of God and of human justice, 'for himself is instead of the whole law, yea he is the law itself, and the only interpreter thereof'.[1] No wonder James I heartily approved of the book! Charles I's administration neglected Parliament, and worked directly through the prerogative courts of Star Chamber and High Commission, the Councils of the North and of Wales, and the church courts. All these courts had their own usefulness, and were tolerable under a monarch who worked with Parliament but became intolerable when operated to enforce the royal will alone. The distinction between these different courts became blurred, and when royal absolutism was abolished they all fell

[1] (4th ed.), p. 140.

together. Although all civilians were not absolutists, most of them were, and they helped the Church to become allied with one particular political philosophy, a philosophy which also guided the continental monarchies with which England was in perennial conflict.

Secondly, however much English nationalism had been moulded in the later Middle Ages in conflict with the French and in other ways, there is no doubt that there was a great upsurge of this nationalism in the sixteenth century. England came to regard the Papacy much in the same way as African nationalists regard the English in the twentieth century—as a foreign imperialist who drained wealth out of the country. Thus the common lawyers took pride in the national origins of their law and ignored the fact that it was less civilized than that of their opponents—as in the subordinate place it gave to women, and in its deficient mercantile law. The Church of England not only had an unreformed judicial and administrative system, papal in origin, but it was also using a law which was foreign to the country. These handicaps added fuel to the opposition to the Church.

After the Restoration the old conflicts died down. Civil lawyers jettisoned the political theories which were associated with their law, and the church courts made a reception of some of the principles of common law. The *ex officio* oath was abolished and a man could no longer be obliged to purge himself of a crime with which he was accused. The standards of common law became more accepted. The final result of all this conflict was that the Church retained courts and laws but her own law (canon law) never developed to meet new needs. It has been tossed about by civilians and common lawyers until today it has no life left in it.[1]

CHURCH DISCIPLINE OVER MORALS

Although there want not,...great swarms of vices worthy to be rebuked, unto such decay is true godliness and virtuous living now come, yet above other vices the outrageous seas of adultery (or breaking of wedlock), whoredom, fornication, and uncleanness have not only brast in, but also overflowed almost the whole world, unto the great dishonour of God, the exceeding infamy of the name of Christ, the notable decay of true religion, and the utter destruction of the public wealth; and that so abundantly that, through the customable use thereof, this vice is grown into such an height, that in a manner among many it is counted no sin at all, but rather a pastime, a dalliance, and but a touch of youth; not rebuked, but winked at; not punished, but laughed at. (*Against Whoredom and Uncleanness*, from *The First Book of Homilies*.)

[1] The writer has heard two diocesan chancellors admit that they knew no church law before their appointment, and he suspects that the same is true of most modern chancellors.

Conclusion

If it was not for the old-fashioned language it might be thought that the above polemic was directed against the permissive society of the 1960s. It was, in fact, directed against the permissive society of the 1550s, and is a good illustration of the thought behind the reinvigoration of church discipline which has been traced in previous chapters. There was, in many places, a feeling that society was decaying, and an efficient discipline over morals was needed. Geneva welcomed Calvin because he promised to 'clean up' the city,[1] but the burghers of Geneva were by no means the only ruling class to diagnose moral rot in the community for which they were responsible. The English local gentry, indeed, applied a moral discipline in their capacity as Justices of the Peace, but the feeling was still common that such work was properly the sphere of the Church. It is not our concern to argue here whether morals were then in a state of decay, or whether indeed every generation is simply convinced that it is more sinful than any that preceded it. People at the time believed that a 'cleaning up' was necessary, and there was enough evidence to confirm that opinion. One example of contemporary scandal may suffice to illustrate the sort of case that aroused the wrath of the preacher and provided the disciplinary courts with their material.

In 1598 there were two prisoners in York castle, William Nelson of Newland in the parish of Drax occupied an outer room, and Charles Barnby, gentleman, the inner chamber which opened out of it. Barnby took a liking to Mrs Nelson and made friends with her when she came to visit her husband. Later, he proposed to Nelson that he should buy Mrs Nelson from him. Nelson agreed and a document was drawn up by a solicitor who was also a prisoner. A divorce was needed, so Mrs Redhead, wife of the governor of the castle, was bribed to take part. Mrs Nelson was invited to a wedding party of two of Mrs Redhead's servants, and when she went to see her husband she accepted an invitation to step into Barnby's room and the door was shut behind her. Later that night, with two servants, Mrs Redhead peered through the door and saw enough to provide evidence in a divorce case. The following morning she went to Barnby with a cock-and-bull story about an agent of the archbishop who had come prying in the night, and who had only been fobbed off by her own resourcefulness. Barnby replied to the hint by sending her to a mercer for further cloth for dresses, but to Mrs Redhead's dismay she found that the mercer was not prepared to grant Barnby any more credit. At this stage she seems to have scented real danger and turned informer, carefully suppressing her own part in the scheme. Mrs Nelson was arrested and charged with adultery, and gradually the High Commissioners ferreted out the whole story. Nelson had sold his wife for twenty pounds and he probably

[1] R. N. Carew Hunt, *Calvin* (1933), pp. 141–2.

241

had the better of the bargain. While he was in prison his wife had been committing adultery with one William Babthorpe of Drax.[1]

The criticism of the first *Admonition to the Parliament* that Commissary Courts were 'but a pettie little stinking ditche, that floweth oute of that former great puddle' [*sc.* the Archbishop of Canterbury's courts] has often been copied in modern books, but the precise criticism of church discipline was that it 'punisheth whoredomes and adulteryes with toyishe censures'. Public penance in church was evidently not a sufficiently severe punishment in the eyes of the Puritans, and the efforts of the Lancashire justices must have come nearer to their ideal. Given the general view that discipline was necessary, the modern student must make up his own mind which of the three contemporary methods was best—Quarter Sessions, Anglican discipline or Presbyterian discipline? Local discipline—by justices or by presbyteries— was cheap, acquainted with local circumstances and flexible. Anglican discipline varied in cost, was more (but not completely) subject to formalities, and was administered by a judge who was less likely to be influenced by local prejudice and pressures. All justice was at that time inefficient by our standards,[2] but Anglican discipline, with its great degree of contumacy, seems to have been even less efficient than secular or Scottish Presbyterian discipline.

The State has always taken notice of the morals of its citizens. In the sixteenth century bastardy was in proportion more of a social problem than it is today, when we have so many problems which welfare workers seek to solve. The mid-twentieth century State provides penalties to prevent racial discrimination rather than sexual immorality. When it was convenient the State backed the Church's moral discipline; when ideas changed the State forgot about seven of the ten commandments and left the Church to find its own way of applying its moral law among its members. The Church in the twentieth century is still trying to find a way to cope with a secular marriage and divorce law which has long since parted company with Christian standards, because it relied for so long on the State; and it still has evolved no common mind about Sunday observance since the State ceased enforcing church attendance and prohibiting a wide range of activities on that day. In the twentieth century it is compulsory school attendance and an ideal of a uniform educational system which inspires our rulers as most necessary for society, rather than compulsory church attendance and a uniform ecclesiastical system.

[1] High Commission A.B.: 17, 20, 21, 29 July, 2 Aug., 3 Oct., 7, 20 Nov., 5 Dec. (a.m. and p.m.) 1598; 15, 16, 17 Jan., 28 Feb., 5 Mar. 1599.

[2] J. Tait in his introduction to the *Lancashire Quarter Session Rolls*, I, xv, records the difficulty sheriffs had in apprehending offenders. They were often reduced to using outlawry, the secular equivalent of excommunication.

Conclusion

The change in the State's ideas about the morals which it should enforce came about partly because of its experience in supporting church discipline. The large numbers of the contumacious formed a group of what can only be termed ethical dissenters. Rather than conform to the Church's standards of morality, men and women of all classes preferred to accept the disabilities of excommunication as a permanent state of life, as later religious dissenters accepted the disabilities of the Clarendon Code rather than conform to Anglican worship. It was partly because of the nonconformity of ethical dissenters that the State had to decide how much of the Church's moral law it would continue to enforce, and how much must be left to the individual conscience. These two factors still dominate England and the fact that the Church has been largely ignored by both the State and the mass of individuals as a moral authority is partly due to the Church's reliance for so long on the State to enforce morals through Parliamentary legislation.

CRITICISMS OF THE CHURCH COURTS

No legal system, including our own, is free from adverse criticism—arbitrary judges, slowness, high fees, inefficient and corrupt lawyers can still be found. The church courts of the sixteenth and seventeenth centuries had them too. They had also to work at the pace a quill pen could travel over paper or parchment, or a horse gallop along a rutted road; they had no corps of police with high standards and professional training; they had no salary scale, but depended on fees for their living. It is worth noting that all lawyers suffered this disability—the more work they had the more money they earned. Common lawyers who forced causes out of the church courts into their own put more fees into their own pockets at the same time.[1] Some modern historians need reminding that the argument from fees is a two-edged one.

It is hoped that this work will have led to a greater understanding of the church courts, and so to a better appreciation of the criticisms levelled against them by contemporaries. Such an understanding is much to be desired, for lack of it has led even such a diligent historian as Christopher Hill into misconceptions. Writing of the Laudian increase in court business he states: '...in 1639–40 1,800 persons came before the 30 sittings of the Archdeacon of London's Court...In the Court of Arches in the 1630s one judge might hear up to 360 cases *a day*. More modestly, the High Commis-

---

[1] In 1627 a judge of the Kings Bench estimated his income as £975. Of this only £148 was by way of salary and allowances, the remainder came from fees (Holdsworth, *History of English Law*, I, 253–5).

16-2

sion heard 80–120 cases a day.'[1] The London court's sixty disciplinary cases a day heard summarily would not be out of place in a modern magistrates' court, particularly if one-quarter to one-third failed to appear, as was usual in church disciplinary courts. There was no comparison between these cases and the formal stages of causes heard in open court in the Arches, taken at speed, or the only slightly less formal stages of causes heard in the High Commission at London. Mr Hill has used an abstract of an act book of the Archdeaconry of Huntingdon to prove his point of the importance of testamentary litigation, but unfortunately the registrar of that court put the receipt of executors' and administrators' accounts (a simple matter of office routine) into his court act book and so inflated the number of testamentary 'causes'.[2] Mr Hill's thesis that the Church attacked property and business life and the common law defended business life leads him to ignore almost completely the importance of defamation causes when considering the work of the church courts. An even more serious omission is any mention of the common law interference with business interests by its attempt to immobilize the Court of Admiralty.[3]

It has been suggested in these chapters that rising fees were due to the employment of lay lawyers, an expanded organization, and an inflation which increased the cost of living by 650 per cent between 1500 and 1640.[4] Probate fees were fixed in 1530, other fees in mid-Elizabethan times, and if the scale could not be adjusted because of political pressure, recourse had to be made to such devices as registration fees for wills. If marriage licence revenue had not been so buoyant, it is likely that other measures would have had to be

[1] Hill, *Society and Puritanism*, p. 307, author's italics. His statement, p. 300, that 'the right of appeal was transferred from Rome to Canterbury and York' is also inaccurate. The right was transferred to a new Court of Delegates on which sat both civil and common lawyers.

[2] Hill, *op. cit.* p. 303.

[3] H. Potter, *Historical Introduction to English Law* (4th ed. 1958), pp. 198–200. The need for documentary evidence is apparent throughout all Mr Hill's criticisms of church courts. E.g. on p. 311 of *Society and Puritanism* he writes 'the well-to-do might get their cases heard *in camera*, or be absolved by proxy'. Court acts show that anyone might be absolved by proxy in disciplinary cases. Sometimes action was taken in chambers (as it is today), but usually only when an absolution or some other act was required in vacation. Very few cases were heard completely in chambers; one of them is described in my *Puritans and the Church Courts*, p. 176, when a Puritan minister, prosecuted by his local knight for nonconformity, made a formal submission in chambers and was then released with a simple admonition.

[4] C. R. Hill, *Economic Problems of the Church*, p. 93. Prof. Stone has reworked Prof. E. H. Phelps Brown's price index of consumables to a base on the decade 1530–9, so enabling the effects of inflation on probate fees to be estimated with some accuracy. Compared with that decade prices had doubled by 1570–9, trebled by 1590–9 and quadrupled by 1630–9 (L. Stone, *The Crisis of the Aristocracy 1558–1641*, 771.) Attempts to evade the frozen fee scale were therefore not entirely unjustified. Similar considerations apply to other fees, e.g. while disciplinary fees at York had almost kept pace with inflation, those at Norwich can hardly have covered costs by the seventeenth century.

adopted to increase the lawyers' incomes. Many judges at that time accepted presents which we should consider improper, and it was only when they overstepped the limits imposed by convention that they were prosecuted. Sir John Benet and Lord Chancellor Bacon were both to the left of centre in their religious opinions, but sought to make too much out of their offices, were prosecuted and removed, while there were others such as John Rokeby who would take no presents at all. The only attack on the courts at York made by the Long Parliament concerned the degradation by the High Commission of Peter Smart from his canonry at Durham, after his famous quarrel with John Cosin.

The main criticism of the Church of England at that time was not that it was corrupt, but that in a missionary situation it presented a picture to the world of a vast property-owning organization, with an infinite hierarchy of officers, endlessly absorbing tithes, fees and 'offerings', regulated by a man-made law, existing only with the support of the State. It was a home for hundreds of officials and their underlings, clerical and lay, who made a good living not by extortion but by drawing the legal fees to which they were perfectly entitled. It is no wonder that many who had read their New Testament sought escape from this colossus in the simple congregations of the Independents, or in the 'spiritual' sects which were later absorbed by the Quakers. A modern, if less pronounced, parallel has been the involvement of the Church of England in the image produced in the popular mind by the Church Commissioners. As long as the average schoolboy has implanted in him the picture of Jesus, his disciples, and the first Christian congregations as poor, simply organized and living on a hand-to-mouth basis, so long will he grow up with an inbuilt tendency to criticize the Church of his day for any involvement in the world—whether that world is organized on a fee-paying or on a capitalist system.

The post-Reformation Church of England allowed itself to be used to support a society which it believed to be divinely ordained but which suffered from increasing internal divisions. The contents list to the Second Book of Homilies, published in 1562, ends with these two items:

Of Repentance and true reconciliation unto God. Three Parts.
An Homily against Disobedience and wilful Rebellion. Six Parts.

A Church which presented the world with a religion comprising three parts of the gospel of salvation to six parts of the sin of rebellion was indeed a Church which was storing up troubles for itself in the future.

APPENDICES

I. THE VALUE OF COURT OFFICES

In the Bishopthorpe MS. there are two papers (bundle 28, nos. 16 and 17) dated at York the 28 and 23 Feb. 1603 respectively, both headed 'The ordinarie profitts of the commissarieshippe of the prerogative courte and of the Exchequer of the Archbp: of York' from Michaelmas to Michaelmas of the years given:

No. 16		No. 17	
1597–8	£346. 16s. 0d.	1600–1	£326. 8s. 9d.
1598–9	£327. 9s. 8d.	1601–2	£379. 9s. 6d.
1599–1600	£337. 14s. 10d.		

No. 16 is in the hand of John Atkinson, Registrar of the Dean and Chapter and Actuary of the Chancery Court.

In the same MS. there is another paper (undated) in the hand of Atkinson (bundle 28, no. 18) headed 'Pattentes of offices and leases granted by the late Lord Archbysshopp of Yorke to his Children'. Seventeen leases are included, with, except in one case, their annual value. Of the offices, the value of the Commissaryship of the Exchequer is not given, the others are:

Registrar of the Exchequer Court, £160.
'Vicar-general' (i.e. Chancellorship), £100.
The Principal Registrar, £120.

The Exchequer commissaryship figure is obviously an accurate one, computed from office figures. The commissary received 2s. 10d. for each will proved or administration granted, according to the 1572 scale of fees printed at the end of H. Conset's *Practice of the Spiritual Courts*. The registrar received 3s. 6d. for each will and administration, 2s. for registering it and for the executor's or administrator's bond, and a fee according to length for engrossing a will. Each officer received fees for other items of work, but it is clear that the registrar's gross income must have exceeded the commissary's gross income. The other figures (which are all rounded ones), must have represented the net profit of these offices to Sandys' sons, after deducting expenses and payments to the substitutes who actually did the work.

II. ADVOCATES OF THE CONSISTORY COURT OF YORK

The advocates of Doctors' Commons represented the élite of the profession of civil law in England and Wales, but that profession was by no means confined to the members of Doctors' Commons. When the records of the church courts are more fully explored it will be possible to trace the careers of some of the rank-and-file civilians who acted as commissaries, archdeacon's Officials or advocates in local courts.

The following list records, in order of admission, those civilians who were admitted as advocates of the Consistory Court of York from 1559 to 1640. The substance of the entries in Venn's or Foster's respective *Alumni* of Cambridge or Oxford is given, followed by what new knowledge can be gleaned from the records studied in this work, enclosed in square brackets.

'Admitted' = the date of admission as advocate at York. The gift of the advocates' places in the court was in the hands of the archbishop. The prospective advocate petitioned him for admission, and when the petition was granted the archbishop gave him a mandate for admission which he then took to the chancellor who admitted him in open court. The act of admission was usually entered in the Consistory Court act book, but some admissions have not been noticed. It is difficult to trace the advocates' activities, but in the earlier and later court acts the actuary has noted the advocates and proctors present in court when sentences in causes, admissions of advocates or proctors and other formal proceedings were enacted. Further, from about the beginning of the seventeenth century advocates endorsed articles (i.e. the libel) or additional articles in causes. From these sources some knowledge can be gained of which advocates actually attended court or were in active practice.

* denotes that the advocate was admitted but did not practise at York. Advocates with entries in this list are referred to elsewhere simply by their surnames.

BESLEY, BEESLEY, BEISLEY, REGINALD. Not traced in Venn or Foster. LL.B. Practising in 1560. Retired *c.* 1564. Case concerning his will ('of York') in Exchequer A.B., 28 Nov. 1571.

FARLEY, RICHARD. LL.B. 1534. LL.D. 1547 (Venn, I, ii, 121). [Commissary of Exchequer in 1549. Practising in 1560. Last court appearance noted 1568.]

FAWKES, EDWARD. Nicholas Hostel, 1548 (Venn, I, ii, 127). B.C.L. (Foster, I, ii, 487). Father of Guy. [2nd s. of William, actuary of Exchequer Court. Practising in 1560. *Ob.* 1579, aged about 46.]

T(H)WENGE, THOMAS. Nicholas Hostel, 1548. LL.B. 1555. (Venn, I, iv, 241.) [Practising in 1560 to *c.* 1582. Judge of Admiralty Court (with Standeven), date unknown. (P.R.O., HCA 50/1, fo. 9.)]

BETSON, WILLIAM. Trinity, 1550. B.A. 1554. Fellow, 1555. Fellow of Pembroke, 1556; M.A. 1557. (Venn, I, i, 145.) [Admitted, 1564. Last court appearance noted, 1574. Custodian of peculiar of Howden in 1571, succeeded by Hudson *c.* 1575.]

*PARKINSON, EDMUND. Foster (I, iii, 118) has one of this name, clerk, Magdalene, 1553, B.A. 1555. M.A. 1559. Chaplain, 1559. Fellow of Brasenose, D.C.L. 1566. Canon of St Paul's, 1565. [Admitted as M.A. and bachelor of laws, 1568, noted as present in court on various days thereafter until 1572. Nephew of Robert (LL.B., a proctor in Chester Consistory Court in 1564: R.VII.G.1000) and joint commissary with him of the Richmond Consistory Court in 1569: still in office, 1608, probably succeeded by Mainwaring. References suggest that Edmund did all, or most of the work of the court. Member of High Commission: attended intermittently 1590–1611.]

PERCY, RICHARD. Son of Walter, of Barton-on-Humber, Yorks. Sometime of Broadgates Hall. Student of Christ Church, 1552, B.A. 1556. M.A. 1558. B.C.L. 1565. D.C.L. 1579. (Foster, I, iii, 1146.) [Admitted, 1569. Living in the Bedern, 1571. Apparently ceased to practise c. 1578. Commissary of the Exchequer, 1570–90. Chancellor, 1585–9. Regular attender at High Commission, 1573–90.] Rector of Settrington, 1591–8 (ob.). Ordination not traced.

CATTERALL, RANDAL. 3rd son of John, of Horton, Cheshire, an attorney of the king's bench. B.C.L. 1570. An antiquary residing at Oddington, Oxon., buried in the chancel of the church there, 1625. (Foster, I, i, 250, as Catherall, Randolph.) [In 1572 was 26 years old. Admitted 1571. Still in his chambers in the Bedern in Sept. 1572, but not mentioned in the court acts after that date.]

HUDSON, RICHARD. LL.B. (Oxon.), c. 1564. Incorporated LL.B. from Peterhouse 1584, LL.D. 1585. [Admitted, 1571; still practising, 1593. Custodian of peculiar of Howden in 1575.] Admitted at Doctors' Commons, Jan. 1595 (Venn, I, ii, 424; Foster, I, ii, 759).

DODSWORTH, MATTHEW. Son of Simon, of Settrington. St John's, 1565. LL.B. from Trinity Hall, 1573. Died at Slingsby c. 1628. (Venn, I, ii, 53.) [Admitted, 1574, not practising in 1592 but practising later. Official of Archdeaconry of Cleveland in 1578, and probably until succeeded by J. Gibson in 1590. Judge of Admiralty Court in 1586. Deputy Chancellor, 1604. Acting Chancellor, 1623. Chancellor, 1624–7. Regular attender at High Commission in 1607 and until 1628.]

CARLILE, JOHN. St John's, 1565. LL.B. 1573. (Venn, I, i, 293.) [Admitted, 1575; last time noted in court acts, 1585. Sued for tithe, 1586. Alive but not practising 1592.]

*STOUGHTON, WILLIAM. The first student of Christ Church, 1561, so elected from Westminster School. B.A. 1565. M.A. 1568. Supplicated for B.C.L. 1571. (Foster I, iv, 1432.) [Admitted (as M.A.), 1577; not noted as attending court after that year.] Probably client of Earl of Huntingdon. Commissary of peculiar of Groby, Leics., c. 1575. Author, *An Assertion for true and Christian Church Policie*, printed in the Low Countries, 1604, in which he argued for the abolition of church courts and canon law, as popish, and replacement by presbyterian system. Apparently envisaged transfer of causes involving civil law to secular courts which would continue to use civilians (p. 39). P. Collinson, *Letters of Thomas Wood 1566–77*, p.x. (Bull, Inst. Hist. Research, Special Supplement no. 5, 1960).

HUTTON, EDWARD. Son of John, of Streatham, Durham. Trinity, 1573. LL.B. 1579. [Admitted, 1579; attended court regularly until 1582; last attendance, 1585. Proctor in Richmond Consistory Court in 1614.] Bailiff of Durham City, 1615. Married Anne, d. of Francis Lascelles of Allerthorpe, Yorks. Buried, 1629, aged 72. (Venn, I, ii, 42.)

SWINBURNE, HENRY. [Born in Micklegate Ward, York, *c.* 1551. (In 1615 gave age as 64: R.VI.H.1171.) In 1567 clerk in office of principal registrar. As notary public acted occasionally as court actuary, 1571—Jan. 1576.] Hart Hall, 1576 (aged 21 says Foster, 16 says D.N.B.). B.C.L. from Broadgates Hall, date unknown. Married at Oxon. Ellen Lant. (Foster, I, iv, 1447.) [Admitted (as B.C.L.), 1581. Statement in sources that he was first a proctor possibly due to confusion with his work in the registrar's office. Auditor of peculiar of Dean of York, 1593. Custodian of peculiar of Howden, probably succeeding Hudson. Commissary of the Exchequer Court, 1604. Commissary or Auditor of peculiar of Dean and Chapter of York from 1613, succeeding J. Gibson; previously acted as Gibson's deputy. Regular attender at High Commission Court in 1607 and until 1622. *Ob.* 1624. Bequeathed 2 sovereigns to Archbishop Matthew, 1 to Mrs Matthew. 'My gold ring with the picture of death' to W. Ingram. Only son Toby (by second wife Margaret) born *c.* 1613, admitted advocate at Durham, 1637, under moderate bishop Morton. Author, *A briefe treatise of Testaments and last Wills* (John Windet, 1590, many editions). *A treatise of Spousals, or Matrimonial Contracts* (1686, 2 editions) printed from the incomplete MS. left by Swinburne, and intended to have a section on divorce.

*DETHICK, HENRY. Son of Sir Henry, Garter King of Arms. B.A. 1569. M.A. 1572. B.C.L. 1578. D.C.L. 1581. Master of Greatham Hospital, co. Durham. Master in Chancery. [Admitted, 1582, attended court until 1586.] Chancellor of diocese of Carlisle, 1586. Archdeacon of Carlisle and Rector of Salkeld, 1588. *Ob.* 1613, aged 67. (Foster, I, i, 398.)

STANDEVEN, THOMAS. Clare, 1576. LL.B. 1582. (Venn, I, iv, 144.) [Admitted, 1583. Judge of Admiralty Court (with Thweng), date unknown, but described as alderman of York. Administration of estate granted, March 1589. The Standevens were an important legal family. The elder Thomas, a proctor and alderman, died 1567. John, a proctor, alderman, and sometime sheriff of York, registrar of the archdeaconry of the East Riding, died Feb. 1588.]

*CROMPTON, THOMAS. Son of Sir Thomas, of London. St Alban Hall, 1577, aged 19. B.A. from Merton, 1579. M.A. 1581. [Admitted, Jan. 1588.] B. and D.C.L. 1589. Of the Inner Temple, 1581. Judge of High Court of Admiralty, 1589–1608. Chancellor of diocese of London, 1607–11. Vicar-general of Archbp. of Canterbury, 1611. M.P. 1598, 1601, 1604. Knighted, 1603. (Foster, I, i, 354.)

SCOTT, HENRY. Of Lincs. St Mary Hall, 1579, aged 18. B.A. from Oriel, 1582. Fellow, 1583. M.A. 1585. Supplicated for B.C.L. 1590. Student of Gray's Inn, 1589. (Foster, I, iv, 1325.) [Admission not noticed. Endorsed articles *c.* 1589–1606 (*ob.*).]

CRAWSHAWE, THOMAS. Born, 1570; brother of William, noted Puritan preacher. St John's, 1585. B.A. 1589. M.A. 1592. (Venn, I, i, 413; P. J. Wallis, *William*

Crashawe (1963), *passim.*) [Master of Southwell Grammar School in 1600 and in 1604. Admitted, Dec. 1605 ('LL.B.'). Practised until death in 1622.]

LYNNE, MARMADUKE. 5th son of John of Bassingbourne, Cambs. Trinity Hall, 1589. Scholar, 1590. Fellow, 1596–1609. LL.B. *c.* 1612. LL.D. 1617. Chancellor of diocese of Salisbury. Admitted at Doctors' Commons, 1628. *Ob. c.* 1640. (Venn, I, iii, 122.) Proctor of Norwich Consistory Court in 1603 (A. Harison, *Vagaria*, I, 28), but not practising. [Admitted, 1607 (LL.B.), and practised to *c.* 1620.]

MAINWARING, EDMUND. Son of Sir Randall, of Over Peover, Cheshire. Brasenose, 1594, aged 15. B.A. 1598. M.A. from All Souls, 1602. B.C.L. 1605. D.C.L. 1629. A civil lawyer on the Council in the North. Father of Sir Wm., sergeant-major in royalist army; brother of Philip, sometime secretary to Earl of Strafford. (Foster, I, iii, 959–60.) [Admission not found but *c.* 1612, practised until *c.* 1634. Commissary of Consistory Court of Richmond, *c.* 1612—*c.* 1634. Official of Archdeaconry of York, 1613–38. Commissary or Auditor of peculiar of Dean and Chapter of York, 1624–37. Chancellor of diocese of York (not active, except in visitation of 1630), with W. Easdall, 1627–37. Fairly regular attender on bench of High Commission, 1612–20. Member of Council in the North, 1629–41, secretary in 1630. Chancellor of diocese of Chester from 1634, but performed duties by substitutes.]

AGAR, ANDREW. Son of Thomas, of Stockton-in-the-Forest, York. Trinity Hall, 1612. LL.B. 1618. Incorporated at Oxon. 1619. *Ob.* 1637. (Venn, I, i, 8.) [Admitted, 1622, and practised until death.]

BRIDGES, RICHARD. Not traced in Venn or Foster. Admitted 1624 (M.A.). Apparently retired from practice *c.* 1635, but still lived in York. Commissary of peculiar of Dean of York, 1624–Civil War.

MOTTERSHED, EDWARD. [Son of Thomas, deputy registrar of High Commission Court, London.] New College, 1618, aged 17. B.C.L. 1626. D.C.L. 1632. (Foster, I, iii, 1042.) [Draft deed of resignation from his fellowship at New College, 1634 (R.VII.P.M.166). Admitted, 1626, and practised until death. Admitted at Doctors' Commons, 1632 (R.VII.P.R.95). Official of Archdeaconry of East Riding, 1632; of Nottingham, 1635. Judge of the Admiralty Court in 1633. King's Advocate in the North, 1635. Commissary of peculiar of Dean and Chapter of York (on resignation of Mainwaring). Commissary of peculiar of North Newbald in 1639. *Ob.* 1641.]

BURTON, GILES. Son of Richard, of Linton, Yorks. Lincoln, 1627, aged 16. B.C.L. 1630. (Foster, I, i, 217.) [Admitted 1632, having observed the courts at York for the last two years; practised until death in 1639. Commissary of peculiar of Barnby in 1637.]

WOOD, RICHARD. Not traced in Venn or Foster. Admitted, 1634 (LL.B.), and practised until Civil War. In list of substitutes, 1638, of Commissary of Richmond Consistory Court. Sometimes acted as substitute in Exchequer Court, 1640–2.

CALVERLEY, TIMOTHY. Son of Sir John, of Littlebourne, Durham. Queen's, 1622, aged 15. B.A. 1625. B.C.L. from St Alban Hall, 1629. (Foster, I, i, 232.)

[Admitted, 1636; practised until Civil War. Succeeded Mottershed as Official of Archdeaconry of East Riding, 1641.]

RIDDELL, GEORGE. Fourth son of Sir Thomas, of Gateshead. Queen's, 1628, aged 19. B.A. 1628. B.C.L. 1629. D.C.L. 1635. Judge-advocate in army of Marquis of Newcastle and died in the siege of Hull, 1643. (Foster, 1, iii, 1256.) [Admitted, 1636, and practised until Civil War. Joint patent (with W. Easdall) of the chancellorship registered by Dean and Chapter, 1637, probably to secure succession to Riddell following resignation of Mainwaring.]

*GLISSON, PAUL. 8th son of Wm. of Rampisham, Dorset. Trinity Hall, 1627. LL.B. 1634. Fellow, 1633–46. Deacon (Peterborough), June 1639. Brother of Francis, Regius Prof. of Physic, Cantab. (Venn, 1, ii, 223.) [Admitted, 1637, at special sitting of court in presence of Archdeacon of Cleveland (T. Thurscross, see my *Puritans and the Church Courts*, p. 284) and Bridges, Archbishop Neile 'having had sufficient testimony from my good friend Dr. Eden' of Glisson's 'skill in the law'. Substitute of judge of Exchequer Court, Jan. 1638–June 1639. Official of Archdeacon of Cleveland, 1638. Thurscross had a conversion from Puritanism to the 'Little Gidding' type of High Anglicanism in 1638, and may have influenced Glisson in the same direction, leading to latter's abandonment of his legal career and to his ordination. No references to him noted after his ordination.]

*WORLICH, TOBY. Son and heir of Thos. of Cowling, Kent. King's, 1624. B.A. 1628. M.A. from Trinity Hall, 1631. Fellow, 1633–40. LL.D. 1639. Married Jane, daughter of Sir Robt. Hatton. Nephew of Wm. Wickham, Bishop of Winchester. [Registrar (sinecure) of Exchequer Court, March 1637. Admitted, Oct. 1637. Official of Archdeaconry of York (his uncle William, son of Bishop Wickham, was archdeacon), succeeding Mainwaring, 1638. Commissary of peculiar of Dean and Chapter of York, succeeding Mottershed, 1641.] Admitted at Doctors' Commons, 1647. Knighted, 1661. Master in Chancery. *Ob.* 1664. (Venn, 1, iv, 449.)

*BROOME, PHILIP. Son of Henry, of Howden, Yorks, mercer. Pembroke, 1632. Migrated to Trinity. B.A. 1636. M.A. 1639. [Admitted Oct. 1639, 'a student of the civil and ecclesiastical laws for 8 years'. Substitute for the chancellor on occasions up to 1644.] Admitted licentiate, Royal College of Physicians, 1657. LL.D. (King's letter), 1661. (Venn, 1, i, 230.)

In addition to the above, Thomas Burton, Chancellor of Carlisle, 1576–7, of Durham, 1578–1608, was listed in the High Commission acts, 1570, and once in the Consistory Court, 1576, among the advocates. Similarly William Turnebull, twice in 1571, and Arthur Ingram, LL.B. (son of Wm., Commissary of the Exchequer, etc.), in the Exchequer acts, 1630. John Gibson, who became chancellor in December, 1572, was listed among the advocates at various dates from July 1571 onwards, yet there is no record of his admission at York, and he was not admitted at Doctors' Commons until 12 June 1572 (Br. Mus. Add. MSS. 24, 463, p. 62. The authority is the notes of his grandson John, born 1630).

III. OFFICIALS OF THE ARCHDEACON
OF NOTTINGHAM AND THEIR
PRINCIPAL SURROGATES

Officials are printed in CAPITALS, to distinguish them from surrogates.

1554 (or before)—1571. CRESSEY, ROBERT. B.Can.L. (probably Cambridge, 1529). Rector of Weston and Wilford. Canon of Southwell and Lincoln. Auditor of Southwell Peculiar Court, 1567–79. *Ob.* 1581. (Details in K. S. S. Train, *Lists of the Clergy of North Nottinghamshire*, Thoroton Soc. Record Series, XX, 1961, 98.)

1572–4. GREEN, ROBERT. Rector of West Bridgford, 1571, of Averham, 1581.

1575–7. HACKER, JOHN. Bachelor of Laws, university not known. Aged 40 in 1588 (Chancery, London, Petty *v.* Booth). Official of the Archdeacon of Derby in 1579 (A 3, 1 March; and on 7 Dec. 1583); 'former Official', 29 Jan. 1595 (A 8). Rural Dean of Newark, Jan. 1582–7. Proctor, 1577–95.

1577–81. BABINGTON, ZACHARIAH. St Alban Hall, Oxford. B.A. 1570. M.A. 1573. B. and D.C.L. 1599. Son of Thomas of Cossington, Leics., baptized 1549. Chancellor of diocese of Lichfield and Canon of Lichfield, 1581; Precentor, 1589; Chancellor, 1598. Held various livings. *Ob.* 1613.

1581. WETHERED, THOMAS. Succeeded Cressy as Rector of Headon. See Train, *op. cit.* p. 98. Auditor of Southwell Peculiar Court, 1579.

1581–3. BYRDSALL, RICHARD.

1583–? PARRATT, SIMON. Literate. Rector of 'Burthorppe' (Eastleach Martin), diocese of Gloucester.

1583–90. PETTY, THOMAS. Literate. Licensed preacher. Probably Vicar of Hault (or Ault) Hucknall. Rector of Langar, 1588–1609 (*ob.*) Canon of Southwell, 1603.

1585–9. BOOTH, REMEGIUS. B.A. from Christ's College, Cambridge, 1575, M.A. (date unknown), Fellow and Tutor of Gonville and Caius, 1581–7.

1589–91. DIGGLES, CHRISTOPHER (with Booth). Of Lincoln, Fellow of New College, Oxford, 1562–73. B.C.L. 1570. Rector of Partney, Lincs. 1585. Prebendary of Lincoln, 1592. Auditor of Southwell Peculiar Court in 1591 (York, R.VII.P.1, 969.)

1591–1600. LEIGH, MILES. Of Lancs. Fellow of Corpus Christi College, Cambridge, 1561. B.A. 1562. M.A. 1572. B.C.L. 1579. Joint Rural Dean of Nottingham and Bingham in 1595 and 1599 (LB 219). Will proved in Prerogative Court of Canterbury, 1601, when of St Michael's, Oxford.

1599–1600. Purefey, Michael.

1600–1. PUREFEY, MICHAEL. B.A. from Magdalene College, Cambridge, 1582. M.A. 1585. Died unmarried, 1627, aged 65.

1601–35. LANGFORD, NICHOLAS. Of Worcs., gent. Born *c.* 1573. B.A. from Christ Church, Oxford, 1590. M.A. 1593. University Proctor, 1600.

1601–4. Petty, Thomas.

1604–27. Purefey, Michael.

1627–35. Greaves, William. B.A. from Corpus Christi College, Cambridge, 1599. M.A. 1602. B.D. 1610. Fellow, 1603–13. Rector of Brailsford, Derbys. 1607, of Nuthall, 1612–46 (*ob.*).

1635–41. MOTTERSHED, EDWARD. See under Advocates, Appendix II.

1635–41. Malham, Robert. Scholar of Trinity College, Cambridge, 1602. M.A. 1606. Vicar of Fen Drayton, Cambs. 1605–14; of St Nicholas, Nottingham, 1611, and of Radford, 1612–51 (*ob.*).

1635–41. Fielding, Christopher. Literate. Licensed preacher, 1605. Vicar of Sturton, 1602–23. Rector of 1 mediety of Treswell, 1614–54 (*ob.*). Rural Dean of Retford from 1618.

1636–9. Laycock, Edmund. Of Notts. B.A. from St John's College, Cambridge, 1626. M.A. 1629. B.D. 1636. Fellow, 1626. Vicar of St Mary, Nottingham, 1635. *Ob.* before 1648. House of Commons allowed him bail in 1643, being in custody of sheriff of Notts.

1641–74. LAKE, EDWARD. See *Dictionary of National Biography*.

IV. PROCTORS OF THE CONSISTORY COURT OF NOTTINGHAM

ALLEN, WILLIAM. Notary public. 1610–28.

BELLWOOD, GEORGE. Admitted 1635 but did not practise.

BERNARD, JOEL. Gentleman. Appeared in a few causes *c.* 1610–12 and *c.* 1634.

BRANDERETH, RICHARD. Notary public. 1610–21. As a clerk, witnessed an act in court, 30 Sept. 1589 (A 5). PB 295 contains a letter to him at Derby concerning a person excommunicated by the court at Derby and now living in Notts, 1620. This suggests that he was registrar of that court.

BREWSTER, JAMES. Vicar of Sutton-cum-Lound. See my *Puritans and the Church Courts in the Diocese of York*, p. 296.

CHARNOCK or CHARWICKE, JAMES. 1578 (or before)–*c.* 1600. B.A. (Oxon.), 1559. M.A. 1562. B.C.L. 1569. Fellow of Brasenose *c.* 1565.

COLBY, Edward. Notary public. 1639–41. Took over causes from Tibberd. One of this name, proctor in Sudbury Commissary Court, in Oct. 1637.

DEPUP or DEEPING, JOHN. 1580–1603. Son of George, 'innholder' of London. Scholar of Trinity College, Cambridge, 1563. B.A. 1564. M.A. 1567. Fellow and Tutor, Gonville and Caius, 1573–5. Master of Nottingham Grammar School, 1578. Rector of Hawksworth, 1585–1603 (*ob.*).

GASCOIGNE, ROBERT. 1628–30.

GYMNEY, RICHARD. 1578–1623. Literate. Deacon, 1572; priest, 1573 (Chester). (Said he was 49 years old in 1602: (York) R.VII.H.124.) Vicar of Stoke-by-Newark, 1578–1635 (*ob.*). Rural Dean of Newark, 1587, deprived, 1606 (York,

Exchequer A.B., 12 March), restored, 1616. Proctor in Southwell court (York, R.VII.H.1169). Licensed preacher, 1611. On various folios in A 3 are records of sums paid to 'my master' by Gymney when acting as judge-substitute for Archdeacon Lowth.

HACKER, JOHN. 1577–95. See under Officials.

HANCOCK. THOMAS. 1608–10. Vicar of Headon. See my *Puritans and the Church Courts*, p. 305.

HOWETT or HEWITT, WILLIAM. 1610–20. Vicar of Farringdon with Balderton, 1596. Probably B.A. (1584) and M.A. (1588) from St John's College, Cambridge.

LUPTON, ROBERT. Literate. 1607–10.

MARTIALL, JOHN, senior. Notary public. 1603–8. See pp. 165, 167, 177–8.

MARTIALL, JOHN, junior. Notary public. 1618–26. Deputy registrar of Southwell.

PARKER, FRANCIS. Notary public. Admitted, 1635. Did not practise. Chief clerk of Mottershed, Official.

RECKLES, HATFIELD. Notary public. 1623–6, 1629–66. See pp. 170–1. Registrar of Southwell. An allegation, 22 June 1632, entered in the Chancery A.B. describes how he stole the records from his predecessor's house when he became registrar of the peculiar. (Also practised after the Civil War, until 1666.)

ROYCE, DAVID. 1634–41. Probably son of Richard of Ayston, Rutland. B.A. from Lincoln College, Oxford, 1625, aged 22. Curate of Kirklington in 1640. Proctor in Southwell court (P 285).

SAUNDERS, GEORGE. 1637–41. Scholar of Trinity Hall, Cambridge, 1631. LL.B. 1636.

SMITH, RALPH. Notary public. 1627–30.

TEILE, LAURENCE. Notary public. Admitted, 1636. Did not practise.

TIBBERD, JOHN. 1628–39. Deputy registrar, 1602–25. See above, pp. 167–70.

BIBLIOGRAPHY

MANUSCRIPT SOURCES

Church court records

The archives of the courts and administration of the Archbishops of York are housed in the Borthwick Institute of Historical Research, St Anthony's Hall, York; those of the Bishop of Norwich and the Archdeaconries of Norfolk and Norwich at the Norfolk and Norwich Record Office, City Library, Norwich; those of the Archdeaconry of Suffolk at the East Suffolk and Ipswich Record Office, County Hall, Ipswich; those of the Archdeaconry of Sudbury at the Bury St Edmunds and West Suffolk Record Office, 8 Angel Hill, Bury St Edmunds; those of the diocese of Ely at the University Library, Cambridge; those of the Archdeaconry of Nottingham at the University Library, Nottingham. Dr J. S. Purvis' description of *The Archives of York Diocesan Registry* (St Anthony's Hall Publications, no. 2, 1952) is the best guide in print to these records.

The basic records of the church administration are to be found in all registries, although many individual items have perished. They consist of the court act books and cause papers, records of summary cases at visitations and of the appearances of clergy and churchwardens at that time; administrative records of institutions (diocesan) or inductions (archidiaconal) and licences; and records of probates and administrations, registers of wills, original wills, inventories and accounts. In addition, all registries had their own precedent books and papers, from which much useful information can be drawn, and sometimes less formal documents have been preserved, such as the account books and Anthony Harison's *Vagaria* at Norwich. The Nottingham act books exist for some years in two series—the actual acts jotted down in court and the fair copy entered up afterwards, but the latter is not a duplicate of the former, and both need searching if the fullest information is desired. Some registries preserve the presentments bills submitted by the churchwardens at visitations, but no bills of the pre-Civil War period exist at York, while most of those for the seventeenth century exist at Nottingham. The practice of individual registries varied, and the student has to be prepared for anything to turn up. His task is also not made easier by the use of different terminology for the same type of document by both ancient and modern custodians. For instance, a 'cause paper' is called a 'libel bill' at Nottingham and a 'deposition' at Norwich; a 'visitation book' may be either the roll call book of clergy and churchwardens, together with formal particulars of the ordination, etc. of clergy (otherwise a 'call book'), or the record of the disciplinary court.

Bibliography

Other records

Dean and Chapter Library, York. Chapter act books. (Minute books of business transacted at meetings of the Chapter.) Note: the court acts of the peculiar jurisdiction of the Chapter are at St Anthony's Hall, York, under the classification R.A.s.

Lambeth Palace Library, London. Acts of the Faculty Office.

Public Record Office, London. Chancery and Star Chamber Proceedings. High Court of Admiralty Precedent Book, HCA/1.

Bishopthorpe MSS. This miscellaneous collection of papers, letters, etc., formerly at Bishopthorpe Palace, York, has been deposited by the archbishops at St Anthony's Hall.

In the possession of Mr K. S. S. Train. The only remaining known volume of the pocket books of Archdeacon Marsden.

PRINTED WORKS

Contemporary

Bayly (or Baily), Bishop Lewis. *The Practice of Piety* (3rd ed. 1613, first publication a few years earlier but exact date unknown).

Clarke, F. *Praxis*. First written in 1596 and circulated widely in manuscript. Printed in 1666, edited by Thomas Bladen.

Conset, H. *The Practice of the Spiritual or Ecclesiastical Courts* (3rd ed. 1708). (A modernized, improved and English version of Clarke's *Praxis*. Conset was a proctor in the York courts.)

Cosin, R. *An Apologie for Sundrie Proceedings by Iurisdiction Ecclesiastical* (1593). (The official justification for the practice of the church courts and the use of the *ex officio* oath.)

Godolphin, J. *Repertorium Canonicum: or An Abridgement of the Ecclesiastical Laws of this Realm* (1678).

Johnson, J. *The Clergy-Man's Vade Mecum* (2nd ed. 1707).

(ed.). *A Collection of The Laws and Canons of the Church of England* (1720; reprinted in the Library of Anglo-Catholic Theology, 2 vols. 1850).

Nottinghamshire, A Petition to Parliament from, against Ecclesiastical Government by Archbishops, bishops, etc. (1641).

Ridley, Sir T. *A View of the Civile and Ecclesiasticall Law* (4th ed. 1675).

Stoughton, W. *An Assertion for true and Christian Church Policie* (1604).

Swinburne, H. *A Brief Treatise of Testaments and Last Wills* (1590).

A Treatise of Spousals, or Matrimonial Contracts (1686).

Modern editions of contemporary works and records

Admiralty, Select Pleas in the Court of. Vol. II. Selden Soc. (1897).

Armytage, G. J. (ed.). *Allegations for Marriage Licences issued by the Dean and Chapter of Westminster 1558–1699.* Harleian Soc. vol. 23 (1886).

Bibliography

Atkinson, J. C. (ed.). *North Riding Quarter Sessions Records*, vols. 1– . North Riding Record Soc. (1884–).

Barton, T. F. (ed.). *The Registrum Vagum of Anthony Harison.* 2 vols. Norfolk Record Soc. vols. 32, 33 (1963, 1964).

Bates, E. H. (ed.) *Quarter Sessions Records for the County of Somerset, 1607–25.* Somerset Record Soc. vol. XXIII (1907).

Brinkworth, E. R. C. (ed.). *The Archdeacon's Court 1584.* Oxford Record Soc. vol. XXIII (1942). (An edition of the court disciplinary act book for 1584.)

Cardwell, E. (ed.). *Documentary Annals of the Reformed Church of England.* 2 vols. (1839).

Charlesworth, J. (ed.). *Wragby Parish Registers.* Yorkshire Parish Register Soc. vol. 105 (1939).

Collinson, P. (ed.). *Letters of Thomas Wood 1566–77.* Bulletin of the Institute of Historical Research, Special Supplement, no. 5 (1960).

Cosin, Bishop J. *Correspondence.* Surtees Soc. vols. 52, 55 (1869–72).

Emmison, F. G. *Abstract of the Act Book of the Archdeacon of Huntingdon's Court.* East Hertfordshire Arch. Soc. vol. VIII (1930).

Grindal, Archbishop E. *Remains.* Parker Soc. (1843).

Hale, W. H. *A Series of Precedents and Proceedings in Criminal Causes, 1475 to 1640* (1847).

Heywood, O. *The Autobiography, Diaries, etc.* Ed. J. H. Turner (Brighouse, 1882–5).

Hutton, Archbishop M. *Hutton Correspondence.* Surtees Soc. vol. XVII (1843).

Jenkins, C. (ed.). *The Act Book of the Archdeacon of Taunton.* Somerset Record Soc. vol. 43 (1928).

King, H. and Harris, A. (eds.). *A Survey of the Manor of Settrington.* Yorkshire Arch. Soc. Record Series, vol. CXXVI (1962).

Lister, J. (ed.). *West Riding Sessions Rolls 1598–1602, etc.* Yorkshire Arch. Soc. Record Series, vol. III (1888).

West Riding Sessions Records 1611–42. Yorkshire Arch. Soc. Record Series, vol. LIV (1915).

Longstaffe, W. H. D. (ed.). *Acts of the High Commission within the Diocese of Durham.* Surtees Soc. vol. XXXIV (1858).

Nichols, J. G. (ed.). *Narratives of the Reformation.* Camden Soc. (1859). (The first narrative is John Lowth's autobiography of his early life and troubles under Queen Mary.)

Notestein, W., Relf, F. H. and Simpson, H. (eds.). *Commons Debates 1621.* New Haven, U.S.A. (1935).

Nottingham Borough Records. 9 vols. (1882–1956).

Parker, Archbishop M. *Correspondence.* Parker Soc. (1853).

Peele, A. *The Seconde Parte of a Register.* 2 vols. (1915).

Puritan Manifestoes. Frere, W. H. and Douglas, C. E. (eds.) (1907). (Contains the First and Second Admonitions to Parliament.)

Purvis, J. S. (ed.). *Tudor Parish Documents of the Diocese of York* (1948).

Stone, E. D. and Cozens-Hardy, B. (eds.). *Norwich Consistory Court Depositions 1499–1512 and 1518–30.* Norfolk Record Soc. vol. X (1938).

Bibliography

Tait, J. (ed.). *Lancashire Quarter Sessions Rolls 1596–1606*. Chetham Soc. vol. 77, N.S. (1917).

Whitaker, T. D. *History of Richmondshire*, I (1823). (Contains transcription of Ralph Rokeby's 'Oeconomia Rokebiorum', 1565, revised 1593.)

White, B. N. (ed.). *Registrum Diocesis Dublinensis: A Sixteenth Century Dublin Precedent Book* (Dublin, 1959).

Williams, J. F. (ed.). *Bishop Redman's Visitation 1597*. Norfolk Record Soc. (1946). (Contains all presentments, but does not fully record all court proceedings.)

Willis, A. J. *Winchester Consistory Court Depositions*. Privately printed (1960).

Wilson, T. *The State of England Anno Domini 1600*. Camden Miscellany, vol. LXVI (1936).

Modern works

'Appeals in Causes of Doctrine or Discipline made to the High Court of Delegates'. *Parliamentary Accounts and Papers*, vol. 57 (1867–8).

Aylmer, G. E. *The King's Servants* (1961).

Barlow, F. *Durham Jurisdictional Peculiars* (1950).

Bowker, M. 'Non-Residence in the Lincoln Diocese in the Early Sixteenth Century', *Journal of Ecclesiastical History*, vol. XV (1964).

Brinkworth, E. R. C. 'The Laudian Church in Buckinghamshire', *University of Birmingham Historical Journal*, vol. V, 1 (1955).

Canon Law of the Church of England, The. Report of the Archbishops' Commission on Canon Law (1947).

Churchill, I. J. *Canterbury Administration*, 2 vols. (1933).

Collinson, P. *Elizabethan Puritan Movement* (1967).

Copnall, H. H. *Nottinghamshire County Records—Notes and Extracts: Seventeenth Century*. Nottingham (1915). (More notes than extracts.)

Curtis, M. H. *Oxford and Cambridge in Transition* (1959).

Dansey, W. *Horae Decanicae Rurales*, 2 vols. (1st ed. 1835).

Devlin, P. *The Criminal Prosecution in England* (1960).

Ecclesiastical Courts Commission, Report of, (1832). (The Special and General Reports made to His Majesty by the Commissioners appointed to inquire into the Practice and Jurisdiction of the Ecclesiastical Courts in England and Wales.)

Fees and Faculties. Report of a Commission of the Church Assembly, 1959.

Foster, J. *Alumni Oxonienses 1500–1714*. 4 vols. (1891–2).

Giles, F. T. *Open Court* (1964).

Harvey, C. P. *The Advocate's Devil* (1958).

Henderson, G. A. *The Kirk of St Ternan Arbuthnott* (1962). (Good description of presbyterian discipline in action.)

Hill, C. *Economic Problems of the Church from Archbishop Whitgift to the Long Parliament* (1956).

Society and Puritanism in Pre-Revolutionary England (1964).

Holdsworth, Sir W. S. *A History of English Law* (vol. I, 7th ed. 1956; vol. III, 4th ed. 1935).

Hunt, R. N. C. *Calvin* (1933).

Jones, W. J. *The Elizabethan Court of Chancery* (1967).

Bibliography

Lawton, G. *Collectio Rerum Ecclesiasticarum de Dioecesi Eboracensi*. 2 vols. (1840).

Maguire, M. H. 'The Attack of the Common Lawyers on the oath ex officio' in *Essays in History and Political Theory in Honor of C. H. McIlwain* (Cambridge, Mass., 1936).

Malden, H. E. *Trinity Hall* (1902).

Marchant, R. A. *The Puritans and the Church Courts in the Diocese of York 1560–1642* (1960).

'John Darrell—Exorcist', *Transactions of the Thoroton Society* (1960).

'The Restoration of Nottinghamshire Churches 1635–40', *Ibid.* (1961).

Moore, E. Garth. *An Introduction to English Canon Law* (1967).

Morris, C. 'The Commissary of the Bishop in the Diocese of Lincoln', *Journal of Ecclesiastical History*, vol. X (1959).

'A Consistory Court in the Middle Ages', *ibid.* vol. XIV (1963).

Neale, Sir J. E. *The Elizabethan House of Commons* (1949).

Owen, D. M. 'Ely Diocesan Records' in Dugmore, C. W. and Duggan, C. *Studies in Church History*, vol. I (1964).

Paver, W. (ed.). *Paver's Marriage Licences*. Yorkshire Archaeological Journal, vols. 9–14, 16, 17, 20, and Yorks. Arch. Society's Record Series, vols. 40, 43, 46.

Peters, R. *Oculus Episcopi*: *Administration in the Archdeaconry of St Albans 1580–1625* (1963).

Plucknett, T. F. T. *Concise History of the Common Law* (5th ed. 1956).

Potter, H. *Historical Introduction to English Law* (4th ed. 1958).

Price, F. D. 'An Elizabethan Church Official—Thomas Powell, Chancellor of the Diocese of Gloucester', *Church Quarterly Review*, vol. CXXVIII (1939).

'Elizabethan Apparitors in the Diocese of Gloucester', *ibid.* vol. CXXXIII (1942).

Purvis, J. S. *An Introduction to Ecclesiastical Records* (1953).

'A Note on Pews and Stalls', *Yorkshire Archaeological Journal*, vol. 146 (1949).

Reid, R. R. *The King's Council in the North* (1921).

Ritchie, C. A. *The Ecclesiastical Courts of York* (Arbroath, 1956).

Ritual, Report of the Royal Commission on, (1868).

Skeel, C. A. J. *The Council in the Marches of Wales* (1904).

Slatter, M. D. 'The Records of the Court of Arches', *Journal of Ecclesiastical History*, vol. IV (1953).

Stone, L. *The Crisis of the Aristocracy 1558–1641* (1965).

Storey, R. L. *Diocesan Administration in the Fifteenth Century* (St Anthony's Hall Publications, no. 16, 1959).

Sturge, C. *Cuthbert Tunstal* (1938).

Thompson, A. H. *The English Clergy* (1947).

Tickhill, J. *History of Kingston-upon-Hull* (1796).

Train, K. S. S. *Lists of the Clergy of Central Nottinghamshire*. Thoroton Society Record Series, vol. XV (3 parts, 1952–4).

Lists of the Clergy of North Nottinghamshire. *Ibid.* vol. XX (1960).

Venn, J. and J. A. *Alumni Cantabrigienses*, vol. I (4 vols. 1922–7).

Winckworth, P. *A Verification of the Faculty Jurisdiction* (1953).

Woodcock, B. L. *Medieval Ecclesiastical Courts in the Diocese of Canterbury* (1952).

TABLE OF CASES

Ch   = Chancery Court of York
Con = Consistory Court of York
RC = High Court of Chancery
Ex = Exchequer Court of York
HC = High Commission Court of York
N   = Nottingham Archdeaconry Court
Nor = Norwich Consistory Court

Ashburn *c.* Lascye (Ch)	*page* 78
Babington *v.* Lowth *et al.* (RC)	162
Barton *c.* Taylor (Con)	74
Bateman *c.* Barwick (Con)	74
Beverleye *c.* Hawkes (Con)	73
Brake *alias* Ledell *c.* Murton (Con)	97
Brearton *c.* Massye (Con)	79
Broadheade *c.* Bull (Con)	72
Browne *c.* Nevill (Con)	72
Carr *c.* Marsh (Ch)	77
Ex parte Chollerton (Con)	64
Clay's Case (Kings Bench)	67, 69
In re will of Constable (Con)	97
Constable *c.* Constable (Con)	52
Constable *c.* Simpson (Ch)	71
Cooke *c.* Lickbarrowe (Ch)	73
Corbet *c.* Churchwardens of Patrington (Ch)	122
Criplinge *c.* Pearson (Con)	72
Crossley *c.* Hutton *et al.* (Con)	107
Dallamye *c.* Brayne (Ch)	73
Dawney *c.* Copeland (Ch)	80
Denton *c.* Woodwarde (Con)	80
Devonshire, Christine Countess of, *c.* Osborne *et al.* (N)	193n
Dinnocke *c.* Lloyd (Ch)	79
Done *c.* Wilbraham (Con)	79
Edmundson *c.* Bell (Con)	126, 141, 167n
In re will of Estofte (Ex)	95n
Farringdon *c.* Hobbs *alias* Meare (Ch)	79
Foster *c.* Daie (Dean and Chapter of York)	74
Freeman *c.* Cullier and More (Nor)	37
In re will of Gravenour (Con)	104
In re estate of Hanson (Ex)	99

Table of Cases

Hart *c.* Smyth (N)	*page* 193n
Harte *alias* Punchon *c.* Punchon (Ch)	79
Hodgson *c.* Nicholson (Con)	124
Hoggerd *c.* Wood (Con)	72
Holmes *c.* Crosthwaite *et al.* (Ch)	109
Holmes *c.* Hanner (Nor)	19, 54, 57
Howe *c.* Hill (Ch)	74
Jobson *c.* Ricard (Con)	52
Ex parte Johnson (Con)	64
Lamberte *c.* Holmes (Con)	74
Mathew *c.* Hudson (Ch)	77
Middleton *c.* Blacket (Con)	79
Milbanke *alias* Emerson *c.* Wharton (Ch)	79
Oldefielde *c.* Adamson *alias* Crosse (Con)	73
Office *c.* Barnby *et al.* (HC)	241–2
Office *c.* Bell (N)	183, 221
Office *c.* Birchall (Ch)	5
Office *c.* Bullock (HC)	106
Office *c.* Burwell (HC)	106
Office *c.* Coates (HC)	223
Office *c.* Crawe *et al.* (Ch)	67
Office *c.* Elithorpe *et al.* (HC)	128
Office *c.* Griffith *als.* Griffin (Norwich Audience Court)	35
Office *c.* Haber (Ch)	77–8
Office *c.* Heighington (Durham HC)	106
Office *c.* Huit (N)	184
Office *c.* Kidd (Ch)	69–70
Office *c.* Lowth *et al.* (HC)	153–5
Office *c.* Oglethorpe *et* Allen (Ch)	60
Office *c.* Redhead (HC)	241–2
Office *c.* Rowley Churchwardens (Ch)	131
Office *c.* Sallowes *et al.* (Nor)	229
Pawson *c.* Cooke (Ch)	76n
Peacocke *c.* Clarke (Con)	74
Petty *v.* Booth (RC)	160, 163–4
In re will of Preston (Con)	95
Ramsden *c.* Staynton (Con)	72
St Saviours, York, Churchwardens *c.* Russels (Ch)	78
Ex parte Shafto *c.* Blenkinsopp *et al.* (Con.)	79
In re estate of Smith (Nor)	108
Smithe *c.* Harte (Ch)	79
Smythe *v.* Leigh *et al.* (Star Chamber)	177–8, 181
Stanley *c.* Salisbury (Con)	45n
Stocke *c.* Tingle (Con)	63
Stringer *c.* Burton (N)	193n

Table of Cases

Steel *c*. Mell (Ch)	*page* 56–7, 78
Talbot *c*. Arthington *et al.* (Con)	89, 95 n
In re will of Tempest	98–9
Thurston *c*. Hobman (Con)	72
Tocketts *c*. Twenge (Ch)	78
In re will of Turnell (Ex)	98
Underne *c*. Lowth (Ch)	151–2
In re will of Warde (Con)	97
Water *et al. c*. Hobman (Ch)	76
Watkin *c*. Westrop (Con)	74
Westrop *c*. Watkin (Con)	74
Wharton *et al. c*. Garthe *et al.* (Con)	63
In re Wilkinson (Ch)	78
Winder *c*. Gill (Ch)	74
Ex parte Wrighte (Con)	64

STATUTES AND CANONS

Archbishop Langton's Constitutions (1222)	*page* 72
21 Henry VIII c. 5	24
25 Henry VIII c. 21	21
5 Edward VI c. 4	71
1 Elizabeth I c. 1	33
Act of Uniformity (1559)	131
Injunctions of Elizabeth I (1559)	129, 131, 153
1 Elizabeth I c. 19	44n
18 Elizabeth I c. 3	224
Canons (1585)	171
Canons (1597)	21, 81, 129, 171
Canons (1603), No. XIV	131
No. XV	131
No. XXXVI	129, 133
No. LVIII	132
No. LIX	131
No. LXXXVI	131
No. XCII	106
No. CI	21
No. CII	21
No. CXVI	180
No. CXX	182
No. CXXXII	25
No. CXXXIII	viii
No. CXXXV	190
No. CXXXVIII	181
7 & 8 James I c. 4	224
13 Charles II, St. I, c. 12	225
Statute of Distributions (1670)	112

INDEX

(This index does not contain names found only in the Appendices)

Absolution (*see* Excommunication)

Act Books (and acts of court), 10, 16 n, 17, 65, 69, 87, 92–5, 104, 172, 206, 209, 247

Actuaries, court, 55–6, 58, 64, 95 n, 138, 209

Admiralty, courts of, 2–3, 9, 38, 41, 190–1, 244 (*and see* York, Admiralty Court of)

Advocates (London), 3, 11, 50, 52–4, 101; (Norwich) 19, 52 n, 53–4, 57; (York) 50–4, 67, 78, 97–8 (*and see* King's Advocate in the North)

Agar, Andrew, 50, 250

Ainsty, New, deanery, 115–17, 123, 207

Ainsty, Old, deanery, 116, 123, 207

Ainsty, rural dean, 93, 128 n

Aislaby, George, 83 n

Alder, Wm., 82

Allerton(-shire), peculiar, 38, 40, 105–6, 119 n

Alne, peculiar, 40, 119 n

Alsopp, George, 25, 200

Andrews, Bishop, 84

Apparitors (or Summoners), 23, 26–8, 31–5, 59, 88–9, 110–11, 116, 135, 139–40, 146, 167, 170, 176–7, 180–2, 185, 188, 199, 223

Apparitor-general (York), 58–9, 67 n, 115, 139

Appeals, 13, 20, 64–5, 79–80, 85, 98–9, 189

Appleton-le-Street, 130 n

Arches, court of, 12–13, 18, 64, 243–4

Arnold, 183, 201

Askew, Hugh, 115

Assessors, 64, 171–2

Assistance, Letters of, 50, 223

Assize courts, 28 n, 164

Atkinson, John, junior, 43

Atkinson, John, senior, 43, 55, 58, 73, 246

Audley, chancellor, 122

Aynsworth, Charles, 172, 196

Ayscough, Henry, 220

Babington, Zachary (Zachariah), 159–63, 171, 192, 252

Babthorpe, Wm., 242

Babworth, 182

Bacon, Lord, 245

Baguley, Robert, 181, 185 n, 199

Bainbridge, Archbishop, 87

Barker, Barnabas, 84

Barnby, Charles, 241

Barnes, Bishop, 66, 119

Barnston, 201 n

Bateman, John, 94

Bayley, Bishop, 86

Bell, Thomas (R. of Beeford), 124, 143

Bell, Thomas (R. of Felixkirk), 141

Benefices, litigation about, 60, 67; personal unions of, 28–9

Benet, Sir (Dr), 44, 46, 48, 64, 73, 78–9, 101, 143, 186–7, 245

Benson, Thomas, 171, 184

Berkeley, Bishop, 150

Berkshire, archdeaconry, 113, 165

Berwick-on-Tweed, 83

Beverley
  peculiar, 40
  rural dean, 128 n
  St Johns, 77 n

Birchall, John, 5, 8

Birth-control, 222

Bishop, Thomas, 172, 196–7

Bishops, as supreme in own courts, 33, 35 n, 37, 52, 76, 78, 85, 102; resisted by lawyers, 55

Blasphemy, 72

Blomefield, John, 18 n

Blythburgh, 30, 229

Book of Sports, 217, 220 n

Booth, Remegius, 162–3, 171, 252

Bonds, executors', and administrators', 25, 91, 109, 111

Bosvile, Wm., 221 n

Boswell, Thomas, 47

Boswell, Wm., 47

Brandereth, Ric., 195, 253

Brewster, James, 181, 253

Briefs, 170

Brook, John, 187

Buckingham, archdeaconry, 222

Bullock, Thomas, 106

Bulmer, deanery, 116–18, 123

Burton, Dr Giles, 121, 197, 250

Burwell, Thomas, 106, 251

Bury St Edmunds, court at. (*See* Sudbury Commissary Court)
Byrdsall, Richard, 162, 252

Caesar, Sir Julius, 11
Calvin, John, 2, 241
Canon law, 1–3, 10, 71–2, 90, 128–33, 240
Canons of 1603, wrongly described as of 1604, 129 n
Canterbury
  Archbishop of, 12–13, 15, 33–4
  archdeacon's court at, 13
  Consistory Court of, 12–13
  Court of Audience of Archbishop of, 12–13, 18
  Prerogative Court of, 12–13, 25 n, 44, 48, 53 n, 109 n, 112
Car Colston, 183
Carlisle, appeals from diocese of, 64; provincial visitation of, 119–20
Carlton-in-Lindrick, 184
Carpenters, wages of, 145
Cartwrighte, Wm., 168
Catechism, mocked, 176 n
Catechizing, 66–7, 131, 213, 218–19
Chancels, 32, 69, 122, 125–6, 130
Chancery, High Court of, 2–4, 9, 52 n, 63, 107, 112–13, 204 n
Charnock, James, 193, 253
Cheshire, 212
Chester
  Bishop of, 14
  Consistory Court of, 14, 51 n, 64, 248, 250
  diocese of, 14, 80, 88 n, 103, 227; provincial visitation of, 120–1, 140, 209–12
Church, attendance at, 138, 159, 218–20, 225–6, 234
Churches, disturbances in, 176, 219, 226; furnishings and decorations, 69, 125, 133, 136, 140, 186, 199–201; inspection of, 126, 131, 199–201
Churchwardens, 10, 31, 75–8, 132, 134–7, 180, 182–4, 200–1, 218–20, 227, 230, 237; examination of, 115, 198–9
Churchyard walls, 184, 228
Churchyards, disturbances in, 8, 71, 219, 226
Citations, 19, 28–9, 32, 116–17, 135, 156, 181, 184, 190, 234, (*and see Quorum nomina*); oral, 69–71
Civil Law, 1–3, 9–11, 87, 91, 108, 237–40
Civil Service mentality, in Church of England, 36–7
Civilians 2–4, 10–11, 46–8, 57, 239–40
Clark, Wm., 48

Clay, Dr John, 67, 69
Clergy, examined, 115, 129, 153, 163
Clerke, Thomas, 58
Cleveland
  archdeaconry court, 122, 124, 126, 137, 139 n, 141–2, 167 n, 207–8, 231, 233–4, 248, 251
  rural dean, 92, 128 n
  rural deanery, 118
Cleveley, John, 89
Coe, Stephen, 172
Coke, Lord Chief Justice, 8–10
Collinson, Henry, 171
Colne, 80
Common law, 2, 9, 90, 105–9
Communion table, 130
Communion wine, dirty, 184
Commutations of penances, 31, 138–9, 154 n, 155, 175–8
Constable, Robert, 71
Convocations, 84, 129–30, 236–7; proctors in, 49, 166
Cooke, Alex., 133
Coombe, John, 171, 180
Cooper, John, 187
Copinger, Edward, 168, 170
Copley, Christopher, 82
Corbett, Dr Clement, 11, 36
Correction, House of, 224, 235
Cosin, John, 124–5, 245
Cotterell, Dr, 150
Coventry and Lichfield, chancellor of diocese, 160, 162
Coventry, Carr, 171
Craddock, Dr John, 49 n
Crane, Wm., 185 n
Crashawe, Thomas, 46, 249
Craven
  Deanery of, 117 n, 120, 207–8
  rural dean of, 88–9, 128 n
Crayke, 40
Cressy, Robert, 158, 187, 252
Crewkerne, Deanery of, 207
Criminal procedure, 4–8
Curates, fees at visitations, 28; licences of, 25–6, 82; stipends, 66, 78, 125

Darfield, 216
Darker, George, 200
Darrell, John, 34 n
Darrell, Robert, 63
de excommunicato capiendo, writ of, (*see Significavit*)
Defamation, 9, 16, 19–20, 54, 57, 61, 63, 65, 71–5, 80, 189, 192–4, 244

Delegates, High Court of, 64, 85, 95 n, 98, 104 n, 105, 113, 120 n

Dennyson, Thos., 181, 185 n

Denton, Wm., 124 n

Derby, Henry Earl of, 209

Derby
  Official of, 159
  archdeaconry registrar of, 167, 195

Devonshire, Elizabeth Countess of, ('Bess of Hardwick'), 151

Dickering, Rural Dean of, 89

Diggles, Christopher, 162, 164–5, 174, 187, 252

Dilapidations, 27, 32, 66, 84

Dinder, 150, 155

Discipline, church, 16, 20, 146, 204–35, 240–3; causes of, 26–7, 60–1, 64, 67, 69, 73, 80, 85, 193–4

Dispensations (see Simony); of laymen to hold ecclesiastical benefices, 42 n

Doctors' Commons, 3, 85, 236

Dodsworth, James, 45

Dodsworth, Matthew, 44–6, 48–50, 73–4, 125 n, 137, 141, 157, 175, 187, 206, 248

Dodsworth, Roger, 45

Dodsworth, Simon, 45

Doncaster, 74, 137, 139, 208, 213, 216, 218–19
  Deanery, 117, 128 n, 136–9, 206–7, 213–19, 228

Drunkeness, 72, 138, 217, 219, 223, 226, 228

Ducke, Dr Arthur, 48

Dunster, Deanery, 207

Durham
  Bishop of, 38, 40, 83, 119–20
  Chancellor of diocese, 49, 64 n, 105, 251
  Consistory Court, 49, 64, 103
  Dean and Chapter of, 38, 40, 119–20
  Diocese, 40
  sede vacante jurisdiction in, 120 n

Easdall, Dr Wm., 47–51, 69, 75, 77, 85, 101–2, 121, 132, 137, 139–41, 187, 202, 208, 212, 220, 232–4

East Retford (see Retford)

East Riding, Yorks., archdeaconry court, 122, 124–6, 142, 144, 249–50

Eden, Dr Thos., 11, 113, 193

Edmundson, Thos., 141

Ely
  Consistory Court, 18, 20, 107 n
  diocese, 142–3, 226

Exchequer Court (York). (See York, Exchequer Court of)

Excommunicates, burial of, 139 n, 220; consorting with, 221–2

Excommunication and Absolution, 9 n, 19, 27, 33, 64, 71–2, 111–12, 114–15, 124, 135, 137, 140–4, 152, 161, 169, 172, 174, 177, 179, 199, 201, 204–5, 209–11, 216, 220–2, 226–31, 242 n, 243, 244

Executors, 86, 144

Ex officio oath, 4–5, 9, 225 n

Faculties, 25–6, 75–7, 238–9; Court of 12, 29, 37 n, 42 n

Farm workers' wages, 145 n

Farmerie, Edward, 171

Fawcett, Edward, 50, 55–6

Fees, 15, 18–19, 21–31, 51–4, 71, 75, 81, 91, 93, 111–12, 124, 134–6, 140–5, 185, 189–92, 199, 200 n, 208, 222–3, 234, 237, 243–4, 246; remission of, 25, 28, 142, 228–31, 234

Felixkirk, 220 n

Fenay, Giles, 58, 73

Fermer, James, 162

Fielding, Christopher, 187, 198, 253

Fines, 175–6

Fisher, Nicholas, 69–71

Fishlake, 216

Floyd, Sir Robert, 53 n

Fortune-telling, 170, 226

Fothergill, Wm., 53 n, 55, 58

Foxe, John, 147

Frankland, Richard, 58

Frodsham Deanery, 121, 207, 210–15, 217, 219, 226, 228

Fryckley, John 56

Gentili, Alberico, 3, 11

Gibson, Sir (Dr) John, 42, 44, 46, 50, 61, 67, 97 n, 119–20, 143, 223, 251

Gifford, Robert, 119 n

Glisson, Paul, 11, 101, 251

Gloucester, diocesan chancellor, 150–1

Golf, prohibited on Sundays, 183

Goodwin, Wm., 101

Gough, Francis, 143 n

Greasley, 152

Great Budworth, 218

Greaves, Robert, 185 n

Greaves, Wm., 166, 172, 192, 195, 197, 253

Green, Richard, 158, 252

Greenfield, Archbishop, 52

Greenham, Richard, *Workes*, pawned, 167

Gregson, Eleanor, 175 n

Grindal, Archbishop, 13, 42, 45, 56, 95, 119, 127–31, 151–6, 158, 173, 179, 186

Grysdale, Oswald, 55

Guardians and Guardianship (see Tuitions)

Guiseley, 77 n
Gymney, Richard, 89, 162, 164, 172, 178 n, 195–6, 253

Hacker, John, 159–61, 164, 193, 252
Halifax, 67, 135, 207–8
Hall, Robert, 59, 83
Handsworth, 119 n
Hardwick, Bess of (*see* Elizabeth, Countess of Devonshire)
Harison, Anthony, 34 n, 35–6
Harworth, 201 n
Harsnett, Archbishop, 119 n, 131, 140, 186
Harthill
    Deanery, 40
    Rural Dean of, 128 n
Hatfield (Yorks.), 136 n
Hawton, 151, 153
Heighington, John (mayor of Durham), 106 n
Helmsley, 208
Henry VIII, 3, 41, 57
Hexhamshire, 64
Heywood, Oliver, 83 n, 135
Hickleton, 136 n
High Commission Court, 4, 33–4, 36, 44, 51, 69, 131, 190–1, 239, 243–4; Durham, 7 n, 33–4, 106; Norwich, 34; York, 5, 7, 33–4, 42, 47–9, 51, 56, 58–9, 63, 66–7, 69, 75, 105–7, 124 n, 128, 132, 140, 152–6, 173, 204, 218 n, 222–3, 236, 241, 245
Hodson, Dr Phineas, 49–50, 101
Holderness, Rural Dean of, 127 n, 128 n
Holgate, Archbishop, 85, 102 n
Holy Tables, railed, 130, 201
Hoods, enforced wearing by clergy, 132, 201
Howdenshire, 38, 40, 119 n
Howson, Bishop, 119 n
Hull (Kingston-upon-Hull), 118, 126, 133–4
Huntingdon archdeaconry court, 244
Huntingdon, Earl of, 115, 166
Hutton, Archbishop Matthew, 42 n, 45, 49, 83, 115, 118, 129, 163, 239

Ilkley, 130 n
Immorality, sexual, 9, 27, 33, 67, 69, 72, 137–8, 159, 177, 181–2, 212, 215–17, 219, 221–2, 224–5, 227, 229, 235, 240–3
Impropriations, 125
Induction, 27, 29, 144
Informations, 10, 54
Ingram, Sir Arthur, 46–7
Ingram, Dr Wm., 46–7, 251
Injunctions, 129–31, 151
Institutions, 15, 27–8, 82–4
Interdict, 75, 140

Ipswich, 16, 30
Iveson, Anthony, 96, 97 n, 98

Jackson, Sir John, 139
Jegon, Bishop, 35, 37
Jennison, Robert, 82
Johnson, Robert, 93–4
Jones, Dr Walter, 41–2, 89, 94–5, 151–2, 155–6, 187
Judge-substitutes, 11, 42, 44, 52, 94, 96–9, 101–2, 113, 120–1, 137, 162–6, 172, 196–8, 200–2, 223
Justices of the Peace (*see* Quarter Sessions)

Kelham, 199
Kendal, 120–1
Kidd, Elias, 69–70
Kilham, 40
Kilvington, 200, 202
King, Archdeacon John, 165, 174
King's Advocate in the North, 7–8, 51, 132 (*and see* Mottershed, Edward)
King's Proctor, 7
Kirk Smeaton, 216
Kirkby Underdale, 221 n
Kirkbymoorside, 124

Lambarde, Wm., 235
Lancashire (*see under* Chester Diocese and Quarter Sessions)
Langford, Matthew, 166 n
Langford, Nicholas, 166, 195, 252
Laughton peculiar, 119
Laws, Doctors of, admission fees, 52
Laycock, Edmund, 197–9, 253
Leake, Luke, 154
Leeds, 77, 218, 220, 230
Legacies, suits for, 16, 20, 63, 112
Legal Secretaries, bishops', 35–6, 82–4 (*and see* Barker, Barnabas; Hall, Robert; Harison, Anthony; Liveley, Edward; Mortimer, Wm.; Theaker, John; Turbatts, Wm.)
Leigh, Miles, 165, 171, 177–8, 187, 252
Levett, Dr John, 101–2, 106
Levett, Thomas, 48
Licences, 15, 25–6, 29–30; in Notts., 174, 179
    marriage, 15, 20–3, 29–30, 80–2, 244; in Notts., 156, 173–4
    clergy, to marry, 153
Lincoln diocese, 14
Lindley, Edmund, 56
Liveley, Edward, 83–4, 195 n
London archdeaconry court, 243
London Consistory Court, 14, 112
London diocese, 121

Lougher, Dr Robert, 42, 44, 63, 79, 96–9, 155
Louth, 133, 150
Lowth, Archdeacon John, 147–66, 173–4, 179, 185 n, 193
Lowth, Edmund, 147–8
Lowth, Humphrey, 165–6
Lowth, Thomas, 165
Lowth, Thomasin, 161
Luddenham, 77 n
Lupton, Robert, 141, 254
Lyndby, 201 n
Lynne, Dr Marmaduke, 46, 250

Mainwaring, Dr Edmund, 46–8, 74, 113, 209, 250
Malham, Robert, 172, 196–8, 253
Malin, George, 185 n
Malton, 45, 117, 208
Mansfield, 159, 161, 196–8
Marches (of Wales), Council of, 4, 109, 192, 239
Maritime law (*see* Admiralty, High Court of)
Marriage licences (*see* Licences, Marriage)
Marriages, clandestine and illegal, 8 n, 32, 66, 125, 140–1, 176 n, 219, 227
Marsden, Archdeacon, 173
Martiall, John, 165, 167, 171, 174, 176–8, 180, 193, 254
Martiall, John, junior, 167 n, 254
Mason, Adam, 55
Matrimonial litigation, 16, 20, 61, 78, 112; offences, 8 n, 137
Matthew, Archbishop Toby, 47, 49–50, 83, 91 n, 121 n, 131 n, 132–4, 140, 157, 163
Middleham, 40
Middleton Tyas, 220
Midwives, 25–6
Milbourne, Richard, 106 n
Mitton-in-Craven, 208
Mollineaux, Francis, 153–4
Money-lending, 167–8 (*and see* Usury)
Monopolies, archiepiscopal, 133–4
Morley, Richard, 154
Mortimer, Wm., 35–6
Mortuaries, 16
Morris dancing, Sunday, prohibited, 183
Moseley, John, 202 n
Mottershed, Dr Edward, 7 n, 51–2, 70, 74 n, 102, 122, 124, 131, 143, 195–202, 250

Nantwich, 218
deanery, 121, 210–11, 228
Navy, not prayed for, 59
Neile, Archbishop, 11 n, 49, 52, 69–70, 77, 81–5, 102, 105, 125–6, 130–3, 136, 139–40, 186, 195–6, 200–1, 208, 213, 216, 223

Nelson, Wm., 241
Newark, 159, 161, 172, 175–6, 186, 196–9, 202
deanery, 181, 200, 203
rural dean, 89, 161 (*and see* Gymney, Richard)
Newman, Wm., 165
Neville, Archbishop, 87
Non-residence of clergy, 32
Norfolk Commissary Court, 18
North, Council in the, 4, 41, 46–7, 49, 108–9, 145, 166, 192, 239
Northumberland archdeaconry, 67
Norwich, Audience Court of, 35, 37
bishop of, 31–7
church court organisation in diocese, 14, 18, 20, 23, 25, 29, 30–3, 35
Commissary Court, 18, 20, 30, 54, 57, 179
Consistory Court, 14 n, 15–29, 54, 61 n, 75, 107 n, 109–10, 180, 190–2, 204 n
diocesan chancellor, 11, 14 n, 19 n, 20–1, 23, 26–9, 33, 229, 238
diocesan registrar, 15, 18–19, 21–9
episcopal privileges, 21, 28–9
visitations, 134, 138–9, 142–5, 227–8
Nottingham, 34 n, 151, 161, 163–4, 166, 169, 176, 186–7, 224
Angel Row, 167, 169
appeals from, 64
Archdeaconry correction courts, 127–8, 132, 134, 141–2, 159, 161, 163–4, 177–86, 192, 218, 228
Bridlesmith Gate, 168–9
Borough Sessions, 166, 225
Chapel Bar, 168
Consistory Court, 8, 16, 54, 173, 185, 188–96, 198–9, 201 (*and see under* Proctors)
Free Lane, 176
Low Pavement, 169
Officials of, 158–66, 171–6, 179, 182, 185–8, 252–3; income, 81 n, 160
Registrar of, 81 n, 152, 155, 161, 164, 167–72, 182–6, 188, 221, 228
(and Bingham), rural deans and deaneries, 161, 165, 172, 185
St Mary's, 151–2, 159, 169, 173–4, 176
St Peter's, 202
Nottinghamshire, 42, 173, 195 (*and see* Quarter Sessions)

Officials, Archdeacons', (*see under* separate archdeaconries)
Okeden or Ogden, Elias, 152
Organs, 133–4
Orston, 176, 183–4
Otley deanery (*see* Ainsty, Old)

Index

Oxford archdeaconry, 165
Oxford university, 11, 176

Padua University, 10
Parish clerk, 21, 69–71, 78–9, 174, 175 n, 184, 185 n, 219, 229
Paris university, 11
Parker, Archbishop, 154–5
Parker, Francis, 51, 195 n, 197, 199, 254
Parkinson, Robert, 224, 248
Parratt, Simon, 162–3, 252
Paupers, 228–9, 234
Paver, Wm., 80
Penance, 28, 67, 124, 127 n, 135, 137–9, 141–5, 187, 225–6, 228, 242, (*and see* Commutations)
Percy, Dr Richard, 44–6, 63, 95, 96 n, 97–101, 104–5, 110, 119, 156–7, 248
Peterborough, diocesan chancellor, 222
Petty, Thomas, 162–4, 166, 186–7, 192, 252
Pews, 25–6, 64 n, 66, 75–80
Philpot, John, 150
Piercy, James, 174
Piers, Archbishop, 44, 83, 100, 167, 186–7
Plague, of 1604–5, 45
Pluralities, 28–9
Pontefract, 137
  deanery, 207
  rural dean, 98
Preachers, 25–6, 28, 82
Precontracted marriages, 137, 220
Presentments, 67, 87, 179–83, 198–202, 212–13, 218–19
Probates and Administrations, 2, 15, 23–5, 29–30, 37, 53 n, 63, 66, 79, 82, 87–93, 103–7, 111–12, 143–4, 161, 237
Probates, enforced, 23, 32, 87, 92; fees, 24–5; in common form 88–9; numbers of, 24, 88, 93, 107; in solemn form, 88, 90, 93, 98–9, 110–11
Proctor, Henry, 55–6, 58
Proctors, Berkshire, 113; Ely, 18; London, 17; Norwich, 16–17, 19, 54, 57; Nottingham, 8, 159, 169–70, 189, 193, 195, 253–4; Richmond, 53, 249; Sudbury, 18; York, 17, 50, 51 n, 53–7, 61, 92, 97–8, 195
Prohibition, writ of, 9, 67, 69, 113, 154
Purefey, Humphrey, 166
Purefey, Michael, 165–6, 168, 170–2, 186, 192, 196–7, 252–3
Purgation, 142, 225, 228, 231
Puritans and Puritanism, 4–5, 7–8, 34, 66, 81–2, 118 n, 119 n, 132, 138, 140, 143, 166, 172, 182–3, 202, 207, 209, 216, 218, 226, 233–4, 242, 244 n

Pursuivants, 34, 59, 175 n, 222; foiled, 124 n
Psalms, illegal singing of, 70

Quarter Sessions and Justices of the Peace, Kent, 235; Lancashire, 224–5, 242; North Riding, 223–6; Nottinghamshire, 174 n, 178–9, 224, 226; Somerset, 223–6; West Riding, 145, 223–4
Quorum nomina, writ of, 92–3, 181–2

Raper, John (organ-builder), 133–4
Rates (church), evasion of, 122; recovery of, 63, 78, 121, 159, 188, 208, 219, 226
Readers, 82, 175
Receiver-general of diocese of York (*see* York, Exchequer Court, commissary)
Reckles, Hatfield, 8, 170–1, 193, 195, 199, 254
Recusancy, 31, 66, 204–6, 208–11, 226
Redhead, Mrs (wife of Robert, governor of York castle), 241
Redmayne, Dr Robert, 35
Requests, Court of, 3
Retford, 161, 172, 186, 192, 196–9, 203
  rural dean of, 127 n, 159 n, 197
  rural deanery, 79 n, 159–60, 180, 200
Revell, Wm., LL.B., 18 n
Richardson, John, 64, 185
Richmond
  archdeaconry, 14, 40
  Consistory Court, 14, 46, 53, 61, 74, 113, 209
Riddell, Dr George, 51 n, 251
Ripon, 40
Rogationtide customs, 135, 140, 216
Rokeby, Dr John, 41–2, 45–6, 50, 60–1, 66, 85, 94–5, 104 n, 187
Rokeby, Ralph, 41
Rokeby, Wm., 93–4
Roos, Peter, 177–8
Rotherham, 137, 139, 208, 213
Rowley, 131 n
Rural Deans, 14–15, 59, 88–90, 95, 98–9, 111, 120–1, 127–8, 141, 143, 151, 158–9, 161, 165
Ryves, John (Archdeacon of Berkshire), 113

St Albans archdeaconry court, 13–14, 224
Sandys, Archbishop, 42, 44, 55–6, 82, 97, 100, 104–5, 115, 119, 155–6, 173, 186, 218 n, 239, 246
Sandys, Edwin, 44
Sandys, Miles, 44, 91, 100–1
Sandys, Thomas, 44
Saunders, George, 193, 195, 198, 254
Savage, Archbishop, 87, 88 n, 91

Savage, Thomas, 202 n
Sawtry (Hunts.), 147
Scadlocke, John, 69
Scarborough, 73, 118
Schoolmasters, examined, 66, 115, 129; licensed, 25–6, 82, 174; visitation fees, 28
Scolds, common, 219, 226
Sede vacante jurisdiction, 157 (*and see* Durham)
Selby peculiar, 40
Sequestrations, 15, 25–6, 32, 59, 82, 93, 125 n; (in Notts.) 153–4, 156, 173–4, 179
Settrington, 45
Sheffield, 118, 207
Sheffield, Lady, 138
Sherborne, Ric., esq., 175 n
Significavit, writ of, 121, 124, 174, 222
Simony, 37
Simpson, Thomas, 71
Slander (*see* Defamation)
Slingsby, 130 n
Smart, Peter, 245
Smyth, Robert, of Laxton, 177–8
Snaith, 40
Sneinton, 169
Somerset, 228
Sorcery, 226
Southwell, 151, 176, 177 n, 186–7
    peculiar, 38, 119 n, 136, 158, 165, 169–71, 173, 180, 195
    Synod, 147, 156–7
Southwell, Sir Richard, 150
Sports, Book of, 220 n, 225
Squire, Thomas, jnr., 40
Standeven, John, 50, 249
Stanhope, Dr George, 50, 102
Star Chamber Court, 3–4, 49 n, 176–8, 239
Stevenson, James (failed examination), 153
Stillingfleet, 130 n
Stock, James, 53 n, 55, 63 n, 98–9
Stockes (or Stokes), George, 59
Sturton, 183, 199
Sudbury
    archdeaconry, 207
    commissary, 11, 179
    commissary court, 18, 30, 54, 107, 113, 192–4
    deanery, 207, 213–19, 228
Suffolk commissary court, 19–20, 25 n, 29–31, 35, 142–4, 180, 182, 207
Summoners (*see* Apparitors)
Surgeons, 25–6
Suspensions, 124–5
Sutton-cum-Lound, 76
Swearers, 138
Swinburne, Henry, 45–7, 49–50, 58, 101, 110 n, 120, 249

Swynburne, John, 45
Synods, 91, 93, 187 (*and see* Ipswich, Southwell)

Talbot, Dr, 54
Taunton archdeaconry, 142–3, 216
Taxes, recovery of, 66, 79
Taylor, Christopher, 98
Testamentary litigation, 16, 20, 63, 65, 67, 79, 90–6, 107–13, 189, 244
Theaker (or Thacker), John, 55–6, 58, 82–3
Theobalds, Robert, 198
Thirsk, 141, 208
Thorne, 130 n
Thornton-le-Dale, 220 n
Thornton, Richard, 48
Thurscross, Henry, 233
Thurscross, Timothy, 124, 233, 251
Thwing, 71
Tibberd, John, 167–71, 176, 180, 182, 193, 198–200, 254
Tickhill, 139
Tithe litigation, 16, 19–20, 63, 65, 80, 112, 189, 192
Tithes, farmers of, 53, 169
Toller, Thomas, 132 n
Tooker, Dr Charles, 113
Topham, Matthew, 226
Trinity Hall, Cambridge, 11
Tuitions, 89–90, 91 n, 94, 95 n, 112
Turbatts, Wm., 58, 83, 84 n
Turvin, George, 172

Underne, Wm., 151–2
Upton (Notts.), 59, 135–6, 180
Usury, 141, 176 n, 180 n, 218–19

Vernon, Granville, 236–7
Vicars-choral (*see* York Minster)
Visitation court, descends into cellar, 135–6; dinners, 134–5; fees, 27–31, 141–5 (*and see* Fees, remissions of); procedure, 115–16, 134–8; provincial, (Canterbury) 15, (York 103), 119–21, 140, 209–12, 223
Visitations, 10; archidiaconal, 122–8, 179–80; Articles of Enquiry, 115; circuits, 30, 116–18, 122–3, 136–7, 196–8, 213; Norwich diocese, 21–3, 26, 28–9, 31, 204, 206; presentments, 115–18, 134, 136–7, 140; profits of, 121 n; records of, 114–15, 206, 209, 212, 230; York diocese, 76–80, 114–21, 155, 158–9, 163–4, 176, 185–8, 195–6, 204, 209, 213, 230–4

Wales, Council in the Marches of, (*see* Marches)

Walkington, 130 n
Ward, Samuel, 143
Wath-on-Dearne, 138
Watson, Bishop, 84
Webster, Wm., 98
Weeks, Matthew, 167, 176
Wells, 150–1, 155
Wentworth, 329 n
Westmorland, 212
Westmorland, Earl of (1564), 94
Wethered, Thomas, 162, 252
Wharton, Sir Michael, 77 n
Wharton, Vincent, 187
Whitby, 208
Whittingham, Wm., 119
Wickham, Henry, 49, 101
Wilmot, Thomas, 167
Withington, Francis, 172, 187, 196
Wizard, consulted, 183
Wolsey, Archbishop, 87
Wood, Dorothy, 168
Worlich, Toby, 11, 251
Wragby, 135 n, 136
Wymondham, 37
Wysall, Stroking Boy of, 183

York
    archbishops: their legal secretaries, 82–4;
        principal registrars, 44, 58, 83, 165, 188,
        246; registry, 45, 55, 58, 81–2, (method
        of filing cause paper), 17; revenue from
        probate jurisdiction, 91, 100
    archdeaconry, 207: court of, 122–3, 128, 134,
        137, 208; Official, 46–7; registrar, 63
    Admiralty Court of, 38, 44, 45 n, 51, 247,
        249–50
    Apparitor-general of archbishop (*see* Ap-
        paritor-general)
    Chancellors of, 38, 41–5, 48, 52, 58, 80–1,
        116, 132, 137, 143–4, 173–4, 176, 188, 226,
        237–8
    Chancery Court, 38, 44, 49, 51, 58, 60–4, 66–
        82, 85, 98–9, 105, 109, 110 n, 118–19,
        122, 140, 151, 153–4, 158, 173, 230
    City, 44, 50, 78, 131 n, 207–8, 218, 226
    Consistory Court, 38, 44, 46, 49, 51–2, 58,
        60–5, 67, 72–4, 78–80, 84–5, 93–8, 104 n,
        105–7, 119, 141, 165, 189, 192, 218, 229
    Convocation of (*see* Convocations)
    Custom of province of, 91, 97, 107–9
    Dean of: 38, 40 (*and see* Hutton, Matthew);
        peculiar of, 40, 59 n, 249–50
    Dean of Christianity of, 88, 94, 115
    Dean and Chapter, 38, 40, 42, 44, 47–8, 51,
        53 n, 58, 60, 73, 79, 81, 115, 119 n, 126 n,
        127, 141, 167 n
    Diocese, *sede vacante* administration, 58, 60
    Exchequer Court: 38, 63, 87–113; actuary,
        56; Commissary, 38, 44–51, 59, 61, 87–
        119, 237, 246–51; registrar, 44 n, 59, 61,
        64, 246; registry, 58
    High Commission Court of (*see* High Com-
        mission)
    Holy Trinity, Goodramgate, 134–5
    Holy Trinity, Micklegate, 69–70
    Minster: Treasurer's peculiar court (*see*
        Alne); Vicars-choral, 52, 64, 115, 124
    Prerogative Court, 53 n, 103–7, 110–11
    St Martins, Coney St, 81
    St Martins, Micklegate, 5
    St Michael-le-Belfrey, 81
    Vicar-general of archbishop, 41, 60–1, 87, 91,
        97, 99, 246 (*and see* York, Chancellors of)
Yorke, Thomas, 59
Young, Archbishop, 41, 60, 94–5, 115, 129,
    151, 155, 186

Zouche, Richard, 11